PUNCHY THROUGH THE COVERS

THE EARLY YEARS
1928-1949

To-

Joe Hardstaff

With very best wishes
– and thanks for the memories!

PUNCHY THROUGH THE COVERS

THE EARLY YEARS
1928-1949

Alan 'Punchy' Rayment

RAYMENT BOOKS UK

First published in Great Britain in 2013 by Rayment Books UK

ISBN: 978 0 9576412 0 4

Printed and bound by CPI Group, Chippenham, Wiltshire SN14 6LH

RAYMENT BOOKS UK
5, Longcliffe, Victoria Road,
Milford on Sea, Lymington,
Hampshire SO41 0NL

Tel: 01590 642693 ~~630442~~
~~Email: office@raymentbooksuk.com~~
~~www.raymentbooksuk.com~~

Contents

	Introduction	7
1	My father in the Great War 1914 - 1918	9
2	Birth – and near death	29
3	Sam and Wyn – family roots	39
4	A young child's memories of home	61
5	Grass – and my early years	69
6	First school and holidays	79
7	Growing and learning in the 1930s	88
8	Born between two Great Wars	102
9	Lord's – first heroes: 1937 - 1939	112
10	Freedom, games and pranks	121
11	People, places and happy events	131
12	1939 – all change	147
13	Last peacetime holiday	154
14	War – and grass again	171
15	New school, no school and Churchill	177
16	Dunkirk and the Battle of Britain	188
17	Evacuation, the Blitz and Mayor's Cup	200
18	Happy days in wartime	210
19	D-Day and Doodlebug summer 1944	226
20	Wartime cricket 1940 - 1944	242
21	Work begins – war ends	250
22	Opportunity	263
23	Dreams come true	271
24	Dancing and courting	287
25	Reluctant conscript	295
26	Called up and called out	304
27	Romance and Lord's in 1947	318
28	Cricket's golden summer	332
29	Flying cricketers	342
30	Two contracts – marriage and Hampshire	357
	Index	378

Acknowledgements

I am immeasurably grateful to my friend, the acclaimed writer and publisher Stephen Chalke, who spent many hours 'imposing' my manuscript and photographs to create a print-ready document, entered a swarm of corrections after my final proof read, and wisely and humorously mentored this greenhorn through the long pre-production process – a big learning curve for me – and fun! Stephen, you made this book happen. Thank you!

I also had fun when gleaning information from old school pals: thank you Dick Nelson; Len Pilditch; Derek Humberstone; Ron Lence; Brian Cross and Dick Seymour. Thanks also to Sir Leslie Sharp, friendly editor of our Old Fincunians bi-annual magazine, The Scimitar, for his advice, information and photographs. Dr Dave Allen, Hampshire's cricket historian and academic, who counselled me about 'audience' after reading rough drafts of two early chapters and has been most encouraging throughout my long writing innings. I greatly value his friendship. My thanks also to family members Den, Martin and Valerie's husband Stephen for reading and correcting some of the early chapters – and to Alison for the first proof-read of the whole manuscript. And to scores of family members and friends a big 'thank you' for your encouragement.

The internet has not only given me direct access to a lot of my research but also to many helpful people – too many to remember but thank you all the same. Special thanks to cricket historian Glenys Williams; to Ricky Gunn of Southgate CC; to staff at the Imperial War Museum and the Royal Air Force Museum and to Mary Wain of Bawdsey. And a big thank you to all my friends at the Dorset Cricket Society for their encouraging banter about my invisible book, especially Peter Jenkins, John White, Chris Finch and Richard Mockridge for supplying information and photographs. Special thanks to my son, Stephen, who kindly gave me his old desktop computer in 2004 and has since steered me through new software programmes – and his golfing friends Cliff Harris and Mark Bridle – New Milton's JPC Tech wizards, who have kept me sane during technical crises and upgrades.

My memoirs contain quotations from the works of several authors: Commander A. Rawlinson RNVR; AJP Taylor; Richard Hough & Denis Richards; James Collier; John Keegan; Winston Churchill; GM Trevelyan; Pat Thane; W Shirer. Also from British newspapers and publications: The Times; London Evening News; Daily Mirror; Finchley Press; Bournemouth Evening Echo; The Fishing Gazette; Wisden Cricketers Almanack; The Economic History Society. I am grateful for additional photographs supplied by Neil Robinson the Lord's librarian; Somerset CCC museum; Middlesex CCC historian William A. Powell; John and Phil Langford; Tom Lee (the late Cyril Perrier's collection); and Peter Haslop. Licensed images obtained from: The Imperial War Museum; English Heritage; The Press Association and Cranston Fine Art.

I have acknowledged the work and support of my niece, Alison Barnes, on the cover flap of this book. Thanks also to Martin and William Barnes for the design of the logo for RAYMENT BOOKS UK – and to Anna Banton of Milford-on-Sea who has designed and implemented the excellent web site.

Introduction

These memoirs depict the first twenty years' experience of a North London kid born in 1928 to wonderful parents who met at fourteen and died within a few days of each other in 1982 at the age of eighty-six.

A year after the funerals I felt strongly motivated to write the story of my early years, both as a tribute to Sam and Wyn and as a family and social record for my children and grandchildren, their progeny and our extended family. I made notes and drafted a rough outline but due to a busy life did not begin the first chapter until 2004 – then focused on research and wrote intermittently until a final edit in February 2013.

There is, of course, an element of ego fulfilment in writing an autobiography but my great hope is that people I know and love in our family – our friends and even strangers too – may be interested and entertained, discover a few facts about our family history in the 19th and 20th centuries and pause, perhaps, to think through the purpose of their own Life Journey.

Volume One is a chronicle that includes some family history, records my upbringing by caring parents, extended family and friends as well as stories about school and sport, our neighbourhood and national events, of life in WWII and growing up in the 1930s and 40s. It is also a preface to a book I am preparing to write about my personal experiences on the long tour of Life from twenty to eighty-plus: tales of marriage, children, divorce and depression; of careers in cricket, dance teaching, school teaching and business; of college at forty and university at fifty; of community work projects and family social work; of counselling and hands-on property renovation; of friends and lovers, travels and social change; of success and failure – and a wholly unexpected, long and bumpy spiritual adventure leading to the inner peace of 'knowing – not believing'.

I extend a warm welcome to you, the reader, and hope that in these memoirs you will come across a few stories of interest – and maybe chuckle or even laugh a couple of times – 'cos laughter is a healthy tonic for body, mind and soul.

Alan 'Punchy' Rayment
Milford-on-Sea
Hampshire

February 2013

~~~~~~~~~~

IN LOVING MEMORY OF

SAM AND WYN

AND IN THE HERE AND NOW

TO BETTY AND OUR CHILDREN

DENIS, MARTIN, VALERIE,
STEPHEN, ANGELA, PETER

WITH LOVE – ALWAYS

CHAPTER 1

MY FATHER IN THE GREAT WAR 1914 – 1918

Samuel Thomas Rayment, RNVR,
and Commander Rawlinson's Mobile AA Unit in WWI.

"Father, what did you do in the First Great War?"

A question I never asked.

So now, in the twenty-first century, I feel cross with myself because I failed to ask my father for details of his interesting military career from 1914 to 1918.

Sam was strong minded yet sensitive and approachable and, according to my mother, I was an insatiably curious child – forever asking questions. So why no questions when Father joined me in games with toy soldiers in the 1930s – or when playing our serious darts matches between air raids during WWII – or when I was a radar operator in the RAF? And why, when my parents were in their 80s and I recorded my mother's childhood background and my own post-natal problems, did I not also record Father's experiences of the first German Zeppelin air raids on London in 1915?

And what was the story behind those small photographs in the old-fashioned family albums depicting Sam in both army and naval uniforms: some in khaki riding horses and manhandling a cart along a muddy track – others in smart seaman's navy riding on motor trucks mounted with six-pounder guns? ˙

And how did Able Seaman Samuel Thomas Rayment become involved in the pioneering adventures of Commander Alfred Rawlinson, CMG, CBE, DSO, who created Britain's first Mobile Anti-Aircraft Unit? And why – when Able Seaman Sam was in action with that unit on Hampstead Heath, London in 1917 – was he sufficiently disabled to become convalescent in the Royal Navy Hospital at Dungavel in Scotland until the summer of 1918?

So many anomalies – so many questions.

Those unanswered questions are intruding on the current writing flow as I record my own clear memories of the Battle of Britain and the Blitz in 1940 – nudging me to focus on my father's military service. So on this June day in 2009 I will digress from writing about WWII in order to satisfy my own curiosity, and that of family members, about Sam's experiences in the First Great War.

May I therefore request your forbearance, dear reader – family member, respected friend or stranger – as I sketch in brief the historical events in Europe that led to those Zeppelin air raids, touch on the fast evolving invention and production of heavier than air flying machines that became weapons of war which, by extension, necessitated the development of new types of mobile artillery to combat the airborne invasion of our homeland.

Samuel Rayment in the Army 1914, front row between the shafts of a cart

British mobile AA gun and crew, London, 1915

Memories of my childhood must wait until the next chapter because ... if Sam had not survived the 1914-18 war my brother and I would not have been born to those particularly wonderful parents and the experiences I share in this book would not have taken place. I am therefore profoundly and humbly thankful to a Benevolent Providence that Sam and Wyn survived, married, birthed two children and were surprised to be the grand parents of five boys and five girls.

LIFE is interesting – an ever-evolving miracle.

General research about the Zeppelin raids reveals that the hotchpotch of primitive air and ground defences cobbled together for London in 1915-18 laid the foundations of policy and systems from which the relatively high-tech air defences of WWII were developed, including radar. In their *Jubilee History of The Battle of Britain*, Hough and Richards underline the link between the 1915-18 experience and our survival in 1940-41:

> History is indeed a continuum, and there is a chain of progression between the innocent half-minute hops in the sand-hills of North Carolina in 1903 and the deadly encounters at 350mph, 18,000 feet above the chequered counties of southern England thirty-seven years later. Of the many links in this chain, few are more important than the experiences of 1914-18, a glance at which will show how victory in 1940 stemmed at least in part from developments more than twenty years earlier.

Given that Louis Bleriot's flimsy monoplane powered by a 25-horsepower radial engine achieved the first flight across the English Channel in 1909, it was almost unthinkable that from 1915 German air raids would cause havoc in London and the east coast of England.

The British newspaper magnate Lord Northcliffe made a profound statement three years before Bleriot's historic flight after reading, in one of his own newspapers, a brief account of Santos Dumont's aeroplane flight in France for a distance of 722 feet – the first real flight in Europe. Northcliffe angrily berated his editor:

> The news is not that Santos Dumont has flown 722 feet but that Britain is no longer an island. It means that aerial chariots of a foe will descend on British soil if war comes.

Coinciding with the rapid though primitive development of aircraft in that era, the German Army and Navy began to build dirigible airships – invented by Count von Zeppelin – as bomb-carrying military weapons. Were Northcliffe's words "if war comes" an intelligent observation or an informed prophecy?

Europe, in the latter part of the 19th century, was awash with tensions created by complex politics and entangled alliances among major nations and lesser nation states. Uncertainty, suspicion and fear triggered an armaments race. International conferences at The Hague in 1899 and 1907 failed to solve disputes or limit rearmament.

During this period the German nation was committed to becoming the dominant military state in Europe and in 1908, with the support of the Kaiser, Wilhelm II (grandson of Queen Victoria), Admiral von Tirpitz began to build a fleet of modern battleships to match the strength of the British Navy. Since the days of Nelson and Trafalgar (1805), Britain's powerful Royal Navy had ruled the global waves, underpinned the expansion of the British Empire, ensured protection of our worldwide wide trading capacity and protected our Island Home against invasion. Thus empowered we remained politically aloof from foreign alliances and developed a policy of 'splendid isolation'.

However, at the beginning of the 20th century the British government, under the premiership of Lord Salisbury, realised the need to counter the worrying threat of Germany's massive military expansion and proposed a minor addition of three army corps to our armed services. But the young Conservative parliamentarian, Winston Churchill, boldly opposed members of his own party in stating that Britain could never match the strength of the French or German armies, that the Royal Navy protected both our shores and world-wide interests and therefore increased military spending should be concentrated on countering the growing threat from the German navy. Churchill's succinct summary:

> Why should we sacrifice a game in which we are sure to win to
> play a game we are bound to lose?

In 1904, the new Conservative government under the leadership of Arthur Balfour appointed the creative and eccentric Admiral Sir John Fisher as First Sea Lord. Respectfully known as 'a turbulent genius', Fisher rapidly and radically modernised the Royal Navy. The bane of politicians and bureaucrats, he scrapped scores of warships "which could neither fight nor run away", thereby releasing money, dockyard capacity and naval personnel to build and crew a new concept of turbine powered battleships. 'Dreadnought', the first of the new class armed with ten 12-inch guns when launched in 1906, immediately made every other type of warship in the world obsolete. The Germans countered by building their own big-gunned, heavily armoured turbine driven battleships and cruisers.

Frustrated by his own party's policy on military expenditure the twenty-nine year old Churchill 'crossed the floor of The House' in 1904 to join the Liberal Party under Herbert Asquith: the latter became Prime Minister in 1906 and promoted Churchill to successive Cabinet posts, first as Secretary to the Board of Trade in 1908, then as Home Secretary in 1910. When he became First Lord of the Admiralty in 1911, Churchill vigorously maintained the development and construction of modern battleships and cruisers. By the time the Great War began in August 1914, the Queen Elizabeth class of even larger battleships – fuelled by oil and bristling with 15-inch guns – ensured that British Naval supremacy over the German fleet was indeed a deterrent against a possible invasion of our shores.

But what of our skies?

How would our armed forces defend the nation and deal with attacks from bomb carrying German Zeppelins and large aeroplanes now in development? How aware of the potential danger from these new weapon delivery systems were our senior politicians and military leaders? Naïve top ranking generals Lord Kitchener (Secretary of War 1914-16) and Sir Douglas Haig declared:

> Aircraft will never have the slightest effect on the outcome of a military campaign.

However, a group of foresighted junior officers persuaded the War Office chiefs to create an air battalion within the Royal Engineers. This unit developed into the Royal Flying Corps and was commissioned in April 1912 to operate airships and aircraft for the Army. Similarly, in July 1914, the Royal Naval Air Service was commissioned to carry out similar duties for the Navy.

Ironically, in 1909 Britain's political chief at the Admiralty, Winston Churchill, received an invitation from Kaiser Wilhelm II to observe German military manoeuvres. From that experience the insightful and pro-active Churchill realised that aircraft would soon develop to become major weapons of war. During the next few years this knowledge motivated him to throw his weight behind the formation of the RFC and RNAS. Typically, to gain first-hand experience, Churchill took flying lessons in 1912, survived a crash, became a competent pilot but never actually held a pilot's licence.

When the Great War began in August 1914 some senior politicians and military leaders were confused by the fact that the Army and Navy controlled separate operational wings of the nation's tiny air-force. Which Service held the major responsibility for air defence? Military pride and tradition held that the duty of the Royal Navy was to prevent approaches to our shores whereas the duty of the Army was to deal with any incursions inland. The Army ordered four of its five squadrons of bi-planes (63 aircraft) to France – the number deemed necessary for reconnaissance and gunnery guidance in support of the British Expeditionary Force of 100,000 men. That left fifteen aircraft to defend the skies above southern England.

Facing the new reality of potential German air raids on Britain, the Cabinet decided to give the Admiralty the responsibility for air defence. But even with mobilisation, military training and industrial production on a wartime footing, defence from air attack was such a groundbreaking trial-and-error exercise that little success was achieved against Zeppelin bombing raids in the first two years of the war.

Vindicating Lord Northcliffe's prognostication – "Britain is no longer an island" – the first lone Zeppelin to drop a few bombs on English soil 'invaded' our shores in April 1915. On the night of May 31st one or more German Zeppelin airships dropped about one hundred small bombs on east and north-east London. Five people were killed and fourteen injured. The effect among the politicians and the general populace was a powerful 'wake-up call' – though this new mode of warfare certainly did not create the panic anticipated by the Germans. How ignorant were they then, as again in 1940-41, of the strength of British character – of our stubborn courage in adversity, our community spirit and our humour.

However, the British press highlighted the anger of the civilian populace who were shocked by their vulnerability to 'bombs from the skies' and bewildered at the inadequacy of the nation's air defences, thus placing the Government, and the Admiralty in particular, under pressure to create a special anti-aircraft defence force for London and the south-east of England. In response the government immediately appointed Commodore Murray Sueter as Air Defence Commander and quickly made several positive initiatives to equip the new air defence units with guns and personnel. Aware of the urgency the dynamic Air Defence Chief became irate with frustration at the grindingly slow processes of 'red tape culture' in Whitehall.

Overall progress was slow until politicians and bureaucrats were again shocked into reality. On the nights of September 7th and 8th in 1915, Zeppelins dropped eighty-five bombs on London which started thirty major fires and caused serious damage to civilian and commercial property. More seriously, a total of thirty-two people were killed and eighty hospitalised with injuries. Coincidentally, public protest rallies had already been organised for the day after the second Zeppelin raid. Supported by The Lord Mayor, thousands of citizens of all classes gathered in central London to demonstrate their anger and frustration at the failure of the Government to defend the nation's Capital.

> Such was the unanimity with which this course was adopted
> that the Government, in vulgar parlance, 'got the wind up and
> got a move on' at once, which without visible public pressure
> would probably have taken still many months to initiate.

Enter a young hero. Captain Alfred Rawlinson was a knowledgeable and enterprising gunnery officer who soon cut a swathe through all the bureaucratic bull-shit and got his show on the road in record time. In the winter of 1914/15, Rawlinson had assisted the French in the organisation of air defences in and around Paris:

> where I had successfully carried out many experiments, both in
> systems of anti-aircraft sighting and in the preparation of fuses
> and ammunition for this entirely novel form of gunnery.

And, importantly, during his secondment to the French army he had made friends with several middle ranking and senior French officers. On June 20th 1915, the British Air Defence Commander sought out Rawlinson, transferred him from the Army to the RNVR with the rank of Lieutenant Commander and briefed him to train and command a newly formed squadron of armoured cars. Such was Rawlinson's energy and commitment that in his spare time he worked on designs for modifications and improvements to the gun-sights and ammunition ... especially timed fuses for anti aircraft shells. Normal shells were designed to explode on impact, not detonate in the air at a pre-set range or height. Rawlinson met with his new chief and complained ...

> ... of the small number of inefficient guns which were then at the disposal of the London air defences. The armament of this force was both inadequate and unsuitable for the purpose for which it was intended, as not only was it quite impossible for it to inflict any injury upon Zeppelin airships, but it was equally impossible that these guns could be fired over London without causing considerable injury to the unfortunate people whom they were intended to protect.

A few days after the September air raids and public protests, Rawlinson was called to the Admiralty for a meeting with the First Lord, Arthur Balfour, to discuss his role and experience with the Paris air defences. Balfour then appointed Lieutenant Commander Rawlinson to assist Admiral Scott in a radical reorganisation of the gunnery defence of London and authorised him to proceed immediately to Paris and negotiate a deal with the French Generals. Admiral Scott wrote a note to confirm the First Lord's instructions, namely, for Rawlinson to procure the loan of the most modern and efficient purpose built French mobile anti-aircraft gun, together with the latest specialised ammunition, in order that British manufacturers might examine the vehicle and weaponry to create their own design for rapid production in our factories.

For me, the researcher-writer, there are so many fascinating aspects – both serious and amusing – within this cameo of the early history of WWI, that I am tempted to go off at a tangent and write another small book – for my own enjoyment and maybe for the edification of my grandchildren. But ... but ... I will reign myself in, stick to the main task and, begging the reader's patience, complete this long preamble to my father's military service in WWI.

Serious and amusing? War, of course, is seriously horrific. Yet for this London kid laughter was an essential every day norm for me and my pals – our parents too – during the Blitz of 1940/41. And I certainly laughed as I read Lieut-Commander Rawlinson's account of his serious adventures when pioneering and operating the Royal Naval Mobile Anti-Aircraft Unit in the autumn of 1915. There was an element of a Keystone Cops style within the dedicated efficiency and energy of this dynamic leader and his troupe; paradoxes contrasting serious endeavour with amusing methods and incidents.

Five days after the meeting with Balfour and Scott at the Admiralty, 'Rapid' Rawlinson (my nickname for the enterprising and eccentric naval officer) drove his own powerful car at speed to Folkestone, boarded the ferry to Boulogne and arrived in Paris that same evening. Next morning, 'Rapid' visited friends at the Paris Arsenal where he had worked on improving high explosives and fuses, discovered that one of the latest 'Canons Automobile' was ready for testing – then rushed off to visit a couple of generals he knew, one of whom was the French Minister of War. Presenting his letter of authorisation from Admiral Scott, our British Naval Officer was informed that the new mobile gun was already allocated to a Paris air-defence unit and that only the French Commander-in-Chief, General Joffre, could authorise its release. Undeterred, 'Rapid' drove immediately – and at speed – to 'Pappa Joffre's' headquarters in Chantilly, some 45 kilometres distant.

Well! In modern parlance, our man had balls – an unbelievable nonchalant confidence – bearing in mind his own rank and that he was dealing with the very top military brass of France. Rawlinson comments:

> I felt so confident that my request would be granted that, before starting for Chantilly, I telephoned the Paris Arsenal to have all the spare parts and equipment of the gun and caisson ready for inspection that evening – and to have preparations made for finally testing the gun next morning – as I was desirous, if possible, of catching the ammunition boat leaving Boulogne that night. I got away down the good road to Chantilly at a speed which could be justified only by the urgent necessities of war.

Rawlinson's meeting with the French Commander-in-Chief was brief and successful. He sped back to Paris, was late to bed, then up early to test the new weapon and ammunition at dawn. The British Lieut-Commander then dispatched the gun and caisson on their 160 mile journey to Boulogne at mid-day, having wired the Admiralty to order his own mechanics from the armoured car unit in London to be at Newhaven the next morning ...

> ... then, after entertaining the French party suitably at the hotel, I tendered them my best thanks for their assistance and got on board in time to sail before midnight, after another somewhat strenuous day. Waking next morning at daylight, I found the ammunition ferry entering Newhaven Harbour where my mechanics from London were ready and waiting on the quay. We were away for London soon after

7am. I drove the gun the greater part of the way myself to have the opportunity of explaining its many peculiarities to the mechanics, who, of course, had never seen anything like it before, and we reached Admiral Scott's house in London safely soon after 11am.

Rapid? I'll say! In less than 72 hours, Rawlinson had received his orders in London, jumped in his own car to Folkestone, ferried the Channel to Boulogne, driven on to Paris and Chantilly, persuaded the French Commander-in-Chief to release the new 'Canons Automobile', inspected, tested and shipped the new machine back across the Channel, instructed his own mechanics and presented the shiny new prize at the door of his Admiral boss's private house in central London. I hear Keystone Cops music.

But wait a bit before you applaud – there was more dramatic comedy to come. Rawlinson had to jump into the driving seat again and race to Horse Guards Parade because Admiral Sir Percy Scott had arranged to display the new French mobile gun under the office window of the First Lord of the Admiralty at 2.30pm *the same day*. Mr Balfour came down from his upper floor office, duly inspected the French 'Canons Automobile' and the attending crew of officers and men, then politely expressed his satisfaction at the *'success and dispatch'* with which the commission had been carried out. Success was obvious, but what did the First Lord mean by his subtle emphasis on the word *'dispatch?'* Rawlinson comments:

> We heard afterwards, however, that such was the 'dispatch' with which our part of the business had been carried out that the gun was actually under the First Lord's window *before the Admiralty's official document asking for it had been written*. And at that very moment London lay defenceless and at the mercy of imminent air-raids.

Three cheers for 'Rapid' Rawlinson the swashbuckling pirate who sliced up red tape, drove his monster car like a rally driver to Paris, sweet talked the French Generals and displayed the loot on Horse Guards Parade for inspection by the First Lord of the Admiralty – all in three days – and without official government permission! 'Forrorr ... he's a jolly good fellow ... and so say all of us!'

Although our hero had achieved his first goal he was extremely frustrated by the slow, piece by piece, allocation of vital resources needed by the newly formed Anti-Aircraft Defence Force. At that time government departments were preoccupied with the increasing hardships being encountered by British forces in France and Belgium, thereby exacerbating the delay of supplies already tied up in red tape.

Given those limitations, Commodore Sueter's officers made every endeavour to locate sites suitable for fixed guns and searchlight stations, organise new telephone links to a central HQ near Horse Guards Parade and train newly enlisted personnel. In September 1915 only 12 fixed guns were in position, but by February 1916 there were 40 fixed guns and, under Commander Rawlinson, 10 mobile guns and one searchlight.

The newly acquired French gun – the only purpose-built mobile anti-aircraft gun in Britain – was garaged in Rawlinson's Armoured Car Headquarters at the Talbot Motor Works in Ladbroke Grove, West London. At 7pm on October 13th 1915, a telephone alert from the Admiralty informed the Lieut-Commander: "Some Zeppelins have crossed the coastline and are due over London at 9.00pm."

From here-on I feel that this lengthy story is best relayed through my edited version of 'Rapid' Rawlinson's own script. The event, and the Commander's intent, was serious. But there is humour too in this tale that highlights London's primitive air defence; scenes we may imagine being projected from a grainy black and white newsreel with piano accompaniment ... for which my imaginary title might be:

French Mobile Gun Chases German Zeppelin
Through London Streets on Dark Night

At 8.25pm I was ordered to proceed to the Royal Artillery Ground in the City, some five miles distant, but was delayed while crew men were rounded up from their civilian billets. As nine o'clock approached – the hour for 'quarters' – the men turned up in batches and we lit the big paraffin headlights of the cars and gun while waiting for an experienced chief petty officer who was vital to the team in case we had casualties. The crew, though well trained and disciplined, were very 'green' and had not, as yet, been 'shot over.'

At 9.05pm we drove out of our HQ into Ladbroke Grove, with myself driving my own fast car and leading the procession – the gun and caisson following at intervals of fifty yards. All headlights were lit and sirens were in use on each car. Not a second was wasted – the fastest pace at which the gun could possibly be driven, with reasonable regard to its safety, being the pace set all the way.

At that time there was no system of air-raid warnings, shelters or maroons, and the streets on this occasion were crammed both with vehicular traffic and pedestrians. In the light of their experience during the previous month, the moment they heard us coming everyone understood that an air-raid was imminent. Pedestrians and drivers had no doubt at all that the most pressing thing to do was *to get out of our way!*

I feel quite confident that no man who took part in that drive will ever forget any part of it, and particularly as we roared down Oxford Street, which presented an almost unbelievable spectacle. I had such an anxious job myself that I had no time to laugh, but I am sure I smiled all the way.

After passing Marble Arch the traffic in Oxford Street became much thicker. The noise of our sirens being *deafening* and the glare of our headlights *dazzling,* the cars, omnibuses and horse drawn transport coming from every direction were seeking safety on the pavement. I also observed, out of the corner of my eye, several instances of people flattening themselves against the shop windows – the public being, at that time, infinitely more fearful of a gun moving at terrific speed than they were of any German bombs – of which they had had little experience to date.

All went well however, until, roaring down the hill in Holborn I glanced at my speedometer and saw that it registered 56 miles per hour. At the same moment I became aware of a 'road up' sign in front of us and that the only passage left open to traffic was hopelessly blocked by a solid mass of omnibuses and other vehicles. To 'stop' at that speed was, of course, quite impossible; the only question to be decided, instantly, was – *'where to go?'* As no other choice was offered me, I was forced to head bravely for the part of the road which was under repair, hoping for the best – although the roadway there was protected by the usual pole supported on two trestles.

As we approached this barrier we could see that the repair was, mercifully, nearly finished and that there was not much to fear from the state of the road surface beyond the pole. However, I did not like the look of the infernal pole itself as, being in a very low car, I was in painful uncertainty as to what would happen – would it hit me, and if so, where? In any case 'we were in for it' and, hoping for the best, I kept my foot down and charged the obstacle without slackening speed. The next moment a relatively insignificant shock reverberated through the car but the steering wheel gave my hands a vicious wrench. Two halves of the broken pole went spinning in the air; as they did so I observed a gallant member of the London Police moving more quickly and less sedately than customary. He was actually running, helmet-less, at top speed towards the other pole which blocked the far end of the road repair. In the nick of time he downed the pole; the car bounded high in the air as we hit it but no harm was done nor was a moment lost.

19

Keeping up our speed we drove on to the Royal Artillery Ground in Moorgate Street, having traversed the whole length of Oxford Street in what must have been record time. I drove straight to the middle of the ground *(oops, the cricket pitch. AR)*, swinging the car round so that the headlights would illuminate the gun position. We immediately became aware that a Zeppelin was in sight from NNWest and making straight towards us at a height of eight to ten thousand feet at a speed of approximately 50mph. The insistent roar of its engines, rapidly becoming louder, was punctuated by the 'boom' of the bombs it was dropping in Holborn and The Strand.

The headlights of my car illuminated our gun in order to bring it into action in the quickest possible manner to set the sights, fuses and load the breach. I had no time to use range finding equipment so estimated the figures mentally; range 5,000 yards at a height of 8,000 feet. As soon as the gun-layer shouted "Ready Sir" I gave the order "FIRE". The 'burst' was short of the target – but must have surprised the Zeppelin crew who, in the light of their experience during the previous month would have been informed, quite accurately, that there were no anti-aircraft *fused high explosive* shells in the London defences.

The Zeppelin then entered our 'dead-circle'; the French auto-cannon could not be elevated beyond an angle of 83 degrees. We prepared, therefore, to catch the airship with a 'corrected fire' as he came out of the dead-circle, waiting expectantly for his bombs to fall. They fell all right – I don't know how many of them – but they made a devil of a noise and brought down several houses on the Moorgate Street side of the Royal Artillery Ground.

"Gun bears, Sir!" ... "Fire!" This time we distinctly saw the shell burst, above and quite close to the Zeppelin. But we saw no more as a sudden fog formed below the airship which had dropped all its water ballast to gain height. Moments later there was a great booming to the east as the enemy dropped the remainder of his bombs. During this raid thirty-nine bombs were dropped of considerably greater power than those used in previous raids, thirteen fires were caused, thirty-three people were killed and seventy-seven injured, whilst the structural damage was estimated at fifty thousand pounds *(many millions in the 21st century)*.

Some idea of the speed at which our unit carried out that operation is the fact that we left the Talbot Works, near Wormwood Scrubs at 9.05pm, drove to Moorgate in the City of London in record time and actually fired the first round at exactly 9.25pm – only twenty minutes later.

1915 recruiting poster depicting a Zeppelin over London

IT IS FAR BETTER
TO FACE THE BULLETS
THAN TO BE KILLED
AT HOME BY A BOMB

JOIN THE ARMY AT ONCE
& HELP TO STOP AN AIR RAID

GOD SAVE THE KING

*Commander Rawlinson's prize:
the French 75 MM Auto-Cannon*

My imagination is exhilarated by the scene: five miles in about 15 minutes through traffic in Central London, which, though not nearly so congested as now, would have been relatively dense and included horse drawn vehicles as well as petrol driven cars, vans, omnibuses – and pedestrians of course. 'Rapid' Rawlinson indeed! He has already reported that the French Auto Canon was powered by "an engine of over 100 horsepower, weighed five tons and did an easy 50mph on the level." Obviously, driving the lead car, his own, he could not outrun the gun. His tale is one of speed and derring-do – all in the cause of duty to "have a shot at a Zeppelin" with the one and only gun in London which had the capability of firing *fused high explosive shells* at a target travelling at only 50mph. 'Rapid' and his three vehicles drove faster down Oxford Street than the lumbering Zeppelin bomb-ship flying overhead!

A baptism of fire for Rawlinson's men – and a 'first night' public performance for thousands of surprised Londoners – including a bit part played by the brave policeman who truly 'manned the barriers.' Imagine the gossip – imagine the hundreds of men and women who 'dined out' on the story for weeks. Soon after that exciting escapade, Rawlinson's Mobile Brigade acquired four British vehicles mounted with guns and another equipped with a mobile searchlight. Rawlinson and a couple of experienced officers trained specially enlisted crews and moved their headquarters to the capacious stables of Kenwood House on Hampstead Heath; that historic house then owned by Lord Mansfield and tenanted by the Grand Duke Michael of Russia.

On November 9th 1915 the six vehicles and their RNVR crews were proudly paraded in the Lord Mayor's Show, cheered by thousands of patriotic citizens lining the rain-wet streets of the City of London. My father witnessed the annual event, not as a spectator, but as a uniformed RNVR rating riding one of the mobile gun automobiles belonging to the Royal Naval Mobile Anti-Aircraft Brigade. He was pleased beyond measure to be in uniform again following a major blow to his pride and social status following his honourable discharge from the Army earlier that year.

In September 1914 Samuel Thomas Rayment, aged eighteen years and eight months, changed from his business suit into the uniform of a Rifleman in the 9th Battalion of the Queen Victoria Rifles. He was one of millions of young men, some under the age of 18, who flocked to the recruiting stations to join the armed services voluntarily before and after the outbreak of WWI on August 4th 1914.

But in January 1915, following a more rigorous second medical examination to determine fitness for service in France, Sam was honourably discharged due to double hernias. Thoroughly disappointed, he reluctantly returned to civilian life in February 1915, lodged with the parents of his fiancé in Hermitage Lane, Hampstead, and went to work on the silk counter at Boyds the Drapers.

Later that year when Rawlinson's mobile unit was authorised to expand, hundreds of volunteers were being interviewed at his new headquarters at Kenwood House, right on Sam's doorstep. He applied, hoping desperately to have a second chance of serving his country in uniform. The massive losses of men in Belgium and France had created a great surge of public patriotism, which, on the negative side, had already caused some young men still in civvies to be given, or sent, a white feather – a symbol of cowardice. I remember hearing my father remark to a friend that after he had been discharged from the Army around the time of his nineteenth birthday he became anxious that some customers at Boyds might think he was a pacifist-coward.

In Rawlinson's book I read with interest the selection criteria for enlistment in the RNMAAB, a section of which was pertinent to my father's situation. Given the numbers of men who applied it was indeed a confirmation of Sam's skills and character – in addition to his Army training and field artillery experience – that he was selected.

> With regard to the mechanics, they were selected from the armoured car personnel and were exceptionally efficient before their selection; and in their case no conditions were imposed as to their physical qualifications, all being classed as A1. The case of the remainder was, however, different, as they were specially enlisted – *and such enlistment was confined to those who were not physically qualified for service at the Front.*
>
> This resulted in the RNVR Anti-Aircraft Brigade becoming a veritable *corps d'elite*, as the number of applicants far exceeded the demand and a careful selection was made in each case. The ranks, therefore, were made up of all classes; each individual having some special recommendation and being exceptionally proficient in some particular line. It was, indeed, frequently astounding to find the extraordinary 'diversity of talent' at our disposal.

Sam reported for duty at the RNMAAB headquarters at Kenwood House on October 27th 1915, drew his kit and proudly donned the dark blue uniform of a Naval Rating, RNVR. I am particularly fond of a photograph of my father, aged nineteen, attired in his dress uniform – a double-breasted, three-buttoned jacket, white shirt and black tie – his handsome young face framed in a peaked cap with white cotton cover.

He was immediately appointed to one of the crews operating a 3-pounder high-velocity, quick-firing, high-angle Vicker's gun, mounted on a Lancia motor lorry. I am fortunate to have a photograph, taken at Kenwood House, of Lieut-Commander Rawlinson inspecting his Brigade: my father, Sam, is standing to attention in front of a row of mobile guns. I can also identify my father in photographs contained in a press article published by the *Daily Mirror* after the war – on January 9th 1919 – with the caption:

We are now permitted to publish these photographs illustrating the work of the (mobile) Anti-Aircraft Corps, which has done splendid service in defending London and provincial centres against the repeated attacks of enemy aircraft. Practically nothing was allowed to be published (in the war) concerning their activities, and their work has hitherto been almost unrecognised.

'Rapid' Rawlinson was promoted to 'Commander' following the recruiting campaign and expansion of his unit. He makes interesting reference to the variety of personnel he commanded: university mathematicians and trained draughtsmen operating complex range finding and navigational devices; skilled electricians dealing with the ever improving technology of searchlights and elaborate telephone equipment; a skilled theatrical artist to organise camouflage for the guns and vehicles and experienced chefs to care for the men's culinary needs. In the opinion of this writer, our hero had pioneered and trained a highly efficient and economical mobile anti-aircraft gunnery unit in record time. He now had to fight the Establishment to keep his successful enterprise from being disbanded.

In May 1916 the Army took over the gunnery defence of the country from the Navy. In his book Rawlinson writes of his tussle with senior officers at Army HQ to keep his unique unit intact and to maintain the efficient team he had recruited and trained. Rawlinson wrote to the Army, explaining why he needed only half the complement of men that would normally be required by their standard regulations.

> The explanation was, of course, that the mobile force under my command had originated from a squadron of naval armoured cars. We had our own mechanics, repair department etc., and took entire charge of our motors. At the same time, the whole force was self-contained; mechanics learning gunnery duties and the gunners rudimentary mechanics, so that each class of 'rating' was able to help the other and all became practically interchangeable when required. All mechanical stores were drawn from the Admiralty on my responsibility without intervention from any other department.

Rawlinson goes on to point out that from May 1916 he was expected to conform to standard Army regulations and methods by which supplies of mechanical equipment were ...

> ... under the charge of the Army Service Corps Mechanical Department, to whom all requirements have to be referred and by whom all mechanical parts are supplied and repairs effected. Much time is therefore lost, and in many cases two

men are required to do the work of one — and the expense is proportionately increased.

Staff at Army GHQ were busily engaged in organising the expansion of anti-aircraft gunnery defences which were now required to cover a large proportion of the country. Senior officers involved in this urgent exercise ...

> ... were familiar with every detail and military requirement of the British guns and men. When, however, it came to the French guns and equipment, and the personnel required for their efficient working, they found themselves entirely at sea; and in the case of the mobile force such as I had the honour to command, they were even more so, as no such class of guns existed in the British Army.

Rawlinson fought a tough battle with the brass hats at the War Office in order to save his unit from being written off. The logic of his case set out in written reports was finally accepted:

> My revolutionary statement was very well received at General Headquarters, and it was allowed to be correct in the case of the quite exceptionally constituted force under my command. The Naval Mobile Brigade was, indeed, entirely outside all the usual customs and regulations of the Army. It was nevertheless recognised as being remarkably efficient, and therefore, in face of the urgent demand for defence, to be encouraged rather than immediately disbanded, especially as no other similar force was then in existence to replace it. The situation, therefore, was accepted, and the immediate result was that I was supplied with some more RNVR officers and informed that I should be allowed to increase the personnel further by special enlistment, as and when more guns became available.

In researching and writing this piece I have become especially proud of my father: that he overcame the disappointment and dent to his self-esteem on being discharged from the army; that he offered his services to, and was selected for, a truly unconventional band of pioneering brothers-in-arms – a disciplined pirate ship fighting for the Country – and at times against the British Establishment. To be a member of Commander Rawlinson's pioneering unit was not only a privilege but a wonderful character-building and formative personal experience for him. In reading Rawlinson's book I have learned much about my father's youth and I now understand and respect him more than ever before. As I wrote earlier, it frustrates me that we never discussed and recorded the details of his brief service in the Army, his embarrassment when having to return to a civilian job, and later, his opportunity to serve in the Royal Naval Mobile Anti-Aircraft Brigade.

Largely unrecognised in the history of World War One is the fact that many civilians and a number of service personnel were killed or injured on home territory by shells from our own anti-aircraft guns. When reading Commander Rawlinson's book, *The Defence of London, 1915-18*, I noted the importance he attached to "systems of anti-aircraft sighting and the preparation of *fuses and ammunition for this entirely novel form of gunnery.*" Against Zeppelins the experiment failed; incendiary bullets fired from fighter planes succeeded.

That I was destined to be the eldest son of Samuel Thomas Rayment is not only due to his double hernias but also to a beneficent providence – and a wall of sandbags – that protected him during a German air-raid in the autumn of 1917. When manning a mobile gun firing at Gotha bombers from a sandbagged emplacement on Hampstead Heath, Sam suffered severe shell-shock when one of our own shells exploded close to the bunker. He was hospitalised at Chatham and later posted to the Dungavel Hospital in Scotland.

One story that my father enjoyed recounting was of his long convalescence: how he missed his recently widowed mother – and of course his future wife Wyn and her parents in Hampstead, but on the other hand, how much he appreciated the care and attention of the hospital staff during his long stay at the Dungavel. He particularly enjoyed the camaraderie among fellow patients; also his involvement in entertaining wounded servicemen and the local people as a member of the hospital's travelling Concert Party.

In my archives I have the programmes of concerts in Strathaven (9th March 1918) and Hamilton (6th April 1918) by 'The Sailors of Dungavel'. Sam played piano solos and sang songs that became familiar to me during our family evenings round the piano at Upton Lodge in the 1930s and '40s. I now feel a lump in my throat as I recall Sam's strong baritone voice, his theatrical style and the twinkle in his eye as Wyn accompanied Sam singing 'Shipmates O'Mine,' 'Trumpeter' and 'Up from Somerset'.

My mother, my brother and I, and our large extended family are so thankful that Sam, having survived the carnage of The Great War, was able to rejoin his sweetheart, sing popular songs with her and 'be joined together in Holy Matrimony' in 1923. As I conclude this chapter I treasure the mind-picture of Sam enjoying his time in Scotland among a jolly crew of land-based sailors, playing the piano and singing 'Shipmates O' Mine'.

~~~~~~~~~~~

Footnote by author: Three years after writing the above chapter I discovered that before WW1 Alfred Rawlinson (nickname 'Toby') was well known as an Olympian Gold Medallist (polo), a racing driver and the third person to hold a Royal Aero Club Aviator's Certificate. Following his pioneering contribution to the air defence of London he was appointed to British Intelligence with the rank of Colonel. When his brother died in 1925 Alfred Rawlinson succeeded as 3rd Baronet of North Walsham, Norfolk. He lived from 1867 to 1934. My apologies for any embarrassment to his family caused by the respectful nickname, 'Rapid'.

Commander Rawlinson inspecting the RNMAA unit at Kenwood House, Hampstead, 1915. Samuel Rayment second from right in back row

Daily Mirror photograph of the RNMAA unit at Kenwood House, Hampstead, released for publication after WWII in 1919

Samuel Rayment
in RNVR uniform, 1915

Wennerloef Carter,
circa 1915

CHAPTER 2

BIRTH – AND NEAR DEATH

JANUARY 1976: AT MY PARENTS' HOME,
'WRAYCOTT', IN BOUNDSTONE, SURREY

Eighty! Father was eighty last week.

Before lunch Joan and I joined Mother in a toast to the birthday boy: raising our glasses of sherry we chorused, "To Sam the Octogenarian!"

During the lively banter that followed, Sam, in jocular mood, accepted the salutation in the spirit of affection in which it was given. Thankfully he was healthy, happily retired and comfortable in his long marriage. Sam and Wyn had been soul mates since the age of fourteen – how far and fast the river of time had flowed since their first meeting, and indeed, since my own earliest memories of family and home in Finchley.

In the early evening, while the ladies were enjoying a tête-à-tête about dressmaking in the dining room, Sam and I chatted about happy times we shared together in 'the olden days': family musical evenings around the piano, darts and billiards between air raids during the war contrasting with peacetime pursuits – fishing at Ryde and cricket at Lord's. Sitting comfortably in his deep arm-chair beside the glowing coal fire, enjoying his pipe and sipping a glass of Scotch, Sam's relaxed reminiscing developed into a brief conspiratorial moment between father and son. My father had rarely, if ever, confided in me. I was therefore pleasantly surprised as he began to share long guarded thoughts in a light-hearted manner and I realised, for the first time, that Sam was really proud – properly chest-puffingly proud – that at the ages 31 and 40 he had sired two sons and thus satisfied his primordial drive to procreate – to become a father.

I was impressed and enlightened – beginning to understand my father at a deeper level than before. With a twinkle in his eye the octogenarian confided: "But you were a surprise my boy – your brother Derek too nine years later." Then in whimsical vein: "Yes, my boy, you were pupped on the Isle of Wight in 1927, born in Finchley – but you didn't know" – pausing to sip his whisky, then whisper – "you didn't know that your dear mother had never seen a nude man until last summer. She was watching cricket on television when that 'streaker' jumped over the stumps at Lord's during the Ashes Test match."

Momentarily embarrassed, I recovered to share his cheerful chuckle whilst inwardly amazed to learn that my parent's traditional Edwardian upbringing precluded undressing in the bedroom. With great respect to Mother we laughed again at our joint conclusion: she had been especially indignant because the 'shocking incident' had been perpetrated on the hallowed turf at Lord's – the cathedral of cricket – with millions of people watching on television.

Father confided: "Do you know what she said, Alan?"

"Disgusting! He'll have to be locked up ... never heard of such a thing!"

Nor seen, evidently.

AUGUST 1980 AT BOUNDSTONE

In the summer holidays Joan and I arranged to discuss and record my early childhood with my parents and, in particular, why I had nearly died when three months old. Studying child development at Sussex University that year had heightened the levels of curiosity about my own childhood and, having gleaned crumbs of information in the past, I was now hungry for the full story. Joan, a nursery school head-teacher, professionally knowledgeable and very experienced in matters of child development was equally curious. During our enjoyable sunlit drive through the leafy Sussex countryside we discussed the potential short and long term effects of infant malnutrition on both child and parents.

A visit to Sam and Wyn at their retirement bungalow in Boundstone, Surrey, always entailed a series of rituals: a Sunday morning pint in the village pub – sherry for the ladies – and on cue, Sam's predictable mantra: "Can't have same ... only similar, my dear" – when Mother responded "same again" as I took orders for the second round. Also predictable, even in a public house: "Quiet now ... THE NEWS" ... when the six pips heralded the BBC's one o'clock news on the saloon bar radio. To Sam the BBC NEWS was sacrosanct.

While Mother and Joan were busy in the kitchen making final preparations for lunch, Father and I set the dining table with a crisply laundered linen cloth, mats, cutlery, water glasses, ringed serviettes, condiments and accoutrements. Settled and seated in high backed chairs Joan and I commented on the delightful aromas of home cooking that accompanied the entry of roast beef on a large oval dish followed by the presentation of Yorkshire pudding, a variety of vegetables in tureens, and a gravy boat emitting a whiff that caused Joan to exclaim, "Reminds me of the *Bisto Kids* advertisement."

From the time I was a small child I had been captivated by the next ritual: Sam, standing at the head of the table, applied carving knife to steel with a theatrical flourish ... skish-skash ... skish-skash ... before plunging the long two-pronged fork into the h-bone joint and placing wafer-thin slices of succulent beef on to warm plates. Wyn, without fuss or flourish, served up the vegetables and gravy – I poured water into glasses and we all passed the condiments. The scene deserved a blessing but Grace was not on the menu.

Mother's apple pie, crowned with delicate pastry, signalled the enactment of a tradition remembered to this day by all who dined at my parents' table. Sam's antique tin spice box containing nutmegs, ginger root and grater was passed round the table, the spices patiently applied to the dessert by guests and hosts, the tin closed and returned to its position in front of Father's place setting. That simple ritual around the family table – of special significance to me and my brother Derek since childhood – seemed to symbolise the stability, strength and warmth of family life that was, thankfully, prevalent in the local community during our formative years. Father and I tackled the final ritual, washing up, while Wyn and Joan had fun playing cheerful duets on the piano – singing along to popular hits from *My Fair Lady* and *The Sound of Music*.

In preparation for recording 'The Story of Baby Alan', Joan and I rearranged the sitting room chairs assisted by a nervous Sam, huffin' and puffin' as he smoked his pipe. Taking time to get comfortable in his deep arm-chair he questioned me as though I were setting up a TV interview. Wyn, more confident and relaxed, breezed into the sitting room, bearing a tray of tea and biscuits. Joan, having experienced many radio interviews when head of the school at The Mayflower Family Centre in East London, joked with Sam in a mildly flirtatious way to put him at ease and cued in the first question: "How long had you been married when Alan was born?"

Sam coughed nervously, but Wyn responded in a clear voice: "Five years ... we were married in 1923."

I pitched the next question in a light hearted manner: "Then I came along in 1928 ... I expect that was a surprise?"

Sam guffawed, "You were a surprise all right ... er ... and a shock, my boy ... 'I'm not going to have it,' she said ... 'Not going to have it' ... so I said, 'Well – you've got it'." Squeals of delighted laughter from the ladies as Sam again intoned, "Well, you've got it, I said."

Wyn, always a good sport, had a chuckle in her voice as she timed her punch line: "And look what I've got now – you Alan with six children and Derek with four. Sometimes I think it's all a dream. At the time I became pregnant I was scared stiff. I was thirty-two ... I'd never had anything to do with young children ... never held a baby in my life. Sam and I already had the responsibility of being guardians to your cousins: Doris was thirteen and away at boarding school – Beryl was seven – and for two weeks around your birth-time she boarded at her local private school. My parents moved in to run the household."

Mother, typical of her generation of women, adjusted quickly to being pregnant, made no fuss and 'just got on with it': *it* being dressmaking, playing piano at evening classes, doing all the shopping, cooking, washing, ironing and cleaning. The five-bedroom house was heated by coal fires and in 1928 there were no modern appliances to ease a housewife's workload.

"Mother, can you recall anything about your pregnancy – especially my actual birth?" I asked.

"Well, the pregnancy was perfectly normal ... in fact, I was playing at evening classes until Easter and nobody knew you were coming because I was conveniently camouflaged ... wasn't any size. Then on the morning before your birth I went for a long walk to Totteridge with Sam's sister-in-law Lizzie, a trained nurse who was staying to assist with your birth. After lunch I had a rest and battle commenced at 10pm. Dr Holmes gave me chloroform in the last period ... so I didn't know anything about the actual birth when you were delivered at 6.00am on May the twenty-ninth."

"Hmmm ... that is so very interesting, Mother. First, that in typical fashion you made no fuss, and second, that your doctor made a home visit in the middle of the night. So as far as Dr Holmes and Aunt Lizzie were concerned, was my birth straight forward: oh, and how much did I weigh?"

"Oh yes ... let me see ... you weighed 6 pounds 15 ounces, and yes, everything during the pregnancy and birth was straightforward ... but the after-effects were troubling because, being so ignorant about babies, I didn't know how to feed you properly ... myself, that is."

Mother, always articulate and still, at 84, quick-minded and lucid, could not bring herself to use the term 'breast feeding'. Respecting her Edwardian sensibilities I joined the game of avoiding the obvious and asked her why she could not feed me 'herself'.

"Because I hadn't got *it* – and didn't know what to do. Dr Holmes kept telling me to feed you with cow's milk – watered down, of course – but you kept throwing that up. Your aunt, Nurse Lizzie, encouraged me to drink lots of water, which I did, but that made no difference either."

The change of mood among the four of us was palpable: our cheerful banter switched to feelings of serious concern for this baby ... and 'this baby' was *me*. My mind teemed with questions. Thankfully, my professional training enabled me to rein in that torrent. "Keep it simple, Alan," I said to myself.

"So ... Mother, right from the time I was born up to, say, three or four days, I hadn't had any 'food' ... or not much ... and the doctor said, "Give him cow's milk." Gee whiz ... that was so primitive and obviously unsuitable. So why didn't Dr Holmes or Aunt Lizzie organise a test feed to see how much, or little, milk I was receiving from you?"

"Oh no ... no ... not in those days!"

"Gee whiz," I exclaimed. "Again that's unbelievably prehistoric! I must have yelled the roof off."

"Oh my ... cry ... you cried and CRIED ... and we didn't get any sleep for weeks," stated Wyn.

Sam, now relaxed and in good humour, added ... "Chuck him out the window, she said, chuck him ... "

"Stop teasing, Sam … but if you remember, it was getting us down … it was so nerve-wracking."

"It must have been more than nerve-wracking," I concurred, "having had six kids with Betty … a baby who cries with hunger night and day can drive parents crazy … so what happened and how long did this drama go on?"

"Well, you were being starved, but in my ignorance I didn't know this. The doctor was old-fashioned, and both he and your Aunt Lizzie were very much opposed to the newly-opened Baby Clinic and told me not to go – probably a bit of professional jealousy – and kept on saying, "Feed him on watered-down cow's milk." Consequently, you went on crying so much – and getting so thin – that by three months old you looked like a scraggy runt of a baby."

I was staggered by this news, yet somehow held back on the stream of expletives rushing from brain to voice box. "Three months … three months! I was starving for three months!? That's preposterous – beyond belief!"

Temporarily shaken up, I became silent as kaleidoscopic pictures whirled through my mind. First, amazement that I had somehow survived, followed by several imaginative scenes depicting the strain, the heartache and exhaustion suffered by my dear parents for three long months.

Sam reminded Wyn that her mother, Emily, had said: "You'll never rear him." Mother responded by turning to me and saying: "Yes Alan, your grandmother was getting very worried and, in her kindly way, urged me to get some advice … 'or you'll never pull him through,' she said."

"Well, Mother, I must have had some food from somewhere to have survived for as long as three months. How about powdered milk?"

"Yes, after a while I did try something else … one of those tinned preparations … Glaxo or something like that which had just come into fashion. But your tummy was in such a state you couldn't digest it. Your breath smelt so sour. All you did was cry … just went on and on crying."

A long silence hung in the air – a silence of sadness and empathy as we all contemplated the dramatic domestic scenes that had unfolded five decades before. With pictures and questions crowding my mind I broke the silence.

"Well, Mother, it wasn't your fault. I don't do the blame thing anyway, but you say this situation went on for three months and that you knew you might lose me … and that you were scared to go to the new clinic because Dr Holmes and Aunt Lizzie told you not to go. I really am amazed at their ignorance and arrogance – and the lack of caring support for you and Father – except perhaps from your parents. Something radical must have happened to change that awful stalemate, some miracle even, because here I am now, fifty-two years later, healthy and noisy – and aching with curiosity as to how we all survived that dramatic ordeal way back in 1928. Thank God for scientific progress because, relatively, that was a primitive era of medicine and child care. Jeepers! … it is hard to take in … nursing a starving baby for three months …

you both deserve the George Medal for survival and rescue. Oh I'll shut-up ... what happened next?"

Mother brightened up: "Ah, but I used to go round to see Mrs Murphy, an educated lady who was wife of the physics master at Finchley County School. I was very friendly with them because they used to run the Evening School where I played piano for the keep-fit and dance classes. Well, for several weeks Mrs Murphy had been urging me to take you to the Baby Clinic, but I was worried that I would upset Dr Holmes. Then one day she said, "Look, Wyn, you be sensible and take your baby to the Clinic. If you don't, you're going to lose him." So, er ... I plucked up courage, ignored the other lot ... umm ... well, Dr Holmes really ... and went ... didn't I, Sam?"

Sam remained silent in deference to Lizzie in Wyn's diplomatic reference to 'the other lot'.

"Did anyone go with you," I enquired, "because, as you said, you were scared?"

"No ... no, I went on my own, with you in the pram. The duty nurse in reception at the clinic was friendly and put me at ease. Then I sat in a line with the other mothers and their babies."

"So did you notice a difference – a friendlier atmosphere than at the doctor's surgery?"

"Well yes, very different. Anyway, my turn came to take you in to see the lady doctor ... I wish I could remember her name ... she took one look at you, asked me a few questions about the feeding and then said, "'This baby is being starved and I want you to have a test feed.' So the nurse in charge took me to another room where she weighed you before and after I fed you ... and this provided the evidence that you were hardly getting anything ... less than an ounce of my milk ... and proved why I was fighting such a losing battle."

Joan and I looked at each other in jaw-dropping amazement. Then Joan, with deep warm empathy, reassured Wyn: "As Alan said before, Mother, it wasn't your fault, just the professional lack of knowledge and general ignorance of those times – though it is hard for me to comprehend that your own doctor, a friend too, should be so un-informed ... and stubborn too."

"That's kind of you to say so Joan, but you can guess how desperately worried I was at the time. Sam and I nearly lost young Alan ... and that would have been devastating."

Wyn then explained that the lady doctor at the clinic taught her how to predigest the recommended Bengers Food by cooking the powdered milk before cooling it and feeding me through a glass bottle with teat.

"Gradually, as you made progress, the scheduled cooking time was reduced until you were able to digest the mixture at full strength."

"Hmmm," I interjected, "a long drawn-out process requiring saintly patience."

Wyn continued, "Thankfully, by that method you gradually picked up, stopped crying and gained weight. I've still got your weight cards in my desk."

I was amazed: "You've still got the weight cards from when I was a starving baby ... incredible. May we have a look because I am fascinated as to the rate of progress in gaining weight and how long it took to double my birth weight, Mother?"

"Well, progress was very slow at first ... let me see ... that first visit to the clinic was on October 4th – so that was eighteen weeks after your birth ... that's over four months."

"Over four months!" I exclaimed loudly, "over four months ... so I was starving and yelling for over four months ... not three as we have been talking about. I can hardly take that in, or understand how I survived. I must have had a powerful will to hang on ... a massive inner drive to live. My intuition tells me that I hung on in there because I received so much love from you and Father in spite of the worry and all those sleepless nights you both experienced. Well, thank you, thank you for your love and perseverance ... I take my hat off to both of you. So back to those weight cards. How much did I weigh at eighteen weeks?"

"Yes, this weight card records that you were 11lbs 9oz on October 4th 1928 ... that was nearly nineteen weeks after your birth. By twenty-six weeks you were beginning to make a bit of progress – and I see that over Christmas you gained one pound in two weeks and weighed 14lb 2oz on January 1st 1929. So working this out from the calendar, it took 31 weeks for you to double your birth weight. Then, on your first birthday you weighed 20lbs. You were strong and fit ... a picture of health as we can see in this photo ... long blond curls, chubby cheeks and holding a book in your hand."

"Ah yes, Mother, I have a copy of that photograph ... very healthy and quite a good-looking child. One more question. Do you remember when you put me on semi-solid foods ... you know ... those baby foods in tiny jars?"

"Oh my! There was nothing like that in those days, Alan. But nine years later, when Derek was a baby, I used to buy them at the local chemist's shop. But to feed you I used to buy a knuckle of veal and boil it down to a thick jelly – then give you spoonfuls of that mixed with some mashed-up vegetables."

"And Mother, that whole experience was a great ordeal for you and Father. You must both have been so relieved when I pulled through and developed into a robust young infant."

"You can say that again, my boy," piped up Sam. "Your mother took the brunt of it all ... took a lot out of her. She lost weight herself – though there wasn't much of her to start with. I was just as worried about her as I was about you. But by the time that photograph was taken she was back to her normal energetic self ... thank God!"

"Well, well, well – what a story. I am still truly gob-smacked that I survived …..and so thankful to both of you. And Mrs Murphy, bless her, played the role of my guardian angel. Maybe I was pre-ordained to live so that Betty and I could create six wonderful children. C'est la vie."

Joan then asked a serious question that provoked much laughter from Wyn and witty comments from Sam: "Did Alan's late physical growth seriously delay his mobility ... his crawling and walking ... and what about talking ... and ... ?"

"Talking!" interjected mother, laughing so much that we had to wait while she got her breath back ... talking ... you ask, dear ... well, Alan was really adept at that from a very young age ... wasn't he, Sam?"

"And he's been talking the hind leg off a donkey ever since," quipped Sam.

"How about walking and reading?" I asked.

"Well!", Wyn replied, exhaling a deep breath, relieved from recounting the most painful part of the story, "well, you took your first steps at fifteen months on the tennis court at Field House, Ripon, when we were visiting Auntie Rose. By eighteen months you were running everywhere and we had to strap you into reins when out walking in town. And about reading, well ... you were always keen on reading ... even before you could actually read."

Having no previous experience of young children Mother had been surprised that I had so accurately memorised the nightly bedtime stories, which after a while I insisted on 'reading' to her. Of course, that knack is common in a high percentage of toddlers – but a revelation to my inexperienced mother when in her early thirties.

The recording session had been long and enlightening ... it was time to wind it up and relax.

"That's it then folks – and thank you all very much. We all need a drink. Is the bar open, Father?"

Sam set up the beers and sherries, raised his glass and called for a toast.

"Here's to Wyn – a wonderful woman!"

Joan and I chorused, "We'll drink to that ... three cheers for a wonderful Mother ... and Father, too!"

~~~~~~~~~~~

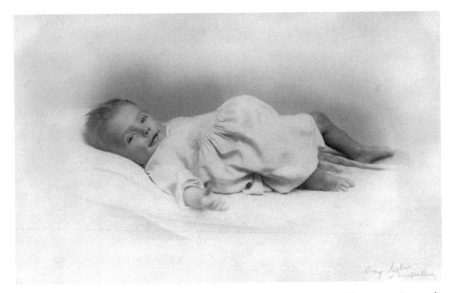

Baby Alan, age 6 months

*Alan, first birthday, with book,
recovered from malnutrition*

Sam and Alan,
Field House,
Ripon, 1929

Wyn and Alan,
Field House,
Ripon, 1929

CHAPTER 3

SAM AND WYN – FAMILY ROOTS

Special thanks to my niece, Alison Barnes, our family genealogist.

Samuel Thomas Rayment and Wennerloef Emily Carter
met in 1910 at 'Weekes The Family Drapers' in Hampstead, London.
As 14-year-old apprentices they worked hard, learned their trade and earned a pittance.

THE RAYMENT FAMILY

Sam, born on a farm estate at Milton Ernest, Bedfordshire in 1896, the youngest in a family of twelve, had descended from a strong line of country stock. His great-grandfather <u>William,</u> born in 1799 at Braughing in Hertfordshire, started working life as a 'carter' (driver of a horse drawn wagon or carriage) and married <u>Emma Barnard</u> in 1820. The couple produced three children, the first of whom was George. In mid-career, William became a Bailiff – a farm estate administrator – near Sawbridgeworth in Hertfordshire. In semi-retirement he was a publican.

<u>George Rayment</u>, born at Clavering in Essex in 1820, married Charlotte Mitchell at Braughing in 1841. Charlotte bore ten children and died, sadly, at the age of forty. George, a gamekeeper on several estates in the Herts-Essex area during his working life, married Susan Ansell in 1863 and was blessed with a daughter Ruth in 1867. In 1850 <u>Albert Barnard</u> Rayment, my father's father, the fifth child in George's first family, was born at Sheering in Essex.

On leaving school at 14, Albert was employed locally (probably as a stable boy) by a Mr and Mrs Chapman and at 16 moved to Thornton Hall in Yorkshire where, at the age of 21, he was registered as a coachman employed by Anne Dodsworth, widow of a baronet and landowner. On March 2nd 1872 Albert married <u>Isabella Johnson</u> at the Weslyan Methodist Chapel in Bedale, Yorkshire. Isabella, who had been employed as the housekeeper at 'Low Barn' in the village of Thornton Watlass, gave birth to their first child, <u>Christiana,</u> at 'Low Barn' on Christmas Day of that year.

Two years later their first son, <u>Henry,</u> was born in Snape, Yorkshire, where Albert was now employed as a gardener. Three more children were born in Snape: <u>George</u> in 1876, <u>William</u> in 1879 and <u>Annie</u> in May 1881. Tragically the children's mother, Isabella, died in the same year on September 7th, aged 39.

Albert, who was now a forty-one year old widower with five children under nine years of age, needed a full-time housekeeper-carer for his family. Given that the lady he employed, <u>Harriet Harrington</u>, was from Pelsall near Birmingham

– a distance of some 140 miles – the author's hunch is that his grandfather placed an advertisement in the *Methodist Recorder* seeking the assistance he needed to cope with the daily needs of his young family.

Four years later Albert moved the family south to Milton Ernest in Bedfordshire where he had been appointed to the post of Bailiff of a gentleman's farm estate. Albert and Harriet were married on June 6th in 1885 at the Wesleyan Chapel in Bedford. Exactly a year later their first child Albert (Bert) Harrington Rayment was born, followed by John (Jack) Barnard in 1887; Mercy in 1889; Charles Frederick in 1891; Frank in 1893; Margaret (Maggie) in 1894 and my father, Samuel Thomas, on January 7th 1896.

As the grandson/author I pause to reflect on the character of my grandmother Harriet: her energy, her fortitude, her love of children and her capacity to cope with the immense amount of work that such a large family would entail. She was 26 when first employed by Albert the 41-year-old widower to run his household and care for five children under nine years of age. When Harriet, 30, married Albert the ages of his five children ranged between 13 and 4. The first child of the second family was born one year later and in the following nine and a half years Harriet gave birth to six more babies. Truly incredible! And, as far as I understood from my father, Sam, he and all his brothers and sisters were born at home in their small lodge house on the Manor Estate at Milton Ernest. I also note that when Sam was born four years were to pass before the eldest, Bert, left home to become a clerk in the wholesale fabric trade in London.

When 'The Squire' of the Milton Ernest estate died in 1901, Albert was entrusted with the sale of the estate and possessions. At the same time he had to move his family to a cottage in the nearby village of Pavenham and find a new occupation. My versatile grandfather drove a horse-drawn cart stocked with books and bibles – and meat slaughtered at a local farm – to sell to villagers around the Pavenham area. Obliged to move again he worked as a caretaker at a girl's school in Bedford before opening a butcher's shop in the nearby village of Clapham. A few years later, probably 1908, Albert purchased 'The Elms', an agricultural smallholding in Grewelthorpe, near Ripon, Yorkshire. He raised a few beef cattle and dairy cows, delivered milk and meat to the local people and thumped the bible on Sundays as a Methodist lay preacher. I clearly remember Sam, with a degree of pride and solemnity, portraying his father as a hard-working and rather stern man – with full bushy beard and powerful voice – proclaiming Christian evangelical theology and narrow Victorian values from the pulpit.

Fortunately, being a diligent pupil, Sam had benefited from a solid grounding in the 3 Rs at a variety of schools and was ready to start work – perhaps as a clerk in a local company connected with agricultural produce or equipment. Sam was a country boy and remained a countryman at heart throughout his life. Cue serendipity – or the outcome of Albert's prayers – or my own romantic view of destiny: to meet his soul-mate, Sam was tossed out of his familiar country environment to start a new life in the hurly-burly of the unfamiliar environment of North London – on his own – at the age of fourteen.

Answering an advertisement in the *Methodist Recorder* in 1910, Albert had negotiated a position for Sam as a draper's apprentice in Hampstead, North London. On the 1st of April 1910 Sam said goodbye to his mother, was driven in a pony and trap to Ripon railway station by his father, shook hands with the bearded preacher, stepped into the gloomy carriage, placed his small suitcase on the luggage rack and settled into the four-hour journey to London.

I remember Sam recounting the story of how frightened he became when, having alighted from the steam train into the hustle and bustle of London's King's Cross station, his elder brother Bert failed to meet him and turned up an hour later. Then another new and daunting experience – down into the Tube. The northern section of London's underground rail system had been extended from Euston to Hampstead and Golders Green in 1907: Hampstead's station was accessed by a lift (elevator) descending 181 feet – or 320 steps. When Bert and Sam walked into the fresh air of Heath Street, my father's new home was a few steps away. Sam lived in at *Weekes The Family Drapers* for three years, received board and lodging plus one shilling per week during the first year, two during the second and three during the third. On completion of his apprenticeship in 1913 Sam obtained employment at *Boyds The Drapers* until joining the Army in 1914.

In 1914 or 1915 Albert's failing health necessitated a move to his son Harry's small farm on the outskirts of Ipswich where he died in July 1916. Harriet, sixteen years younger than her husband, lived on in Ipswich until she died aged 79 in 1934. I was six and have only the faintest remembrance of my grandmother – of an old lady smelling of lavender water, wearing a long voluminous black skirt. However, I hold her in great honour: a truly amazing lady who, from the age of twenty-six, gave dedicated care and service to her husband, to five step-children and seven born and raised during her marriage to Albert.

I am so grateful to my brother Derek's eldest daughter and our family's genealogist, Alison Barnes, for providing nearly all the facts associated with members of our ancestral tree including some interesting details about the lives of Albert and Isabella's children.

The first born was <u>Christiana</u> – known as Chrissie – married Thomas Tolton with whom she bore three children: Annie, Thomas and Mabel. My aunt was widowed in 1933 and married George Manyweather in 1938. I remember meeting Chrissie and George in the 1940s before my aunt died in 1950 at the age of 77. Annie married Hubert Hanks in 1923; their only daughter, Betty, became Mayor of Milton Keynes in the 1970s.

My religious grandfather, Albert, must have been delighted that his eldest son Henry – known as Harry – became a Christian missionary in Africa. Harry's wife, Eliza, bore three children and was the first white woman to enter Nyasaland (now Malawi). When Harry died in Ipswich in 1916 Eliza purchased a boarding house in Felixstowe. She moved to the United States in 1930.

George and William boarded the SS Victorian in Liverpool on June 7th 1906, sailed into Quebec and travelled west across the vastness of Canada to British Columbia. George found employment as a coachman but sadly, in December 1907 – when still a young man of 31, he was killed in a landslide accident in Coykendahl, British Columbia. William was able to reach the tragic scene and accompany George's coffin on the 250 mile journey to Vancouver and arrange the funeral.

Prior to the Canadian venture William had joined The Imperial Yeomanry, a newly warranted cavalry regiment formed in 1900 to reinforce established British army units engaged in the Second Boer War in South Africa. William was wounded, discharged and returned to England before he joined his brother in Canada. After George was killed, William joined the Royal North-West Mounted Police and met a young English widow, Alice Cropp, who was visiting her brother in Vancouver. They married in Canada on November 11th 1911, then travelled to Nyasaland to join Harry Rayment and his wife, not as missionaries but as owners of a tobacco plantation. Their first daughter, Doris Alicia, was born in Nyasaland in 1912.

In 1916 William and his family returned to England - a journey that took several months due to the war. The family settled in Thornton Heath, South London: Doris went to a local school and William worked at the War Office in Whitehall. Their second daughter, Beryl Constance, was born in 1918. Tragically, a year later Alice died on the voyage back to southern Africa, having suffered a heart attack following peritonitis. She was buried at sea.

William brought his baby Beryl and her sister Doris back to England and left them in the care of his younger brother Bert and his wife Margaret at their home in Thornton Heath where they were joined by Phyllis, Alice's daughter from her first marriage. William returned to his tobacco farm in Africa – two years later he took Beryl and Phyllis back to Africa and Doris went to boarding school in Hitchin. From 1925 Doris and Beryl lived with my parents, Sam and Wyn at Upton Lodge, Finchley: both went to boarding school and later married in North London. Their father, William, died in Nyasaland from Blackwater Fever in 1929 and Phyllis, having married and settled in the colony, died in 1933.

Annie, the fifth child of Albert's first family, died in 1899 at the age of 18 in the County Hospital in Bedford where she was receiving treatment for anaemia and thrombosis.

In the following account of my grandfather Albert's second family – seven children – I have combined Alison's research with happy personal memories of three uncles and one aunt. It is sad to record that tragedy and sorrow struck the family twice: first in 1896 when seven-year-old Mercy died of acute bronchitis at Milton Ernest, followed in 1914 by the death of 21-year-old Frank who had recently volunteered for war service in the Army. Stationed in Woolwich, London, Frank was playing football with his mates when he was either hit by –or headed – the heavy leather ball. Later that day he was admitted to Woolwich Hospital where he died from a brain haemorrhage soon after his brothers Bert and Charles had rushed to visit him.

Albert Harrington Rayment – or Uncle Bert as I knew him – established a business career in London. He impressed me as a self-educated, sophisticated city gent – always immaculately dressed – grey spats over shiny shoes, hair sleeked down with brilliantine and sporting a moustache in the style of Hollywood star Clarke Gable. Gifted with a fine baritone voice he was in popular demand as a soloist at soirees in London before and after the Great War in which he served as an Army Lieutenant. In a photograph taken in 1915 he looks particularly handsome in uniform.

Successful in the wholesale textile business between the wars Bert fell from grace in the 1960s due to his love of horse racing and inevitable gambling debts. Separated from his kind-hearted but rather snobbish wife Margaret (my godmother), Uncle Bert lived out his later years in a Margate bed-sit, maintained immaculate personal and domestic standards, kept fit by taking long walks and aimed to live to one hundred. He was 90 when I visited him in 1976 – healthy and cheerful, smartly dressed – always a tie. I enjoyed his lively mind but did not share his confidence that the complex mathematical theories he produced would beat the bookies. He died when 91. Peter, my cousin, who was partially crippled by polio when a young child, was the couple's only child.

John Barnard, my Uncle Jack, was a tall, powerfully built man who served as a Private in Royal Army Service Corps in the First Great War. Thankfully, Jack survived the fierce battles of the Gallipoli (Turkey) campaign in 1915 – one of the most disastrous campaigns in British and Commonwealth military history. Before the war Jack learned his trade under Mr J Williams, a butcher in Newport, Isle of Wight and in April 1907 married Minnie Peachy at East Cowes Wesleyan Church. Their son, Bernard, was born on 8th September that year and daughter, Alice Maud – known as Tilly – on September 29th 1908. However, the 1911 census shows that the family were already living apart; the children with Minnie's parents in Newport and Jack boarding with a family named Spanner. After the war, Jack built-up a successful butcher's business at 173, High Street, Ryde, Isle of Wight, and brought up his two children with the assistance of a housekeeper. As well as being a popular butcher, an all-round fisherman and excellent shot, Jack played a leading part in the affairs of the Vectis Boating and Fishing Club, serving as Captain and later President.

He was also a member of the IW Meat Trader's Association, the Rivers Board, the Southern Seas Fishery Board and the IW Conservative Club. He died in 1957 at the age of sixty-nine and was buried in the private cemetery on the Gatcombe Estate. Uncle Jack features in Chapter 13 of these memoirs.

<u>Charles Frederick</u>. In Chapter 18 I have written of happy holidays with my Uncle Charles, his wife Kezie and cousin Doris (born in 1916) on their farm near Finningham in Suffolk. Charles served as a private in the Army at Felixstowe during the First Great War: his health was not deemed robust enough to be sent abroad. Charles' brother Bert, together with a Mr Warrener, set up a company to purchase Elmer Farm, and in 1927 Charles and his family moved there to manage the agricultural enterprise to which other properties were added, including a 500-acre dairy and arable farm bought by Mr Prescott, an American director of Woolworths. In 1952, Charles and his daughter Doris – a hands-on farmer – purchased the freehold of the thatched farmhouse, surrounding barns and chicken houses together with twenty-five acres of arable and pasture land. In 1961 the family moved to Norwich Road in Ipswich. Charles died in October 1987 at the age of ninety-six. From 1961 Doris gave dedicated service to her community as an auxiliary nurse and an elder in her Baptist church. She died in Ipswich in 2007, aged 91.

<u>Margaret.</u> Aunt Maggie, who was born twenty months before my father and grew-up in Bedfordshire and Yorkshire, married Arthur Newman, lived in Ipswich and gave birth to two daughters, Gwendolin and Joan. Unfortunately, neither Alison nor I have specific details regarding her life journey. Although I met Aunt Maggie at Upton Lodge – and after the war at Elmer Farm – my only recall is of a warm-hearted lady with a strength of character and humour matching her brothers.

In writing up the brief histories of the Rayment family's more recent ancestors I have been struck by the consistency of their family loyalties, their strong work ethic in hard economic periods, their ability to adapt and survive the disruptions caused by two world wars – and the fortitude of the mothers who bore so many children. I find it interesting that in the reign of Queen Victoria two male Rayments, George and his son Albert, sired twenty-two children. I am also fascinated by the range of occupations brought to light by Alison's research: carter; gamekeeper; carpenter; coachman; publican; workhouse overseer; school caretaker; farmer, bailiff; butcher; lay preacher; missionary; Canadian Mounted policeman; tobacco farmer in Africa; soldier; naval gunner; wholesale textile salesmen; wartime Special Constable.

In comparison, and bearing in mind that Wennerloef was an only child, Alison and I have far less information to hand in writing about my mother's family, the Carters.

Albert and Harriet Rayment with family, circa 1905

from the left, standing: Charles; William; Albert H; Margaret; John B; Christiana; George seated: Samuel; Harriet; Albert; Frank; Henry

William Carter, circa 1874

Emily Carter, circa 1874

THE CARTER FAMILY

My mother, Wennerloef Emily Carter – usually called Wyn or Wenner – was born at Willesden Lodge in Willesden Green, North London, in 1895, the only child of <u>William and Emily Carter</u>. By 1900 the family had moved to 'The Hermitage' in Hermitage Lane, Hampstead, the residence of a wealthy elderly bachelor. William was employed to manage the small estate and to look after his 'old guvenor'.

<u>William</u> was born in 1853 in Essex. His parents were Absolam Carter, born in 1813 at Stisted, Essex, and Sarah Ann Everitt, born in 1815 near Writtle in Essex. Absolam worked as a farm labourer and gardener and the couple brought up six children: Hannah, Harriet, Emma, Sarah, William and Charles. Wennerloef spent a lot of time in school holidays with Kate and Herbert who were the children of her father's sister Sarah who, with her husband Walter Sitch, lived at The Hall Lodge on the Great Baddow Estate near Chelmsford where Walter was a gardener. Alan, the writer of these memoirs, remembers visiting mother's cousins Kate, Herbert and their friend Rose in the 1930s, and regular visits by Kate to our house in Finchley during and after WWII.

<u>Emily</u>, who was born in 1854, was also a native of Essex. Her father Robert Wakefield was born in 1810 at Fairstead and her mother, Hannah Swallow, at Springfield in 1812. Robert worked as a husbandman and cowman: the couple raised five children; Emma, Robert, Louisa, Elizabeth and Emily.

My grandparents, William and Emily, were married on the 12th of January 1878 at St. John's Church, Moulsham, near Chelmsford in Essex. They were both in service, at one time to the Freeman family who had a large town house in Kensington, London, and a country house near the sea in Hastings, Sussex. William looked after the horses and stables – Emily was the housekeeper.

WENNERLOEF

Until very recently I had no idea at all why my mother had been so named by her parents. However, Alison – through her diligent research – has discovered that my grandmother Emily's sister married a Swedish man named Andersen. Wennerloef is a Swedish name. Alison has discovered other Swedish names in the Wakefield side of the family.

Although, stupidly, I never did ask my mother to explain the source of her first name, I did record her early history in an audio interview at 'Wraycott' in her 85th year. I have, of necessity, edited the eight-page, close-typed script – though not too severely because her story lights up interesting and amusing contrasts to my own childhood – and even more so to that of my younger grandchildren growing up in the 21st century.

Wennerloef's parents came from rural stock in Essex, were soundly educated in the 3 Rs, and, though they held strong family values, were not particularly religious. I have fond memories of both maternal grandparents who were living with Sam and Wyn at Upton Lodge when they died: William in May 1939 and Emily in July 1940.

Warmed by the coal fire in the comfortable sitting-room at 'Wraycott', Mother and I recorded the following interview on the 26th of February 1981.

"Thank you, Mother, for doing this interview and ... and I wonder if we are telepathic because I'm sure you are saying to yourself, 'About time too – we've been talking about it for a long time so let's get on with it.'

With a chuckle in her voice Mother quipped: "Yes, something like that...I've been looking forward to seeing what I do remember of the past but now I'm eighty-five I may be past it!"

"Mother, you still have a sharp mind ... got all your marbles ... so, starting at the beginning, what do you remember of your early childhood?"

"I can remember some things in my life at Willesden Lodge from when I was three years old. We lived in the stable house next to where Father worked looking after the stables and horses."

"What did your mother do?"

"She was not employed but used to help out in the house if staff were ill. I always went with her when she had to cook the evening meal. Mr Worth, who owned the house, had a business in Great Moulton Street, and Father used to drive him up there in a horse-drawn brougham. Father used to say the journey home was slow and difficult in the winter – thick pea-soup fogs and ice on the road at times. And I remember Mother playing with me in the garden at Willesden Lodge: when I was four she took me to a little private school over a shop in Willesden High Road."

"Interesting, sounds like a nursery school: how many pupils?"

"Only about half a dozen; a preliminary stage before I went to a proper school. And about that time the Boer War was on, and I can remember the songs and troops marching through London before going over to South Africa. Then old Queen Victoria died when I was five and a bit; my parents went to the funeral and left me with friends who were corn merchants. Lovely people – they let me play in the shop, scooping oats and wheat from sacks into the big bins. Then the old gentleman at Willesden Lodge died, and we moved to Worn Lane for a short while before Father took up with his old governor that he had worked for, over many years, long before I born. We lived at an old house called 'The Hermitage' in Childs Hill, Hampstead – that was when I was six – and I went to All Saints Church School at Childs Hill until I left at fourteen."

"What was your father's job at The Hermitage?"

"He was in charge of the small estate, three staff, the house and grounds ... and looked after the old gentleman who was quite frail. Father used to drive him about in a horse and trap, look after the horses ... I remember a bay mare and a dappled mare ... and Father had a full-time assistant and a gardener. The old gentleman had a property in Barnet, and Father, who drove up there on Saturdays to pay the wages, used to take me with him sometimes – even let me take the reins for a while on the quiet roads – with the gentle bay but not with the frisky dappled mare."

"Quiet roads, Mother ... you said ... on that trip to Barnet?"

"Oh, Alan, in those days Childs Hill, Golders Green and up Finchley Road all the way to Barnet was just a country road."

"Gee, Mother, certainly not in my earliest memories – say thirty years later. May we return to life at school ... your teachers and the subjects they taught?"

"Well, at All Saints Church School we had a very strict headmistress. Although she was a little woman with round shoulders she had a booming voice and when she came into a classroom we all stood up ... you could have heard a pin drop. One of the other teachers I remember was Miss Pratt ... she was a forbidding-looking woman – very austere and always very strict with us. Desks were wooden benches – no individual desks – wooden plank floors and only a few round coal stoves on the premises, so everywhere in school was really cold in winter. There was no gymnasium, no swimming, no physical activity except for a little bit of drill or marching on the rough gravel of the playground. All we learnt was reading, writing and arithmetic ... oh yes and needlework".

"My-Oh-My Mother, the environment sounds Spartan, the discipline frightening and the education basic – to say the least."

"Well, I was good at those basic subjects, loved reading especially – and needlework too – and later music. That very strict headmistress was keen to ensure we learnt needlework skills from an early age – probably seven or eight – and by ten I was very good at drawn thread work on linen and Irish pattern crocheted lace. Just before I left school at 14 we were sent to a new school in Cricklewood Lane to receive cookery lessons."

"Very interesting, Mother ... do you have memories of friends, of holidays, of entertainment?"

"I was very friendly with some girls in my class and went to their birthday parties, but otherwise had a very quiet childhood. My parents were in their early forties when I was born – I had no brothers or sisters – so I went everywhere with Mother and Father: long walks over the Heath, regular visits to their friends … one such couple had no children, so from the age of ten I used to visit them on my own to have interesting conversations and play their piano. In the long summer holidays we used to visit my cousins – all older than me – on Father's side of the family at a big estate near Great Baddow in Essex where Uncle was the Bailiff. I used to stay on for the whole holiday … never went anywhere else … and just loved the freedom, and games with Kate and the others in the huge park on the estate. Then back to school in busy London.

Ah! It's coming back to me that I played the ghost in the Shakespearian play *Macbeth* … ah yes, and one of my pals had a rare treat – she had her hair specially done at the hairdressers in a high sort of Victorian arrangement to play Lady Macbeth – but she looked no more like the character than my foot. My pals and I loved being in concerts and plays – all centred around the school or church and attended by all the parents. I can remember opening a concert with a pianoforte solo called 'Ida' and singing 'The Last Rose of Summer' on stage in a small choir with classmates. Of course, being at a church school meant we were expected to attend All Saints on Sundays; mattins in the morning then Sunday school in the afternoon … and when I was older I used to have to go again in the evenings. That was the ritual for Sundays."

"Hmmm, too much of a good thing, Mother! From what you have shared so far it seems to me you must have spent a lot of time alone."

"Well, I was always a great reader – used to read a lot. If I could get hold of a book I was always quite content. Although my parents had few, if any, books they used to buy me children's books when little and when I started work at fourteen I joined the library down Frognall Hill. And the piano – I always wanted to play the piano from the time I was five or six. I used to love going to parties held by my godmother in a big drawing room over their ironmongers shop. Everyone performed – played an instrument or sang – and 'Auntie's' daughters always played the piano and sang. I used to sit like a little mouse beside the piano, overawed by what they were doing, until I wanted to play …

more and more than ever. So at home in The Hermitage I used to creep into my parents' bedroom where my mother had a big tin trunk for clothes, prop a book on the trunk against the wall, sit on a little fold-up seat and bang on the trunk for all I was worth, pretending to play the piano."

"When did you have your first lessons?"

"When I was twelve: my parents bought me a piano for my birthday and a piano stool the next birthday. Mother had asked one of my godmother's daughters to teach me and used to pay her ten shillings for twelve lessons – and that was a lot of money in those days. I don't suppose Father was earning more than three or four pounds a week."

"So to buy a piano must have been a big item for them."

"Well, the piano was second-hand and cost fifteen pounds, and yes, that was a lot of money for my mother to find so I suppose she must have saved up for it. I had a lesson every week for two years. I learnt very quickly so that by the time I left school I could play a variety of pieces. After that I taught myself."

"Gee, you taught yourself, Mother! One of my many happy memories, both as a young child and an adult, was watching ... and listening intently ... to you playing the piano. From sheet music you could play any new score, including light classical music, but it always amazed ... and still amazes me that you sat on that old stool and reeled off songs and sonatas, hymns and marches and dances from memory, and with colour and a verve that delighted young and old. Moving on, who or what influenced you to apply for an apprenticeship at *Weekes The Family Drapers* when you left school at fourteen-and-a-half in 1910?"

"I'm not exactly sure – but, when I think about it, Mother used to buy a few things in that shop when she visited friends who lived in the centre of Hampstead. She must have heard they were seeking apprentices, arranged an interview and I went there on March 1st. Your father arrived on April 1st. For two years I was an apprentice milliner: I sat in a tiny alcove – about six feet square – with the milliner Miss Oldham beside me – no window and only the light from a distant part of the shop. A lace curtain was drawn to hide us from the main shop – so we couldn't see out but used to draw it aside when there were no customers in the shop. My first task was to prepare all the materials: to frill up tulle and pleat and fly georgette using a hand-turned sewing machine. My hands used to get hot and sticky because I was scared of getting into trouble if I didn't get it right. This was a period when old ladies wore bonnets with ribbon strings under their chins – the hats were decorated with little stones, feathers, and tiny bunches of flowers. I had to learn to make a wire hat frame, cover it in straw – which we had in packets – stitch in the straw and trim with flowers or strips of taffeta – often creating big bows held up with ribbon wire. When King Edward VII died everybody went into mourning and the buyer had to go into the City and East End to buy as many black hats as she could find – we had stacks and stacks of black hats. I had to stand on some steps to dust the boxes stored on a high shelf – thankfully they were soon all sold."

"How much were you paid and what were your hours?"

"Two shillings a week, with lunch and tea, plus supper on Saturdays. I was in the shop from 8.30 in the morning until 8.00 in the evening on Monday, Tuesday and Wednesday; 2.00pm on Thursday; 9.00pm on Friday and 10.00pm on Saturday."

"Gee, Mother, that adds up to sixty-six hours per week, less, shall we say, eight hours for lunch and tea during the week and supper on Saturdays – makes a total of fifty-eight hours every week in your confined work space with, I presume, occasional errands to other departments in the fairly extensive premises. I am amazed at the hours you worked for two shillings a week ... what could you buy for two bob?"

"Well, you could buy a pair of cashmere or woollen stockings for one-and-eleven-pence-three-farthings: I had to wear black – Mother made me a long black dress that hung down to my toes – and had to pin my hair up."

"But ... but one pair of stockings consumed your week's wages ... if you can call that a wage ... so how did you dress yourself and...oh so many questions ... what about bus fares to and from work?"

"My parents used to buy some items such as shoes and underwear and Mother used to make all my clothes – that is how I learned to dress-make. I used to walk to work – and home again – across Hampstead Heath in all weathers. Took me about twenty minutes."

"So you would walk across West Heath on your own ... in the dark ... even after leaving work at ten o'clock on Saturday nights? Gee, Mother – was it safe ... weren't you a bit scared?"

"Oh no, there was no fear of not being able to walk across Hampstead Heath. ... and Father used to meet me with a pony and trap when we had really stormy weather."

Alfred Weeks, Family Draper's and Outfitters, Hampstead, where Sam and Wyn met as 14-year-old apprentices in 1910

"Then you and Sam became friendly ... he was a 'boarder' so I guess you first met at meal times."

"Yes, that's right – we had marvellous food – always a hot roast with lots of vegetables and roly-poly puddings with custard – very filling. But the housekeeper in charge of the apprentices was a stern old lady ... no hanky-panky with her around and she didn't like it because Sam and I became friendly – she thought it was 'a bit too much' and told old Mr Weekes. Didn't make any difference and by the time I left ... when I was sixteen ... Sam and I were 'walking out'. Although my manager, Mr Symes, wanted me to stay-on at Weekes, I said, "No, I would rather break out and go somewhere else." I was very grown-up at seventeen – we weren't children for very long in those days, Alan. So I got a job as an 'improver' in the blouse department at BB Evans in Kilburn for a year and was paid £15 per year – about six shillings per week. I then moved on to TR Roberts, General Drapers of Islington where I worked in the millinery showroom, was paid eight shillings a week and lived in. We used to have our meals in a room behind the shop, and I shared one bedroom with two other girls in a house the firm owned in Orford Road. Mother was very upset when I left home.

The buyer in charge of our department was a little grey-haired women who would get into a rage if a hat made upstairs in the workroom had the tiniest flaw. I saw her, in front of a customer, tear off all the trimmings: "That's not what I ordered for madam." Well, I had to take it back upstairs to the milliner: I said, "You aren't half in for it," and she replied, "I'll throw the flat iron at that old woman one of these days." The customer was always right you see ... and you used to get some really 'tabby' old women come in who would wear you flat ... and you dare not let anybody leave the shop without selling them something so if you were really failing you had to refer that customer to the shop walker or the buyer. One day the temperamental buyer came up to me and said, "Miss Carter, you are far too independent to be a saleswoman." I explained that I didn't like having to toady too much to those really difficult customers ... and remember, Alan, how stiff and strict the rules were in business in those days ... so the buyer said she thought I would be better suited to dressing out and doing the window. I said I would love to do that."

"A window dresser – much more creative, Mother: how old were you now and how much were you paid?"

"I was nineteen, coming twenty, and earning ten shillings a week, I think, and now able to make my own clothes and hats, or pay for things like shoes. I used to make Mother's clothes too, and, of course, I could buy materials and other things in our shop at a good discount."

"During this period, Mother, did you have time to keep-up with your music?"

"Oh yes! I was always so keen and always played. We used to make our own amusement anywhere we visited – with my parents or with several girl friends in all sorts of venues ... it was all home entertainment. A year after the First World War started the Zeppelin air raids began and Mother worried so much because I travelled by bus to visit them at The Hermitage once a week. So I agreed to change my job and live at home, but soon after that decision the old gentleman died and The Hermitage was sold. Mother and Father decided to move back to their roots near Chelmsford in Essex, so I moved in with two of their old friends who ran a high-quality guest house in Hampstead. By that time I had decided to leave the trade and try office work for a change. I followed up an advertisement for office workers in the local paper: many businesses were opening up to train and employ women because so many men were being called up in to the forces. So although I had never worked in a office I applied for a job at the Inspector of Taxes in Dollis Park, Finchley."

"Quite adventurous, Mother."

"It was, really, because I didn't know the first thing about it. I was interviewed by an Inspector of Taxes, Mr Blunden. I told him what I had been doing, that frankly I had no office experience but was sure I could learn ... I flannelled him a bit I suppose. Anyway, he put my application forward and on my second visit he told me I had been turned down on account of my lack of education. Mr Blunden said he was very sorry and that he had a good mind to try again. "You rather impressed me," he said, "and I think you might stand a chance."

"Well, if it doesn't work out, that's that," I said to myself. I don't know how I had the courage to try for that job because I never had much initiative in that direction – I was always a bit scared of teachers and bosses – but in the end Mr Blunden took me on. I found the work very difficult at first because there were only two other girls in the office; both taken on recently and better educated than I was. The chief clerk was a real so-and-so – he would not show us how to do a thing and income tax was very complicated – different to an ordinary office job and we really had to feel our way, even how to find the correct wording for a letter."

"Were there a lot of forms?"

"Oh no – no forms, we had to write everything by hand ... pen and ink ... no typewriters or forms. However, I managed to scrape through, kept my eyes open and copied correspondence in the files, asked experienced male staff and, if blocked, then asked someone else. One of the other girls – a lady really because she had two little boys – helped me a lot. Within a year of starting the job, the offices were full of girls because more and more men were called up due to the awful number being killed in France. So, apart from the Inspector of Taxes, the only male in the office was the chief clerk who, now swamped with women, had to knuckle under – give in and co-operate – which meant we had a really good time.

At the beginning of the war income tax schedules were revised which meant that many more people were taxed on earned income, including factory workers. Several factories in Finchley switched to producing essential war-time supplies, one of which was a branch of the big French motor firm, De Dion Bouton. So at the tax office we used to deal with an increasing number of tax returns sent in by wage earners: they all had to be scheduled up, then worked out for the tax due and the paper work sent to the Collector of Taxes. I worked at the tax office for six years and became head of the Schedule E Section, dealing with wage earners. At first I earned two pounds ten shillings a week – then three pounds – and eventually three pounds ten shillings. That was quite a lot of money to me then and I was able to save forty pounds by the time Sam and I were married in 1923."

"And all that work that you and the other girls did in the tax office was by hand, with pen and ink and blotting paper?"

"Yes, I never touched a typewriter. All our figures and correspondence had to go to the Inspector's office to be checked and signed. I was good at the figures, and my good grounding in spelling served me well. So once I had mastered the official wording, the phraseology, I didn't trip up very often."

Samuel and Wennerloef at Upton Lodge, Finchley,
following their wedding at St. Luke's Church in July 1923

Samuel and Wennerloef and wedding reception guests at Upton Lodge, July 1923
Samuel's mother, Harriet sitting on his right; brother Bert further right
Wennerloef's father to her left and mother Emily sitting below William
The bridesmaids are Tilly and Beryl Rayment

From the outbreak of WWI to the end of WWII, a period of thirty-one years, life for my parents, Sam and Wyn, and their peers was charged with change and uncertainty. Understandably prone to anxieties, they were, thankfully, both strong of character and stable in employment.

In the 1920s Sam earned £2.50 per week plus commission in the textile trade and Wyn £3.50 as a section leader in the local Inspector of Taxes offices. Having no capital, they saved their shillings for five years after the war and married in 1923 when they could afford to buy furniture and rent a house in Finchley for one pound per week. The wedding was celebrated at St Luke's Church, Mountfield Road, Finchley on July 28th 1923, and the reception held at the couple's new home: Upton Lodge, Manor View, Finchley, N3.

'Upton Lodge' was a nine-roomed Victorian semi-detached house situated on the corner of Briarfield Avenue. The house was owned by Mrs Edridge, a business lady who was proprietor of an hotel in St Leonard's-on-Sea, Sussex. She was associated with our extended family network in some mysterious way, but the connection offers a clue as to why my parents, as a young married couple, took on a house with so many rooms. In all probability the surplus accommodation could be offered to other members of the family as and when needed. This proved to be the case regarding two of my female cousins, Doris and Beryl, who lived at Upton Lodge until Doris married Larry Bolger and Beryl left home to train as a nurse in the Women's Royal Air Force. Mother's parents also lived at Upton Lodge from time to time in the 1930s and both died whilst in residence.

It amazes me that, even though Sam and Wyn had limited funds, they were able to express their good taste and artistic tendencies in the furnishings of their marital home. They would certainly not have borrowed money but hunted for bargains at auctions and second-hand dealers. Also, as was the custom in that era, in addition to wedding presents, senior members of both families gifted items from their own homes.

And so, with harmonious good taste, Sam and Wyn built their nest and launched a stable home environment that proved to be a blessing for my brother and me, for our cousins Doris and Beryl, for our maternal grandparents and many friends and visiting relatives.

Thank you Sam and Wyn!

~~~~~~~~~~~

*Sam and Wyn
on honeymoon,
Isle of Wight, 1923*

*The family home:
Upton Lodge, Manor View,
Finchley, London*

CHAPTER 4

A YOUNG CHILD'S MEMORIES OF HOME

I wonder how much I remember about the family home and the community where I was born, and lived and played and learned until twelve years of age?

UPTON LODGE

I chuckle to myself as, in both memory and imagination, I slide back into childhood to enjoy the ambience of that household as it was in my early years – or olden days. For the opening scene my mind floats through the substantial front door that faced Briarfield Avenue – half-glazed with lead framed stained glass – into a narrow gloomy hall dominated by a tall and elaborate hallstand with mirror, and in the long glove drawer, a real but damaged flintlock horse pistol. That gloom lifted by a few watts throughout the house – especially in the hall – when electric lights replaced the gas lamps in the early 1930s.

Looking left, there are heavy doors to a dark dining room and a small study used by Mother for dress-making. Straight ahead in the corner of the hall the stairs mount the party wall of the conjoined houses. Turning right a less substantial door opens into the busy family room we called the kitchen: straight on at the end of the passage the Drawing Room – a room of delights that led to the small south facing garden – a place of fond memories and happy times. The Drawing Room? ... a puzzling name for an inquisitive three-year-old.

"Mummy, you and Daddy don't draw in here ... you play the piano and Daddy smokes his pipe and reads the paper. I do lots of drawing, but nobody else does."

Recounting this story many years later, Mother said: "I was tickled pink ... you could be so old-fashioned with your questions sometimes ... and I couldn't answer you for a minute or two because I was laughing so much. My answer often confused you even more and set off my giggles again. When I said, "It used to be called a *withdrawing room* ... a room where people could be quiet, and read or sew and not talk," you replied: "So that's why I mustn't talk when Daddy is reading his paper." I was still puzzled and announced to my bemused parents, "I'm going to call it the Music Room."

Whatever the title, the furnishings were delicate in design and colour, enhanced by the warm glow of the coal fire on winter nights and by sunlight streaming through the south facing french doors in summer. I sense again my infant fingers exploring the feel of the full-drop, pale-gold damask curtains and the matching upholstery of two splendid Victorian settees. Ah, those settees: memories bubble-up from the depths as I see myself again in that room as a child of four or five, fascinated by the smooth curves of their moulded wood frames and cabriole legs – and the delicately turned struts of two semi-circular elbow chairs. I touch again the inlaid leather desktop of Mother's walnut davenport and the brass candelabra that swivelled from the facia of her upright piano. I even dared, when I was on my own, to twiddle the knobs on that brown wooden box next to Father's chair because, if I twiddled long enough, the box would make music or talk about things I could not understand. Ah! Father's new pride and joy ... the wireless.

Gee – memories from aged eight or nine emerge in pastel shades and contrasting highlights: the cream-painted, four-inch architraves and even wider skirting boards that framed a sedate floral-print wallpaper tastefully enhanced by several small landscape water-colours in carved gilt-frames. But my eye was always drawn to a larger picture – an oil painting depicting a beautiful young Victorian lady in full-length cream satin dress shyly opening a billet-doux. A mahogany framed oval mirror above the pale coloured mantelpiece reflected light from an unfussy chandelier and – yes, I remember now – that other picture in the corner above the small Edwardian display cabinet was a still-life water colour by a budding artist who was too busy to bloom – my mother.

Father's imprint on the Drawing-Music room was a rack of briar pipes and the aroma of St Bruno tobacco impregnated into the upholstery of his comfortable fireside arm-chair – a Viking throne that disturbed but did not overpower the pervading artistic atmosphere. Odours and aromas stay longest in the memory – the warm smell of wax polish, of burnt toast held too long in the coal fire on the delicate tines of a brass fork, and the sensuous smell of new mown grass wafting through the open french doors on a warm day in May. The garden, the dog kennel, the chicken house and Father's tool shed feature in later chapters.

The airy feminine atmosphere of the drawing room was in sharp contrast to the masculine vibrations that pervaded the north facing dining room, evoking in me memories of Father performing formal culinary ceremonies before an obedient audience on wet winter Sundays. My cheeky inner gnome is saying, 'Heavy man, heavy.' But paradox, so beguilingly present both in matters that matter much or matter little says yes – the scenery was heavy – yet the people bright and conversation light with laughter when I was nine and left an imprint on the child awed by *The Monarch of the Glen*.

The Monarch, a huge oil painting of the great stag standing proud on heather-ed Scottish crag – offset on the opposite wall by *Mafeking Relieved* in even bigger gilded frame – dominated our small suburban dining room choked with heavily carved dark Victorian furniture in the style of the 16th century Stuart period. Six high backed chairs and a prominent carver stood around the extended table like an escort of Grenadier Guards; the guardhouse a foreboding carved dresser with high canopy supported by dark pillars. In my young child's imagination I was hunted by the Monarch, captured by the Boers and imprisoned in the Stuart Castle. I feel a shudder even now.

Alan, age 2½,
with Mother

Mother's piano and the canopied dresser
Alan's art homework in 1944

I was also fearful, when very young, of stepping on the cold stone tiles to enter the dark scullery where, above my eye-line, gruesome domestic contraptions and blackened iron pots overwhelmed my imagination and tender courage. The main culprits were a grey-black gas cooker – built to last a century – a large stoneware sink paired with a huge wooden draining board, a giant mangle and a big walk-in food pantry with marble shelves – one displaying gauze-wire dish covers that sufficed to cool and protect food in days before a fridge was even available. Scariest of all, in the gloomiest corner of that scullery, the forbidden door to the coalhouse that remained unconquered until I was five. Access to the scary scullery was from a room full of light – a happy family room that witnessed creative activity and family interaction every day.

The focal points of the family room were two large, west-facing sash windows, the table, the dresser, the wireless and the coke-fired range. The large solid pine table – dutifully scrubbed with carbolic soap and water every Saturday – was a surface for all tasks according to need and season: for skinning rabbits, gutting poultry and preparing vegetables; rolling pastry and mixing Christmas puddings; being set with table cloth and cutlery for breakfast, lunch and evening meals; at other times covered with a blanket and pristine sheet for use as a dressmakers work table ... and occasionally with newspapers when Father set about repairing a valve wireless or a malfunctioning household gadget.

Father's electrical tools, together with dozens of old tobacco tins containing 'bits that might come in useful', were tucked away in the deep cupboards under the long high dresser – a solid pine fixture so capacious that to this kid it seemed to be a magic storehouse for all domestic paraphernalia. Competing for prominence on the opposite side of the room, the temperamental black coke-fired range that emitted sufficient heat irregularly, puffed smoke into the room capriciously, supplied the hot water system occasionally – but faithfully boiled pans of water and warmed a collection smoothing irons used to press clothes dried on the overhead rack.

I remember one very cold winter when for weeks we, the family, lived totally in that room by day. In the evenings, wrapped in blankets and sipping hot cocoa we huddled round the stoked-up range before scampering upstairs to bed with hot-water bottles – still to shiver under ice-cold sheets piled high with blankets. Father even lit a coal fire in my bedroom but it was out in the morning, my bedside glass of water frozen, the lino floor threatened frostbite to my bare feet: which reminds me that the main bedrooms as well as the drawing and dining rooms all had a linoleum surround framing the Axminster carpets. The three double bedrooms were warmed sparingly by gas fires: no heat at all in the capacious bathroom and separate bench-seat toilet. Except in high summer I always felt cold upstairs, but downstairs I loved the glowing heat of coal fires and the tactile enjoyment of shovelling new fuel and poking the embers.

Maintaining solid fuel fires in the drawing room and the kitchen-cum-family room was a labour intensive chore tended by Mother on weekdays. At weekends Father ritualised that duty, adding the preparation of a fire in the dining room. Carpets and runners were swept regularly with a Bex Bissell and, in another ritual every April and September, were hung over the washing line to be beaten with a cane contraption shaped like a long-handled tennis racquet. The stair carpet received weekly attention from a stiff hand brush and dustpan. In the late 1930s a Hoover vacuum cleaner and an electric iron modernised the domestic equipment but my parents had neither a refrigerator nor a washing machine until the mid-1960s.

A third ritual, washing day, was performed every Monday in the scullery. The old black range was fuelled and stoked up to its highest efficiency, except in the summer months when hot water issued from big kettles and saucepans heated on the gas stove. All the family clothes and domestic linen were virtually hand-washed in a large galvanised tub. How fit my mother – and other women – must have been to handle the three-legged wooden 'dolly' to swish the laundry to and fro in a brew of hot water and copious amounts of Lux Soap Flakes. Several rinses in warm and cold water were necessary, to be followed by hand wringing and the mangle. Towelling nappies and soiled items of clothing were rubbed energetically on a wooden ribbed washboard … beware the knuckles.

The piece-de-resistance was another 'test your fitness' contraption: The Mangle. Set in a huge cast-iron frame the hand-operated, cog-geared machine drove two thick wooden rollers – each about six inches in diameter. When I grew big enough and strong enough I pretended I was at the helm of a pirate ship as I turned that large mangle wheel. I remember that while in my pirate phase I enjoyed the chore of hanging out the sheets on the long washing lines in the garden – or hauling aloft the five slatted airer in the kitchen: "Aarrrgghh ye lubbers … fly der Jolly Roger … an' 'oist t'mainsal me'arrrties." My mother, though so busy, joined in the fun of her child's piratical and other imaginative games – bless her.

Good mothers are all-round amazing people. Reflecting back to those years of innocence before World War II, I realise that all my pals had wonderfully kind and hard-working mothers – but how did they cope? Of course, my mother was the best – certainly the most energetic and cheerful. In the years following my birth, her income from dressmaking and piano playing eased the financial strain of maintaining an ordered lower middle-class lifestyle. But the physical effort to maintain that household was immense, therefore Mother – a cheerful worrier – was always on the go: shopping, cooking, cleaning and tidying; making beds, fires and cakes; washing, mangling, folding and ironing; speedily peddling the treadle of her Singer sewing machine and fitting visiting lady clients with part finished garments. Pins everywhere.

At weekends there was extra cooking, washing up and tidying when entertaining family and friends. Sam, the countryman brought up in a large family, certainly did his share of the chores. Thankfully, life was not all work for my parents: they enjoyed singing and playing the piano at regular musical evenings, we rotated visits to and from relatives and friends, walked miles and spent quiet evenings reading, listening to the radio and playing card and board games.

Was my mother a super multi-tasker? Absolutely!

NORTH LONDON

Sam and Wyn never drove or owned a car. We walked everywhere locally or travelled by bus or Tube train. Shopping involved a quiet half-mile walk from our house along Litchfield Grove to enter the hustle and bustle of Regent's Park Road in Church End, Finchley. As a young kid I was particularly attracted to the skills of the stylish assistants and the distinctive aromas that emanated from the traditional range of foodstuffs in a pre-war Sainsburys.

I loved entering the narrow shop with high ceiling, gliding over the shiny tiled floor and touching the cool marble topped counters – being particularly fascinated by the style and manner of smartly uniformed male and female staff wearing straw boaters and blue striped aprons. The customers were served individually, cheerfully and politely by that squeaky clean crew of attentive assistants, one of whom, 'the butter man', I watched with open mouthed awe as he performed his ritual. First he cut a chunk from a squat cylinder of butter and slapped the portion into shape with small wooden paddles ... then shaved, weighed, slapped with flat or corrugated paddle and weighed again before wrapping the delectable result in grease-proof paper. For a year or so he was my hero. I was also entranced by the bacon-slicing machine and the scoops used to fill the blue paper bags with tea, sugar, oats – all weighed and packed into a large brown paper carrier bag with string handles. The fact that every straw-hatted assistant could so rapidly add up the figures on the pencilled list of purchases made a lasting impression and encouraged my interest in mental arithmetic.

No arithmetic on pencilled lists in my favourite shop, Halls the Drapers and Haberdashers' Why? Because Halls shop assistants used a 'whoosh machine'. From a very young age I visited Halls regularly with my dressmaking mother; when old enough I became her willing errand boy to buy urgently needed cottons, trimmings and needles. Having listed and priced the customer's purchases, the shop assistant deposited the invoice and cash into a rubber buffered metal cylinder, placed the cylinder in a pneumatic tube at a nearby despatch station of the 'cash railway' and whoosh ... in seconds the cylinder arrived in the accounting office upstairs. The process was then reversed ... and whoosh again, the cylinder with receipt and loose change arrived back at the despatch station. What fascinating gee-whizz fun when I was eight years of age!

More fun was readily available when riding on the noisy old trams and studying the driver's technique as he wound and unwound the control handles attached to vertical spindles that linked with the motor and the brakes ... 'the wind-up man', I called him. In the mid-1930s the tramlines around Finchley were dug up and replaced by silent trolley-buses – interesting but not so exciting. But I also remember the joy of riding on the old red double-decker buses with outside staircases: 'Room outside only,' called the uniformed male conductor. Ah yes – more pictures float to the front of my brain – I was fascinated by his hand-held wooden ticket dispenser which had six sprung wire clips holding the tickets, his bell-ringing ticket punch and large leather money satchel. By the late '30s I loved travelling 'up to town' on the double-decker buses, often unaccompanied on a No.2 or No.13 to watch the cricket at Lord's or to meet my father at his office in Cheapside. As a treat we would go on to Gamages Emporium to buy clothes or have lunch in a City sandwich bar. On one such visit when I was about ten, Father surprised me as we walked down Fleet Street and entered a sports shop – to me a treasure trove. While I was engrossed in checking the grain on several size five cricket bats Father had a chat with the shopkeeper, then tapped me on the shoulder. As I turned round Father said, "Alan, Mr Hobbs would like a word with you ..." ... and there was *the great cricketer*! I was in awe – absolutely speechless. I do not remember what he said to me but can still recall his kind eyes and polite soft-spoken manner.

But one of the best treats – apart from meeting Mr Jack Hobbs or watching a day's cricket at Lord's of course – were the rare occasions when Mother or cousin Beryl took me to Lyons Corner House at Marble Arch after a shopping expedition in the West End. The opulence was glamorous: chandeliers and palm trees, waitresses in smart black and white uniforms crowned with frilled coronets – Nippies they were called – and a string orchestra playing light classical music and show tunes. I always pestered my mother to ask for a table near the orchestra ... "and please may I have a knickerbocker glory?" An hour of middle-class heaven – then back into the discordant thrum and distasteful smells of London's traffic. Even then there seemed to be too much traffic in central London. At the end of the 1930s there were approximately one and a half million motor vehicles in the United Kingdom.

By 1930 the major commercial companies had converted from horse to motorised transport but many local traders, such as bakers and milkmen who made daily house to house deliveries, still used horse drawn wagons or even hand carts until changing to small electrically powered vehicles. Though scared of the coal-man in blackened leather cloak with hood, I loved his beautiful shire horse. In contrast I felt sorry for the sad nag that plodded our streets hauling the rag-and-bone man's wobbly cart – but was always filled with wonder at the sight of a team of thoroughbred cart horses drawing brewer's drays – a glorious romantic image etched forever on my mind. Less romantic was the knife-and-scissor grinder; an old man in ragged clothes with a hunched back who called out, in a high lilting voice: "Knives o'grind 'n scissors t'sharpen" as he pushed a heavy handcart containing his tools and a pedal-operated grinding stone. From push cart to 'white van man' is an example of accelerated change in the second half of the 20th century.

Since those pre-war shopping days with Mother and Beryl in the West End, motor traffic on Britain's roads has increased twenty-fold to the current thirty million. In the same period the population in the UK increased from forty-five million in 1931 to sixty million in 2006. Hold it – I am digressing into the social history of that era around my childhood and I need to return to personal memories and family history. However, in an appendix not included in this book I have written an extensive, though by no means definitive account of some of the men and women whose inventions, pioneering endeavours and enterprising deeds certainly affected my early life – and radically changed lifestyles in Britain and the rest of the world from the beginning of the 20th century.

Reading through this chapter again I am hoping that I have been able to convey to my family, grandchildren and friends some sense of the environment of my early years – and especially my heart-felt gratitude to Sam and Wyn for their loving care in difficult times ... and there is more of that to come.

Meanwhile, let's have some fun with the story of how I fell in love when I was in my nappies.

~~~~~~~~~~~

'The Grass' at Upton Lodge: Alan with grandfather William Carter, his first cricket coach and mentor

CHAPTER 5

GRASS – AND MY EARLY YEARS

I have always loved grass. Not the euphoric weed but nature's emerald cloak eternally caressing the undulating contours of England's green and pleasant land.

Grass and I first met and fell in love when I was in nappies. Crawling over the vast expanse of the small lawn at Upton Lodge I tugged at the tiny blades, enjoyed the different shapes and textures, puzzled over the fat leaves of plantains, the petals of daisies and dandelions and an occasional long slimy thing crawling in the miniature forest. Oh, and the delightful smell of the cuttings in Father's mower box caused me to ask unanswerable questions. As a toddler the green carpet became my favourite playground – even more so from the time that Grand-dad Carter patiently played throw-ball-and-catch with me for hours on end.

My mother once told me the following story:

Sitting on the lawn near the old apple tree one sunny Sunday afternoon early in May, several adult members of the family were enjoying tea and a chat while Sam was busy tending his beloved vegetable plot. Alan, soon to be three, was playing contentedly with a pile of new mown grass at the edge of the lawn. Suddenly, the energetic child ran over to the group of adults and announced, "I wanna morlamba!"

Engrossed in their adult conversation, nobody took much notice of the child at first but he repeated the demand in a loud and insistent manner: "I wanna morlamba ... I wanna morlamba!" Having gained their attention he repeated the demand, "Mummy ... Mummy I wanna morlamba!"

The now silent and puzzled adults all looked to my mother who, in her gentle way, proceeded to teach her son the mannered version of such a request. "Alan, please say, 'I would like' ... whatever it is ... and ... 'please Mummy'."

Alan complied – falteringly. "I would ... like ... er ... er ... morlamba ... please ... please Mummy dear ... like Daddy's."

Grandparents and cousins simultaneously asked each other the question: "What does he mean ... I don't understand what he means by a 'mor ... something ... like Daddy's'. Do you know what he means, Wyn?"

"Sam," Mother called out, "come and have a cup of tea and help us with something young Alan is asking – he says – whatever it is – is like Daddy's." Sam downed tools, grunted as he straightened his back and joined the family tea party. "Sam, what on earth does Alan mean by that strange word ... 'morlamba'? He insists he wants one ... like yours."

Sensing confusion, Alan ran across the lawn towards a long-handled, two-wheel machine with a curved metal box attachment. Plunging his tiny arm into the box, he grabbed a fistful of grass cuttings, held them aloft as he ran back to the adults and exclaimed, "Like Daddy's, like Daddy's" – and pointing to the mower – "that one that one ... a morlamba."

"Oh!" chorused the grown- ups, expressing surprise and laughing. "He means a lawn mower ... a morlamba is a lawnmower!"

"Isn't that sweet – a 'morlamba'. Who'd have thought it?" exclaimed cousin Beryl.

"And he seems to like playing with the grass cuttings," observed Wyn.

"Hmm," humphed Sam, "so that's why there's been such a mess around my compost tip. I thought it must be the birds but it's young Alan. Well, well – such a mess, such a mess. I'll have to put up some chicken wire to stop him."

Sam did fortify his compost heap – but also thought about 'a morlamber like Daddy's.'

Although I have only fleeting conscious memories of my third birthday on May 29th 1931 my parents recounted the occasion in their later years – also I do have a feel for the story and claim artistic licence to combine reported facts with imagination.

Alan felt really excited when he woke up on the morning of his third birthday, a Friday. Washed and dressed by Mother he was allowed to bottom-bump his way down the stairs, pausing occasionally to inspect the shiny brass carpet rods fixed to the brown varnished border of the stair treads. Lifted into the wooden high chair beside the well-scrubbed kitchen table, a large Terry-towelling bib tied around his neck, the birthday boy attacked his porridge with gusto and random distribution. "He's making a mess on the floor again," noted Sam, as he applied himself to the serious business of bacon, sausage, eggs and fried bread. "Never mind, I'll clean it all up in a jiff," replied Wyn protectively.

Breakfast, normally a formal and rather dull affair at 7.30am seemed more colourful that morning. Wyn slit open several envelopes, naming the senders of a dozen birthday greetings from relatives and friends. "Look, Alan, this one is from Uncle Charles, Auntie Kezie and Doris at the farm ... and look ... pictures of baby lambs."

"Baaaa ... Baaaa," chortled Sam, now feeling full, satisfied and cheerful. Reaching under the table, he produced a brown paper parcel – then, to increase his son's bubbly excitement, rustled the paper as he unwrapped it and mumbled, "Hmmm, I wonder what we've got here, my boy?"

"Daddy, Daddy, what is it ... what is it?" piped Alan.

"Oh don't tease the boy so, Sam," interjected Wyn. "Let him see it."

Sam raised the bulky object from below the rim of the table, slowly ... theatrically.

"Look Alan, look … do you like your birthday present from Mummy and Daddy?" queried Wyn, wide-eyed with excitement herself.

"Er … er ffinjin," squealed Alan, "ffinjin ffinjin … Alan do it."

Wyn lifted her impatient son from the high chair as Sam knelt down on the floor to wind up the clockwork mechanism of the big red fire engine. The two 'boys' played with the all-metal toy on the floor whilst Wyn cleared the breakfast dishes to wash up in the scullery, using a cotton-headed dish mop and soda crystals to soften the water.

Alerted by the excitement in the kitchen, Judy, the family's cuddly Old English sheep dog, emerged from her gloomy lair in the scullery to join in the birthday fun. Judy was adored by everyone – especially Alan and Tig the black cat. Sam ushered Judy into the garden through the back door, affectionately ruffling the neck of her shaggy white coat with black patches: "Wait there, we're coming out in a minute … you're a lovely girl."

"We're going into the garden, Wyn," called Sam, "to open the big box for Alan."

"Another box," thought Alan, as he followed his father into the hall, bursting with excitement. Delving into the capacious cupboard under the stairs, Sam hauled out a mysterious looking object – long parcel wrapped in brown paper tied with coarse string – and carried it through the french windows to the middle of the well-manicured lawn.

The crisp scented air of a bright spring morning greeted Wyn as she emerged from the dreary environs of the scullery. "Oh my … what a beautiful morning," she chirped, holding Alan's hand in a futile attempt to restrain him from interfering with Sam's impromptu ceremony.

"Got to untie the string, my boy … no use trying to pull it off you know." Sam was good at parcel tying – and untying – patiently rolling up each strand round his hand and fastening the loop with yet another knot, the slow ritual adding to the agitation of the three-year-old. Wyn released Alan's hand as Sam prised open the lid to reveal a toy replica of his lawnmower.

"My morlamba … my morlamba," whooped Alan as he dived into the box to haul out the shiny metal machine with curvy green bin and smooth wooden crossbar handle at the end of the shaft.

"Daddy, Daddy … Mummy … my morlamba!"

"What do you say?" questioned Wyn, softly. Alan glanced quizzically at his parent's feet whilst continuing his energetic attempt to stand the machine upright.

"What do you say, Alan?" commanded Sam. The strong, deep voice stilled the boy who stood up, raised his fluttering eyelids toward the heads of his seemingly giant parents. "You say 'thank you'," prompted Wyn.

Throatily and impatiently, Alan croaked, "Thank you … Mummy dear …

Daddy," then grasped the handle to race the morlamba up and down the lawn exclaiming, "Alan do grass ... Alan do it!"

Sam and Wyn linked arms and smiled at each other, silently sharing warm feelings of pride, admiration and happiness as they watched their first-born son tear around the lawn pushing his new pride and joy. Alan completed three laps of the lawn imitating the brrr brrr noises of the whirring wheels and cutting blades, then slowed down to experiment with the push-pull movement he had observed whilst helping Daddy in the garden. He was having the time of his life until ... until the sturdy blond child realised that there were very few bits of grass in that important curvy green bin.

Puzzlement led to a serious inspection and frowned expression which developed into a tearful exclamation: "Daddy Daddy ... morlamba broken!" Floods of tears. But Sam had anticipated the scene. With some small planks he had already built a mini compost site next to his tool shed. Taking the sobbing child by the hand, he patiently coaxed his son towards a heap of fresh-mown grass in a newly boarded play area. Tears switched off, eyes lit up, hands thrust deep into the green aromatic mound.

"Daddy, Daddy ... box, box!" called Alan as he stumbled along the crazy-paved path, fell, got up – no tears – yanked at the handle of the toy mower and hurriedly dragged it back to his new play area. Frustrated, and becoming fretful again as he tugged vigorously with both hands at the rim of the curvy green box, Alan cried out, "Off, off. Daddy do it, off, Off!"

Daddy did it. Alan filled it. From his very own pile of fine cut grass.

I have always loved grass.

In my childhood years I was fortunate to be surrounded by kindly adults. When not at school my delightful cousins, Doris and Beryl, cared for me like big sisters, changing nappies and playing games in house and garden. Soon after my birth their father, William Rayment, had insisted that he pay for a domestic help to assist Wyn with running the household. My mother engaged a fourteen-year-old school leaver named Lyle, of whom I have no conscious memory but sense that she was very caring and that I was fond of her.

"Lyle was ever so good with you ... she loved children," Mother remembered. "She was with us five days a week from eight until five. She did the domestic chores in the morning, then she'd help prepare the lunch and look after you in the afternoon when I had to play for a class. Occasionally I would go to Doris's boarding school in Hitchin to attend Sports Day or Founder's Day. Lyle knew roughly when I was due home and would stand you on the table by the front window, which, you'll remember, had a view down Lichfield Grove. She told me that you would get excited and jump up and down, exclaiming repeatedly: "Mummy Dear coming." Evidently it was Lyle who initiated that term of endearment.

Mother, recounting these stories when aged 82, still found that term of endearment amusing and rather pleasing. "You always called me Mummy Dear until you were eight or nine."

I do have a conscious memory of standing on that same table in the bay window when I was about four, waiting for another of my first loves – two pairs of beautiful Suffolk Punch carthorses, festooned with gleaming brasses on their elaborate leather harnesses, drawing pneumatic-wheeled dustcarts back to the stables at Deard's Yard in East End Road. I used to jump up and down on that table shouting, "Clippity-clops ... oh look, here come the clippity-clops ... Alan go look ... go look," and, when the weather was fine, Mother used to take me out through the front door and hold my hand as I stood on the pavement. I adored those proud, beautiful horses – fascinated with the frills of hair festooning their fetlocks and their huge clippity-clop feet. "Hoofs," Mother insisted. "Horses have hoofs, not feet, Alan dear."

Later, from the age of eight, I used to collect the huge droppings often deposited by the clippity-clops when they passed our house at tea-time. "Good for the garden that horse-dung, my boy, good for my vegetables you know," Father confided. Now, as I type this moment of memory, I am wondering how much shit I shovelled in those suburban days when there was a romantic country aura associated with the collection of horse dung. And what an odour!

Shovels? ... shovels trigger another mind picture of my pre-school childhood – the road menders. The tarmacadamed surface of the crossroads adjacent to our house was regularly attacked by workmen to lay electric cables or repair leaking water mains. Mother allowed me to stand on the pavement to watch the fascinating rituals performed by huge men attired in sleeveless vests with wide belts a'midriff and protective leather spats tied with string above the knee reaching down to heavy hob-nailed boots.

Their first job on arrival was to light up a coke-fuelled brazier crowned by a huge iron kettle balanced on metal bars. Meanwhile, wooden struts were quickly slotted together and covered with a tarpaulin; a shelter from the rain ostensibly, but primarily a hide-away for tea breaks and lighting up Woodbines. While the heavies unloaded the tools from a small Bedford truck, the foreman studied the tarmac and marked out the dig in chalk. Then three muscled giants picked up sledgehammers and a relative midget of five-foot-nine, the comedian of course, gripped a three-foot-long cold chisel in a pair of five-foot iron tongs. Then the show began.

One-two-three-one-two-three-one-two-three as hammer hit chisel-head, driving its point deeper through the tarmac. Then, without command, the routine ceased. Two men played croquet with the chisel, loosened it, and Mr Tongs withdrew the pike to place in a new position. The routine was repeated again and again until pick-axes replaced sledgehammers and shovels filled wheelbarrows – up plank into the lorry. "Br'u'mate," called Mr Tongs – often. Pouches produced Rough Cut for pipes, fags were lit, the brazier stoked and the kettle filled with water from a small milk churn.

Already somewhat skilled at swinging a cricket bat I was captivated by the rhythmic movement and timing of those broad-shouldered sledge-hammerers – and a bit concerned for the safety of the wicket-keeper, Mr Tongs. When his role became redundant due to the introduction of ear-shattering pneumatic drills, I transferred my spectator allegiance from the noisy navvies to the groundsman at Arden Field applying manure to the cricket table or mowing the outfield. I much preferred the rural scene – the grass to tarmac.

In the early 1930s pre-school education was a relatively unknown and singularly private resource in North London. Earlier pioneering work by the Macmillan sisters and other visionaries of nursery education influenced a section of the Hadow Report on Education of 1927 which recommended the establishment of nursery schools in addition to the main goal of raising the school-leaving age to fifteen. However, political procrastination, financial constraints and the Second World War imposed such delays upon the latter initiative that the worthy aim was not implemented until the Butler Education Act of 1944. Few mothers in suburban Finchley went out to work, and child-minding, if required, was undertaken by neighbours or members of the extended family who lived nearby. The Cowling household next door became a second home for me: exciting excursions in their big car included trips to Regents Park Zoo and a boat ride on the River Thames. Grandpa Carter spent many hours playing inventive indoor games with toddler Alan and, on sunny summer days, cricket on the adjacent Arden Field in Briarfield Avenue.

In that quiet community the 'learn through play' kindergarten experience evolved through a series of natural social processes. Pram-pushing mums would stop and chat, with pride or anxiety, about their child's progress in teething, crawling, toddling, first words and bum rash. Young parents who met socially at church or the cricket club, adult education classes or the newly opened health clinics – or serendipitously wherever – developed tentative friendships sealed only by the invitation to tea. Edwardian customs still held sway among the lower-middle classes of suburban London prior to the Second World War.

The polite ritual of afternoon tea eased the ladies through the 'getting acquainted right of passage' while the children began playing together ... until. Until three or four crawlers-cum-toddlers started screaming and yanking favourite teddy bears and dolls from visiting intruders. Intruder wars calmed down as the matresfamilias ganged up to instil fair play (very much in vogue) and encourage their as yet undisciplined offspring to share and not fight.

Discipline and politeness were taught with uncompromising consistency. 'No' really meant 'NO!' Wyn never spanked me: Sam rarely.

I happily recall burgeoning friendships among half a dozen boys whose homes were located in the tree-lined streets around the cricket ground. Between the ages of four and five we were allowed to 'go out to play' in each other's houses and gardens. We grew to be self-assured and confident – and sometimes mischievous – a band of little brothers by the time we were due to be corralled in a classroom.

Our organically grown kindergarten had provided rich soil for strong core values and healthy psychological roots. Play in houses and gardens established unshakeable foundations in the first five years of this man's life. Many years later I began to really appreciate, understand and to be truly thankful for those core values laid in childhood by my parents, our extended family, neighbours, young friends and the ambience of our neighbourhood.

In those early years of my development live music at home stimulated my senses and founded a love of harmonious sounds and rhythmical lyrics. At four, I was allowed to stay up late to join in the family musical evenings and perform my mini-repertoire of songs: *There's something about a soldier* and *The sun has got his hat on, hip-hip-hip hooray, the sun has got his hat on and he's coming out today*. The modern technology of the era – the wireless and the gramophone – provided instantly accessible 'canned music': "But there's nothing like the real thing, my boy," stated Father, even though he was a wireless enthusiast who built valve sets as a hobby. This boy showed such an interest in singing that my prosperous godmother, Mrs Beswick, fascinated by my solo performances, kindly presented me with an expensive portable gramophone for Christmas in 1932. I became fondly and possessively attached to that mechanical device and was especially intrigued with the detachable handle. After all, that Z-shaped, chrome-metal tool with shapely, black-lacquered knob was essential to the functioning of my music box and *must not be lost*. The wind-up machine was my most treasured toy. Teddy Bear came first, of course. But then he was my friend, not a toy.

Gee, I was so proud – my own gramophone! Even now, as though watching an old magic-lantern show, I can picture the scene and hear the sounds as I sat on the Axminster carpet of the drawing room floor with Teddy at my side. I see the ornate furniture, sense the aroma of wax polish and the sooty smell of the open coal fire. I visualise my actions as I wind the handle, push the turntable lever to 'on', carefully place the heavy arm containing a thick needle on to the rim of the solid shellac record, and listen: *If you go down to the woods today, you're sure of a big surprise ... de dum ...*

I sat for hours and hours on that floor between Father's chair and the french doors, listening and singing along until I knew all the words of all the songs in my small collection. The lyrics of *Camp Town Races* were tongue-twistingly difficult to mime to the fast tempo of the music, but I performed the song for Mother around my fifth birthday. Her patient tuition and accompaniment at the piano enabled me to add several 'grown-up' songs to my repertoire, including *Danny Boy*, *O For The Wings of a Dove* and *God Be In My Head*, so that by the age of six I was a star turn at the family's musical evenings.

Looking back, I realise now the intrinsic value of those formative musical experiences in relation to my development as a child: the many hours spent by myself, enthusiastically listening and singing along to my records established a natural discipline and a long attention span. I also realise that music was a catalyst for family bonding and hours of enjoyment spent together with adult relatives and neighbours; that the encouragement of my parents instilled in me a confidence to perform and a sub-conscious pride in their musical talents. My good fortune is almost beyond thankfulness.

In writing this fragment of personal history I am surprised to discover that, though later overtaken by the passion for outdoor sports, singing preceded cricket as an enjoyable expression of innate ability. Singing, however – in terms of practice and performance – was still ahead on points when, at the age of eight, I joined the choir at St Mary's Parish Church at Finchley. The prime mover for this initiative was Father, who relished playing the piano, leading the singing of *Jerusalem* and popular hymns from *Ancient and Modern*, all of which I sang with zest but naïve religious intent.

In general, the parents in our neighbourhood were tolerant towards their children's friends, opening their homes and gardens for play space in winter and summer. My mother was very friendly and kind, allowing us to make an untidy mess as long as we cleared up after our play activity. Good manners were de rigueur; therefore we always asked our parents if it was convenient for friends to come round to play and remembered to say 'thank you' to the host parent upon leaving.

There were no girls among my friends in the 1930s, only one pal had an older sister, only one family was formidably religious and only one owned a car. Walking everywhere was the norm; buses a treat, trams and trains exciting. To a five-year-old, a day trip to St Albans on a Green Line coach was as exciting as a flight from Gatwick to Malaga today. Parents had little money to spend on toys or treats because they had to save their spare shillings for the greatest treat of all – the summer holiday. Every year from my birth to August 1939 we spent two weeks in Ryde, Isle of Wight, lodging with Father's brother – my Uncle Jack.

While I have no recall of my earliest adventures on the sands at Ryde, I do hold the family collection of black and white photographs taken with a Box Brownie camera; snaps that record many happy scenes with my parents and several cousins older than me, one of whom probably saved my life.

Cousin Beryl and Alan
at Sandown, IOW, 1931

Alan at Ryde, 1931

Father held the memory and told the tale that when I was four, and contentedly playing sand castles on my own near the family group, I decided I needed a bucket of water and wandered off to find the sea. The tide retreats a very long way at Ryde, exposing vast acres of sand, but then returns very quickly. Suddenly the adults were in a mild panic because I had disappeared; Father spotted me at the water's edge some two hundred yards away – and the tide was coming in – fast. Eleven-year-old Beryl won the race to rescue me, and return the naïve child to worried and rather cross parents.

Father loved the lifestyle enjoyed by his older brother on the Isle of Wight. He had a wish-dream to live there and wrestled with his emotions when having to return to life in the metropolis. Mother also enjoyed the island for holidays, but by the end of the fortnight she was itching to return to London, to her home, to dressmaking and piano playing. But while on holiday, both Sam and Wyn revelled in the change of environment and devoted themselves to holiday pursuits with the family.

Thinking about those holidays in the early thirties I do have clear memories of playing cricket on Ryde sands with cousins Doris and Beryl, local cousin Tilly – and many young male admirers of the three good-looking girls. Also, happy memories of many hours spent with Father fishing from Ryde pier – having first dug lugworm and ragworm from the soft wet sands surrounding that iconic Victorian structure. Paddling – sandcastles, of course, and later swimming on warm days in chilly waters – donkey rides, bumpy bus rides and long walks ... oh, and another favourite ... train rides to Sandown and Freshwater travelling through beautiful countryside in ancient carriages pulled by my beloved 'Puffin' Billy' steam engines.

I loved the Isle of Wight, the seaside, the countryside and villages – even the quaint little towns. And as I shall be writing more about experiences on the island in later chapters, I'll leave the bloom of the earliest memories in the 'once upon a time' mists of a really blessed early childhood.

When my pals and I returned from our summer holidays in August 1933 we shared stories about where we had been, what we had seen and done – talking over each other in loud voices – each claiming the best adventure. Little was said about what might happen next week when we would lose our accustomed freedoms to become corralled in the classrooms of those forbidding institutions called schools. We felt fear and foreboding on the one hand: on the other, excitement at the prospect of becoming 'big boys' going to school. But as we soon discovered, being the minnows in a pond of much bigger children was a bit scary at first.

Change, change, change – the challenge to learn, and learn to adapt, is constant throughout our life journey. So how did my minnow pals and I adapt to life in the scary Big Pond of School Life?

~~~~~~~~~~~

CHAPTER 6

FIRST SCHOOL AND HOLIDAYS

*"Mummy, I don't want the big boys to think I am a sissy
…please … please don't come with me, Mummy Dear!"
"Alright, I'll stand at the gate and watch you to the corner;
now you be careful crossing the road, Alan."
"Yes, Mummy Dear."*

Manorside Infants in Squires Lane was only five minutes walk from home. On the Monday of my second week at my first school I refused to let my mother accompany me.

Freedom! I ran down Manor View, stopped, turned and waved. Mother waved back. Bursting with energy, I ran on, up and over the slope of the railway bridge until I caught up with a couple of my pals. Our natural high spirits were tempered with apprehension because, during the previous week, we had tasted the restrictions and formalities of the classroom for the first time. I clearly remember that we all fell silent as we passed through the formidable iron gates into the commotion of the boys' playground.

The intake of sixty boys and girls came from a wide range of social backgrounds. A dozen or so parents were professional and posh – upper-grade civil servants, a doctor, several teachers, a vicar and a few successful businessmen. The majority of parents were either 'in trade', or clerks in banks, insurance and shipping offices in central London. A few children came from 'rough homes'. Father had impressed upon me: "It would be better if you did not play with those rough boys."

However, in common with my pre-school pals, those exhortations soon faded. Any boy who would share his ball to throw or kick around in the playground became a mate. The new social mix stirred the vernacular pot and levelled it to a common parlance ... 'norf lunnun spik'. Consequently, in my second year, Mother shepherded me to a private tutor – a terrifyingly posh dame – for elocution lessons.

"Why, mummy….why do I have to go to 'looshon' lessons?"

"Because you are not speaking properly. You have picked up bad habits from those other boys, Alan, which your father and I don't like."

"But Mummy, I like playing with Fred and Bill ... and ... and I don't like that 'looshon' teacher," I pleaded.

After three lessons with the terrifying dame I began to wet my bed. This problem escalated when the posh witch produced a children's show performed to an audience of parents at Manorside School. Mother quickly ran up my costume on her sewing machine; an all-in-one, head-to-toe 'bunny rabbit' outfit in light brown cotton material, complete with close-fitting hood and big ears.

I became so angry at the thought of having to wear the stupid costume that at the final fitting in Mother's dressmaking den I kicked up a great fuss – a stomping, yelling paddy: "I hate it, I hate it ... I'm not going to do it!"

'Doing it' in school clothes at rehearsals was bad enough – hopping around on all fours in a type of chorus line in that awful costume in front of lots of adults would be "stupid, stupid! I don't wanna do it!" And I didn't do it ... in showbiz parlance, 'it was *not* all right on the night': I bolted down an imagined rabbit hole behind the back-drop curtain and stayed there.

My disappearing trick was not due to stage fright because, even at the age of six, I would sing anywhere in public at the drop of a middle C. No, not stage fright, but I have a clear memory of the show being silly and childish, so my reaction was probably associated with the fact that I had always been surrounded by adults who performed 'proper music' and were in no way mamby-pamby. That 'bunny rabbit' incident seeded a negative conditioned response that affected me throughout my adult years: I always avoided fancy dress parties.

I was still wetting the bed weeks after the calamitous children's show, so Mother, thinking I had an intestinal infection, made an appointment with Dr Holmes who examined me but did not prescribe the anticipated bottle of medicine. Wisely he asked my mother if I was having any problems at school.

"No, Alan loves going to school."

"Has he fallen out with any of his friends?" queried the doctor.

"No," replied Mother, "but he has fallen in with some of those boys from the council houses and is now talking just like them."

Mother was certainly not a snob but as musicians both she and Father had 'an ear' for nuances of sound and became concerned that my newly acquired accent had already changed my singing tonality. But wetting my bed had become an even more serious problem, highlighted by The Accident.

The classrooms at Manorside were tiered; the gangways between the desk platforms sloped at about fifteen degrees. My desk was situated on the third of four tiers. Immediately after the bunny rabbit fiasco the intervals between my needing to pee decreased alarmingly. Wriggling in my seat, hand aloft, my frequent and insistent pleas annoyed our class teacher: "Miss ... please, Miss, may I be excused?"

Sitting in class soon after school dinner one day I became really desperate. Up went my hand, "Please ... "

"No," came the immediate and stern reply, "You should have gone at dinner time!"

Desperation powered my imagination: 'Oh crickey, what shall I do? Dare I run down the gangway and through the door, into the hall past the gym class and outside to the toilets across the playground? No, too far!'

That I improvised so quickly and riskily – at the age of six – amazes me now as I recall the scenario. I was the proud possessor of a real leather satchel. As soon as Miss turned her back to write on the blackboard, I surreptitiously removed a couple of books from the satchel, and pretending I was reading the lesson book, held the receptacle between my knees. With one hand I undid the buttoned flies of my short trousers, extracted my willie with the other and hosed. Oh! ... such relief! Pints! ... well, a lot anyway.

I propped the satchel carefully against the cast-iron leg of the desk; then paid full attention to Miss, who was now addressing the class in her authoritative manner. "Bring your books to me as soon as you have finished."

Finished? Yes, I had finished – but not my lesson book.

Maurice The Brain, who sat behind me, always had to be first up for marking at teacher's desk. As he rushed down the gangway his left shoe nudged the strap of my satchel. Over it went and out poured the contents. Horror! Slowly, ever so slowly, a tiny stream trickled down the gangway to form a mini-pond beside teacher's desk. Perched on her high chair with foot rest, mind focused on Maurice's lesson book, Miss gradually became distracted by discrete tittering ... boys and girls were not allowed to titter in class in 1934. "QUIET!" she commanded, scanning the classroom, her sharp eyes alighting on the mini-pond beside her desk: (it seemed like Regents Park Lake to me).

Blushing and crying I stood up and pleaded: "Please, Miss ... I'm sorry ... I had an accident."

"AN ACCIDENT!" boomed Miss, as dramatically as Lady Bracknell in Oscar Wilde's play – "AN ACCIDENT? This is not an accident ... it's ... it's a vile breach of good manners! Why didn't you ask?" "But ... bu ... " Fear and tears drowned my mind and closed my throat.

"Maurice ... MAURICE ... stop looking at that horrible mess and go ... GO NOW, BOY ... find the caretaker and tell him to come here with a bucket and mop," commanded Miss. "YOOOUU, you filthy boy, are coming with me to Miss Mustard – NOW!"

Hoisting me by the collar of my jacket so that I was on tiptoe, she dragged me, terrified and screaming, through the gym class in the hall and down the dark passage to 'that room'. I remember no more – except a stinging bum from the cane administered by the Deputy Head Teacher with the hot name. On receiving news of the incident my bewildered parents again consulted Dr Holmes who advised them to cancel the elocution lessons. Bedwetting, so embarrassing, decreased but did not cease altogether until I was ten.

In writing about my early years I have discovered – often to my amazement – that I have clear memories of scenes and situations that impacted my emotional memory. In general, however, I have only vague memories of the two years in the infant school. It is logical that I settled into the restrictive regimen, made average progress in the 3 Rs, looked forward to holidays and made new friends. More memorable are activities I enjoyed at home: drawing cars and aeroplanes, many solo hours with my Meccano set and Dinky toys and lots of time with friends playing simple board games indoors when the weather was inclement. Naturally, given reasonable weather, my pals and I took every opportunity to be outdoors playing cricket and football. My physical energies seemed boundless, and I remember that I used to run everywhere except when curtailed by adult company and authority. Until the age of nine I often challenged myself to a running race when walking to the shops along Lichfield Grove. On hearing a car behind me I would try to beat it to the next lamp post or telegraph pole ... short, sharp, flat-out sprints. There were not many cars in our area in the 1930s but, unconsciously, my game laid a foundation for skills at cover point in the years ahead.

Home life was stable – my parents kind and supportive. Mother encouraged my reading and singing; Father patiently taught me gardening skills and bought me a fret-saw set to divert me from spoiling his precious carpentry tools. When Grandpa William stayed with us he encouraged my batting by patiently bowling underarm, and my cousin Beryl began teaching me to swim at the indoor baths in Squires Lane.

In retrospect, I realise now the value and importance of imaginative play in those early days. My pals and I treasured our basic toys which, though few in number, gave us hours of pleasure. But whether playing on our own, in pairs or small groups, we had a lot of fun inventing games that stretched our imaginative skills, often competing with each other to dream up a new idea.

For instance, I remember a game of 'hunt the treasure' played in our gardens, whereby we hid clues in trees or buried in the soil, leading finally to the treasure – three wrapped humbug sweets hidden in the most unlikely locations. This game became so popular that the competitive 'Final' was held around the vast perimeter of the cricket ground, each of us in turn hiding clues in the bushes, under the fixed wooden seats, behind the tea hut and under the raised deck of the old wooden pavilion. Daringly, we tried out a similar game in the botanical gardens of Avenue House Park but were soon caught out and evicted by the vigilant head-keeper, Mr Thomson, who wielded a sergeant-major's drill stick with voice to match.

More seriously, I evoked my father's admonitory tone and rarely used strap on my behind when, still in the infant school, I was caught out stealing the milk money. Mother gave me four pennies every Monday to pay for school milk – a daily one-third of a pint drunk through a straw from a glass bottle with a cardboard lid. I liked the milk but preferred sweets and pomegranates, available at a corner shop near the school. So for two weeks I kept the money and indulged myself with wine gums and fruit on the way home at tea-time. At first I lied when Mother asked why I was not hungry – and lied again when questioned by my teacher as to why I was not drinking milk at morning break.

Tears flowed when Mother confronted me with the contents of a letter from the head-teacher, and more painful tears when Father arrived home from work. I have avoided pomegranates since that day because they are associated with Father's strap. I deserved it and learned a valuable lesson. The fact that that memory is clear over seventy years later proves to me that selective and mild corporal punishment, very occasionally administered by parents for serious misdemeanours by their own children, helps to define boundaries more effectively than other forms of reprimand. On the other hand I accept that modern legal restrictions have thankfully eliminated physical abuse caused by cane and strap in schools and a minority of homes.

However, the balance of my personal opinion remains intact regarding the right of parents to administer mild corporal punishment as a last resort. While I am an advocate of 'tough love', I accept that much depends on the nature and self-control of individual parents. The debate goes on. There was no debate in our household following the incident of the milk money. The subject was never mentioned again.

Father taught me to fish on our family holiday to Ryde in the summer of 1935. On previous holidays I had dabbled enthusiastically, but now that I was seven Sam decided it was time to impart knowledge and skills of his favourite sport. We spent many hours together in various locations on Ryde Pier seeking a variety of species: he was very patient, and I was an enthusiastic pupil. It was a proud moment for both of us when he presented me with one of his rods and a wooden reel with ratchet. Yes, I loved fishing, yet there were so many other exciting things to do on those memorable holidays before the war. Beryl, local cousin Tilly and her boyfriend John played cricket with me for hours on the sands – Sam and Wyn joined in from time to time. We had fun in the sea, throwing and catching a beach ball, splashing each other and swimming when the tide was up. To travel by 'Puffin' Billies' to the beautiful beaches at Sandown and the picturesque bay and pier at Shanklin was a special treat for this young boy.

As a kid our holidays on the Isle of Wight were always an adventure: so many places to visit and explore, exciting activities with my parents and cousins and Uncle's Jack's interesting friends to meet. I enjoyed talking with grown-ups and was always asking questions ... my-o-my, those adults were so patient ... and they really listened. One of my greatest joys was to sit near the ornate bandstand on Ryde's Esplanade, listening to brass band music, fascinated by the big instruments whose names I could not pronounce ... 'u fon eemum' ...

Sam and Alan fishing
on Ryde Pier, 1933

Sporting passions:
bat beats rod anytime.
Sam and Alan
on Ryde Pier, 1933

and as always, captivated by the variety of expressions, often humorous, on the face of the conductor. I enjoyed amusing the adults when we walked from Ryde to Puckpool – along the promenade – by singing the chorus of a popular song whilst imitating a marching drummer: *'As I walk along the promenade with an independent air, you can hear the girls declare, he must be a millionaire'* ... but not in French. Puckpool triggers memories of delicious ice creams plopped atop enormous cones and fun times playing crazy golf.

At Sandown I enjoyed rides on the narrow gauge steam railway on the beach side of the Esplanade wall and bumper cars in an amusement arcade. I spent hours on the tranquil boating lake at Ryde where I learned to row in a tiny clinker-built dinghy. I thought canoes rather sissy – couldn't go fishing with Father in a canoe. The day before we returned to London I was invited by Uncle Jack to join him and my father for an afternoon's fishing from his boat – my first at sea in a dinghy. Preparations to tackle up in the Vectis clubhouse seemed to me to take a long time, but eventually four men carried the ten-foot clinker-built dinghy to the top of the slipway and eased it down the slope into the cool waters of the Solent.

I was chaperoned aboard and noted that there was no outboard engine, just two pairs of oars. None of the anglers I met in the 1930s wore life jackets – I could now swim and that was why I was permitted to board Uncle's boat. Big burly Jack, an expert angler and Captain of the Vectis Fishing Club, knew the best spots to catch different varieties of fish. On that sunny August day we dropped anchor west of the pier on an incoming tide. We soon caught half a dozen dabs and four edible plaice – then at high tide Jack and Sam changed tackle for the sport of catching gar fish. I was enthralled as I witnessed the thrashing fight put up by those slim green-silver fish with a long needle-like beak. I managed to land a few inedible small fish and crabs before finally feeling a strong tug on my line and, with lots of advice and encouragement, hung on while I reeled in a whopping plaice that Father carefully coaxed into the landing net. I was more than excited – I was hooked on fishing.

At the end of a day I shall always treasure, Father gutted the flatties, the ladies prepared a succulent fish supper and the family gathered around Uncle Jack's dining table to enjoy the meal, the banter and a special moment of family togetherness. For me, the seven-year-old kid, the abiding memory is the feeling of being grown up among the grown-ups, and a sense of belonging in a warm and caring family.

Holiday over, we returned to London: Father, as always, reluctant to change roles from countryman to businessman while Mother, refreshed by good company and sea air, looked forward to getting back to her weekly routines. I was excited to meet up with friends at home to regale them with my fishing stories, but not so excited at the prospect of returning to Manorside where I was about to move up from the Infant to the Junior School.

~~~~~~~~~~~~

Cousin Tilly, Wyn and Alan in Ryde 1933

*Alan sits well but finds
people more interesting,
Ryde, 1933*

*Sam, Wyn and Alan,
Ryde, 1935*

*Alan on the grass in
beloved Arden Field,
Finchley, 1935*

CHAPTER 7

GROWING AND LEARNING IN THE 1930s

CURIOSITY

To learn, to grow, develop strong
in mind and heart, become, belong
'tis said that curiosity is key,
deep thirst to understand, to know, to Be:

So rich were we, though money poor,
in Finchley Town, before the war,
green fields and parks, quiet streets to stray
to learn through play – to seize the day
To Live – with constant curiosity.

And so we grew and learned, developed strong
home ties and friends, to neighbourhood belong,
to school, to church and sport – the Nation too –
their influence all essential, true
For Life – a constant curiosity.

'Tis now in twilight years I understand
a little more of life than then, the hand
of Destiny dealt full when young and green
fulfilled beyond all hopes, all dreams –
yet Life remains – a constant curiosity.

----

*As far back as I can remember I enjoyed spending time on my own so that
I could 'have a think.'*

I don't remember ever being bored because, when alone, I would happily
spend hours making useful things with my few tools – also drawing, reading,
collecting stamps – and studying a big old atlas to identify those far-off colonies
and foreign lands represented by those stamps. Above all, I was curious about
people and places: why did people in Africa and China look so different, dress
so strangely and live in buildings so unlike ours? Though never a scholar I had
a strong desire to find out and to understand so that by the time I was eleven I
was a strange mixture of athlete, performer and solo student. I ask myself now:
'Why was I such an enigma?'

Given the lottery of genetic inheritance there are many factors surrounding
the development of a young child that determine the foundations upon which
that individual's life is built: the influence of parents, family and neighbours,

of peer-group pals, the quality of local schools, the community environment and national mood – of family economics, local facilities and opportunities. The positive and negative influences of so many circumstances mould the child's character and effect the unfolding journey ahead – a journey as yet unknown.

I was indeed fortunate to begin my journey surrounded by caring adults, who, for all their own frustrations and limited capabilities, nurtured me with loving care in an environment favourable to the development of my natural inclinations and abilities. Some of those abilities surfaced and developed when very young. Others lay dormant until experience and circumstance – in some instances necessity – opened new and unexpected pathways to a fuller life. In my thirties the furnace of disappointment and hardship removed some of the gloss of the past to temper the core of character, reveal latent talents and offer new goals. Later, from my mid-fifties onwards, a free-spirited, free-wheeling, serendipitous peregrination blew me into situations that in previous life situations I had not even considered.

Nor were the key influences that laid profound and permanent foundations during the seven-eleven period of my development in any way engineered. Personal self-analysis concludes that in addition to the 'given' of parental influences, family interests and community environment, I assimilated, osmotically, the mores and values extant in the particular historical period in which I grew up. Within that framework the quality of the local school, the church choir and excellent recreational facilities contributed significantly to my general development and influenced my future – for better or worse.

The standard of education proffered at Manorside Junior School was neither of the above – but middling. But then, to be fair to the teachers, I was a middling student – never a scholar at school. I got by in a day-to-day sense: then accelerated unexpectedly when faced with an exam – a mystery probably connected with my sporting instincts and adrenaline when faced with a challenge.

Today, sitting in my attic study seeking inspiration from my view across the Solent to The Needles, fingers poised over the keyboard, my mind begins to formulate a question: "What on earth was junior school really like way back then in the 1930s?"

Fortunately I am blessed with a surprisingly good long-term memory. Those happy days and tough moments of yesteryear remain sharp and easily accessed – although today when I move from desk to kitchen I may forget the purpose of the visit. So, in the period under review some memories will pop up on the screen of my mind – while others will have to be dredged and then dressed up with a smidgen of colourful imagination.

Manorside Junior School? Big windows but dull interior colours: grey clothes and grey pavements, black tarmac roads and black tarmac playgrounds, faded cream paint and brown wall tiles inside drab red brick buildings. No grass! The green of our garden, the public parks and the cricket field were refreshing oases within the suburban desert surrounding that educational establishment. Manorside breathed an atmosphere of regimentation and strict discipline conducted by conscientious female teachers who patiently hammered home the 3 Rs. I enjoyed reading and quite liked sums but preferred drawing, singing, gym and sport because those activities were artistic or physical – and fun.

The promotion of good nutrition, hygiene and physical health was a national priority in that era of high unemployment and general ignorance of healthy living. Tuberculosis and diarrhoea were killers, rickets debilitating and lice catching. Many school periods were allocated for physical activities in the gym and, weather permitting, in the playground. Keep-fit classes proliferated throughout the country; exercise in the fresh air for all age groups became fashionable. At school we did 'physical jerks' – today known as 'warm-ups' before gym classes and sports events.

School lunches were ... school lunches ... not very tasty but relatively nutritious: real meat, soggy greens and mashed potatoes, followed by rice pudding or apple pie and custard. I still enjoyed the small bottle of subsidised milk sucked through a straw at mid-morning. The visiting Matron, a formidable character, was square of body, military in bearing and uniform; dark blue tunic with a starched white apron, wide blue belt and perky cap perched precariously on tightly permed mouse-blond hair. Her aura and aroma seemed to dispel germs in her wake as she swept through corridors and classrooms. She insisted that we wash our hands regularly, using carbolic soap and drying on laundered roller towels. And sneezing! Woe betide a sneezer without a clean handkerchief.

We learned 'times tables' by rote, games in mental arithmetic became competitive and reading aloud embarrassing to the shy – I was not shy. Pages and pages of sums were marked on the spot with a thick blue pencil. Silent reading, writing and spelling were the other main staples in our learning diet, with the addition of basic grammar at a later stage. Simple geography, mainly about the British Empire; drawing, painting, singing and gym were programmed into the curriculum.

Evidence of my modest level of attainment at 7 years 10 months is contained in a letter that my brother and I discovered in a box of child memorabilia and cricket press cuttings after the death of Sam and Wyn in 1982. Written to my mother when she was in hospital undergoing a mastectomy operation in 1936, my letter indicates a surprising interest in schoolwork, a real affection for my parents, concern about friends and amusing spelling. The writing is looped, large, neat and legible.

March 25th 1936.

My Dear Mummy

I hope you are getting on all write in hospitle.

I have chicken pox as you said. I think you are

mour like a doctor and better stay and be a nerse.

I want to go to school and work. I have not got

the Hornby badg yet but I am looking forward to it.

Daddy has given me his bible to reed.

Dick has got chicken pox and Bill cort it and then Peter.

Mss Churchill is going to give me some sums to do.

With much Love from Alan.

Comment: the composition and spelling is well below the standard attained at a similar age by my youngest grandchildren.

With life at home being stable and my social-sporting activities stimulating, school terms folded seamlessly into holidays and weekends into the school week. Three easy-going school years rolled by without a hitch ('pressure' had not been invented) until, in the autumn term of 1938, the senior teachers made it clear that we had to work especially hard because we had to sit for an important examination next May. My grades in the 'B' stream were average. Mother was perceptive and, anxious that I should go to grammar school, arranged for some private coaching in my weaker subject areas. I had a think: "Exams in May are a nuisance because they mess-up the cricket season." The private coaching helped but I did not 'step on the gas' until a week before that important Eleven-Plus Examination.

Would I progress to grammar school? Maybe – maybe not. Would my passion for sport distract me from swatting for the exams? Probably. Did my parents and teachers express concern? Definitely. Was I given a stern lecture regarding the consequences of my confident laissez-faire attitude? No. Was there a surprise factor? Yes, unbeknown to me before that time, I discovered a trump card in my pack – I enjoyed exams. Naturally I was nervous, but once in the arena of the examination room the light of concentration switched on, the adrenaline flowed and I got into 'the zone' – to use the vogue terminology in sports today. The habit – the learned behaviour of the concentration required in sport lit up as though I was playing an important innings to win the match. I was amazed that I won – that I passed. I have always been amazed when I have passed exams.

Looking back, I am thankful to those dedicated female teachers at Manorside School for the basic foundations they implanted. The focus on the three Rs, combined with the contemporary discipline in schools in the 1930s, squeezed me into grammar school and finally paid dividends in later years when I attended college aged forty and university at fifty.

In April 1936 I joined the choir at St Mary's Parish Church, Finchley. The Reverend SF Bernays led a theologically middle-of-the-road Anglican congregation – no bells and smells of Catholicism or evangelical bible-thumping in the old Parish Church. Although my musical parents did not attend church they were aware that I had a promising soprano voice and were keen for me to benefit from the vocal training available in a church choir.

As soon as I was able read the soprano line of a music score, Mother prepared me for an audition. I remember standing by her at the piano and following her lead as she played single notes to test the accuracy of my pitch; then scale after scale before finally rehearsing my audition piece: the hymn *God be in my head, and in my understanding* to the musical score by Henry Walford Davies.

Satisfied that I was well prepared, Mother accompanied me to the home of the choirmaster, Mr Ivor Richards, whose gracious welcome eased my nervousness and boosted my confidence. Sitting at his grand piano the choirmaster tested my pitch, then the range of my voice and proceeded to run through all the scales within that range. He seemed pleased, turned to my mother and whispered something about 'perfect pitch' before inviting her to accompany me at the piano to sing my favourite hymn.

"Excellent, Alan, excellent – would you sing that again, please, and emphasise all the 'ds': it is not 'Goh be in in my heh' ... but ... 'GoDh be in my heaDh' ... do you see ... like that. Oh, and Mrs Rayment, would you mind playing the piece a little more slowly this time, thank you."

At the end of the audition Mr Richards took Mother aside for a chat: I heard nothing but noted the smiles and nodding of heads. Mr Ivor Richards invited me to join choir rehearsals for the next four weeks and, if I made good progress in learning the structure of the services, the chants, descants and anthems, I could sing in church with the choir on Whit Sunday – a few days before my eighth birthday. I remember feeling really embarrassed, dressed up in an Eton collar, black cassock and white surplice as we walked slowly through the aisles singing the processional hymn. 'You look such a sissy,' whispered the sporting me to the sensitive artistic self within. However, 'having a think' during the sermon, I concluded that in addition to loving the music there was something about lots of people singing and praying together that I quite liked. In later years I realised that I took to the social and theatrical ambience of church and choir like the proverbial duck to water. Until I was ten, singing in the choir competed with cricket as twinned enthusiasms.

No-one at St Mary's, not even the amiable Rector, was more highly respected by the boys than The Choirmaster. A gifted musician and teacher, his enthusiasm and transparent love of church music inspired his mischievous choirboys. He also coaxed a full complement of serious, and at times temperamental male singers, to ever higher levels of performance. Ivor Richards was a popular man who produced a standard of choral singing that undoubtedly lifted the moral and religious spirit of the large congregations attending St Mary's, especially during the second world war.

During the period called 'The Phoney War' I was privileged to represent our church in a diocesan choir to sing alongside the choristers of St Paul's Cathedral at the Service of Enthronement of the new Bishop of London, Dr Geoffrey Fisher. I recall travelling by Tube to the City for several rehearsals prior to the colourful religious ceremony in November 1939. To sing glorious choral music in the vast amplitude of Wren's architectural masterpiece was a great honour and a great pleasure. Happy days!

In writing about 'singing in the choir' I realise how much I benefited from the self-discipline required when learning the score of a new anthem or chant: the requirement of clear diction, breath control, spot-on timing and concentration. Those years of regular attendance at St Mary's deepened my love for music – and for the sound of words too – not only from the repertoire of choral music but also from listening to readings from the King James Authorised Version of the Bible. I was introduced to ceremony and communal order, to new friendships and a sense of belonging to something important, both in the local community and in the 'big world out there'. I did not become hooked on religion, although when singing *God be in my head and in my understanding*, I felt I was expressing my desires to 'someone up there'. Later, in my thirties, I was to encounter a heavy dose of spirituality and religion, but during those choirboy years sport soon took precedence above all other interests – and 'churchy' things faded when my voice broke.

Being committed to a church choir was not only a serious responsibility but a lot of fun too! Choirboys 'muck about', of course; play pranks, rustle sweet papers, shake tiny tins of throat soothing Meloids and whisper loudly. They make up and sing alternative lyrics, ('most highly flavoured gravy' is a line I remember in a Christmas carol), and are regularly berated by the grumpy old tenors in the stalls behind. We were paid half-a-crown for weddings and funerals and a whole pound at Christmas and Easter – an enormous sum for a young boy in those days – some of which I saved for the choir's summer outing to Brighton.

Picture the scene, in the present tense, inside Victoria Station early one Saturday morning in August 1937:

> The drab and noisy concourse is bustling with people – smoke and steam billowing aloft in the canopy. I am nine, one of a flock of excited choir-boys yakking like geese as we storm the slam doors of the Brighton train and pile in heaps on the hard upholstered seats of an open third-class carriage. Mr Ivor Richards and his grumpy tenors are attempting to restore order with little success, but the sudden appearance of a beefy-looking uniformed ticket collector reduces our excited activities to prayer-like stillness.

"Nah then ... nah then ... tickets please all ofyer ... an' mind yer behave yooo lot," commands Mr Collector, standing in tall authority over us and waving two index fingers from his extended right arm as though he is about to pronounce the Benediction – which he's not. As he moves on to the adults our restrained whispers are suddenly overpowered by shrill whistles, powerful steam blasts and stuttering steel couplings ... uncoupling our temporary self-discipline with cries of 'WE'RE OFF!!' Unable to restrain ourselves we resume our yakking – sotto voce.

Brighton Pier – ice creams and the sea – heaven! As I skip along the planks over the water with special mates Bill and Charley I start singing – they join in: *Oh I do love to be beside the seaside ... where the band plays on, tiddly-om pom-pom ...* and I insist that we go to the end of the pier where I anticipate there will be old men and young boys fishing.

"You caught anything, mate?" enquires Charlie of a dark-haired kid about our age – no reply. "What can you catch here ... plaice ... sea bass?" I query in a tone that, hopefully, gives the impression that I too have fished from piers.

"Nuffink yet, just bleedin' crabs, mate," ventured a twelve-year-old ... "Yer lot darn frum Lunnun?"

"Yes," says Bill. "We're choirboys on an outing."

"F'ort yer'er bleedin' posh lot ... stuck-up bloody Lunnuners," chimes in an even bigger boy three rods up ... "Piss orf, willyer ... yer'll upset'n der bleedin' fish."

Too big to argue with, we cross the pier to look down at a boat tied up to the landing stage: 'Day Trips to Worthing Pier', states the chalked caption on a small blackboard.

The narrow-beamed, elegant steamer draws whistles of admiration from Bill and Charlie. "Cor! what a wizard boat, Al, I'd like to have a go on her," exclaims Charlie.

"Cor, she's a posh one, mate," adds Bill. Fascinated by the scene below we stay awhile, commenting on the gleaming varnish of the wooden fore-deck, the highly polished brass fittings, the tall slim funnel and a scallop-bordered, white canvas awning on the aft deck sheltering well-dressed landlubbers from the heat of late morning. Several gents dressed in waist-coated grey suits or blazers, white shirts and club ties are chatting to slim young ladies wearing calf-length, floral-print cotton frocks – some sporting wide-brimmed lacy hats. "Gee, that's really posh," I say out loud to my friends, then continue with a question to myself: "What's posh – and what's not? ... hmmm; that big Brighton kid called us 'posh' and 'stuck up', but his lingo sounds just like ours ... hmmm: I thought Sussex people spoke country-like ... broad and round like that actor Bernard Miles we've seen in films. But the people on the boat look really posh – they probably talk like some of those rich business people in the cricket club. Well, Bill and Charlie are not posh – but we're not rough either."

As we move away from the pier-head some older boys in our party call out, "Come on, you kids, come and have some real fun on the slot machines." We follow dutifully and enter the noisy smoky annexe housing the money-gobbling pin-ball tables. We are soon lost in animated competition, shouting and arguing about 'cheatin' and 'that's not fair', while losing pocketfuls of big old pennies saved up from half-crowns earned at summer weddings. Hungry, we sit on a bench in the sunshine, eat our sandwiches, buy more ice-creams and, as instructed, report to Mr Ivor Richards in the Tea Rooms on the hour. Free again, we join up with the main adult-boy group for several thrilling sessions driving bumper cars.

Time whizzes by, and it is now four o'clock. The whole party gather for a sumptuous feast of Tizer and big cream cakes – yum! The choir-men and their wives who serve us join in the fun and banter – even the grumpies seem cheerful for a change. Out of respect for our charismatic choirmaster – and because we were brought up that way – we behave reasonably well and do not disgrace our 'posh choir' during the Annual Outing.

Happy Days indeed!

As I look back I realise, once again, that through our upbringing in suburban London in the 1930s my pals and I learned 'to take thought for others' and to 'behave in public'. Not to do so would be letting down your family or your team, your school or choir ... and yourself.

From music with words to words between covers of books. I bless my mother for her initiative when, in April 1936, she introduced me to the library at the corner of Regent's Park Road and Litchfield Grove. Although my parents read the newspapers and occasionally borrowed a book from the library, there were few books at home. However, Mother's academic friend, Mrs Murphy – whose influence had saved my life as a baby – had become the family mentor in matters of child upbringing and education. She suggested that it was time for young Alan to become a junior member the Public Library.

In writing about that memorable first visit to a library I have to remind myself that I was a child whose imagination was, at that time, influenced by my hobby of battles with toy soldiers. I was also energetic and talkative so, as Mother opened the swing door she placed her index finger to her lips and said: "You must *not* talk in the library, Alan dear."

First in view was a slim, bespectacled, female librarian – her brunette hair in a bun – sitting behind a large desk stamping index cards quietly – ever so quietly. Then open-mouthed in wonderment I surveyed regiments of book spines standing to attention on tiered shelves as though waiting to be dismissed from their parade grounds to spend leave on the arm of a comfortable chair beside a blazing coal fire. I was also awed by the silence – and a distinct smell that, subconsciously, became mildly intoxicating. Ever since that initiation I have loved libraries: the miracle of thousands of books containing millions of words sweated over by hundreds of authors – and that smell! Is it the newsprint or the sweat – or both?

That first profound experience stimulated my thirst for reading, and I was soon transported to other worlds through tales written by Crompton, Defoe, Stevenson and Burroughs. I have fond memories of a leather bound edition of *Black Beauty* given me one Christmas by my parents, and two large books I discovered in the cupboard under the stairs, *Aesop's Fables* and an old encyclopaedia titled: *Enquire Within About Everything*. And naturally, by the time I was eleven I had consumed every cricket book I could borrow or buy second-hand. A life-long love affair with books had begun. Even my enthusiasm for cricket was overtaken by books from the advent of my first mystical experiences when I was twenty-nine. The personal renaissance that followed energised and motivated me to devour books on religion, theology, psychology, philosophy, literature and biography – any book that might give me a clue as to what the heck was happening to me! I had to *understand!* A long flirtation with the church did not enlighten me, but further experience – and brilliant authors of a wide variety of books – did feed that hunger *to learn, to know, to grow and to understand.* Thank you authors ... everywhere! I still experience a special buzz when I walk into a library or a bookshop – they are temples that satiate the appetites of the curious.

Three Graces of Nature's prolificacy have charmed me since early childhood and stirred my creative senses: grass, the sea, and trees. Heaven on earth, for me, would be to live in a self-built timber hut with reed-thatched roof situated on a grassy bank surrounded by palm trees overlooking a tropical seascape – very Robinson Crusoe. It is possible that my imagination tripped off into fantasy to associate Defoe's character with my father, his garden shed and tools, because I was always in attendance as a Man Friday helper when he was engaged in building or repairing timber structures. I remember the time when he dismantled his old garden shed to build a new one. I was surprised and excited when he added a small lean-to as a playhouse for me and my friends. Also joining in the fun when he built a new dog-house for Judy and extended the wired enclosure for our growing population of chickens. Father was always in jocular mood when applying his carpentry skills, and his enthusiasm rubbed off on me.

To prevent his nine-year-old son from messing up his precious tools, Father bought me a basic carpentry kit to augment my much-used fret-saw set. Thus encouraged I made a small bookcase and set of shelves for my bedroom and improvised additions to my own small garden shed. However, I had longed for a small second-hand billiard table and became upset when Father refused to buy one: "Can't afford it, my boy." I then challenged him with a bold reply: "Well, I'll make one, Daddy." He laughed: "You can't make a billiard table, my boy – that's preposterous."

I did not understand 'preposterous' – maybe daddy meant impossible. The word sounded nasty, made me feel angry and determined to prove 'I can do it!' Having obtained a large piece of box-wood from the greengrocer's shop, I sawed it down, 24 by 12 inches, sanded the surface and glued catapult rubber to six strips of wood that I screwed to the sides and ends. Mother, co-operating in the secret mission, supplied some rather rough green baize and crocheted six ball-receiving pockets. I threaded strips of garden wire through the top of the pockets, fixed them in place with bent-over pin tacks – then stood back to admire the result. Wizard! Paring down a length of old broom handle to make a cue took an hour; a cue tip and three large marbles cost a few pennies.

I was very proud of my achievement and immediately challenged my pal Dave Limbert to a game of billiards at our house. The table looked good but the density of the marbles slowed the game to a snail's pace. When Father came home that evening I was almost afraid to show him my masterpiece but, rather ceremoniously, and with Mother standing beside me, I removed a towel covering my mini-billiard table. For a moment Father was speechless, but then a grin developed into congratulatory praise as he took hold of the cue and attempted to pot a marble. "It's a bit slow, my boy, but well done – I didn't think you had it in you to make such a thing – and at your age, too!"

I was so relieved that Father was impressed. Years later Mother told me that the story became a major topic of conversation in the offices of Martin & Savage for the next couple of weeks. Six months after presenting my masterpiece I was overjoyed when Father produced a half-size portable billiard table that was to provide hours of fun for family and friends before and during the war.

Charles and Kezie Rayment
at Elmer Farm, Suffolk, 1935

Brothers Charles, Sam and Bert
at Elmer Farm, 1935

Farmer Doris and her mother Kezie at Elmer Farm

Alan helping with the harvest at Elmer Farm, 1937

From seven to eleven my physical growth enhanced natural abilities with willow blade and leather ball. Balls really: the small hard variety with proud stitched seam and that large, wickedly laced, leather panelled soccer sphere ... and soft tennis balls for my throw-catch wall game or to kick around in the school playground. Balls symbolised fun in the open air and freedom from the strictures of the classroom. Whether playing alone or with pals – throwing, catching, hitting, kicking, chasing – I seemed to be powered by an inexplicable inner drive to desire more of the same until it was bedtime or too dark to see the ball. That drive enabled me to grow in confidence and skill before becoming involved in organised games.

On entering the Junior School I was introduced to team games by the female PE teacher who organised competitions between forms A and B. Ingenuously, because of my enthusiasm and aptitude, I soon became a team leader. Two years later I was playing first-team soccer and cricket under the leadership of the dynamic Dick Nelson, a neighbour and friend whom I succeeded in my final year as captain of the school cricket team. One event evokes a chuckle now as I recall those happy days of Junior School cricket. Our all-conquering team played a full game against another school every week. One evening, when playing away at Martin School in East Finchley, we bowled out our opponents for nine runs. My good pal, Johnny Loosemore, took 5 wickets for 0 (zero runs): I took 5 for 4. There were five byes. That night I sat up in bed feeling cross with myself because Johnny had a better average and debating who was our best bowler – Johnny or me? Obviously I can laugh at myself now, but at the time I felt it was a serious matter. My pride was hurt, and I needed to get in the nets to practise and improve my bowling.

I will digress for a moment to record a recent and relevant happy experience – about a photograph that fell out of a Christmas card envelope in 2008. Wow! my first cricket team ... Manorside Junior School in 1938. Gee, how blond I was, aged ten. Actually, I had a copy in my collection ... but ... but ... who could be sending me this team photo now – seventy years later? The card was from Dick Nelson, one of my great childhood friends – the captain of that team in the photo – sitting front centre with two old, bandaged cricket bats crossed in front of his knees. In modern terminology ... I was gobsmacked!

Dick and his wife Norma had moved from London to Winchester and heard of my whereabouts through the Hampshire Cricket Society. I phoned – we met for the first time in over sixty years and could have reminisced for a week – a very happy occasion. One issue raised by Dick is important in comparing our background in sport to the facilities available to the present generations of young children. Dick remembered that there were no male teachers at Manorside School in 1938 and '39. The female staff, bless them, organised and supervised the school cricket and soccer teams to home and away matches, often umpired and occasionally refereed. Dick is still miffed that our popular teacher, Miss

Weiss, gave him out LBW to a ball pitching outside his leg stump. Yes, 'out' for a right-handed batsman ... but Dick batted left-handed.

The competitive spirit between teams playing inter-school matches was friendly and well mannered; good behaviour on the sports field was a norm throughout my playing career. Cricket matches in those days were never of the limited-over variety. The aim was to win the toss, make a big score then time the declaration to give the bowlers an opportunity to win the match. Old-fashioned maybe, but as batsmen we had time to build a big score or, if our team were batting second, to attack the bowling to win – or play a long defensive innings to draw. A really good bowler might bowl throughout the innings and regularly take six or seven wickets.

Importantly, we learned the game by watching and imitating adult players, by helping each other, through reading and studying photographs. From the pull-out sequence of pictures in Don Bradman's *How To Play Cricket* I learned the cut strokes and the pull shot – by trial and error and through practice, practice, practice. I received no coaching until I was nearly seventeen: even so, given the facilities available to the average young sports person of today, I have absolutely no regrets that 'I did it my way.'

> At Manorside and Arden Field
> I gambolled free with bat to yield
> alone – oh no, for spirit of the team
> I learned when young supplants the solo dream
> of glory in success – and shame in failure too,
> for none can play alone: eleven be the body true.
>
> Eleven boys in white, enthusiastic fight
> bold to win, flash blade and spin with flight
> red leather ball – dive catch with bruis-ed hand
> to out the batsman – clapped by brother-ed band.
>
> All one we grew, and one for all, though few remain
> in latter years a toast to drink to wisdom gained
> as boys in white, once green to values high,
> we learned – win, lose or draw – to laugh and not to cry.

In my formative years a core of adults at the Finchley Club became my second family and Arden Field my second home. Father often said, "I think you'd better take your bed over there, my boy." Later in this book a chapter or two will be devoted to my early years in cricket, but for now, I will make one observation. From childhood, through adolescence into mature manhood in my late twenties, the sport of cricket was a primary educator, my only career goal and blessed me with many wonderful friendships.

Thank you cricket – most enigmatic temptress of all team sports.

~~~~~~~~~~~

Manorside School 1st XI 1938
Standing: D.Young; T.Rawles; H.Hutchins; K.Holt;
G.Tugwood; J.Loosemore; G.Stanley; A.Bowness (scorer)
Sitting: A.Rayment; J.Creighton; R.Nelson (capt.); D.Limbert; A.King

Manorside School's cricket captain, R. (Dick) Nelson
with Alan at Hampshire's Rose Bowl, Southampton, 2009

CHAPTER 8

BORN BETWEEN TWO GREAT WARS

Yesterday is history
Tomorrow a mystery,
Today is a gift we call
THE PRESENT.

Today is a new moment of history.

Every yesterday and yesteryear was 'a modern time' in its own moment.

Change, a constant throughout The Universe, evolves moment by moment in every individual, every family, community and nation. The changes through which we evolve are imprinted in our personal and communal memories, gathered in the collective consciousness of the human race and chronicled by all forms of ancient and modern media.

My humble endeavour in this chapter is to sketch outlines of the historical, political and socio-economic events that influenced my upbringing in North London in the 1930s ... to paint a cameo of a bygone era so very modern in its time ... and to honour my parents who adjusted to, and coped with, constant and fluctuating change.

Her Majesty, Queen Elizabeth II, born in 1926, made the following comment during a tour of Pakistan in 1997:

I sometimes sense the world is changing almost too fast for its inhabitants, at least for us older ones.

Yes, we 'older ones' have witnessed, survived, and thankfully adjusted to an incredible volume of change through eight decades of the 20th century into the second decade of the *now* century. Personally, I am thankful that I was a happy and energetic child blessed with a degree of awareness that sensed, at family gatherings, an underlying sadness among the adults when they talked softly about national affairs and international crises.

The aftermath of the First World War was a time of grieving and the rebuilding of family and community life. In the 1920s and '30s the world was still recovering from the disastrous consequences of *the war to end all wars*: that gruesome conflict in Europe had accounted for the deaths of more than ten million people. Even more millions were injured – many disabled in body or mind. To begin to comprehend those figures, in 2011 the total population of Portugal was 10,781,459.

Families at all levels of our class-ridden British society were grieving – painfully adjusting to the deaths of over 750,000 fathers or husbands, sons or lovers, brothers, sisters and friends – and coping with another one and a half million who were physically crippled or impaired among whom were a proportion of women. My father had suffered shell shock; my future mother-in-law lost a beloved husband and her second husband, my wife Betty's father, never fully recovered from being gassed in the trenches in France.

On November 10th 1920, the coffin bearing 'The Unknown Warrior' was brought from France and solemnly paraded through the streets of central London before being interred the next day in Westminster Abbey. On that day the nation fell silent at 11 o'clock to commemorate 'The Armistice of 1918': to pay homage to the men and women of Britain and the Commonwealth who had died in that needless and tragic war. Throughout four days and nights thousands of mourners filed past the new Cenotaph Monument in Whitehall, London, laying so many wreaths and flowers that they covered the magnificent memorial designed by Sir Edwin Lutyens.

We Shall Remember Them.

The immense organisational task to demobilise millions of men from the armed services was efficient but slow, creating understandable frustration among the majority who wanted to 'go home and get on with life'. The Government ruled that priority for release be allocated to men whose skills were essential to the rebuilding of industry and commerce. However, a high percentage in that category had been called up in the later stages of the war. That prioritisation caused discontent among the longest-serving troops and provoked a mutinous rally in London that involved three thousand uniformed officers and men who occupied Horse Guards Parade. Trouble! Who would disperse these wartime heroes? Winston Churchill, then Minister of State for War and Air, ordered an immediate change to the existing scheme, declaring, with Cabinet approval, a 'first in, first out' system.

People involved in all aspects of national life desired 'to build a land fit for heroes'. Industry and the economy boomed for a while – jobs were plentiful but wholesale prices tripled from 1914 values. In January 1920 the government launched a programme to build 100,000 houses in the coming year which led to the clearance of major slum areas in a few cities. However, the majority of new-builds were in virgin suburban sites around London, Manchester and Birmingham. One-third of those 1920 houses were funded privately; local councils funded another third to rent and the others were paid for through government subsidies. Awash with money the building industry flourished, employment and wages boomed and costs overheated. For example, houses built with grant aid in 1921 cost £900 to build. A year later the same types of houses were being built for less than £400. The government grant scheme ended in 1922.

Some of the families who relocated to the new suburban neighbourhoods from the gloomy environs of inner cities felt uncomfortable in the country. Even though the new houses were equipped with every modern convenience including a bath and indoor toilet – and a garden that provided healthy play spaces for children – those families feeling alienated in their new environment returned to the emotionally comfortable hustle, bustle and grime of city living among old friends and relatives.

Given those exceptions, the majority of private owners and council tenants had realised that the new suburban estates represented a giant leap in social conditions including opportunities for better health and education. Schoolteachers, bank clerks and skilled tradesmen earning £400 a year could well afford a new three-bedroomed semi costing £900: deposits were low and mortgages in plentiful supply. The one and a half million new houses built by the end of the decade significantly enhanced the social conditions and living standards of thousands of families.

However, on the downside, the fluctuating economy caused unemployment and hardship to millions of people working in the major industries, giving rise to bitterness and strikes that affected people in all walks of life. The resulting frustration developed into a national mood of disappointment: 'is this what we fought for?'

But again, life is full of paradoxes. On the lighter side the 1920s witnessed a revolution in music and dance, in dress fashion and entertainment, in new consumer goods and gadgets. The need to blot out memories of the war popularised modern dance music that heralded 'The Jazz Age', accompanied by new-style fashions exhibited by the Bright Young Things. The bobbed hair, flattened bosoms and pelmet hem-lines of 'Flappers', combined with the uninhibited behaviour of louche-living, night-clubbing rich kids, caused outrage among members of the Establishment. The less well-off young people expressed their exuberance in hundreds of newly built dance halls, performing the Charleston and Black Bottom in a jazz dance craze that swept the country. The young were letting their hair down – living dangerously in reaction to the loss of so many contemporaries who had missed out on life's youthful pleasures.

The fluctuating post-war economies of the major industrial nations culminated in the Wall Street Crash in 1929. Panic trading on the New York stock exchange triggered an immediate worldwide economic downturn followed by the Great Depression of the early 1930s. Political and economic unrest in Europe presaged gathering storm clouds of territorial conflict. Then in 1939, after only twenty-one years of unsettled peace, the Second World War brought six more years of death and destruction in Europe, Russia, the Mediterranean, North Africa and the Pacific Far East.

War in the Pacific began dramatically with the unanticipated and devastating aerial attack launched from Japanese aircraft-carriers on the US fleet in Pearl Harbour, Hawaii. To effect closure of that war in 1945 the United States made controversial use of the atom bomb to annihilate the Japanese cities of Hiroshima and Nagasaki. World peace in 1945 heralded the Cold War between the Western Allies and Communist Russia – and too many more hot wars: Suez Canal, Korea, Vietnam, Israel-Egypt, the Falkland Isles, Afghanistan and Iraq, genocide in Africa – and today, terrorism.

The tragic consequences of 'man's inhumanity to man' in the last hundred years of human history have been offset and balanced by exponential developments in all areas of creative human endeavour. Since the 1920s multitudinous aspects of positive change have been recorded and debated in thousands of weighty tomes, endless film documentaries and forests of publications. Changes that immediately spring to mind as personally significant include vastly improved standards and resources in education, in health and hygiene – also amazing developments in telecommunications and transport systems.

For me, the most beneficial modern influences have been the plethora of information available since the 1960s in the fields of social history, personal growth and spiritual discovery; also the practical advantages afforded by motorised transport and the jet airplane to travel in comfort to places near and far. And I especially rejoice that in the last five decades we have witnessed improvements in racial harmony and female empowerment – and a greater understanding of human sexuality. In that time span, men and women dedicated to scientific research have decoded DNA, succeeded to accomplish human organ transplant operations, created space travel, satellite technology and the World Wide Web.

However, let us be aware that when I was born there were two billion people inhabiting our planet: now, in 2012, there are seven billion and rising. The ever-present paradox is that rapidly increasing population and successful economic growth have led to rampant consumerism, plundering of the planet's natural resources and irreversible damage to the climate of Mother Earth – our Home. For better or for worse we, the human species, are immensely creative and immeasurably destructive.

Ninety years ago nations as well as families struggled to recover from the universal consequences of the First Great War. In the next few paragraphs I will attempt a very brief sketch of the links between the political, economic, national and international events that coloured the backcloth of my childhood – and thereby influenced my future life journey.

In the aftermath of WWI many factories in Britain had to scrap and re-tool wartime production lines, raise capital to invest in new products and retrain existing employees, returning servicemen and women. Commendably, given the many new inventions and advances in design and technology, industrial and economic recovery was swift. For example, the aircraft and motor industries were expanding rapidly; radios were becoming a necessary luxury and hundreds of new cinemas catered for the growth in popularity of silent films. 'Going to the flicks' changed the pattern of 'the night out' and our own cockney actor-comedian, Charlie Chaplin, was the biggest Hollywood film star.

And, as in Chaplinesque dramas, national success alternated with failure at home and abroad. For a few years our exports boomed in fluctuating world markets: then over-production in 1921 caused more than two million people to be unemployed. 'One of the worst years of depression since the industrial revolution,' stated *The Economist*.

Serious international or economic crises often energise social unrest that escalates into political upheaval, changes of leadership and party affiliations, whether through the ballot box, revolution or putsch. In Britain, between 1919 and 1924, there were four general elections and five governments led by four different Prime Ministers.

In Germany, only five years after the end of that 'war to end all wars', disturbing signs of social, economic and political unrest were heeded by the wise, Churchill among them, but unheeded by the majority of politicians in Britain and the rest of Europe. The peace treaty between the Allies and Germany – the Treaty of Versailles in 1919 – had created harsh economic and financial sanctions on Germany. The French felt insecure vis-à-vis Germany and provided the majority of Allied troops who occupied the Rhineland for fifteen years. The League of Nations, an organisation conceived at Versailles in 1919 to monitor disarmament and, hopefully, to prevent war through collective security, failed to arbitrate in disputes over reparations, particularly between France and Germany. The collapse of the latter's economy led to inflationary meltdown: in 1923 one British Pound was worth three trillion German Marks.

After the 1914-1918 war the United States maintained a policy of 'isolationism'* while in Britain and Europe the politics of uncertainty and see-saw economics prevailed. Following the 1917 revolution in Russia the new political philosophies of Karl Marx and Vladimir Lenin led to the establishment of a Communist government. Joseph Stalin, Head of State from 1924 to 1953, turned Russia from an agrarian to an industrial economy. But during his harsh dictatorship tens of millions of people were persecuted and died, either from starvation or were shot during Stalin's 'Purges' of ethnic minorities.

In 1922 Mussolini's Fascist Party bullied their way to power in Italy, and their influence became a growing threat to democracy in Germany. At a political meeting in a Bavarian beer-hall in 1923 a group of armed German Fascists belonging to the emerging Nazi Party made a farcical attempt to seize power. Their leader, reported to be 'an obscure corporal named Adolf Hitler', claimed he that was supported by war hero Field Marshal von Lundendorff. Both principals were arrested and charged with high treason. At the trial, Lundendorff was acquitted and Hitler given a light prison sentence during which he wrote the first volume of his book *Mein Kampf* (My Struggle) – part autobiography and part political ideology.

David Lloyd George led Britain's post-war Coalition government from 1919 to 1922. In the aftermath of Turkey's crushing defeat of Greece in 1922 a crisis developed on the Asiatic side of the Dardanelle Straits where British peace-keeping troops were stationed to protect the neutral zone and ensure safe passage for shipping. The diplomatic crisis was abjectly mishandled by Lloyd George and his Cabinet. Conservative MP's and peers in rebellious mood met at the Carlton Club and voted 185 to 88 to end the Coalition. Lloyd George resigned: King George V asked Andrew Bonar Law to form a Conservative government. Bonar Law called a general election, won a workable majority then, sadly, became terminally ill and resigned.

To many MPs, as well as the general public, it came as a surprise that King George V invited the Chancellor of the Exchequer, Stanley Baldwin, to form a Cabinet. Baldwin, determined to reduce unemployment by seeking support for a policy of 'trade protection', called another general election in December 1923. The result was a 'hung Parliament' (no single political party having an overall majority of elected Members of Parliament). When Parliament reconvened after the Christmas recess, the Conservatives were defeated and Baldwin resigned. According to constitutional precedent, the King requested the attendance of the Labour's Ramsey MacDonald, leader of the party then holding the second highest number of parliamentary seats.

Conservative and Liberal MPs alike were aghast at the thought that any Labour politician should ever become Prime Minister: a reaction to radical change by old-fashioned traditionalists that led to several cabals proposing 'hair-brained schemes to avert this terrible outcome'. However, King George V made it clear that the Labour Party 'should be given a fair chance'. Ramsey MacDonald, heading the first Labour government with only a flimsy majority of seats in the Commons, held on to power for eight months before the electorate were again called upon to visit the polling stations. On November 6th 1924, the Conservative Party were returned to power with a large majority of seats and Stanley Baldwin as Prime Minister. Winston Churchill, having regained a seat, again crossed the floor of the House from the Liberal benches to join Baldwin's Conservatives. He was duly appointed Chancellor of the Exchequer. In his Budget speech the following year Churchill announced a return to the Gold Standard as Britain's monetary exchange mechanism for international trading purposes. Sterling strengthened: one pound purchased 4.86 US dollars.

The economic roller-coaster climbed and dipped: cinemas, dance halls and nightclubs boomed, skirts and economic hopes were high but so was unemployment at one and a half million. A long-running dispute between the coal miners' union and the mine-owners eventually drew support from other major unions. The resulting General Strike in 1926 crippled the nation for a while, but the economy recovered relatively quickly to herald a short period of uncertain prosperity. In June 1929 the electorate voted in Ramsey MacDonald's second Labour Government, but by October 1929 the Wall Street crisis triggered the worldwide economic avalanche of 'The Great Depression.'

The weak American economy destabilised world trade. British industries reliant on exports were paralysed. Our shipbuilding, steel and textile industries went into severe recession, creating knock-on effects to coal, transport and general manufacturing – then spiralling down the economic chain to the pub and the local corner shop. Unemployment in Britain increased to over three million; poverty, both visible and invisible, was on a scale beyond anything that later generations would experience – or could even imagine. The dole queues were long; hand-me-down clothes became rags, charities were overwhelmed and soup kitchens became essential. Poverty breeds poverty, and long-term poverty breeds mental and physical ill-health. The workhouse was the end of the line for many of those who fell through the few safety nets available. One historian wrote: 'The workhouses of the Thirties were a living archive of 19th century squalor.'

To deal with the crisis in August 1931, Ramsey MacDonald announced the formation of 'a Government of Co-operation that will take whatever steps may be deemed necessary to restore confidence in sterling, upon which the well-being of a large part of the civilised world rests.'

[I am editing this passage on 27th September 2008: the President and Congress of the United States are holding meetings to determine a solution to the nation's, and the world's, greatest ever financial crisis.]

A small Coalition Cabinet of ten members – four Labour, four Conservatives and two Liberals – aimed to balance the budget and save the pound. They succeeded with the former but a run on sterling in September 1931 caused the value of the pound to fall by more than twenty-five per cent. Parliament voted to suspend the 'gold standard' and the electorate was asked to approve the continuation of the National Government. The voters who went to the polling stations on October 27th 1931 proved to be patriotic rather than party political during troubled times, and although the Conservative Party won 473 seats to Labour's 52, Ramsey Macdonald remained as titular head of the new National Coalition Government.

The 1930s proved to be a decade in which the turbulent winds of change in international trade, economics and politics rumbled into a storm that burst into the Second World War. To begin to understand the complex reasons for that war would require a major study of European history, but to sniff the acrid aroma of that bubbling cauldron of political upheaval on the continent of Europe I will offer a brief summary of critical events from 1933 and 1936.

Adolf Hitler became chancellor of the German Reich in 1933. The German economy was in ruins, democratic government had collapsed and civil war loomed. When Berlin's Reichstag (parliament) was set on fire it was seen by many as symbolising the funeral pyre of German democracy. Hitler's Nazi officials and troops began a systematic persecution of Jews who, in Nazi philosophy, were classified as being inferior to the Aryan Race (Nordic type of Caucasian Gentile). Thousands fled abroad, but millions of German Jews were killed before 1939, followed by the greatest crime in modern history: in WWII the Nazis exterminated more than six million European and German Jews in the gas chambers of Auschwitz, Belsen and other 'vernichtungslaga'.

[Six million men, women and children is an incomprehensible number of living, breathing, running, singing, dancing, laughing, crying human beings. In 2008 the entire population of Scotland was five million people].

Spanish politics and economics had been turbulent since the middle of the previous century and in 1923 lurched towards fascism when General Primo de Rivera followed Mussolini's example and seized power. The Spanish General and his military cohorts suspended the constitution, suppressed political parties and set up a form of dictatorship. Rivera began to modernise industry and transport but the world-wide trade depression after 1929 stirred the political cauldron again and Spain became a republic once more – though without the titular monarch Alfonso VIII who left the country. Continuing conflicts between republicans, liberals, communists, nationalists (fascists), the army and the Catholic Church led to a bloody civil war from 1936 to 1939. Left-wing republicans (or loyalists), armed and supported by communist Russia, fought General Franco's nationalists (or fascists), supported and armed by Germany and Italy. Mercenaries from many nations were involved on both sides of this horrendous war between Spaniard and Spaniard.

The most macabre event of that civil war was the infamous destruction of Guernica by German bombers on April 26th 1937. General Franco had colluded with Hitler and the Luftwaffe's Air-Marshal Goering to obliterate the small market town in northern Spain as a rehearsal of tactics planned for Germany's 'blitzkrieg' methods in the inevitable European war ahead. That murderous event with intent underlined Hitler's ruthless determination to conquer Europe and, of course, caused an immediate international outcry. One report stated:

> The German bombers appeared in the skies over Guernica in late afternoon of April 26, 1937, and immediately transformed the sleepy Spanish market town into an everlasting symbol of the atrocity of war. The residents of Guernica did not know they had been chosen by their attackers to become guinea-pigs in an experiment designed to determine just what it would take to bomb a city into oblivion.

The legendary painter, Pablo Picasso, immortalised that Spanish tragedy in his painting, *Guernica*. The shock-horror of Herr Goering's 'blitzkrieg' experiment reverberated throughout every free and democratic nation in the world. Adults around me were enraged that an estimated 1,650 people were killed out of a population of 7,000. And, though I was only nine, I remember being affected by articles and pictures in the newspapers and bewildered by discussions on the radio. In the cinema I really felt sick as I witnessed dramatic newsreel footage showing Heinkel bombers releasing their lethal load, screaming Stukas dive-bombing residential streets, and innocent people running for shelter being machine-gunned from low-flying German aircraft. The dangerous power of those *real events in the now* contrasted starkly with the safe fantasies of reel wars in the cinema: of cowboys and Indians and WWI 'dog fights' between fragile bi-planes in Howard Hughes' film *Hell's Angels*.

In October 1933 Hitler withdrew the German delegation from the Disarmament Conference in Geneva. Germany and Italy immediately began massive rearmament programmes. Mussolini's troops invaded Abyssinia in October 1935, and in June 1936 the Italian dictator declared, "Italy at last has her empire." In March 1936 goose-stepping, jackbooted Nazi troops occupied the Rhineland. In the same year Nazi showmanship and propaganda dominated the Olympic Games in Berlin. In March 1938 Hitler was triumphantly accepted in Vienna as his troops occupied Austria. Following futile negotiations between Germany, France, Italy and Britain at Munich in September 1938, Hitler's troops invaded Czechoslovakia, and the scene was set for inevitable armed conflict in Europe: Germany and her ally Italy against France and Britain. The governments of the latter nations – and of their 'sit on the fence' American allies – were shocked beyond belief when Hitler and Stalin signed a non-aggression pact on August 23rd 1939. Two weeks later, following Hitler's invasion of Poland, Britain and France declared war on Germany.

Before the commencement of WWII there was a degree of all-round stability in mid-1930s Britain, show-cased by expanding consumer industries and a major house-building boom. The expansion of the British motor car industry widened the leisure interests of the middle classes and facilitated the planning of new suburbs around major cities. However, unemployment swung between 9% and 15% of the labour force; the trade unions grew in strength and supported industrial strikes. Hunger marches symbolised human poverty and insecurity throughout the decade.

A general election in 1935 returned another National all-party government under Stanley Baldwin. There was not to be another election until 1945. Neville Chamberlain, who replaced Baldwin as Prime Minister in 1937, failed abjectly to rebuff Hitler's territorial ambitions and reluctantly formed a War

Cabinet in September 1939. Winston Churchill took over the Premiership from an enfeebled Chamberlain in May 1940 and with inspired leadership led the country through a crippling war to victory in 1945. He then lost the post-war election in 1945: the Labour Party gained a landslide victory under the leadership of the wartime Deputy Prime Minister, Clement Attlee.

I have written the above thumbnail sketch of British political and social history in order to emphasise how uncertain and worrying life was for my parents from 1914 to 1946. They were both eighteen in 1914 and fifty in 1946 when there was, at last, a relative sense of peace and security – though no prosperity. My sketch also underlines their strength of character: how they coped with the turbulent changes that buffeted young people who became young parents between those two awful wars. Their stability and caring commitment created the warm and safe environment in which my brother and I were nurtured.

I raise my glass of red wine and call for a toast…

"Thank You ... Thank You ... Sam and Wyn ... Wonderful Parents!"

DEFINITION OF USA ISOLATIONISM IN 1930s:
involvement without commitment – advantages without obligations. Keep U.S. sovereign, free and at peace: U.S. unique, none of its interests threatened; U.S. superior to a corrupt world. U.S. impregnable to attack.

A.J.P.Taylor

CHAPTER 9

LORD'S – FIRST HEROES 1937 – 1939

I'm enjoying a wistful day-dream as I quietly sing ... 'love and marriage ... go together like a horse and carriage' ... for I loved Arden Field in my toddling years and was married to cricket when seven.

A dream, like a stream, has a source – a place of origin. Upton Lodge and Arden Field are twinned as my birth-place and the cradle that nurtured me towards the fulfilment of my longing to play cricket every summer's day. In human terms the origin of opportunity is often a matter of coincidence or unfathomable destiny. By whatever serendipitous design, my place of birth and childhood environment happened to be adjacent to an established and vibrant cricket club. What direction, I sometimes wonder, would my life journey have taken if the family home had been adjacent to a tennis club or golf course?

On a rare visit to Finchley in the winter of 2005 I was surprised by the powerful vibrations of deep and thankful happiness that reverberated within me as soon as I stepped on the verdant carpet of Arden Field and sat under the chestnut trees reliving scenes from the past. At that moment I felt more powerfully rooted to that *place* than anywhere else on the planet.

So, whatever the science or parapsychology of vibrational associations concerning *place and person,* the fathomable reality of parental support and adult encouragement is easier to account. I am therefore forever grateful to the senior players at Finchley Cricket Club who inspired, encouraged and supported me as I developed from a naturally athletic kid of ten to a competent all-round cricketer who was selected to play for Middlesex County 2nd XI as an amateur at the age of 18.

Although my parents had never played competitive ball sports my maternal grandfather, William Carter, enjoyed village cricket in Essex in the 1870s.

"It was your grandfather who got you started when you were three, Alan," my mother once told me. "He bought you a tiny bat and stumps, to which you became much attached, and would bowl a tennis ball to you for hours over in the cricket field. He had the patience of a saint. You became so keen and pestered him so much, "Please, Grand-dad, can we play cricket today?" When available, your father and teenage neighbour Lesley Cowling took over the role of bowler-cum-ball-chaser."

I remember when seven years of age trying to recruit two pals as ball-throwers and chasers, but Dave and Kenny were too easily distracted by their own hobbies – or bored. I was serious and wanted to bat, bowl and field all day. Then, one memorable July evening in 1936, aged eight, I played my first proper cricket match for Finchley CC Juveniles on a side pitch in Arden Field. I was so excited that I wet my bed the night before the game – and cried the night after because I was bowled out for a duck. However, a ten-second triumph sparked a fire that burned within me throughout my cricketing days. Fielding at square leg, I threw down the one-stump-to-aim-at from ten yards, running the batsman out by several feet. Yes, I received a few polite verbal plaudits, "Well done ... good show" – no hugging or dancing in American Indian style at the fall of a wicket in those far-off days.

Most significantly, that mini-success as a fielder implanted something so memorably real, so deep within me that it is almost beyond self-analysis. My interpretation of a process that became programmed through years of practice combines physical, psychological and artistic elements. First, a focus beyond concentration and hunger for the ball – I always wanted every ball to be hit in my direction. Second, the spontaneously choreographed movement from the walk-in, the instinctive anticipation of the ball's direction from the batsman's body movements, the sideways push off the left or right foot to change direction, the angled run towards the ball, the bent-knee swoop to pick up, the gun-sight eye-focus on the stump or keeper's gloves, the orchestrated harmony of eye, brain and body to execute the muscularly balletic throw and follow-through – the eternity of the slightly arced two-second trajectory – the hit – the elation – the satisfaction of achievement. Does that suggest the implantation of a 'conditioned response' à la Pavlov?

Whatever theory may fit, fielding at cover point became one of the greatest joys of my young and adult sporting life.

My batting heroes and cover-point models at the Finchley Club were a star batsman named Frank Hobbs and a dashing teenager from Christ's College, Geoffrey Davidson. Whenever they were batting or fielding I watched with rapt attention and admiration, absorbing their playing styles and cheerful demeanour. In particular I noted that whether they had scored fifty or a duck they conducted cheerful banter with players and members as they leapt up the pavilion steps with a smile on their faces. Frank and Geoffrey epitomised the amateur spirit prevailing in London club cricket before the war – a spirit of enjoyment that I soaked up like a virgin sponge. And virgin I proved to be next summer, aged nine, in my first few games with Manorside School second eleven: top score ten, one caught-and-bowled and no run-outs.

The clearly memorable highlight of 1937 was my first visit to Lord's Cricket Ground. My parents, bless them, aware by now that their nine-year-old son lived, read and dreamed cricket, decided that they would initiate me into the game's holy of holies to watch the great Patsy Hendren play his last game for Middlesex. Of course I had read about Patsy Hendren in a couple of books and the newspapers, knew he was quite old and had been a hero for Middlesex and England since the Great War. I was so excited ... so excited the day before that I could hardly eat, slept fitfully and woke before dawn on Saturday August 28th. Gee whiz! – I was going to see Middlesex play Surrey at Lord's! For Sam and Wyn it was a special day out too, for they had not been to a game at Lord's since their courting days.

What do I really remember about my first experience of Lord's? Lots of things! First, having alighted from the No.2 bus in Wellington Road, I was surprised by the bustle and chatter of spectators hurrying towards the long queues funnelling slowly through the turnstiles. Second, I had never seen so many people and held on tight to my mother's hand. Inside the ground, Father bought a scorecard and rented three small green cushions from a bearded steward plying his wares in a loud cockney voice. The hubbub of people scurrying to their seats increased my wide-eyed excitement as we eased our way through the benches half-way up the old Mound Stand.

My first panoramic snapshot of Lord's is still clear: the arena looked huge, the wicket strangely brown, the outfield a luscious green and the pavilion a palace. Again, the people! There were *so many* people – and I was asking so many questions ... "Daddy, daddy, what is that 'thing' on top of the roof above the scoreboard?" "A weather vane, son ... they call it Father Time." "Why, daddy?" ... "Oh, you'll understand one day ... look my boy ... the captains are tossing a coin to see who will bat first ... hmmm ... looks like Surrey have won and decided to bat."

Because Middlesex took to the field on the Saturday we did not see Patsy Hendren bat. I do have vague memories of Laurie Fishlock scoring runs (127), and how very fast Big Jim Smith bowled – I thought he was a bit frightening really – but have no recall of Barling scoring a hundred. Checking the records I see that Surrey scored 448 for 8 wickets. Ah yes, I also remember my hands being held very tightly by Mother and Father as we shuffled through the exit gates into St John's Wood Road surrounded by lots and lots of big people – and a very long queue for the bus to Finchley.

"But Mummy ... Daddy, I wanted to see Mr Hendren bat ... you promised!"

"I have to go to work on Monday, my boy, but your mother will take you to Lord's."

"Thank you ... oh thank you, mummy ... I'm so excited ... it's so long to wait till Monday."

Yes, Sunday passed so so slowly. In the choir vestry at St Mary's I jabbered on to my mates about the big match at Lord's. The hymns seemed too long and the sermon interminable. Over in Arden Field that afternoon, still excited about seeing Mr Hendren bat tomorrow, I lost interest in the game Finchley were playing and bent the ear of my young cricketing pals with exaggerated tales of the wonder of cricket at Lord's.

Exaggerated maybe – but haven't thousands of players and millions of spectators been deeply affected by something inexplicably ethereal permeating the environs of those hallowed grassed acres framed by the intricate miscellany of historic architecture and commercial artefacts? Except for the pavilion the architecture is now totally different, but the sights and sounds of yesteryear are etched in my memory. Cranky old turnstiles drummed a broken rhythm ... 'tlich tlich tlich k k k' ... hurrying feet scuff-shuffled an impromptu sand dance accompanied by animated murmurs between seat seeking aficionados. "Scorec'd ... scorec'd ... latest scorec'd, mista," shouted the diminutive cockney boys – in numerical terms members of a club more exclusive than its colourful upper-class parent. The Ground Staff Boys Of Lord's wore proudly their lowly but highly esteemed status – the few who achieved glory in their time have become legends to the many.

Elias Henry Hendren is one such legend. He began his career as a member of that exclusive boy's club and in retirement was elected to an Honorary Life Membership of the MCC. Born in Turnham Green, Middlesex in 1889, he joined the Lord's ground staff in 1905 and made his first class debut for Middlesex in 1909. Due to his inborn Irish sense of fun – always the dressing-room joker and crowd entertainer – he was affectionately known everywhere in the cricket world as 'Patsy'. Given that there was no first-class cricket in England for four years during the First World War, it is remarkable that he played in 833 first-class games, scored 57,611 runs, made 170 centuries and represented England in 57 Test matches.

As I research Patsy Hendren's playing career, deep memories are stirred that rekindle awareness of how privileged I was, at the age of nine, to witness the farewell of one of England's truly great and much loved cricketers. And because, as I write this piece, part of me is able to become that nine-year-old boy again, I know that that boy would have been both embarrassed and unbelieving if he could have 'seen' a few years into the future when he would meet, play cricket with and seek career advice from Mr Patsy Hendren.

Whilst I have a few clear mind pictures of events at Lord's on that special Monday, August the 30th 1937, for facts and colourful detail I depend on research kindly undertaken in 2006 by Glenys Williams, historian and archivist at Lord's – and contemporary reports in *The Times* newspaper.

Playing to a full house on Monday morning the Surrey innings continued until they were all out for 509. With only four runs on the scoreboard the Middlesex openers Hart and Price were back in the professional players annexe to the north of the pavilion. The hushed crowd waited with excited anticipation for their hero to emerge from the professional's side gate on to the hallowed turf – then burst into loud applause, even some cheering – unusual at a cricket match in the 1930s. The Surrey players formed a 'guard of honour', clapping and no doubt expressing sincere congratulations as he walked through their midst.

THE MASTER ON HIS HEATH, headlined *The Times*.

Wisden records:

> When he came out to bat at Lord's on the occasion of his last appearance in a Championship engagement, the Surrey team joined with the large crowd in according him a vociferously affectionate reception that must have touched him deeply.
>
> Unfazed by that emotional reception and the fiery fast bowling of Gover and Watts, Patsy Hendren focused on the serious business of building an innings, displaying all the great strokes of his illustrious past ... though for a long time he had little of the bowling, benignly encouraging his young partner Bill Edrich as they exposed the limitations of the Surrey bowling. The pair built a stand of 182 before Edrich was out just four short of his century, but Patsy, the 48-year-old veteran, celebrated his farewell to his admirers and to Lord's with exuberance and authority in an historic innings of 103.

Patsy Hendren's biographer, the Middlesex and England leg-spinner Ian Peebles, records the joyous moment:

> When Patsy reached his century there was a rousing chorus of *For He's A Jolly Good Fellow* ... the singing led by MCC member Denis Noble, the famous operatic baritone, who once said that he would have sooner played at Lord's than sung a single note.

Interestingly, years later when playing county cricket, I was to hear that same sentiment expressed by several well known actors and musicians – and dozens of successful lawyers, accountants and businessmen. But I must return to the memorable scenes of that very special day in 1937.

My first mind-video clip is of Surrey's fast bowler, Alf Gover, charging down the hill from the pavilion end: long run-up, arms bent at the elbows and pumping high – bowling so very fast. My young brain was abuzz with thoughts: "How can the batsmen see such balls and still have time to drive, cut or glance to the boundary?" I remember that I was 'worried' when some of those fast balls hit Patsy on the body, including a glancing blow to one side of his head. Is it a figment of my imagination that after the tea interval the hero sported a white bandage beneath his Middlesex cap? Another quirk of memory, but a factual one, is that although I cannot conjure up the image of Bill Edrich at the wicket I distinctly remember young Denis Compton batting with the veteran. I was already a Compton fan, having read in the newspapers of his promise as a soccer player with Arsenal and that he had already won an England cap in a Test match.

Alan's first cricket heroes:
Patsy Hendren and
Denis Compton,
The Oval, 1936

Alan's inspirational hero, Learie Constantine

How could I have failed to have been impressed by the scenes and events of my first visit to Lord's because, for me, the experience was two days of heaven on earth. Just to watch one match played in that Cathedral of Cricket would have sufficed to kindle a warm fire of devotion. Add the privilege of a contest between London rivals; add my first sight of hero Denis Compton; then add the historic climax of Hendren's 170th century in his farewell match at Lord's, topped by the singing of *For he's a jolly good fellow* by the huge crowd of people when their hero reached his hundred ... then you, dear reader, may understand how that warm fire filled my inner being and thrilled my senses that day – and remain a glow in my heart to this day.

I now loved cricket beyond all else in life. Veteran Patsy Hendren was my new hero: Denis Compton his young counterpart. A third all-time cricket legend was added to my collection of heroes two years later.

The following season, both at school and with the Finchley Juveniles, I matured into a 'young hopeful.' I was particularly encouraged by an older boy, my friend and neighbour Dick Nelson, who was captain of the school first eleven and a young star in the Juveniles. What a difference a year makes at that age. In the 1939 season I became school captain and a young star myself; scored runs aplenty, opened the bowling and scalped many a run-out from cover point. And to cap all that success and excitement I watched the electrifying West Indian touring team play my county Middlesex at Lord's – followed by the thrill of my first Test match.

I had read so much about the exuberant nature of West Indian cricket and cricketers that I began wishing the hours away on the Friday before their match against Middlesex. Fortunately we had no school game that Saturday, and now we were eleven years of age my pals and I were allowed to travel to St John's Wood without adult escort. The three of us were bubbling with excitement at the prospect of seeing the dynamic all-rounder Learie Constantine in action but were disappointed when the West Indians won the toss; this meant we were unlikely to see Mr Constantine perform as a fast bowler and brilliant fielder. Perhaps the West Indies would lose a few early wickets so that he could entertain us with a swashbuckling innings.

Our disappointment abated when the great George Headley, nicknamed 'The Black Bradman', joined JB Stollmeyer and they proceeded to dominate the Middlesex bowlers to build a partnership of 216 before Stollmeyer was given out 'lbw' to Big Jim Smith for 117. Exquisitely timed cuts, cover drives and nudges through mid-wicket flowed from the bat of the wondrous George Headley who scored a magnificent 227. JED Sealey, another superb attacking West Indian batsman, remained not-out at the close of play.

We were back at school on Monday when Sealey reached 181 before being 'caught Price bowled Compton'.

What an unforgettable display of batting on an unforgettable day at Lord's. I count it as a great privilege to have witnessed the greatest of all the pre-war West Indian batsmen score a double century. My enthusiasm for the game of cricket rose exponentially towards a passion on that beautiful summer's day before the gloom of war tarnished the bloom of youthful enjoyment of watching first-class cricket at Lord's: the last was my first Test match – England versus West Indies.

Alas, on a very cold day my new hero, Learie Constantine – cheered when he emerged from the pavilion – scored only fourteen runs. However, I relished every moment of his short innings in partnership with George Headley who was on his way to his seventh century against England. I was impressed by the run-up and action of fast bowler Bill Copson who took five wickets, but thought the action of Bill Bowes to be ungainly and out of rhythm ... whereas his Yorkshire colleague, the spinner Hedley Verity, had a beautifully precise action. Doug Wright made the greatest impression of the England bowlers as he bounded through his long run, arms whirling, to bowl medium paced leg-spinners and googlies. "How odd ... how odd," I kept muttering to myself ... "Never seen anything like that before." First Test match ... Lord's ... heaven ... even on a cold day.

I had to go to school on Monday and Tuesday but my mind kept drifting back to the Test match ... "I wonder what is happening ...?" Then I rushed home at lunchtime to hear the BBC commentary on our radio. Oh, what a feast I missed: a second hundred in the match by George Headley as well as centuries by Len Hutton and the twenty-one-year-old Denis Compton.

Those never to be forgotten experiences of cricket at Lord's in 1939 inspired a heightened ambition to play first-class cricket when I was grown-up – but would I ever be good enough? The dream would develop from 'maybe' to 'perhaps' six years later at the end of the war. But I am running on to events of the mid 1940s and must return to memories of my childhood in the 1930s and place on record some of the people, places and events that were of interest – to me anyway – in those days of false calm before the storms of war.

But first a few 'boys will be boys' stories that may or may not have been influenced by the *Just William* tales. Comparatively tame exploits by 21st century standards but for me the stories evidence a healthy experimentation with adventure that tested the boundaries of acceptable behaviour to which, by the age of seven, I was conditioned by my home and school environment and the mores of the lower-middle class in that pre-war era.

What were those tame exploits?

〜〜〜〜〜〜〜〜〜〜〜

Middlesex CCC, 1938: back row, from left: L.D'Arcy; L.Hart; L.B.Muncer; C.I.J.Smith; W.T.Nevell; L.H.Gray; D.C.S.Compton front row: W.F.F.Price; E.H.Hendren; H.J.Enthoven; W.H.Webster; J.H.A.Hulme inses: R.W.V.Robins (capt) and G.O.B.Allen. The author was inspired by Patsy Hendren and Denis Compton, mentored by Walter Robins and Gubby Allen, signed for Spurs Juniors by Joe Hulme and befriended by Len Muncer

CHAPTER 10

FREEDOM, GAMES AND PRANKS

How blest we were, children of my generation in all levels of society, to play in urban street and spacious park, by country stream and sandy shore – unsupervised.

From about the age of five we were trusted by the parents in our community to visit each other's homes; from the age of seven to go further afield to play on the swings in the park and ball games in Arden Field. Knowing we were trusted we did not venture beyond generally accepted limits, nor misbehave to extremes that would restrict our freedom in the future. I am thankful beyond measure that I experienced that era of liberty without anxiety and thus developed, unconsciously and without tutelage, a sense of responsibility. After all, I would be embarrassed if I caused my parents to be anxious – and angry with myself if I did something for which I was punished: not a beating but worse – to stay indoors and not go out with my pals.

Without exception our parents and elders expected high standards of behaviour. Good manners, honesty, duty, loyalty and a respect for authority were the norm for people in our family and, in general, in our neighbourhood a child or young person grew-up in an environment in which adults were respected. We were polite, did not answer back and 'No' really meant ... well ... 'NO!' How grateful I am that I grew up in stable circumstances in those unstable pre-war years. Therefore, a boyish prank or naughty deed needs to be seen in the context of that era and personal background.

So, apart from cricket and football, what did my pals and I get up to between the ages of seven and eleven? In general we were well behaved but none of us were 'goody-goodies'. We were curious, adventurous and athletic and ... and boys. Boys will be boys.

When seven or eight one outdoor activity was 'larks in the parks'. Nearby Victoria Park in Long Lane provided a large open space for impromptu games of soccer, flying kites and racing our child-sized bikes: the leafy botanical gardens of the posh park, Avenue House, provided hours of fun tinged with danger.

When we had had our fill of swings and see-saws our small group of eight-year-olds played 'hide and seek' in and around the network of winding paths, clusters of dense bushes, grassy mounds and sub-tropical trees – sometimes daring to taunt the vigilant park-keeper.

Mr Thompson was quite scary: a man of military bearing, suitably moustached, resplendent in dark blue uniform and smart peaked hat, shiny-

shiny boots and a silver-knobbed cane. Mr Thompson patrolled the Park with the fervour of a gamekeeper seeking poachers. We were fast, agile and would split up to create diversions. We were never caught but one day became really scared when Mr T walked the winding paths accompanied by a local copper. We scarpered.

Our boyish pranks in the second half of the 1930s were partly motivated by natural curiosity and partly by a normal need to test adult authority. Age nine I 'borrowed' a short fat cigar from my father's secret stash atop the high canopy of the repro-Stuart sideboard and dashed to Kenny Brunskill's house at the other end of Briarfield Avenue. My young conspirator's mother had gone to the cinema that afternoon, giving us time to pretend that we ourselves were film stars enjoying the pleasure of smoking cigars. After all, Errol Flynn and Douglas Fairbanks portrayed cigar smoking as something special and luxurious – like drinking champagne.

The location of my first smoke, Kenny's too, was in his kitchen. I knew from the films that I had to snip off one end and light the other with a match – not a lighter. I drew a few puffs, disliked the taste but enjoyed the aroma. Kenny's turn ... puff-puff ... grey smoke hung in wispy clouds below the kitchen ceiling. Click-clack ... Kenny turned doubly pale and whispered, hoarsely: "the front gate... Mum's back!"

I grabbed the cigar, drowned it under a running tap, opened the outside door next to the sink and jammed the five-inch sodden mess between the soil pipe and the wall with one hand while fanning the door to and fro with the other. Meanwhile, Kenny opened the top lid of the Ideal boiler into which he threw some socks that were drying on the rail above ... burning wool and coke fumes combined with cigar smoke created an acrid cocktail. The front door clicked shut and Kenny's mum entered the kitchen saying, "The queue was too long ... I wouldn't have got in until the next ... the next ... er ... perform ... BOYS, what is that smell ... and what on earth are you doing, Kenny? ... PUT THAT LID BACK ON THE BOILER!"

Mrs Brunskill, destined to be Mayoress when her husband became Mayor of Finchley in 1956, looked me up and down, raised her eyebrows and with a quizzical smile said, "And Alan, why are you swinging the door? ... Have you boys set something on fire?" Well, of course, the fibs poured forth from our wide-eyed faces ... amazingly well-coordinated impromptu explanations that seemed to satisfy Ken's cuddly mum. No reprimand, no mention of the incident to my parents – just a wry smile. Fifteen years later I bumped into Mr Brunskill at a social function. We had a pleasant chat about the time when his son and I were best buddies, then, as we shook hands on parting he said – with a twinkle in his eye: "Still smoking cigars, young Alan?"

Alan enjoying Finchley Lido, 1933

*Alan and
Kenny Brunskill
at Upton Lodge*

I was bursting with curiosity about so many things in life around the ages of nine and ten and therefore sub-consciously tested the boundaries of acceptable behaviour. I have a clear memory of a couple of exploits that caused me to worry and feel guilty. The inner emotional power of shame and guilt was new to me – and in a sense good for me – because that power burned itself into my psyche at an early age. In the future those conditioned memory responses triggered the 'no entry' barriers regarding several areas of behaviour and activity.

One spring day when rummaging for a fishing rod deep inside the capacious dark cupboard under the stairs at Upton Lodge, my outstretched fingers touched a hexagonal metal pipe of rod-like dimensions. Curious, I tugged and tugged until suddenly the heavy object was released from the entangling jumble. In the light of the hall I was amazed to see that I had dragged out a very old air rifle. "Gee-whiz! an air rifle ... a very heavy air rifle ... I wonder if ..." I muttered to myself. Then I remembered: I had seen a large round tin of air-gun pellets in one of Father's tool boxes and as both parents were out, I grabbed a handful and took the gun upstairs to my bedroom.

What happened next is a minor yet interesting insight into learned behaviour through unconscious observation – from both real life and the cinema. I had seen dozens of 'cowboy and Indian' films in which Winchester rifles and Colt pistols were cleaned and oiled. I called the big old air rifle 'Hex', and though Hex was dusty rather than rusty I thought I should clean the barrel. But how do I thread a piece of thick string down the narrow barrel? 'Ah,' I thought, 'boats and docks.' My mind drifted to the scene of a seaman aboard an Isle of Wight paddle steamer throwing the thin rope line to his counterpart on the dock, then the docker winding in the line to which was tied the heavy rope painter to be looped over the bollard to secure the ship to the dockside. I found some catgut line from the fishing tackle to which I tied a length of thick string, applied cycle oil to the string and pulled the simple device through the barrel of the air gun several times.

Acting out my cowboy film fantasy I opened the lower half of my bedroom window and fired a few pellets at a stack of earthenware pots in the back garden ... 'pot shots' ... sorry – but I missed. How about a longer-range target to test this heavy old gun? Hmmm ... fifty yards to the green-painted, iron gate-post at the entrance to Arden Field. Making sure that nobody was walking along Briarfield Avenue I aimed, fired and missed ... but! ... but the pellet hit the pavement and made high-pitched screeching noise ... pweeow. This is fun, so I aimed at the tarmac surface further along the road ... pweeow. 'Gee whiz, this airgun is powerful.' A longer range shot ... pweeow ... oops, a lady resident walking through her front gate looked startled. Gee ... more fun.

When alone during the next two weeks I played at 'cowboys scaring the Indians, firing pellets at the pavement and tarmac on the cricket field side of the road to startle old ladies (everyone over twenty-five was old) ... ladies tending their front gardens or walking along Briarfield Avenue on the opposite side to Arden Field. Pweeow! Then one day I reacted to the annoying 'caw-caw' of rooks busily nesting high in the trees just inside that iron-gate to the cricket field. So I took a few pot-shots in their direction which caused them to flutter about when I hit an upper branch – clack ... flutter ... rooks settle again. Lots of fun.

A few days later, when Mother went out to a dress-fitting appointment, I filched some more pellets from Father's tin, pulled the air rifle from the under-stairs cupboard and opened the sash window in my bedroom. A new imaginary Texas cowboy game: 'those rooks are vultures hovering over my wounded horse ... I have to frighten them off .' Load-fire-clack-flutter. But one large rook-vulture did not flutter – he had the temerity to cling to one of those high branches. "What a cheek ... I'll get him!" Never in a month of Sundays did I think I would actually hit that particular rook at that distance. I aimed carefully, fired ... no clack ... but horror of horrors ... a black-feathered 'thing' was falling through the branches and disappeared in the long grass at the base of the trees. "O God I've killed it!"

My heart pounded, my palms and forehead felt cold and clammy as my life seemed to pause for a few seconds. Then fear and guilt pumped adrenalin into my circulation. Action! I flew down the stairs, threw the rifle to the back of the cupboard, dashed to Father's shed, grabbed a spade, yanked the side gate open and rushed across the road through the iron gates and searched for my victim. I made a big effort to hold back the tears while frantically digging a hole big enough to bury the dead bird. I kept looking, furtively, through the gate and up the street to ensure nobody would catch me in the act and report me to the police ... I've murdered a living creature! After treading in a few tufts of turf over the fresh soil of the grave – and again making sure there was no one in sight – I ran the fifty yards to our side gate, cleaned the spade with a piece of slate and returned the tool to its special nail in the shed. Indoors, I washed my hands, ran upstairs and lay on my bed ... howling.

From the next experiment I learned, intuitively rather than consciously, that stealing an object from Woolworths was just as guilt-inducing as the demise of that rook but far less gut-wrenchingly emotional than the outcome of my unintentional killing of a living creature.

At Manorside School one of my pals had a pal who was not a pal of mine. The pair of them challenged me to join them one Saturday morning to steal three items from Woolworths. In 1937 ninety per cent of the items for sale in that store were priced at sixpence (worth about one pound today). There were hundreds of small items to nick and lots of shoppers to provide cover on Saturdays. I had a problem: what if I was caught stealing – would I go to Borstal? My parents would be very upset and my good reputation at school ruined. So many questions.

Why did I agree to join this mini-criminal adventure? I had no need to gain credibility among my peer group because I was already a leader in all things physical and sporting. And this was not an impetuous act on the spur of the moment but rather a considered decision made during a couple of sleepless nights. In retrospect, I think my need to be loyal and maintain the close friendship outweighed the fear and guilt associated with being conscious of the misdemeanour.

The day came when three nine-year-olds walked into Woolworths in Ballards Lane. Going in, I was really nervous: on leaving my heart was thumping and my head bursting with guilt. Inside the shop I was calm. No, I didn't steal sweets, or a ball, or padlock for my bike. I stole an adjustable date stamp and an ink pad in a tin box. We were not caught for shoplifting, but I caught a big dose of guilt that lay buried in my sub-conscious for many years until, when sorting out 'stuff' before joining the RAF, I discovered both items and chucked them in the dustbin. I felt relieved – like having a good crap after being constipated.

The fourth of these mini-stories is about a practical improvisation rather than an errant deed. But I was caught out – by a copper. I was a little older, in fact over eleven because Father had rejoined the Special Constabulary at the beginning of the war. As I have mentioned, our house Upton Lodge was on a street corner. The front gate in Manor View opened to a pathway bordered by a four-foot-high fence parallel to Briarfield Avenue. The entrance porch, front door and dining room window were only five feet from the pavement and therefore very much on public view.

Returning home from school one day ... parents out ... key left in my room – I climbed up on the wide sill of that side window and, using the long blade of my substantial penknife, proceeded to slide the window catch, open the window and begin to climb in. Now honestly, the deep male voice behind me did not say *'ello 'ello 'ello, wha are you adoin' of 'ere*, as would be written in the script of a British film comedy of the era. He did say, in educated London speak: "Get down from there, nipper, I'm going to have to arrest you for attempted breaking and entering."

A photo would have been interesting – me with my knees on the sill, bum up in the air, hands on the stool inside the window. I couldn't see the face of 'The Voice' until, having reversed and my placed my feet back on the tiled front path, I turned. The man standing there was neither young nor old, dressed in a sports jacket and tie – not a uniform. Since I was inside my own home boundaries I was not only a bit annoyed by this civilian, but also, as a confident young lad with a bit of the gift of the gab I challenged 'The Voice' who wore a dark brown Harris Tweed jacket.

"This is my house – I live here and I've left my key indoors. Anyway, you're kidding me – you're not a policeman."

"Don't you be cheeky with me, me lad ..." as he pulled out his warrant card from his inside pocket.

"I'm off duty, but I'm taking you to the station when I've had a word with your mum or dad ... where do you really live?"

I was cross: " I've told you, mister, I live here! Anyway, my dad's a policeman too – in the Specials."

"What's your name then, son?" I knew I was winning – and played my trump card.

"I'm Alan Rayment, and my father is Sergeant Samuel Rayment," I pronounced proudly.

"Then who lives next door?"

"Mr and Mrs Cowling and Leslie," I replied, knowing I had won. "I expect they're in. Do you want to ask them?"

"Yes, but you are coming with me. I'm not letting you scarper while I go next door."

Knock-knock at number thirty-six. Mrs Cowling opened the door: "Hello, Alan ... you want to come in until your mother comes home. Oh, and this gentleman, is he one of your friends from the cricket club?" Game, set and match.

My parents were amused by my story and, of course, Father was curious about the identity of the off-duty policeman in civvies. "He might be a senior officer, or even a detective, my boy."

Early one evening a few days later I heard a knock on our front door and ran to open it ... Mr Tweed Jacket.

"Hello, young Alan ... is your father home yet?" he asked in a cheery voice.

"Yes, he is in the garden – I'll take you through," I replied, grinning a polite smile but feeling victoriously mischievous within. Hearing voices on the garden path, Father emerged from his shed holding a pair of shears and a whet-stone. "Arthur, so you must be ..."

"Yes, Sam, I'm the one who collared your lad. Looked very suspicious at first but he gave a good account of himself ... should be proud, Sam." I left the coppers and found Mother standing at the open french doors – "Is that the man who ...?"

"Yes, Mother." She smiled – and we both crept upstairs to make sure that two-year old Derek was fast asleep. The next morning at breakfast Father announced: "That was a detective friend of mine who came last evening, my boy ... he thought you were up to no good."

I've forgotten his full name but not the experience – and I still chuckle to myself about it. Ah, sweet memories of innocent days in a happy childhood before the bombs began to fall.

When I woke up in my small bedroom on Christmas morning 1937 I really was surprised – and delighted, of course – to see a gleaming new bicycle (eighteen-inch wheels) propped against the tiny fireplace. My first bike – and a new one too! Father had bought it on the 'never-never' from a friend who owned the bicycle shop in Church End – a Mr Ames, I seem to recall. Freedom! My bike was a passport for extended local travel and, given the relative low density of traffic in the suburbs of North London, only the Great North Road, Regent's Park Road and the North Circular were banned. My pals and I relished our cycling adventures to Mill Hill and Totteridge, to Alexandra Palace and Hadley Woods, and through the Garden Suburb to Hampstead Heath and Whitestone Pond. Cycling on errands for my busy mother made me feel useful and proud: to Hall's the drapers, to her clients to deliver dresses, blouses and small repair jobs – and chat politely with the customers – occasionally being tipped with a shilling or a chocolate bar.

Tip, or being tipped up, conjures up adventures with four-wheeled carts from around the age of nine – carts my pals and I made using old pram wheels and planks. Our nearest paved downhill run was from the railway bridge on the North Circular road sloping down towards Long Lane. During the next two years many models were made and crashed, or had design faults that caused their early demise. The best and last was the Super Model, created with great enthusiasm by yours truly with friends Dave Limbert and Grant Stanley. I think it was Grant who acquired a pair of bath-chair wheels for the back-end, which, allied with pram wheels for the front steering axle gave the appearance of a modern dragster. I made a pair of hand brakes to control the big wheels, and Dave devised a steering system with small pulleys and rope. Pushing each other along the flat roads in Briarfield and Rosemary Avenue – and even free-wheeling down the gentle slope of Dudley Road proved that the brakes worked reasonably well.

The day came for the big test ... the steeper slope from the railway bridge. Grant sat in front to steer, I perched at the back to operate the brakes and Dave stood behind to give us a push. Between the busy road and the pavement there was a grass verge about fifteen feet wide; a chain-link fence formed the boundary between the pavement and an unkempt open space called the Back Field. Dave pushed – maybe too hard – and we rapidly gained momentum ... fast ... very fast ... too fast – brakes! The lever in my right hand ripped out of its fixing, causing the Super Model to career towards the fence. Grant counter-steered and for twenty yards we zig-zagged at high speed ... then crashed into the wire fence. I am laughing now as I write this, but at the time 'it' was serious. 'IT' is the ten-second movie I have in my head ... Grant flying head-first over the five-foot fence, hitting the grassy slope with a thump, then rolling on his side to the ditch at the bottom. Dave and I climbed the fence and rushed to Grant's aid: "It's my bum ... I landed on my bum ... gee, it hurts." Relieved, the banter and the giggles quickly turned to laughter – the sort of laughter that you can't stop, that opens the tear ducts and makes you roll around on the ground. Eventually we climbed the slope to inspect Super Model, parts of which were enmeshed in the bulging wires of the chain-link fence, the planks splayed awry and the big wheels buckled.

Little wheels negotiated that same slalom with ease when roller skates were popular during the last two summers of pre-war normality. For me there was no contest between ball and skates when both were leisure options, though I must have rolled a few miles because I remember having to buy new metal wheels. But sometimes, on chilly damp winter days, my pals and I were keen to strap on rubber-wheeled skates at the Arcadia Indoor Rink. The exercise warmed us up as we whizzed around the floor, skilfully dodging slower skaters when playing tag. I became aware that I really enjoyed skating to music – canned and repetitive but full-on, big-band harmonies of melodic tunes I'd heard on the radio. Dave, Kenny and I would stay warm by running home through drizzle or snow, lunch on hot tomato soup with crusty bread, then stay indoors all afternoon to play Monopoly in front of the glowing coal fire.

But sometimes Kenny and I went back to Church End in the afternoon to the small cinema that had slack rules about unaccompanied children. Next to the Arcadia the Bohemia cinema offered escape in several forms: the darkness shut out the grey-brown gloom of a cold foggy day, the central heating cosseted the legs and feet in unaccustomed indoor warmth and the films transported the senses to comforting non-reality. We cheered both cowboys and Indians, laughed with Donald Duck and fidgeted with embarrassment if the 'A' film was a long sloppy romance, unless, between yukky kisses, we could quietly cheer the swashbuckling Douglas Fairbanks when he ripped the baddie's shirts with the tip of his sword.

Fighting – do I remember fighting against other boys in the years before I went to my next school? Definitely not, in our neighbourhood or at Junior School in the 1930s there were no gangs, no personal enemies and no serious aggression on the sports field. Tests of strength included friendly wrestling and competitive races – running, climbing trees, roller-skating and cycling.

What I do remember is 'having a look' during the summer of 1937. Our neighbourhood group, mostly the little cricketers aged around nine, built a pretend pavilion in the bushes next to the old wooden clubhouse on the north side of Arden field. Those bushes bordered the rear gardens of houses in Manor View and concealed a shallow dry ditch that we extended to create a camp floor. There was enough space for half a dozen boys to play cards or five-stones, to drink Tizer and eat anything anyone could 'borrow' from their mum's cake tin. We talked, argued, wrestled, ate ... then talked some more.

I hope the reader will comprehend that, compared with the computer proficient children of the 21st century, my nine-year-old mates and I had almost no access to information regarding human anatomy, emotions and sex. No boys in our little group had a sister who was a year or two older ... or even younger. Recently introduced to the cinema we cringed when confronted with mild love scenes on screen, and were blushingly embarrassed when cycling past a real-life courting couple canoodling in the park.

So inevitably, squatting in our pretend pavilion one summer's day, 'the little cricketers' had to settle an argument about 'what girls had down there'? We had dared to invite a non-cricketing schoolmate to our secret camp – but only if he would bring his ten-year old sister and she was willing for us to 'have a look – just a look'. Sated with Tizer and rock cakes – and with curiosity overcoming red-faced embarrassment, the little cricketers gasped when the young girl hitched up her skirt and dropped her knickers: "Cor, she ain't got nuffin' dunvere," exclaimed Charlie who was born in Hackney. "Do you have to pee out of your bum?" another mate enquired, politely. Anti-climax all round, curiosity satisfied and interest in female anatomy shelved for several years.

Although I remember my pals with affection, enjoyed our naïve experiments and all the games we played, it was the freedom to venture abroad around our suburban neighbourhood without fear or serious reprimand that at first seems to be of the greatest personal value in those pre-war years of childhood innocence. Yet that value cannot stand alone because, as a close knit group of friends, we consciously and sub-consciously learned from each other – we grew up and evolved together in the healthy physical and social environment of our community. Therefore, in my opinion, the bonding in our relationships was the greatest value gained from those freedoms and joint experiences: learning to trust, to depend on each other, to give and receive without counting, to work together, be serious in thought at times – at others to banter, wrestle, to have fun, to laugh and to cry – and still like each other. Within the ins and outs, the ups and downs, the give and take, the work and play – the laughter and the tears of every day life – we were un-wittingly learning to trust and care for each other ... learning that people need people.

I believe we were happy: I know for sure I felt both secure and happy.

And because of that foundation I have always really liked people!

~~~~~~~~~~~

CHAPTER 11

PEOPLE, PLACES AND HAPPY EVENTS

Cue ... Barbra Streisand ... singing......
> *' Memories ... like the corners of my mind ...*
> *misty watercolour memories ... of the way we were ...'*

Naturally, my memory can only recall a soupcon of daily life in my childhood years. However, I am truly surprised that I remember so much.

Without doubt the process of writing stimulates the mental and emotional senses that enable the scribe to delve into the deeper archives of bygone memories. Exploring those *misty watercolour memories* is fun – one discovery reveals clues to forgotten pictures in another *corner of my mind*.

Even faint sketches, when enhanced, unfold a story of interest to the writer, if not the reader. So please allow me, dear members of family, old friends and new acquaintances – if you have not yet succumbed to yawning boredom – to indulge in a few more sketches from my life in the 1930s.

Cue Barbra again ...
'PEOPLE ... people who need people, are the luckiest people in the world ...'

I was lucky – though I prefer the term blessed – because I had many young pals with similar interests in the neighbourhood ... *'children, needing other children ...'*

What about the grown-up people who filled the background of my young life? Again, I was blessed by their positive influences: middle-class in speech and manners without being posh; strict, yet kind and caring – mostly good fun to be with. Good role models from whom I learned respect and responsibility.

Our next-door neighbours, for instance. Mr and Mrs Cowling had been minders for baby Alan from a time before I could walk. My mother once told me, "When you were a toddler I would wait at the Cowling's front gate while you walked up their front path, knock on their door and ask, 'Is it compeenant?' When about three you were given a bus conductor's set and played buses with the very patient Mrs Cowling, insisting that you clipped the tickets to 'S'norgans' or ''itchin'."

'The Plank': I have such fond memories of a six-foot plank that gave me hours of pleasure at the Cowlings when four years old. A simple game that extended my imagination and abilities to improvise: prop the 'The Plank' on the arm of the settee and run Dinky toy cars down the slope to crash into toy brick barriers or through improvised tunnels. When eight I became a Hornby train enthusiast – the large clockwork 'O' Gauge series. Twenty-year-old Leslie Cowling constructed wooden scale models of an engine shed, a platform with ticket office and two sets of signals – all beautifully painted. He spent hours with me, building bridges and cranes with Meccano, assisting with complicated jigsaw puzzles, teaching me chess – and even playing cricket in the garden. Special treats included car rides when Leslie drove his father to business meetings in central London in their big American car, a Hudson Terraplane.

Two exceptional treats were holidays with the Cowling family on the Norfolk coast at Easter time in 1938 and 1939. We travelled in the latest model of the American Hudson to a small cottage overlooking the shore at Mundesley in Norfolk. Leslie and I searched the tide-line detritus, climbed the crumbling clay cliffs and played cricket on the hard sandy beaches when the tide was out. 'Auntie' Cowling organised picnic adventures to interesting places, ensuring we all had gum boots and rainproof gear stowed in the Hudson's capacious boot together with delicious home-cooked food packed into real-wicker hampers. We investigated the esplanade and pier at Cromer, the ruins of Walsingham Abbey and fascinating fishing boats at Wells-next-the-Sea. As ever, I was insatiably curious – constantly asking questions. Thankfully, the patient adults were always willing to listen and answer intelligently. I learned a lot from Leslie, who, for a few years before the war was a surrogate big brother – an excellent role model.

Beyond even the rare delight of travelling everywhere in a luxury car the pièce-de-resistance of those Norfolk holidays were day trips to 'The Broads', a vast network of navigable rivers and lakes renowned for their quiet beauty, abundant wildlife and – according to Mr Cowling – "too many boats disturbing the peace." Leslie helmed the broad-beamed motor cruiser, Mr C navigated while Auntie C whispered the names of the birds and water-fowl I was trying to snap with my Kodak Box camera. Fortunately, on both occasions the weather was warm enough to moor in a quiet spot and lay out all the paraphernalia required for the sumptuous picnic. I so loved the natural environment and mystery of 'The Broads' that I day-dreamed I would one day live on a boat and work as a wildlife photographer.

Travelling anywhere by any form or transport always excited me. The prospect of a day visit involving a bus journey across London, a Green Line coach into the Hertfordshire countryside – or further afield by steam train – never failed to stimulate my mental and physical energies. How did my parents cope with all those questions and abundant energy?

Visits to my mother's family in Cheshunt were especially enjoyable. Grandad and Grandma lived in a sweet old cottage surrounded by a beautiful garden: Mother's cousin Kate was nearby and her close friend Rose lived with her husband on a farm near Great Baddow in Essex. All the adults were very kind to me and, as I have mentioned before, I was comfortable in grown-up company, able to hold conversations and, of course, ask questions – and more questions – and be blessed with patient answers and dialogue. I also succumbed readily to second helpings of the delicious farm-style cooking.

I must have been very young and impressionable when I first travelled with Mother on a Green Line coach to visit my cousin Beryl at boarding school because, as Mother told me in later years, I was mildly obsessed with Green Line coaches until the age of seven. Why? Was it that I associated journeys in a Green Line coach with trips into the countryside and red buses with the busy streets in London? Or was it that I was excited about seeing Beryl at her big school in Hitchin? I also dimly remember Green Line coach trips to St Albans that caused – so I was told – much mirth among my parents and their friends because I talked excitedly about going to 'Snorgans Katdrill'. On my first visit to the cathedral I may have been as awed as my grandson Sam who, on entering Salisbury Cathedral when four years old, exclaimed to Angela in whispered tones: "Mummy, this is a big big church! Do very big people live here?"

Writing about big churches brings to mind a visit to Ripon Cathedral with Mother and Father in 1936. We were staying with Auntie Rose and her father, Old Mr Taylor, at their spacious house by the canal in Ripon. Inside the cathedral I became puzzled by a series of glass-topped display cases showing sections of wooden beams decimated by deathwatch beetles. A volunteer steward tried to explain to me that the congregation had to raise a lot of money to replace the roof timbers being eaten away by the nasty hungry crawlies. I tugged at my mother's hand, insisting, "Hurry, Mummy and Daddy, we've got to get out of here before the roof falls down" – a fair assumption for a child who, the previous day, had seen the ruins of Fountains Abbey.

So many things in Ripon stimulated my curiosity: the really old-fashioned shops around the Square; the Town Crier in traditional costume who rang his hand-bell before declaiming public announcements prefaced by a self-amplified "O Yea ... O Yea". My persistent questioning paid off when late one evening Mother and Aunt Rose walked me to the Square to witness the 'Wakeman's Horn', blown every evening at nine o'clock on all four corners of the Obleisk in Ripon Market Place to set 'The Watch' – a traditional ceremony unbroken since AD 886.

I was also fascinated by the character of Old Mr Taylor who drove the sumptuous Vauxhall Six on our day excursions from Field House. He was the epitome of an Edwardian Yorkshireman, sporting a bushy moustache and a chunky gold fob spilling from his waistcoat pocket, indicating ownership of a gold half-hunter watch. And of course, being a Yorshireman, he loved cricket and bowled underarm to me as I batted on the well-kept grass tennis court at Field House. He was a kind man, but his rather gruff Yorkshire voice and mannerisms scared me a little.

Whilst I am not able to recall every historic site we visited during that Yorkshire holiday in 1936, I do remember a day trip to York that resulted in a constant stream of questions: "When were those (timbered) houses built ... they are so very old ... look, some are falling over ... and why are the streets so tiny ... why is this cathedral called a Minster ... is it going to fall down too?" Again, Mother, Father and Aunt Rose must have had endless patience and deserved a quiet interval in Ye Olde Teashop where, hushed by the posh environment and a large ice-cream, I uttered not a word.

Harrogate? Yes, we strolled around that historic spa town too, though I did not understand what the adults were talking about when they tried to explain to me why people went there to 'take the waters'. And though the breathtaking scenery in the Lake District was truly impressive, again I was puzzled why some of the lakes were called 'Waters'.

Aunt Rose drove the big Vauxhall on the long excursion to Keswick. We stayed for two nights in a guest house, ate a full English Breakfast – I only remember the sausages – and toured the beauty spots during the day. As we hiked through lakeside woods I was captivated by the beams of sunlight reflecting rainbow hues into the blue-hazed waters through tall trees lining the shore.

Thinking about that trip recently I searched through my parents' photograph albums and discovered several black and white snaps taken in 1936, some showing the family group picnicking on a rocky outcrop by a step-stone waterfall in the Lake District. The photographs triggered scenes long buried and drew me into a gentle regression that opened up colourful mind-pictures of the wonderful scenery witnessed by my eight-year-old self.

We drove through the hills and dales, walked awhile beside another glorious lake before returning to Keswick by early evening, eager for the hearty home-cooked meal. I asked for 'seconds' but was too full when offered 'thirds' of ginger pudding with treacle and custard. More memorable than the food, however, was my first experience of long distance travel by car ... the freedom to plan the route, stop anywhere anytime to picnic, to feast on the panoramic views ... to pee into a ditch when necessary. To me that Vauxhall Six epitomised a temporary taste of a lifestyle I knew my parents could not afford.

Thankfully, Sam and Wyn were able to afford short holidays to places other than the Isle of Wight, and again their albums of black-and-white photographs stimulate memories of some, but not all, the places and events recorded in those pictures. I have no recall of a vacation in Minehead, Somerset, nor of time spent at Henley-on-Thames. Although we visited Sam's brother, Charles, on several occasions before the war, I will save a detailed account of happy times at Elmer Farm in Suffolk until a later chapter. A few days on the Isle of Wight in May 1936 are especially memorable but family fun at St Leonard's-on-Sea in 1933 require the snaps to augment the few wispy mind pictures I retain.

I could excuse myself and say, "Well, I was only five," but I have already recorded several clear memories of events at home in Finchley before I was five

– and of my first year in school. The holiday photos show me frolicking in the sea with cousin Beryl (15); record Larry and Doris as a lovey-dovey courting couple and my parents as being happy and carefree. And I am surprised that I looked so strong and athletic in those photos; smug too, holding Father's best rod over the ornate railings of Hastings pier. Ah! the little grey cells are oiled by the writing – I 'see' myself standing on a stool, leaning over a table ... holding a cue ... yes, a billiard table, not full size ... in the fusty basement of an hotel. Of course, I remember now, this terraced hotel belonged to Mrs Edridge, the owner of our house, Upton Lodge. She was a rotund lady with a jolly smile who wore wide black hats dressed with feathers ... black feathers. Maybe our family were offered a special rate; I'm sure that was our only family holiday at ... ummm ... 'Westgarth Hotel' ... gee ... where did that fact pop-up from?

No aide-memoire is required to recall the special holiday on the Isle of Wight during the Whitsun half-term holidays of 1936, specially organised by Sam and Wyn so that, with family and friends, we could witness the spectacle of the maiden voyage of the Cunard Shipping Company's new eighty-thousand-ton super-liner, the RMS QUEEN MARY.

We were staying in Uncle Jack's home above his butchers shop in High Street, Ryde. On his advice we planned a picnic on the beach at Puckpool rather than join the crowds on Ryde pier or the Esplanade. In the early afternoon of May 27th, two days before my eighth birthday, cousins Beryl and Tilly helped Mother make sandwiches and fill two rucksacks with food, thermos flasks and small bottles of Tizer. Equipped with rugs, buckets and spades – and of course a cricket bat and tennis ball – we strolled down Union Street, turned right along the Esplanade, continued the long walk past the boating lake to the beach at Puckpool Park where we camped by the sea wall, facing north across the Solent towards Portsmouth.

The Queen Mary was due to set sail at four o'clock from the Cunard Terminal in Southampton. We had time to play beach games and cricket before the tide swamped our playing area, then enjoyed a swim before tucking in to the sandwiches, cakes and tea. Meanwhile, more and more families and children arrived until the beach either side of us was quite crowded: there must have been many thousands of people gathering at vantage points along Southampton Water to Lee-on-Solent, to Southsea and beyond, as well as spectators on the north and east shores of the Island.

We waited and looked ... looked and waited until ... sometime after five o'clock the low buzz of general chatter developed into excited shouts of "there ... there she is ... look ... look, there she is!" I looked, could see nothing special in the Solent to the west, then after repeatedly tugging my father's shorts and calling "where ... where, daddy ... ?", he hoisted me on to his shoulders and pointed to a big blob surrounded by lots of little blobs. Slowly ... slowly ... the distant mirage evolved into one of the most memorable scenes in my childhood years: the enormous, glisteningly beautiful ship with three uniquely symbolic funnels, dressed overall and escorted by a galaxy of Consorts: tugs and steamers powering water-jets into the air – all surrounded by a fleet of Maids of Honour – yachts and motor cruisers, fishing boats and tiny sailing dinghies – all bedecked in celebratory finery and singing their praises in a choral cacophony of high-pitched horns, trumpeting hooters and deep-throated sirens.

Majestic! In full broadside The Queen seemed to fill the Solent: I was transfixed and speechless with awe until ... until the powerful waves of her wash anointed us with lashings of salt spray. All in all, a truly wonderful experience ... a scene I have never forgotten. In 1949 I was privileged to walk beside the immense ship cradled in her dry dock at Southampton: more than fifty years later I walked her decks when, sadly, she was a pensioner at Long Beach, California.

I am fortunate to retain a few clear images of royal events in the mid-1930s – events that caused temporary fluctuations of joy, sorrow and bewilderment in the national mood. Just before my seventh birthday the nation celebrated the Silver Jubilee of King George V and Queen Mary. In every city, town and village bunting festooned the streets, shops, houses and schools. At Manorside Infant School we were treated to a Jubilee tea party, received mugs, sang patriotic songs and waved flags. At home we sat round the wireless to listen to BBC broadcasts of exciting events in central London attended by huge crowds of spectators. Mother took me to the cinema a week later to experience Movietone News footage of the Jubilee celebrations; scenes of their Majesties riding in an open horse-drawn carriage from Buckingham Palace to St Paul's Cathedral, cheered by thousands of flag-waving adults and children lining the streets.

Tragically, seven months later, the streets of Westminster were again lined with crowds for a Royal Ceremony when thousands of solemn people, silent in their black attire, waited patiently to witness the King's funeral cortege process to Westminster Abbey where the monarch, who had reigned for twenty-five years, Lay In State until his burial at Windsor Castle on January 28th 1936.

In 1917, during the Great War with Germany, King George V had relinquished all German titles and styles (inherited through his grandfather, Albert, husband of Queen Victoria) on behalf of himself and members of his extended family who were British subjects. He announced that in future his family's generic title would be known as the 'House of Windsor'.

Following the funeral and a respectful period of mourning the nation rejoiced again at the accession to the throne of the 41-year-old Edward, Prince of Wales. Edward had served with the Grenadier Guards during the Great War, and had travelled more extensively in Britain and the Commonwealth than any previous heir to the throne. He was a good communicator who enjoyed meeting the general public. He became interested in the welfare of miners and dock workers, the plight of the unemployed and disabled people. In contrast he was also known as the Playboy Prince, a bachelor who loved parties, women and sporting occasions – popular with the people and, of course, the press. But suddenly he is the King: he is not married – there is no direct heir to the throne – and for four years he has been romantically and sexually involved with a twice-divorced American lady.

Early in December 1936 the British press broke a self-imposed silence when it became known that the King intended to marry Mrs Wallis Simpson. A constitutional crisis erupted: Parliament was in uproar and the Church adamant in opposition. The British Constitution and Church of England Canon Law distinctly precluded the marriage of a monarch to a divorcee. Trapped between duty and love, King Edward VIII abdicated the throne and sailed to France on December 12th to join his future wife. Prince Edward's married brother, George, reluctantly acceded to the throne supported by his able and popular wife Elizabeth and two young daughters, Elizabeth and Margaret.

The Nation and peoples of the British Empire rejoiced in the crowning of King George VI and Queen Elizabeth at Westminster Abbey on May 12th 1937. All our family gathered around Father's valve radio set again; being Londoners, we could dress the excellent commentary with mental pictures of the streets, the Abbey and the Palace. On my next visit to the cinema a special Movietone News 'Coronation Documentary', filmed during that day of pageantry and celebration, was so moving that a trickle of tears expressed feelings of joy – and a strange new feeling: I was proud to be British.

> How swift the gods of change new destinies do create,
> And sacrifice for love parts waves in history's seas of fate.

The imprints of those historic events were sealed in my mind by bold headlines and dramatic photographs in Father's newspapers and memorable newsreels in the cinema. I remember cutting out pictures from the newspapers during the time of the abdication crisis, and later, the Coronation of King George VI and Queen Elizabeth. The main features in my scrapbook were photographs of horse-drawn carriages in royal processions, wonderful Daimler cars and Rolls Royces – also a long, black, American Packard. I must have made a score of pencil drawings of that Packard in which Mrs Simpson was chauffeured from place to place in Britain. Even though I was so young, that black Packard symbolised something that stayed with me as I grew up: something to do with 'luxury can be sinister' and 'divorce means a whole lot of trouble'.

Weddings were a much more powerful positive influence on my impressionable young mind. As a choir-boy I really loved singing at weddings, sensitive to the happy energies bouncing around in the church ... *'with one person – one very special person'*... ... and people enjoying other people in the now of the celebrations even if, maybe, tomorrow's realities dulled the euphoria.

Sam, Beryl and Tilly,
Ryde, 1935

Brother and sister cousins,
Tilly and Bernard Rayment

Within our family my dear cousin Doris's wedding in the Spring of 1935 is forever memorable. Larry Bolger married Doris Rayment at St Monica's Roman Catholic Church in Palmers Green; the bride and Beryl, her seventeen-year-old sister and bridesmaid were both radiantly beautiful. Larry, outwardly calm as ever, seemed to be melting with pride.

I was so proud to be honoured with the role of the Page Boy – my chest puffed out and my head seemed to grow. Mother had made me a smart outfit in pale-green velvet, matched with a silk shirt and bow tie. Twelve months after the wedding another big family gathering attended the same Catholic Church to witness the christening of Michael, the first of four children raised by Larry and Doris. I have a special coloured photograph depicting yours truly, aged seven, sitting on the lawn cradling baby Michael wearing his christening gown.

Larry worked for Barclays Bank and played soccer for that institution in the Southern Amateur League. A tall left-footed defender, he turned down an offer of professional terms with Brighton F-C in order to continue the safer career path that culminated in the post of Chief Clerk at Barclays Head Office. A delightful, very intelligent and soft spoken man, Larry was the only active ball-playing sportsman in our extended family and, when visiting, he always took time to play ball with me. During the war years Tottenham Hotspur shared their ground at White Hart Lane with Arsenal. Larry was a life-long supporter of Spurs, and I was an Arsenal fan – lots of banter and leg-pulling. In cricket Larry supported Surrey and I was closely associated with Middlesex. When, in my mid-teens, I began to make my mark on the sports field, Larry was wonderfully encouraging, able to converse knowledgably about cricket and soccer.

Although there were no more family weddings during the 1930s, regular visits to family and friends were part of the social norm. Sam's eldest full-brother Bert and his wife Margaret lived south of the Thames in Streatham. I had to be on my very best behaviour when we visited them because they were deemed to be 'posh' – a façade actually, as I learned when older. Long-term friends of my parents, the Beswick family who lived in Hendon, were more realistically posh and well-off: Mr B owned a bed-manufacturing business and could afford two cars. Mrs B was the godmother who gave me my beloved portable gramophone – bless her. The only other car owners I knew personally in the 1930s were the Cowlings next door; the Taylors in Yorkshire; Uncle Charles the farmer in Suffolk and Mr Robins, father of cricketing pal Ray. Interestingly, apart from Uncle Bert and the Beswicks, who both had sons several years older than me, there were no children anywhere near my age in my parent's social group, underlining the fact that adult people filled the background of my young life.

During the mid-to-late 1930s I enjoyed being taken on day outings by Mother and Father 'to see the sights of London' – often accompanied by Beryl, country cousins and visiting aunts. At first the dark interior of the Tower of London scared me a bit but I cheered up when I saw the wondrous Crown

Jewels and became wide-eyed and silent when I first witnessed the raising of Tower Bridge. Streams of whispered questions in the inspiring museums in Kensington contrasted with my respectful silence inside Westminster Abbey and St Paul's Cathedral – though I was shushed when testing 'the whispering gallery'. I was animated by everything in Regent's Park Zoo, showed off my rowing skills on the Serpentine and was 'lost' for a while in glorious Kew Gardens.

First visits to Selfridges, Peter Robinson's and Gamages were interesting but thereafter tedious. Later, in my twenties, I realised that I had never been inside Harrods, Liberty of Regent Street or Fortnum and Mason, all too posh and expensive for my dear parents as customers – though Father made regular appointments with their buyers. Twice in the late 1930s Father arranged special invitations for Dick Nelson and me to attend Christmas parties for children of veterans of WWI. Held in a big hall at the Honourable Artillery Company Headquarters next to the Royal Artillery Cricket Ground in Moorgate, London, Dick and I remember running around the vast indoor space, eating jelly and ice-cream and enjoying physically competitive party games ... thank you, Sam and military friends.

'Thank you' also to all the parents of friends at Manorside School who arranged Christmas and birthday parties in their homes, including of course Sam and Wyn. My birthdays were celebrated with a few close mates – all keen on sports: David Limbert, Kenny Brunskill, Dick Nelson, Len Pilditch, David Young, Johnny Loosemore. No girls, no photographs – I find that interesting – but the one picture I do have is really interesting in that there are girls as well as boys at a birthday party for Alan Bowness. And, amazingly, I remember all but one of the names.

The photograph appears on page 153. Oh how smart we all are at the age of ten or eleven: boys in suits and ties, girls in fancy cotton frocks.

I'm chuffed that I have warm memories of those friendships formed at school before 1939 and move on to thoughts about two significant adults – the family doctor and the dentist. Dr Holmes was a Scotsman, small in stature with a stocky body – I can imagine him playing scrum-half in his days at medical school. His tight wavy hair framed blue-green eyes set in a square-jawed face. Probably in his early fifties by the beginning of the war, he was, even in those days, a family doctor of the old school. I was not aware of course that Dr Holmes had played a negative role in the debacle of my near-death experience as a baby, so I remember him as a kind and cheerful man who was friendly with my parents. Of course, I contracted the usual childhood illnesses; chicken-pox, mumps and measles – I was prone to ear ache and nose bleeds – and it seemed to me that the doctor always visited me at our house. I cannot picture myself visiting Dr Holmes' surgery near St. Mary's Church until I was twelve.

Doris Rayment (William's daughter) marries Larry Bolger, Southgate, 1935
left: Larry's parents; right: Sam and Wyn with bridesmaid Beryl; Alan the page boy

Alan with the Cowling family, Norfolk Broads, 1938

On the other hand I have clear memories of visiting Mr Foster, our dentist, whose surgery was somewhere in Hendon. Another small urbane, wiry and energetic man who had been a friend of my parents for many years. Some of my baby teeth had rotted early and had to be extracted. I remember 'the mask' that induced what I would now describe as 'out-of-body' dreams or experiences. Oh, and the Drill, a noisy giraffe with whirring wheels driving thin tubular belts – and that spiky thing on the end grinding into my tooth and making me bounce in the chair as I gripped the arms white-knuckle tight when drill hit nerve. No anaesthetic! I do not remember having injections until the late 1950s. But Mr Foster always rewarded me for 'being a brave little chap' – the prize being a sample-size tube of toothpaste – sometimes two. Good psychology, because in later years I was always confident and cheerful when sitting in a dentist's chair.

When my second teeth came through, Mr Foster became concerned that a lateral incisor was growing behind its intended position: evidently a common problem because at age nine or ten the mouth may not have grown sufficiently to cope with a whole set of full-sized teeth. So one day early in 1939 Mother took me to Guy's Hospital near London Bridge, where my mouth was examined and a cast taken in order to make a corrective denture. On the third visit the contraption was fitted; a 'partial' with sprung wires to shunt the wayward tooth into position – slowly. Thereafter I travelled up to Guy's on my own every month for a check-up until the Germans began bombing London in 1940. That wayward tooth finally docked close to, but not in its actual berth.

By far the most important event in our nuclear family in the 1930s was the birth of my brother, Derek, on June 9th 1937 at a nursing home in Hampstead. I remember being very excited earlier that year when Mother told me she was expecting a baby sometime in June. Father and Mother were obviously very pleased too, though somewhat concerned because Mother would be approaching her 41st birthday at the time of the birth. Mother was slim with narrow hips: thankfully, all went well and there were no complications even though Derek's birth weight was just over eight pounds.

There are some lovely pictures of Mother in the family collection of studio portraits and Kodak snaps taken in the 1930s. Wyn was a gracefully good-looking and naturally slim woman who displayed a dynamic energy in a quiet, creative and friendly manner. She had trained as a milliner, was highly skilled as a dressmaker and when younger had had the time to produce some quite good paintings. For me, her most memorable artistic expression was as a musician, a versatile pianist who often surprised me with the rich quality of her mezzo-soprano voice.

Very occasionally Wyn allowed herself to indulge in a repressed desire to experience the classical arts. But the family budget held in check 'unnecessary' indulgences and Wyn was, of necessity, an all-round busy lady who had little time for extraneous pleasures. Given those restrictions, yet always keen to

Sam and Wyn with
young Derek,
Upton Lodge 1938

Alan and Derek,
Upton Lodge 1938

encourage my general education, Mother ensured that we visited many of the historic buildings in central London as well as the museums and art galleries. I did not care much for the waxwork models at Madam Tussauds but, with both parents, enjoyed the Lord Mayor's Show and the Changing of the Guard at Buckingham Palace. But for Mother's own pleasure and my enlightenment one special cultural experience lights up on the screen of my mind. A Promenade Concert.

I was eight: my early love for music had grown exponentially at home through regular musical evenings round the piano, playing records on my own gramophone, listening to a variety of music on the radio – then leapt ahead after joining St Mary's choir in the Spring of '36. In September of that year Mother mentioned that we, just she and I, were going to a concert to see, and listen to, one of the great classical orchestras: "We are going to a Promenade Concert in London next week, Alan."

I was puzzled: I often sang – ... *as he walked along the Promenade with an independent air ... the man who broke the bank at Monte Carlo* – and I had walked along the Promenade beside the beach at Ryde.

"But Mummy, is there a beach on the River Thames beside a paved bit where people walk ... and music from a bandstand?"

"No, Alan," Mother replied, laughing, "we are going to the Queen's Hall to listen to a big orchestra conducted by a famous man, Sir Henry Wood."

"Oh, I see – like the big band I saw in that film *Broadway Melody*."

"No, no dear, a symphony orchestra is ... is ... well, just wait and see."

Bouncing with the energy of anticipation as Mother and I entered the foyer of the Queen's Hall I was overawed by the décor and the people ... so many people! People chattering in upper class accents, men in bow ties and women wearing posh frocks ... even at eight I knew what a posh frock looked like because Mother was a dressmaker ... and when I looked at her I was proud to notice how smart she was too. We eased our way through the throng to search for our aisle seats near the rear of the stalls. The constant murmur from hundreds of voices rumbled through the audience until musicians started walking on to the platform: so many musicians carrying every type of instrument – some I recognised and several I had never seen before. I was so over-the-top excited that Mother had difficulty in keeping me seated. So much to see ... so many questions. Finally I blurted out, "Mummy, Mummy, may I go down there to have a look at those trumpets and drums and things, Mummy ... please, Mummy?"

Patient as ever, she said, "No, no dear, that's not allowed ... and the concert will start very soon ... as soon as the conductor comes on." Confused again, I interrupted, "Mummy, Mummy ... will he be dressed like the man with the tickets on the bus?"

144

Mother quickly pulled a lace handkerchief from the long sleeve of her beautiful dress and thrust it over her mouth. 'Oh dear,' I thought, 'have I upset her?' But I could see her shoulders shaking ... I thought again, "Oh, she is laughing – I wonder why?"

"Mummy," tugging at her sleeve, "why are you laughing?" She kept the cream silk square firmly to her lips, at the same time pointing her other hand towards the platform from whence strange squeaky sounds were floating into the auditorium and quelling the hubbub of chatter. Now, using words I would not have known at the time, the strange sounds crescendoed into a cacophony before resolving into tuneless harmony. Mother, now recovered from the giggles, whispered, "The musicians are tuning up."

"Why – what for?"

"Rather like my piano tuner ... so that they play in tune with each other ..."

"Oh, I get it now, all those different instruments have to have the same pitch," I whispered back, showing off a word I had learned from our choirmaster.

"Shushsh" – a hushed whisper in my ear as everyone stopped talking as though a radio had been switched off ... then the glad sound of clapping that grew louder and louder and went on and on ... confused again ... until I saw a bearded man in a very posh suit with tails standing at the front of the platform, holding a small stick and looking straight down our aisle. I was sure he was looking at me.

Sir Henry Wood turned his back on me – and the audience – and waited. Silence absolute. The vibrant energy of anticipation was palpable ... then tap, tap, tap of baton on lectern, strings tucked under chins, wind and brass raised to lips. I was on the outer edge of my seat in awed expectation. Baton aloft in right hand, left arm extended – waiting.

Then, with energetic caresses, Sir Henry's arms gave life to the instruments – oh such glorious harmonies – waves of sound beyond my experience yet so beautiful that I felt a warm shiver coursing through my body. I was transfixed emotionally and spiritually – though not fixed physically in my aisle seat as I leaned to the left and stretched my neck to gain a full clear view of 'the bearded man and his band'.

"Orchestra, Alan dear," Mother insisted during the interval treat of ginger beer; "a symphony orchestra plays classical music. A band plays dance music, my dear."

I have no memory of the music played – only of feelings and actions – especially feelings – incredible feelings that inspired me for days. Actions? Even into her eighties, Mother would tell the story about young Alan's performance at the Queens Hall ... mainly out of pride but tinged with the embarrassment she felt that evening so long ago.

"Well ... well, all through the first half of the concert Alan had been silent ... lost in the music as he leaned out of his seat to get a full view of the orchestra.

In the interval he was *so* excited and couldn't stop talking about ... about everything. After the interval the orchestra played a symphony ... I think one by Beethoven ... it might have been the Fifth. Anyway, Alan ... always so energetic, my dear ... couldn't hold back any longer, got on his feet and stood in the middle of the aisle waving his arms about ... conducting. I was so embarrassed but daren't call him – I could only move into his seat and beckon him to come and sit down. Then the lady sitting behind me tapped me on the shoulder and mouthed, 'It's all right', and nodded her head. So I left Alan standing there, lost in a world of his own – at one with the music – and in his childlike innocence copying the actions of the conductor. Fancy ... he was only eight ... and trying to copy Sir Henry Wood. At the end, when the famous man did not return for yet another curtain call and the musicians began to walk off the stage carrying their precious instruments, several people spoke kindly to me, saying complementary things and reassuring me that Alan had not misbehaved. "It was so lovely," said one elderly lady, "to see such a young boy so lost in the music. He was 'gone', my dear ... you understand?"

"Yes," I replied, "he is in a choir and loves singing at home, too."

"You're a lucky mother, my dear. Maybe one day he'll play in an orchestra."

"I wish," I am now thinking – or rather talking to myself as I rattle the tabs on this keyboard … "Yes, I would have loved to play in an orchestra; if not an orchestra then to create beautiful harmonies by stroking the keys on a piano keyboard – just like my wonderful mother!"

> *... so it's the laughter*
> *we will remember*
> *whenever we remember*
> *the way we were ...*

CHAPTER 12

1939 – ALL CHANGE

All changed that summer '39
from shorts to longs striped blazer mine,
Eleven Plus meant change of schools –
much talk of war – no flannelled fools
we boys so free to roam and play
who say we have no fear – display
bravado, skill with bat and ball,
how changed all that if bombs do fall:
Will courage fail or courage make us men
before our time: that time may come – but when?

In March 1938 'That Time Had Come' for the Czech and Slovak peoples when German administrators, backed by the Gestapo, installed a Nazi dictatorship in Prague.

Reaction in the British Parliament escalated into longer and more heated debates between the appeasers seeking a treaty with Hitler and the realists backing rearmament. Thankfully, within limited budgets, the armed services chiefs had been urgently preparing for war since 1936. The majority of the politicians and the general public objected to the phoney agreement between Prime Minister Chamberlain and Hitler at Munich in September 1938. With heavy hearts and worried frowns the adults around me accepted that war with Germany was inevitable.

On Easter Day 1939 I processed with the choir through the aisles of a crowded St Mary's Church singing triumphant hymns. As I strolled down Squires Lane a few days later to commence my last term at Manorside Junior School, my mind was teeming with thoughts about being captain of the cricket first eleven. Such a terrific summer ahead: athletic events at the School Sports Day; a chance to win prizes at the swimming gala and above all, the honour and responsibility of leading a bunch of very keen young cricketers against traditional school rivals.

Out-of-school hours we enjoyed cycling to Hendon aerodrome to watch Handley Page Hampdens and Boulton-Paul Defiants take off and land; we pedalled all the way to Hampstead Heath and Totteridge Ponds to fish for nothing much and roared around our neighbourhood on roller skates with metal wheels, even on the paved verge of the North Circular Road past the fields leading down to Henley's Corner. On rainy days in the holidays we still frequented the Arcadia Indoor Rink: round and round but dry and warm and, oh yes, the Bohemia cinema next door – cosy and exciting and Tarzan. My pals and I were having so much fun both on and off the sports field that I was oblivious to my parent's anxiety about the anticipated arrival of *that envelope*.

The warmer weather in April heralded spring and the cricket season. As nature's energies burgeoned with bloom, scent and song, so my energies – bursting with enthusiasm – pitched into everything that took place across the road on Arden Field. I pestered the grounds-man preparing the wickets ... "Mr Joy, please can I help" ... so eager to learn and thrilled when he gave me a chore ... to get rid of me. Lots more enjoyable chores at weekends: scoreboard boy peeking at the match through a narrow metal slot beside the rattling white-numbered, black-canvas rollers; kick-folding the deck chairs in the Members Enclosure and stacking those finger-pinching traps in the old wooden shed beside the smelly gent's toilets. And, of course, watching every ball, every stroke, noting all the fielding positions and changes: and listening, huddled in a quiet corner of the bar as *they*, the men, agreed and disagreed about cricket theory, about women, about business and increasingly, about war.

At that age I was in awe of the club's first team players who practised in the nets on tranquil summer evenings. They seemed so big and strong – bowled so fast and hit so hard. Every ball whacked out of the nets was mine to chase and return. Every moment of those evenings in the fading light was a joy: my enthusiasm, curiosity and focused observation enabled me to learn and develop my own game.

Above all else I loved the fielding practice organised by older boys in the Colts. No fancy warm-ups or fitness games. Simply, thrillingly basic! A boy with a bat hit a full-size cricket ball high in the air to catch, or drove it hard along the outfield towards a boundary line – to pick up on the run and throw above the one stump to a mate wearing keeper's gloves. For hours and hours we ran and caught and threw – so often having to pack it in because it was too dark to see the ball. Keen, we were *so* keen ...

KEEN

Keen, we boys of ten with tender dreams, so keen
to run for hours and hours to field the hardest ball, wield
willow blade, hit catches tall 'til darkness fall on Arden Field,
that brightest summer long before the gloom of war felled men and dreams.

Keen, this boy of ten with tender dreams – so keen
a cricketer to learn the art and for a County play, one day –
or coach or teach in school? ... now School is so routine –
a time to fill, until the years ahead unfold life's destined way.

Keen, or not so keen this sport-mad boy of tender age, to swot,
compete with scholars bright in grammar school next term and learn
the rules of algebra, of chemistry and foreign verbs – and not
to play all day: yet even now I for those school days yearn.

Mother eagerly awaited the postman's delivery that usually plopped on to the doormat just after Father left the house to catch the 143 bus to the City. But morning after morning *that envelope* failed to arrive and, as she sorted the letters, Mother could only express her frustrated anxiety.

"Well! I don't think it's fair to keep us waiting so long. *They* should have let us know by now. Really! Maybe it's this war hanging over our heads and *they* haven't decided about evacuation yet. Well, I don't know ... it's all so worrying."

The morning arrived when frustration was replaced by anticipatory anxiety as Mother tore open *the* envelope and called me to her side. Hushed tension, then a squeal of delight ... and tears: "You passed! ... you did it ... well, you scraped through, but you passed, Alan ... and you are going to ... let me see ... er ... Finchley County School. Well done, oh I'm so pleased for you!" Mother gave me a long, warm, joyful hug and I burst into tears – tears of disappointment.

I was *so* disappointed ('gutted' is a more appropriate modern idiom) that I had not gained entry to Christ's College, the premier grammar school for sport. That I was to enter a co-ed grammar school with a lesser reputation in sports horrified me. Mother phoned Father at work and after an animated conversation wept a little more – tears of relief and happiness. "You did it ... you really did it, my dear!"

"Oh well," I replied nonchalantly and flatly, "I wrote down everything I could think of and just hoped for the best ... but Mother, you know I wanted to go to ... "

"Oh, never mind," Mother interrupted, "I think it's better to go to a co-ed grammar school, it's more natural somehow."

My parents left secondary school aged fourteen, solid in the three Rs, but through considerable innate intelligence, observation and practical application had developed into multi-skilled adults who were also good communicators. Though not bookish their conversational and writing skills were fluent; both were competent in basic maths, Mother in particular as she had managed a section of the local Inland Revenue office during and after World War I. However, though they were proud that their son was to enrol at Finchley County School in September 1939, they were unsure of their ability to give me adequate academic support.

"I don't know how much your father and I will be able to help you with homework, Alan – I expect you'll have a lot of studying to do," stated Mother, frowning.

"Please don't worry so, Mother – I expect I'll cope – and I'm sure you'll help me with my sums. And Father, he knows quite a lot about history."

Sam returned from work and boomed, "Well done, my boy," ruffling my hair as we stood beside each other in Mother's sewing room. Having recently been recalled into the Special Police, Wyn needed to alter his sergeant's uniform – last worn in 1930.

"You've put on too much weight, Sam. Now ... let me see ... I've let out this tunic as far as I can ... try it on." Sam's strong fingers could not persuade buttons into buttonholes ... "You'll have to requisition a new one, Sam."

Then, in playful mood, he clasped his hands behind his back, puffed out his chest, rocked on his heels and turned to me: "Mind you look after your new uniform, my boy ... it's going to cost a lot you know – blazer and long trousers and all that sports gear."

"Stop teasing him Sam," laughed Mother, "you know you're as proud as Punch ... maybe even a tiny bit envious?"

The teasing and banter expressed their pride in my unexpected success and temporarily smoothed the furrowed brows of a couple whose stable lives were now threatened by the upheaval that war would cause – should it come.

Given the limits of my capacity to comprehend the complexities of current affairs aged ten-eleven, it seems that I was driven by a natural and thirsty curiosity to *try to understand the big world out there* as the adults around me discussed, worriedly, the inevitability of war with Germany.

"Again?! ... we haven't got over the last lot yet – can't afford to have another war!"

"Anyway, we're not ready, not tooled up for a war with anyone, let alone that war machine of Hitler's!"

As a healthily sensitive child I didn't like people looking so worried and sounding so frustrated and angry. Few seemed really afraid, but some sounded apprehensive about the possibility of German air raids. I observed and I listened, particularly to conversations among the grown-ups both at home and at the cricket club.

In the old timber pavilion, the bare-board floors impregnated with a heady mix of hops and trodden in fag-ends – and walls bedecked with sepia photos of heroes past – I would often stand within earshot of a group of adult players: London businessmen, lawyers, civil servants and local traders supping their pints as they discussed the latest crisis and the possible effects on their families and careers. To satisfy my hungry curiosity about Life, I also absorbed information in an osmotic way from listening to the wireless, reading *Picture Post* and headline stories in the *Daily Mail* – best of all watching newsreels in the cinema.

By the age of ten I was already hooked by the action-packed and sometimes scary 'other world' available in the cavernous cosiness of an Art Deco-style cinema. From the age of seven my pals and I queued up outside the local Odeon or Gaumont on Saturday mornings to lose ourselves in the make-believe adventures of Roy Rogers and Tarzan; the slapstick antics of Laurel and Hardy and the hilarious brilliance of Walt Disney's animated characters. Saturday film going had to be sacrificed to school soccer and cricket matches from age nine, but parents often gathered a small group of juveniles for an outing to see suitable feature films. Children under fourteen had to be 'accompanied,' so at least once a week in school holidays, usually on my own, I would tout the cinema queue asking, "Please will you take me in Miss – or Sir". Polite address was normal – the socially accepted practice in that era. The black and white films, horribly grainy by modern standards, always included 'A' and 'B' feature films, a cartoon and a newsreel. And, at the big Odeon cinema, the organ. Ah! ... *The Organ!*

I looked forward to the organ recital as eagerly as the main film. Rising from the depths below the orchestra pit the luminous Wurlitzer thundered a popular march – or *Happy Days Are Here Again* ... I can hear it and feel it now ... the power, the vibrations, the jolly tunes. Happy days indeed ... well, four hours of reel-life escapism. I am still addicted ... and must shut down this computer immediately to catch a favourite 'Fred and Ginger' film on TV.

More seriously, the cinema newsreels presented powerful images of grim events in Europe as the Fascist menace spread – then exploded. Scenes from some of those newsreels are indelibly printed on my mind. Footage from the Spanish civil war depicting screeching Junkers 87 dive bombers was terrifying, bi-plane dog fights were fascinating and General Franco – in full military regalia with 'baddy' moustache – seriously comical. The controversial militaristic scenes filmed at the 1936 Olympic Games in Berlin were worrying – Hitler's manic, mind-bending, screeching speeches to the black-shirted, goose-stepping Nazi hordes at Nuremberg Rallies – chilling!

In direct contrast Prime Minister Mr Neville Chamberlain was a man of peace: an appeaser. He was politically and psychologically naïve when trying to negotiate 'peace' with Hitler and Mussolini at Munich in September 1938. Recalling those cinema newsreels I have an inerasable image of Neville Chamberlain alighting from the plane at Heston airport, pale in face and tremulous in voice, waving a piece of paper – a copy of the new Anglo-German Accord and saying, "I believe it is peace for our time." Politicians who were realists called for rearmament – the appeasers buried their heads in the sands of denial.

Writing stimulates the memory ... I recall snippets of a friendly argument with my pal's mum as we exited the Bohemia cinema after watching a newsreel showing particularly scary bombing scenes in the Spanish civil war. Ken's mum insisted that the Nazis would not attack Britain because we were an island and we would be protected by our very powerful Navy. Kenny and I protested loudly that we had just been watching scenes from Spain where German dive-bombers sunk ships and knocked out airfields.

Obviously I was too young to understand the nuances whirling within the complexities of the international political see-saw. However, the headline issues and major personalities involved were of great significance and impacted on everyone around me. My dear cousin Beryl – big sister really – left Upton Lodge and her job as a secretary with the Provincial Insurance Company to become a live-in nursing student at St John's and St Elizabeth's Hospital in St John's Wood. When trained she joined the Women's Auxiliary Air Force and served as a Nursing Sister with officer rank through the war until 1947. In the late 1930s thousands of intelligently perceptive young men and women like Beryl prepared themselves for military duty by undertaking specialist training or by joining cadet and territorial units.

These were seriously worrying days! In London some serious practical measures brought home to neighbours and friends – and to the mildly inebriated debaters around the cricket pavilion bar – the probability that 'We Brits' were preparing, if somewhat half-heartedly, for a war against Nazi Germany.

In the autumn of 1938 a few civilians were conscripted for military service, including one member of the cricket club. That reality unsettled the complacent members. In London's major parks air raid shelters were being built, trenches dug and anti-aircraft gun emplacements installed, surrounded by walls of sandbags. Such visible preparations, supplemented by the eerie wail of air-raid sirens tested on BBC wireless programmes, emphasised the reality of the Nazi threat to peace.

Millions of gas masks were manufactured and stored in warehouses near ports and cities thought to be vulnerable to German air attack. Ironically, on Chamberlain's orders, Britain's massive naval fleet was mobilised on September 27th 1938. Over eighty per cent of parents in the Greater London area registered their children at Local Authority offices in preparation, should the crisis deepen, for evacuation to safer rural environments. In January 1939 the press released the fact that production in aircraft factories had been increased fourfold in one year, with 400 aircraft being delivered to the RAF every month. The House of Commons reluctantly endorsed an order for the general conscription of essential personnel to the armed services – announced the distribution of Anderson air raid shelters to houses with gardens in districts most likely to be bombed if war came – and ordered ration books to be printed.

Among the already bewildered British populace anxiety escalated into anger when the IRA exploded bombs in London, Manchester and Birmingham. The British Fascist leader, Sir Oswald Mosley, continued to organise rallies in London. The Germans made a peace pact with Russia, flew the first jet aircraft and split the atom. Even my young mates and I took notice of such perplexing events and shared our romantically unrealistic ideas of how a war would affect us.

To war – or not to war? That ominous question hung in the air like a dark thundercloud. But life was certainly not all gloom and doom and, in general, our daily routines continued as usual.

On the lighter side, Portsmouth beat Wolves 4-1 to win the FA Cup in 1939; *'a tub that does its own washing'* was displayed at the British Industries Fair; the young singing star Judy Garland stirred hearts in *The Wizard of Oz* film; Hutton and Compton both scored centuries at Lord's in the Test against the West Indies – and I had seen, with my own eyes, the great stars George Headley and Learie Constantine perform in my Theatre of Dreams. Those joys not only shielded me, temporarily, from the darkness of the thundercloud but inspired me to dream ... dreams that floated me across the seas ... to see myself playing cricket on the famous grounds in the Caribbean Islands. In reality, my overseas cricket that year was to be played on the beaches of the Isle of Wight during the last peacetime holiday of my childhood.

~~~~~~~~~~

Manorside School friends at Alan Bowness's birthday party, Finchley, 1938
From the left, standing: ? (apologies); Alan Rayment; David Limbert;
Johnny Loosemore; Tony Wallace; Vivien Smith; Alan Manship; David Young
Sitting: Betty Plumley; Margaret Smith; Colin Bowness; Bowness sister;
Alan Bowness; Pat Manship; Margaret Peeling

CHAPTER 13

LAST PEACETIME HOLIDAY

Summer time in thirty-nine,
primetime childhood richly mine,
peacetime fading, darkening sun,
playtime beckons, holiday fun,
daytime fishing, joy sublime:
A glorious time in thirty-nine.

In August every year Sam relished his annual escape from the hurly-burly of the rag trade in London's City to enjoy the quieter seaside ambience of Ryde, Isle of Wight. Wyn also enjoyed the change of pace from her busy-ness in suburbia. In their later years my parents remarked that even in the 1930s, Ryde and the Isle of Wight felt so utterly Victorian: "So behind the times, my dear – it was so peaceful after London."

Waterloo, the Southern Railway terminus in London, symbolised for me the opening scene of a new holiday adventure every summer from my birth in 1928 – though, of course, my earliest conscious memories are from age four or five. Bored by the stuffy Tube train journey from Finchley, my enthusiasm rose in harmony with the slow-moving escalator until, at last, we emerged into the daylight mayhem of that vast people's auditorium – the concourse of Waterloo railway station.

August 6th 1939: my last childhood holiday at the seaside had begun.

Even though I was now eleven I insisted that Father and I observe a traditional ritual he initiated when I was a toddler. Leaving Wyn comfortably settled in her seat on the train, Sam carried my wide-eyed brother Derek as we strolled down the long platform, side-stepping busy porters trundling steel-wheeled sack-trucks piled high with luggage. We *had* to examine the engine – up close and personal – and chat with the driver and fireman of the mammoth locomotive – a dark green-and-black Nelson Class 4-6-0. I was allowed to stand on the step below the footplate and watch the sweating fireman with coal-smudged face shovel the jagged black lumps into the blazing red furnace.

"That's wachyer call hard work, young-un," observed the friendly engine driver in a rich cockney accent as he unfolded and refolded an oily rag. With a nod and a wink to Sam he added ... "Don' s'pose yer still wanna be'n engin droiver, eh, smar blond kid lik'n yu eh?"

"No, a cricketer I hope," I replied, confidently.

"Oi, for Surrey wiv Fishlock n'Gover n'awl that lot, I s'pose."

"No," softly, sensing his allegiance, "Middlesex."

"Eh! ... them uver lot ova riva ... naahh ... Surrey's best mate ... bu'h goo'luck to yer kid ... see yer at the Oval one dayh, eh?"

With Derek fidgeting in his father's arms, over-stimulated by all the imposing sights, sounds and smells around him, we retreated from the steamy soot-filled air by the engine to the comparative luxury of hard seats in a third-class coach. The Kid had 'a think' about engine drivers ... "a real friendly bloke, likes cricket too ... see yer at the Oval one day'h eh? ... I really hope so, it's my second dream – the first of course is to play at Lord's! Hhmmm, salt-of-the-earth those steam engine drivers, or soot of ... er ... something?"

Still fascinated with all the hectic activity on the platform, I leaned out of the carriage window to watch railway guards in dowdy uniforms blow whistles and wave green flags to signal our departure. Friends and lovey-dovey couples waved and shouted last farewells, porters leaned on their trolleys and the vast canopy over the platforms echoed the thunderous release of pressurised steam. Steel wheel fought steel rail as the massive power of the 4-6-0 caused steam pressures to exhaust in frighteningly unsynchronised bursts.

"We're off," announced Father, stating the obvious in an authoritative manner. "Better come in from that window, my boy, and shut it because of all the smoke." I ducked inside as Father tugged at the long leather strap and slipped a hole therein over a stout brass knob to secure the thick wood-framed window. Sam disappeared behind the *Daily Mail* whilst Wyn concentrated on the task of calming down my excited brother. A ditty which popped into my head ... *We're on our way ... to our holiday* ... kept pace with the clickity-clack rhythm of steel wheels dancing over track joints – the distinct beat disconcertingly overwhelmed by un-syncopated drum rolls as the long train rumbled through a series of points until, freed from Clapham Junction and the inner suburbs, my dotty lyrics were outpaced by the power and pace of steam-driven locomotion.

Gripping scenes flashed by my window: glimpses of the River Thames between Vauxhall's grey Victorian streets packed with tiny terraced houses; offices and shops among the factory chimneys belching thick black smoke at Battersea; the huge cemetery at Earlsfield contrasting with neat gardens on new housing estates – and a school with a large and luscious green sports ground. On and on into the country ... Brooklands the car racing stadium streaked by ... then farms with tiled barns and undulating fields of variegated colours ... cows drinking at a shallow stream – and quaint village stations whizzed by in such a blur that I could not read the name boards. My short-lived grunts of frustration changed key to squeals of delight as my eyes framed *the* most picturesque village cricket ground – with thatched roofed pavilion enclosed by a low white picket fence:

"Daddy ... Daddy look at that ... no, its gone."

Happy again, I began to realise that although I liked London – especially my suburban home patch around the cricket club – I really loved the green and golden acres, the hedgerows and woods of the countryside.

Nelson 4-6-0 slowed as we approached Guildford station, halted, expressed steam as though sighing with relief from effort – or pleased to be free from the busy-ness of London. Carriage doors clicked open and clanged shut, another holidaying family joined us in the narrow compartment just as Sam attended the leather strap again: "Got to open the window, my boy ... let some country air in."

Derek was asleep, leaving Mother free to focus on her knitting – she always had to keep her hands busy. Then, soon after the train pulled away from the station, I spotted a large ugly-looking building under construction in the middle of acres of green fields:

"What is that, Father ... that over there ... that horrible big thing in those lovely fields?"

"I think they're building a cathedral, my boy," he replied.

"What, a cathedral in the middle of the country ... that's a bit daft ... why?"

"Don't know, young Alan. Have to wait and see."

I waited – a long time – but in 1973 I attended a large gathering of happy-clappy charismatics in the huge redbrick Anglican cathedral. Those lovely green fields had disappeared, swamped by the need for new housing estates and a sprawling university.

As our rumbling train picked up speed, the parents of the other family were having difficulty in controlling their exuberant seven-year-old twins, thus spoiling my enjoyment of the ever-changing scenes kaleidoscoping past *my* window. The verdant farmland and rolling hills of the South Downs gave way to the blackened jumble of ancient slate-roofed terraced houses – and glimpses of sleek-grey naval ships – as we chugged through Fratton into Portsmouth City station. My excitement rose as the hissing, rail-grinding, slow-moving Nelson dragged its family of green carriages past the United Services Sports Ground and snaked round the final tight bend to expire in a cloud of steam at the harbour terminus. "Yippee, we've arrived!"

My excitement was accompanied by the rat-a-tat-tat of doors being opened and slammed – cries of "hello hello" – shouts of "porter, porter" followed by the hullabaloo of mums, dads and squeaking children scurrying down the platform towards the paddle-steamer ferries. Father and I paused on reaching the now passive steam monster, thanked the cockney driver and fireman – then we rejoined the chattering mob of people moving slowly down a narrow, sloping corridor to the dockside.

Portsmouth Harbour – a different world! Ah ... the Solent's bracing tang of salted breeze wafting sounds of deep-boom horns and whistles shrill amid the sight of cranes and ropes and anchor chains – and sea!

The noisy melee of mums with kids and dads with baggage shuffled forward towards the dock-edge until we became an orderly British queue marshalled by cheerful smart-capped stewards: "Single file now – single file and hold the rail," bellowed the boss steward, "an' hold on to yer kids." Some kids were frowning and nervous but others, like me, were making jokes about 'walking the plank' – in reality the precarious gangways bridging that frightening chasm twixt ship and shore. 'All Aboard!' We were, at last, aboard the PS Whippingham. Beyond excitement – I was in a seventh heaven of calm happiness.

Aboard a paddle steamer! Gee! Much as I delighted in steam engines I adored paddle steamers. The Whippingham was spotlessly maintained by a disciplined crew who 'turned to' at every turn-around, dutifully sweeping rubbished decks, clearing crockery and polishing brass rails. A carefree holiday spirit burbled among the crowd of adult townies and their exuberant wide-eyed kids. So much to see ... too many new sights to savour on both sides of the ship. Which side has the best view?

As paddles spewed froth and spray to get underway, the older children ran from port rail to starboard and back again, competing to claim sight of the biggest warship or busiest tug – even the chug-chug of the little Gosport ferry provoked excitement as the helmsman skilfully avoided the great grey ships of the Royal Navy. With white-grey smoke belching from our black-tipped yellow funnel the ponderous paddles caressed the waters on 'slow ahead' as Whippingham's helmsman eased the proud vessel through the narrow harbour mouth, past the famous Spice Island Inn and historic Round Tower into the open Solent. The open sea! I loved being at sea. I have always loved the Solent: for me it spells and smells – *freedom and adventure.*

For The Kid from London, this forty-minute sea crossing was always a prime adventure – a holiday highlight – with one exception. The Clarence Pier funfair. From the age of seven I had consciously and vocally detested that gaudy construction which spoilt the shoreline's landscaped charm. Old Portsmouth, regal Dame of the Realm, wearing brash jewellery from Woolworths? "Outrageous my dear!"

I distinctly remember my reaction in 1939: I turned my back on 'that thing', that aberration, and said to my father, "I wish they'd take that horrible thing down; it spoils the view ... and ... and if there's a war I hope it gets bombed!" Yes, a sensitive child, prone to get angry even then when beauty perceived meets insensitive deed. However, my gripe dispersed a few seconds later as I marvelled, once again, at the large copper globe balanced on the pinnacle of the Naval War Memorial, rising proud on Southsea Common as though it were standing to attention in honour of the thousands of lives lost at sea in Freedom's Cause.

A strong south-westerly breeze blended with the warm mid-day sun sparkling on the rippling aquamarine sea to create an ineffably bracing tonic, lifting the spirits of pale-faced Londoners as though it were an elixir. PS Whippingham changed course forty-five degrees to starboard, the wind swirl adding puffs of coal smoke to nature's aromatic mix on deck.

A noisy group of inquisitive youngsters had gathered on the port rail to marvel at the dark doughnut of 'Spitbank Fort'. "Waas dat bleedin' fing stuk owt 'ere fer?" shouted a cockney nipper on his maiden voyage – causing heads to turn. "Sumfink to do wiv guns – but it's secrit, so shuhit 'arry," replied his all-knowing older sister. "Looks mor loik bleedin' St Paul's wivowt its lid sat in fik bleedin' soup, Sis," came the sharp retort. I chuckled, admiring the cockney kid's witty imagination, then still amused I looked down at the broiling foam wake stirred up by the rhythmically beating paddles … mesmerised. Looking up again I focused on sails – some taut, some flapping – of fast, sleek racing yachts as they 'went about' to avoid the determined ferry steaming upwind, beam-on to the incoming tide. Rarely did a paddle-steamer ferry give way to sail.

Rejoining my parents, I discovered they were sitting near a large air-intake funnel … my imagination pictured it as a broad-stemmed, white mushroom with a vertical face … but, of course, an engine-room ventilator … another traditional ritual. "Father, may we go down to the engine room now?" I asked. "Won't be long, Mother … no, Derek, you can't come 'til you're older," said Sam.

As we descended into the bowels of the ship the pungent, throbbing combination of coal-fired furnaces and pounding oil-scented steam engines ascended to meet us. The scene is impregnated upon my memory: a snapshot of giant steel flywheels whirring in perpetual motion; of hissing valves and huge thrusting piston rods gleaming with oil … a steam-driven dream of orchestrated synchronicity that transfixed all my senses. Four minutes in yet another world: four priceless minutes of holiday happiness below decks on a paddle steamer which, only nine months hence, was to save 2,700 British troops at Dunkirk. War cancelled our holidays to Ryde.

Fast-forwarding this tale for a moment to 1947, my next Solent crossing was, coincidentally, on PS Whippingham. Memories of that pre-war four-minute moment in the engine room flooded my senses as the paddles sank their broad teeth into the choppy seas. When the heroic old ship passed the Naval War Memorial, the scene of my 'steam-driven dream' flashed before me, but with it, a new and deeper understanding. I now understood something of the reality behind the dream; the fact that ships were built by hundreds of men from thousands of components, which beforehand had been manufactured by thousands of people in factories up and down our land. Now I truly appreciated the inventiveness of our nation's naval architects and engineers; the skills of sweat-drenched men labouring in the cauldrons of iron foundries and rolling mills; of deft hands turning intricate parts in lathe-lined factories in Scotland's shipbuilding heartland; and welders – perched on gantries high, come rain or shine – hammering red-hot rivets through holes in plates of inch-thick steel.

Now nineteen, the war behind us, and with it, thankfully, the tragic loss of so many ships and their crews, I felt a high regard for the skill and physical hard work of those men, and women too, who laboured in our shipyards. During the war they had worked long hours for low pay to replenish those losses, and then, together with designers and draughtsmen, office cleaners and management bosses, they proudly cheered the fruit of their collective labours down the greasy slipway into the mist-hung waters of the River Clyde.

Sadly – now in the 21st century – Britain no longer has a major shipbuilding industry. Long gone too are the days of steam-paddle power, that romantic meld of grace and utility which ferried Wight-bred 'caulkheads', migrant residents and holidaying 'ov-ners' fro and to a small peaceful Island hanging loose below the pouch of its parent Isle. The tune of 'thanks for the memory' wafts through my mind.

Memory rewinds again to August '39 aboard the Whippinham to picture two-year-old Derek, safe in his father's arms, agog at all the new sights and asking endless questions in his then limited vocabulary. "What's that, Daddy – that – no that?" Sam enjoyed his son's curiosity and maintained his patience admirably. Mother said we should go for'ard to enjoy the fast-approaching shoreline of Seaview and Puckpool, of Ryde sands and the long pier. Mimicking the first syllable of its name, the ferry's paddles whipped the sea into a white frenzy as the helmsman, battling the strong tide, manoeuvred the ship within rope-throwing distance of the pier-head. Intrigued, I watched the crewman coil the long, slim heaving line in cowboy fashion, then hurl the snaking rope across the void from ship to pier where it was expertly caught by the waiting docker. The catcher then proceeded, with energetic speed, to haul in the heaving line to reveal the thick hawser attached to it and place that hawser's eye over the stout steel bollard. Aboard the ferry, crewmen at bow and stern operated motorised winches to ease the rolling Whippingham alongside the buttressed landing stage until, at last, the graceful ship was made secure. 'Ding-ding ... ding-ding' ... signalled bridge to engine room. Our Whippingham adventure was over.

Friends and relatives had been waving to each other from ship's deck to pier and vice-versa. Mother spotted the distinctive broad back and balding pate of Sam's burly brother, Jack, who was engrossed in conversation with an angler reeling in his line to avoid entanglement with the ship's bow. "He's not seen us yet," exclaimed Mother, disappointedly. Sam replied cheerily, "You'll see him soon enough ... and soon get fed up with his teasing." The Rayment men flirted mildly and teased maddeningly.

"Let's check our luggage, Wyn: I've got my rods and the big case ... you carry Derek," stated Sam. Our main luggage had been forwarded a week earlier, so I only had to carry a small haversack and an old cricket bat. Jostling holidaymakers squeezed patiently down the narrow gangways as busy little cranes swung cargo from the hold in rope net slings to rail trucks. I ran over to Uncle Jack, grabbed his hand and pulled him away from his weather-beaten fishing mates. Jovial as ever, he hoisted me for a piggy-back through the crowd to welcome his pale-faced London relatives. The family's mutually warm and jocular greetings set the tone for my last and best seaside holiday as a child.

We were guests of Uncle Jack in his spacious home above the butchers' shop atop the steep hill rising from the Esplanade. Number 173, High Street, Ryde is forever memorable: the home comfortable and warm contrasted with the clinically cool and hygienically clean shop – yet the latter was filled with friendly banter and bonhomie through my uncles' booming energy and bold humour. Jack was a well-known and popular personality on the Island: Captain of the Vectis Boating and Fishing Club, a respected businessman and a member of the shooting fraternity – friendly with farmers and the landed gentry.

Of course, The Kid was fascinated by everything in and about the shop but most puzzling of all: 'why was all that saw-dust on the floor?' Although I was a little bit scared of Uncle Jack I plucked up courage to ask my question one morning as I stood just inside the back door of the shop. For a short while I was captivated by the skills and rituals being displayed by my butcher uncle who, dressed overall in a white long trouser tunic, chef's hat and a blue striped apron, was showing off to a couple of smartly dressed lady customers. On sighting me out of the corner of his eye he picked up a gleaming chopper, brandished it in my direction and boomed, "to soak up blood dripping from my sheep's carcases, young Alan ... and if you ask any more questions this morning I'll chop off your head and give you a one of these instead!" Bang went the chopper into the wooden block as he held up a sheep's head with his other hand. I scarpered – half scared and half laughing – upstairs to the tiny attic bedroom I enjoyed so much because of the privacy and the views. From the small north-facing window I could scan the exciting variety of ships traversing the Solent: big cargo ships and full-sail yachts, majestic liners and sleek naval cruisers ... ferries, fishing boats and motley small craft going about their daily business.

Best of all I could see the end of 'My Ryde Pier': the smoky paddle steamers disembarking passengers and essential supplies at the busy wind-swept pier-head ... oh ... and the electric trams mimicking grounded ski-cars trundling back and forth to the Esplanade servicing holidaymakers and their luggage. Also glimpses of the trains I loved – the bustling green-and-gold-painted 'O2 Class' tank engines, each with their distinctive domed steam-boiler hat between the smoke funnel and Pagoda cab –'My Puffin' Billies'. When fishing at the head of the pier I would sometimes need to stretch my legs and stroll into the station to adore and absorb their powerful beauty at close quarters on the turntable. I was also enamoured with their 'music' – their unique sounds and rhythms as they shunted – hissing, panting and clanging before coupling with the front coach of the outgoing train. Oh, happy summer days high above the surging double tides of Solent seas – a miniature Water-loo.

Ryde Pierhead, circa 1930,
showing the Vectis Boating and Fishing Club and slipway

PS Whippingham,
Portsmouth to Ryde
passenger ferry and
one of the Little Ships
of Dunkirk in 1940

As I reflect on the multifarious activities that I engaged in during that unforgettable fortnight, I feel the urge, if you dear reader can bear it, to describe two events at length and give brief mention to others. The stories are a reminder of how much could be achieved with relatively little money in those far off days: days neither better nor worse in comparison with today – just different. Different era, different culture, different values, different expectations.

As I begin to visualise places, people and events experienced during that special holiday I seem to be able to regress myself to become 'Rainbow' again – my nickname ascribed by school mates for no logical reason; to be again that athletic blond kid who also loved to stop and stare – and 'have a think'. So I'm there, in and around Ryde, running everywhere – yet also standing or sitting still for hours and hours – fishing. Two fishy tales are long – they usually are – and I'll speed through a few of the other 'many splendoured things' which gifted me with youthful joy on that last peacetime holiday.

From the age of five I had learned to row miniature wooden dinghies on Ryde's oval boating lake a few yards from the beach east of the pier – in those days a charmingly natural environment as yet unsullied by the advertising gimmicks and gaudily painted fibreglass novelty boats of today. For very few pennies I filled a vacant hour or three playing rowing dodgems on the lake's shallow waters in preparation for the 'big one" – a wish that came true unexpectedly soon – though I had pestered my father and uncle long enough for Sam and Jack to conspire to shut me up 'good and proper'.

One glorious August afternoon, with a light westerly breeze wafting up from the Needles, my father and his brother launched Big Jack's ten-foot clinker-built dinghy from the Vectis Fishing Club's pier-side slipway. Two pairs of stout oars were eased into their salt-tarnished brass rowlocks by the two fifteen-stone brothers. I relaxed on the hard seat astern, left hand dangling over the side caressing the briny while the flat-capped adults rowed in unison, joking and laughing, to round the pier on an incoming tide from the Needles. For Sam – this was heaven!

A fishing trip – but where? I had often fished from this boat with Father, inshore either side of the pier on changing tides. But this time we headed for Seaview. Of course, there continued to be lots of banter and leg-pulling, boasting reminiscence and anticipation of the catch to come. My ears were red hot from all this 'man talk', yet having a double-whale-of-a-time (excuse the pun). But I was puzzled: "Uncle Jack, where are we headed?" "Ayee ... we'ra goin' to ancherrr orf No Man's Land Fort," barked Jack, mimicking Long John Silver, "an' catch some o dem big thornbacks young Arlen." No Man's Land Fort was one and a half miles from Ryde pier: to me it seemed to be in the middle of the Solent. It was – almost.

We dropped anchor about fifty yards west of the imposing sea fort, baited our tackle with juicy lugworms whilst Jack and Sam continued their juicy tales of yard-long fish caught yesteryear. The brothers were close: men bonded by love of family, the English countryside and field sports. Their values were imprinted by their upbringing in a large family on farms remote from city life and grime ... I hear a ditty forming in my mind – I trust, dear reader you do not mind – excuse me, please, while I ... er ... sneeze ... that's better ... coffee poured, milk, sugars two – then scribble dotty lines afew:

Sam's mask peeled off
away from City life so tough,
the countryside he loved, the charm
of field and tree, the sea, the farm –
Especially!

On holiday, a wider smile
in boat with Jack off Wighted Isle,
true man revealed, at last at one
with self, and me, the sea and fun –
Especially!

Where was I? Ah yes – fishing. We caught a few: cut dabs for bait, threw back the crabs, reeled in a skate or two apiece – the biggest catch to Master Angler, Jack. Warm day, blue sky, small boat, calm sea – brothers and son at one with nature – much laughter, too – a paradise glimpsed – then lost as a squadron of grey warships steamed east at speed close by Spitbank Fort: foreboding shadows of war on the near horizon.

Time passed in a whisper before 'Captain Jack' announced that high tide was turning: "It's time to pack it in ... clean up and stow the tackle tidily, you landlubber townies," he quipped. Then, as the brothers had planned, they gave me the honour of the oars, alone. "OK, young 'un," commanded Jack, "let's see if you've got the muscles to row us home to the clubhouse. You come and sit here in the centre ... be careful not to rock the boat as we change place ... don't want to go swimming before supper." Father, though in good form, made a negative comment about my boyish muscles, questioning my ability to row the heavy cargo all the way to the pier. My reaction to the negative was – and always has been – positive.

New challenge – quick think: "My sports intuition says rhythm is the key, not strength ... no hurry, just enjoy ... row slow and win." And win I did, secretly aided by my wise uncle who knew that on a calm day at slack water I would have little opposition from wind or tide. Plaudits all round as I shipped oars alongside the Club's slipway as the brothers smiled and slapped my back. "Well done, young'un," boomed Jack.

The rite of passage passed, though small, was big to me. To crown the day, eight Rayments – such a noisy lot – sat round Big Jack's big table for supper. I feel a warm glow within as I 'see' that scene again, feel the energy, hear the deep-shrill laughter, smell and taste the fresh deliciousness of grilled skate caught by the brothers and the boy that glorious afternoon aside the sea-fort called 'No Mans Land'.

So what about the little stories ... hmmm ... too many tales of yore could bore the browsing reader to a doze. Here goes – in brief, I hope.

At low tide the sands at Ryde provide a vast arena for games with ball or kite, for bucket, spade and playtime inventiveness – and a worm farm. I dug for bait every day, lug and rag – a healthy, patient exercise. Cricket too – with Father, cousins Beryl and Tilly and her fiancé John – and boys young and old attracted to three sticks pushed into the sand as though we were about to perform some ancient magic ritual – which we were, of course – to attentive rain gods. As a family we swam in the sea most days when the tide was high and enjoyed playing sandcastles with young Derek when low. I walked or ran everywhere, along the beach and up and down the hills of Ryde, sometimes alone to fish from the pier or run errands to the shops, but mostly with family, rediscovering places like Puckpool Park to play on swings with Derek or kick a football. On a longer walk to Seaview we indulged in a posh cream tea whilst watching yachty types race their small sailing boats, seriously and competitively. Were they really having fun? I was – we were – lots of outdoor family fun, come rain or shine: no car to mar our exercise.

Train rides: I could wax long in praise of the Isle of Wight steam railway because it was ... well ... *so* Isle of Wight before the butchers of Whitehall chopped out its heart. But no, another time maybe ... although the practicality as well as the romance of the Puffing Billy trains was a premier feature of a holiday on the Garden Isle – so I'll take a peep.

Twice we ventured far on across the Wight Isle's rolling Downs – long Dragon spine of chalk from Culver Head far east to Needles Point out west. From Ryde Esplanade station up north to Ventnor down south – 'Back-o-the-Wight', the locals say – beyond famed sandy seaside halts at Sandown, Shanklin, green Puffin' Bill trundled on through tunnel long to emerge in clouds of steam and grey-black smoke ... as though blessing the picturesque Ventnor station with holy-railway incense. We cleared our lungs on a long walk down zed-bending roads granting veiled glimpses of the sea and into the town both small and quaint – Victorian to the core in stone and soul – shale beach, small pier, deck chairs, ice-cream – a seaside dream crowned green above by summit Boniface. Ventnor, a smuggler's haven not long ago, an artist's retreat back then and now where ghosts of Dickens, Swinburne and their like haunt grand manors in nearby Bonchurch. In adult years I've visited the area often, and in the mid-nineties lived high on Ventnor's escarpment for a year. The vibes were always gently inspirational.

For our second railway jaunt we ventured west, to Yarmouth's pretty station beside the River Yar, where, on rising tide, I spied week-end sailors – men and femme – launch their dainty craft and tack up-wind towards the harbour mouth. "They're going to race ... we must get to the pier so we can watch," I pleaded – tugging Father's arm to speed the go-stop stroll of the adults who were more interested in arty-crafty gifts displayed in tiny shop windows. Yarmouth seemed ancient, neat and tiny – and almost Lilliputian. Father, in charge of Derek and pushchair, empathised, "You run on, my boy, we'll see you on the pier." I ran fast and wriggled through a knot of spectators to the furthest rail to witness the dinghy sailors – a score or more – jockeying for position to time their gybes and tacks for a full-sailed run across the line on starter's gun. "Away": we cheered "hurray! hurray"! The sight of sailing fun impressed me some – "one day I'd love to sail" – I heard me say.

Attempting brevity once more – an art I've yet to master – I'll relate two forgettable memories from that golden holiday. Shooting and slot machines. Fishing and shooting were Uncle Jack's passions, and, having several pals among the farmers on the Island, he arranged an early morning shoot – just Jack, Sam and me. Duck and pheasant were out of season so we hunted rabbits.

Uncle Jack handed me a '410' double-barrel shot gun and gave me a stern lecture on safety and etiquette. Hmmm, as I type I find myself humming, *If you go down to the woods today, you'll be sure of a big surprise ... da dum.* Big surprise! I missed. Everything! Even the rabbits laughed – perhaps their ancestors had told them the story of the 'terrifyingly posh dame' and the six-year-old boy in the rabbit costume. Cheeky lot. No wonder I've never been interested in shooting as a sport.

Neither have I been interested in gambling – well, the football pools and the National Lottery at times but arcades, race tracks and casinos, no! But ... but at the end of Ryde pier there was a small arcade containing a variety of table and wall-mounted pin-ball machines that gobbled large old fashioned pennies. Whilst I dared not wind the handle to see 'what the butler saw', I did spend far too many precious pennies on the mechanical bagatelle games, had fun – never won. I was used to winning more often than losing on the sports field at home and was about to win away, at sea, unexpectedly.

The second big fishy story, enacted exactly two weeks before Britain declared war on Hitler's Germany, juxtaposes a minor personal triumph in those last days of freedom with the impending strictures of wartime living in Britain: from fun in the sun to bombs in the blackout.

The Fourth Annual Angling Tournament at Ryde, sponsored by the *News of the World*, was held over the week-end of August 18th to 20th 1939. The Fishing Gazette of August 26th reported:

... the tournament produced a record crop of entries for both the pier and boat sections, the total number of competitors reaching close upon the 600 mark.

Father and I fished all three days from Uncle Jack's dinghy. On the Friday and Saturday we caught some decent plaice and several garfish for which we won five small prizes. Uncle Jack could not compete because he was one of the organising officials and a judge. On the Sunday we anchored west of the pier in line with the old ornamental bandstand and baited up to fish with float for gar: green, slim body with spear-like snout; when hooked they wriggled violently, thrashing their tails on the surface of the sea, before unwillingly succumbing to the landing net. The rules of the competition stipulated that no assistance be given to the person playing the fish.

Two hours passed by with nay a bite, when suddenly my float disappeared and the ratchet on my old wooden reel screeched like a muted Bren gun. "Let it off ... let it off," shouted Sam, "... give it line ... play it ... take your time, don't reel it in yet!" Sam, unusually excited yet commanding, even forgot to add 'my boy'.

Action! Concentration ... I hung on to the rod ... totally focused in the moment ... speechless ... unable to ask Father what the monster might be. Nessie? Hours passed – well five minutes. Locking the ratchet again I gradually reeled in the line, held the rod in my right hand, landing net in the left and hooked one leg under the dinghy seat to steady my balance before leaning over the gunnel. First sight of my monster caused mixed emotions – triumph and disappointment – impostors both. My monster was a minnow – a mackerel.

Scooped safely into the net and hauled aboard I detached the hook from minnow's mouth and said to Father, "Such a fighter, I thought it would be much bigger."

"Know what thought did, my boy ... it's not a bad size for a mackerel ... hmmm, might win you something if you're lucky, my boy."

Feeling hungry, we ate our sandwiches with fishy fingers and drank bottled beer – ginger for me – then resumed the cause of our intent, to catch fish unseen below the gently lapping waves green-grey that bright blue day in peacetime's holiday. Applying bait to hook again we cast in hope, as man has done through endless time for food and sport – at times when faced with hunger in desperate last resort. How favoured we, my dad and I, to share such precious hours so free of need, enjoying manly love unconsciously – the bond grows stronger longer be the memory.

Into action again we landed several small garfish, changed tackle to fish on the bottom and bagged five decent plaice for supper. I had lost interest in Mr Mackerel, hoping to catch something really big. Getting bored I questioned, "Is it nearly time to weigh in, Father?" "Another half hour ...", his answer left in mid-air as he struck his rod, expecting plaice – then cursed the crab that flattered to deceive.

"Let's pack it in then, young Alan: you see to the anchor and row us back for the weigh-in ... we've had a good day, my boy," said Father, patiently dismantling his tackle and sliding his favourite two-piece split cane rod into its brown linen case. Approaching the club house complex beside the pier I was surprised to see so many people milling around on the deck; officials and judges already weighing and recording the days' catch entered by hundreds of competitors. Shipping oars, I leapt out of the dinghy and held it steady against the seaweed-encrusted timbers of the slip-way, then, aided by two strong club members, Jim and Tom, we manhandled the heavy craft up the slope to the boat shed. "Didya catch much, Sam?" enquired Jim, a local copper.

"Not a lot, Jim – nothing big anyway but young Alan caught a decent mackerel – you never know, might win the special prize for youngsters under fourteen again." Naturally curious, Jim and Tom inspected my fantasy monster-turned-minnow, mumbling approval, nodding heads, "Hmmm, you never know, Sam."

I did know that I was having a wonderful time, enjoying animated chats with Mother and cousins about several fish that Father and I had entered for the weigh-in. A hubbub of chatter rippled through the large crowd of competitors and spectators thronging the club's deck, above which the pier's main promenade provided a natural balcony overlooking the stage of the forthcoming prize-giving ceremony.

The Superintendent of Ryde Pier, Mr R Lugg, swung a large hand-bell, town-crier-style, to hush the crowd and announce the order of proceedings. In both pier and boat sections several categories of parallel prizes were to be awarded, for example: the heaviest gross catch; the greatest number caught; the heaviest fish. The person landing the 'best specimen fish' would receive first prize – a split-cane rod given by the national Sunday paper, *News of the World*. The enthusiastic crowd applauded every winner as they received their awards, in reverse order, from the Mayor of Ryde. Cheers rose to a deafening crescendo when Beryl Sweet, a 14-year-old from Ryde, stepped up to accept first prize for the Pier Section.

"In the Boat Section ... for the heaviest fish", announced Mr Lugg, "Mr FG Hawkins of Portsmouth for a thornback skate of 4lb 8 oz" – and so on through all the categories. "And lastly, for the 'best specimen fish', a mackerel of 1lb 4dr ... and winner of the first prize, a *News of the World* rod, is ... (suspense) ... Alan Rayment of Finchley."

Applause? The roof came off ... except there was no roof ... and no prize winner either. Heads were turning and mutterings were mounting because the crowd could not see the winner approaching the dais. To get a good view The Kid had been standing on an upturned dinghy on the periphery of the gathering. For about ten seconds I was transfixed – 'Me? … I've won? … gee-whizz!' Invisible to the puzzled crowd I squeezed between tightly-packed adult bodies and emerged, eventually, at the foot of the podium.

"Oh, at last, there you are, young man," said a relieved Mr Lugg, introducing me to the Mayor as the clapping and cheering crescendoed for me as it had done for Beryl Sweet. A mix of pride and embarrassment caused this small blond kid from London to blush bright red as Mr Mayor congratulated me, shook my hand, presented me with the linen-cased rod and urged the crowd to applaud again.

"Thank you, sir … gee-whizz … gee-whizz … I've won … gee-whizz!" I could think of nothing else to say.

Best Specimen?! Wow! My minnow had transmogrified into a monster fishing rod … monster as in quality and value. Mother, Father, cousins, friends, even strangers, gathered round to congratulate me and examine the beautiful two-piece cane rod with agate rings and cork sheathed butt. Then Uncle Jack, with big strong arms and beaming smile, picked me up and held me aloft as though I were the FA Cup and pronounced the highest compliment: "Young Alan, I'm very proud of you because you're a real sportsman – and a Rayment to boot – well done, my boy!"

Sam Rayment was also effusive in his praise – "I'm as proud as Punch, my boy! … do you know that rod is worth more than my week's wages?"

Now, as I reflect on that scene in far-off '39, I chuckle at my luck and the consequences that followed when *that* fish took *that* bait on *that* hook – and The Kid hooked the prize rod.

An article published in the *Fishing Gazette* the following week is filed in my archive. The accompanying photograph shows a couple of kids who had beaten hundreds of adults in both pier and boat sections of the tournament. And there we are, Beryl and Alan, side by side, rods held like sentries 'at ease', standing next to the Mayor, his wife and the judges. Such is Life and five minutes of fame.

The *Fishing Gazette* reporter wrote:

> There was quite a good percentage of ladies and juveniles amongst the competitors, and youth undoubtedly had its day on Sunday, when Alan Rayment of Finchley, aged eleven, and Beryl Sweet of Ryde, aged fourteen, proudly went to the platform to receive the *News of the World* rods from the hands of the Mayor of Ryde, Alderman AF Wright, who attended on Sunday evening for the prize distribution. The Isle of Wight Angling Society and the Vectis Boating and Fishing Club co-operated in a very enthusiastic manner to make the festival a very enjoyable and successful event.

Uncle Jack at his butcher's shop, High Street, Ryde, 1939

Alan and Beryl Sweet, surprised winners of the fishing competition, Ryde, 1939
Big Uncle Jack to Alan's right

The next evening another celebratory family supper was followed by the anti-climax: holiday over, we packed the suitcases early in the morning, boarded the ferry and train and returned to the hubbub of Waterloo, the crowded Tube and suburban air of Finchley. Sam left the island reluctantly – Wyn almost cheerfully, because as much as she enjoyed the family's traditional summer holiday she preferred the pace of suburban life. "Got to get back because I'm so behind with my dressmaking orders," she declared.

And The Kid? I was split, reflecting both my parent's preferences. Gut-wrenching to leave the Solent, the beach, the pier, the fishing and the Puffin' Billies: yet head-spinningly exciting to anticipate the remaining cricket matches, seeing pals again, a new school and the soccer season.

Life was wonderful in that summer of 1939. Captain of Manorside School cricket team; watching my heroes Constantine and Compton at Lord's; a good season with Finchley Cricket Club Colts; success in the 11-plus exams; excitement about starting at Finchley County School; first prize in a prestigious fishing competition and a glorious holiday in a place I really loved: the Isle of Wight.

FREEDOM – WAR – PEACE
Tis Thirty-Nine and all is fine,
sunshine, sea, fun family time
on Island Wight so loved –
the trains, the sands, and Solent thrill
to fish with Sam in Big Jack's boat.

From boat to date with waiting whore,
A War – we Brits abhor,
avoid if be – it be too late
to stem the hate –
the arrogance of Nazi gait in black jackboot.

I wonder long how long the wait
to walk the sands and dig for bait
again on Island Wight so loved –
the pier, the trains, and Solent thrill
to fish again with Sam in Big Jack's boat.

~~~~~~~~~~~

CHAPTER 14

WAR – AND GRASS AGAIN

Sunday September 3rd 1939

I was angry! Woke early, got dressed and charged out into the garden to 'have a think'.

But I was too angry to think. I paced up and down the lawn muttering to myself, bursting with so much energy I had to *do something* – picked up a tennis ball and threw it, hard, at the trunk of the old apple tree – missed! ... retrieved, threw, missed ... again and again until I scored a direct hit on a branch. The ball ricocheted into the neighbour's garden. Lost ball! More angry! I was rarely angry but occasionally had a fit of pique caused by frustration, uncertainty or not getting my own way. This morning – all three!

"Why do we have to have a war??!!"

I was really cross with that screaming Nazi, Adolf Hitler. But I was also cross with our weak Prime Minister, 'Chamberlain the Appeaser', and with that stuck-up Foreign Secretary, Lord Halifax. Listening to Father's wireless on Friday I had learned that half a million children and teachers were being evacuated to rural areas from cities vulnerable to air raids. I also heard the announcements about immediate general mobilisation and blackout after sunset. I so desperately wanted to *understand.*

"Why a war? Why now?"

I was, of course, too young to have any real clues, any real insight to formulate even small answers to the big questions burning in my mind. But I did have the common sense to realise there would be big changes in the way we lived. I already had a gas mask. Now we were to be blacked out: no street lights, masked lights on cars and bikes, no lit window displays in shops. And food rationing!

I could not stop thinking about it: 'IT' ... THE WAR!

But again, another part of me didn't want to think – but TO DO!

I searched Father's shed for another ball, then returned to the lawn and began my game of wall-ball-catch. The target wall was above the french doors and between two large bedroom windows. Since I was eight I had spent innumerable hours throwing a ball at that twelve-by-twelve-feet area, never smashing the glass, and catching the ball on the full – most times. I had developed throwing techniques to make the catches difficult so that I had to dive or jump to succeed and invented imaginary contests between famous cricketers ... Hammond versus Bradman: Constantine versus Compton.

The rhythmic pattern of enjoyable exercise temporarily relieved my mind of 'IT' and Hitler. Feeling calmer I went indoors to the family room where

Mother and Father were engaged in a serious discussion. I crept past them as quietly as possible to polish my shoes in the scullery – then whispered, "I'm off to choir now."

"You come straight home, Alan," said Mother in worried tone, "and don't go off playing with Bill and Tony after church because we don't know what's going to happen ... it is dreadful ... if there is a war we don't know what we'll do." Father was silent: puffing on his briar pipe, head buried in the Sunday papers, deeply engrossed in gloomy reports by leader writers and correspondents in Europe – all concluding that Great Britain and the Commonwealth, together with our European allies, would soon be engaged in war against Germany. Mother stood at the front gate waving me goodbye – her face a pale mask of anxiety.

Action! I felt as free as the wind as I ran at top speed down the wide footpath that linked Manor View with Regents Park Road, whizzing past Smith's Sports Ground and Avenue House Park. I was soon in the church vestry chatting animatedly with my pals, noticing that the tenors and basses were gloomily wordless as we all donned black cassocks and white surplices. Robed and ready we formed a line in pairs, waited for the Rector to announce the first hymn as the church clock chimed the eleventh hour, then processed round the aisles singing: *Praise my soul the King of heaven ...*

The church was packed: regular worshipers augmented by uncomfortable irregulars hoping that God would provide some answers to their prayerful fears. The choirmaster signalled 'forte ... forte' as we approached the choir stalls and our soprano voices rejoiced in the high notes of the glorious descant, descending into the final line ... *Praise with us the God of grace.* We all needed grace on that solemn historic morning.

The mood of the congregation was quiet and anxious, their singing muted and their prayers heartfelt in hope that war might yet be averted. Some expected to receive solace from the ceremony – or words of comfort from the Rector – and probably did.

The ordered grace of the traditional Anglican mattins service proceeded fluently until ... until at eleven-thirty, in the middle of congregational prayers, that ordered grace was shattered by the deafening wail of air raid sirens. As the kneeling worshippers resumed their seating positions, a soft involuntary murmur rolled through the pews as the Rector ascended the pulpit steps.

Silence!

The hush was pregnant with anxiety as choir and congregation alike awaited the words of the Reverend Prebendary S Bernays. He addressed his bewildered flock with calm authority:

"I have been informed that the Prime Minister has announced on the wireless that our nation is at war with Germany. It is unwise that we should be gathered here ... a large body of people ... during an air raid. I therefore ask you to leave the church in a calm and orderly fashion ... and return to your homes. Thank you. I will pronounce The Blessing:

> *The peace of God, which passeth all understanding, keep your hearts and minds in the knowledge and love of God, and of his Son, Jesus Christ our Lord ... and the blessing of God Almighty, the Father, the Son, and the Holy Ghost, be amongst you and remain with you always. Amen."*

Worshipers old and young filed slowly towards the exit doors but before we reached the vestry their whispered conversations had become a mezzo-forte babble. In the vestry, sombre adult choristers shared troubled thoughts while we boys quickly disrobed and exited into the bright shadows of the sunlit churchyard. Bill Macey and I threaded our way through small groups of adults in serious discussion who were blocking our pathway into Hendon Lane. "You scared Bill?" I asked as we crossed the road.

"Don't know really Al, just want to get home ... see you at choir practice if we ain't been bombed."

Our eyes, sharing unspoken doubts, met for a second before we scurried off in different directions.

I crossed Regent's Park Road at walking pace, then ran along the Avenue at full speed until I slowed to a stroll on reaching the park gates. Inside the grounds of Avenue House I felt safe, embraced by the canopy of tall trees and prolific evergreen bushes crowding the winding path. At the next gate I rejoined the Avenue – but my thoughts were unjoined – teeming with questions: "an air raid ... so soon ... so soon." I felt calm enough in my body but needed to clear my head – to stop and 'have a think'.

With my fingers gripping the wire-netting fence bordering Smith's Sport's Ground I surveyed the tranquil scene, drank in the greenness of the outfield and began to watch the groundsman, seemingly oblivious of the air raid warning, rolling the cricket pitch in preparation for the afternoon match. My mind relaxed, lost in a day-dream, visualising myself running up to bowl ... mmm ... "I've never played there ... wonder if it's a good wicket?"... when WHAM ... the day-dream was shattered by the banshee shriek of the 'ALL CLEAR' siren! My heart raced and nerves jolted as though I had been zapped by an electric shock from the wire fence ... "Jee-eepers!!"

Hundreds of screeching birds flapped into the air from surrounding trees – even the trees themselves seemed to rustle in bewilderment. For interminable seconds I was transfixed ... my mind frozen ... then re-engaged all my senses to kick-start my legs and run my fastest ever two hundred yard sprint. Phwew ... Home!

Mother and Father were relieved to see me. Obviously troubled and tense, they talked in hushed tones while preparing vegetables for lunch. "You'd better go in the garden, my boy," said Sam. "Your mother and I need to talk about what we're going to do."

"Do?" I thought, not daring to speak my own worried thoughts: "oh no, not evacuation ... I don't want to leave mummy and daddy ... or Derek ... or the cricket field." My tennis ball hammered the Wall ... again ... and again ... and again ... as I took refuge from all worries by focusing on my throw-dive-catch game. Mother called me in from the garden to join the Sunday ritual: lunch in the dining room around the long table dressed with white damask cloth, place mats, best cutlery and white linen serviettes rolled in silver plated rings. Father, as always, in a performance worthy of Stewart Granger in an Ealing Studios drama, duelled steel with steel to sharpen the carving knife before slicing the succulent joint of beef, allocating generous portions to three dinner plates – and a small well-chopped portion into Derek's bowl. Mother served home-grown vegetables and poured thick brown gravy from an elegant oval jug.

Banging his pusher and spoon on the tray of his high chair, two-year-old Derek was sternly 'shooshed' by Father as he waited for the wireless to broadcast the 'six pips' – his cue to command absolute silence in a tone worthy of an army chaplain about to say Grace: "The News!"

Even I ate slowly as we listened intently to the grave voice of the anonymous BBC announcer who stated that our government had not received a reply to their final ultimatum demanding that Hitler withdraw his troops from Poland. From the sonorous depths of his upper-class accent the announcer reported statements and opinions given by political leaders and establishment pundits. Then at 1.19pm the recorded voice of the Prime Minister, Neville Chamberlain, drearily intoned: " ... no such undertaking has been received ... consequently this country is at war with Germany."

Silence – a long deep silence!

A muted croak escaped from Mother's taut lips, "dreadful ... dreadful ... what are we going to do, Sam?"

To reassure himself, Father applied knife to steel again and proceeded to carve more slices from the joint: hushed seconds hung in mid-air before his throaty voice managed, "We'll have to wait and see, my dear, wait and see."

Mother cleared the dirty plates and escaped to the scullery, returning red-eyed with the traditional apple pie and a large jug containing thick custard. I tucked in and asked for a second helping, but such was the pall of gloom pervading that dining room I dared not say anything. I looked up at the huge gilt-framed lithograph depicting *The Relief of Mafeking* which hung on the wall to my right – a present from one of Sam's older brothers who served in the Boer War. "Real war must be awful," I thought, "and now there are bombers and tanks in a modern war." I was both frightened and excited and – as ever – needed 'a think'.

"Please may I be excused, Father?"

"Where are you going, my boy?"

"To the cricket field, Father. I'm on the scoreboard this afternoon."

"Well, all right. The match may be cancelled because of the war, my boy. If it is, you come right back ... and if those sirens go off again ... you come right back!"

"Yes, Father."

Derek, quite naturally, sought some attention and was demanding, "Dadda garden ... Dadda garden." Sam unstrapped his lively young son from the highchair and carried him, caringly and playfully, through the drawing room to the garden.

Mother, attired in a halter-necked floral apron she had made for herself, retreated into the scullery to wash up the big pile of plates, the saucepans and greasy utensils.

"You be careful, Alan, and come back here if there's no game."

"Yes, Mother, I'll come back ... but I hope they'll play ... I get two shillings for scoring on the board."

With that optimistic parting I escaped through the scullery door and side gate into Briarfield Avenue and sprinted the few yards to enter the haven of my happiness – my original theatre of dreams – 'That Field'.

But where were the people – the early-bird members and spectators – the players? Well, maybe Arden Field was mine alone – for a moment. Suddenly, for no reason at all, I felt I just had to run right round the ground, which I did, fast. Almost back to the starting point I paused, looked around me – still nobody in sight – sat on the grassy slope behind the boundary line next to a mound of grass cuttings tipped from the big Dennis mower on Friday ... "Hmmm, now I've had a run I need a think." So many questions tumbled around in my head. My earlier anger about the war had eased to annoyance. I felt strangely safe here ... sitting on the verge of the familiar green acres imagining ghosts of players past ... of great centuries and hat-tricks ... of tightly drawn games where no-one wins and nothing is lost but pride.

Momentarily I became lost in my cricketing reverie ... then shocked into awareness by the staccato rata-tat-tat of a motor bike as it accelerated down Briarfield Avenue within feet of my grassy haven ... "Machine guns! War! God!" I exclaimed out loud.

Annoyed again, I flung handfuls of grass into the shallow ditch behind me, murmuring, "Why does God allow war?" No answers. Playing with the grass for several minutes calmed me down; even my busy thoughts eased as I began to burrow one hand deep into the warm belly of that lightly compacted aromatic mound. Relaxed, burrowing deeper, my mind floated away into a spiritual day-dream half-way to somewhere else.

Rolling some warm grass between the palms of my hands to make a green hay-ball I seemed to be having a quiet discussion with God about the war ... as though He was one of the cricket club elders. Strange – but so real. I only

175

remember my closing words in that short discussion ... never-forgotten words burned deep into my memory:

"God, You understand why I'm so cross ... this war is really going to mess up my cricket career!"

I was eleven.

Now in my early eighties I am both amused and amazed that at such a young and naïve age I experienced, consciously, that powerful innate drive 'to understand'. Cricket and friends were the outward expressions of creative passion in my youth and young adulthood: 'to understand' was, and is, a lifelong inner desire beyond passion.

> *When I was a child, I spoke like a child, I thought like a child, I reasoned like a child; when I became a man, I gave up childish ways. For now we see through a mirror dimly, but then face to face. Now I know in part; then I shall understand fully, even as I have been fully understood.*   [Corinthians 1, Ch 13, verses 11-12]

Oh, and by the way, I have always loved grass.

Sergeant Sam Rayment rejoins the Special Constabulary, 1939

Alan St Mary's Finchley choirboy, 1938

CHAPTER 15

NEW SCHOOL, NO SCHOOL AND CHURCHILL

"We shall defend our island, whatever the cost may be."
Winston Churchill, June 1940

False alarm! The air-raid sirens that wailed in London and south-east England at 11.28am on Sunday September 3rd 1939 were switched on because Britain's pioneering 'chain home' radar system had picked up an unidentified aircraft flying from the Normandy coast towards Kent. The owner pilot of the small private plane had 'forgotten' to register the flight details before departure from the French airfield – an innocent mistake that created minor mayhem for millions of Brits and delayed the cricket match at Arden Field. But I did earn my two bob on the scoreboard.

After we had collected and stored the member's deck chairs my young pals and I had a serious natter about 'this war'. The only thing I remember is that we kept saying, "Messed up! ... everything's messed up!" By the time I went home for supper I was quite fired up and rabbited on about, "everything's messed up for everybody by that nasty little Nazi who has the impertinence to grow a Chaplinesque moustache and the arrogance to think he can invade the British Isles." My passionate oratory seemed to amuse my parents and, for a moment, ease the worried looks on their faces.

My first thoughts were that Hitler and his gang of militaristic thugs had not only wrecked my cricket career and education but nearly everything else in my young life except, thankfully, the stable home life provided by my parents. However, by Christmas 1939 my pals and I realised that we, and people in our local community, had adjusted and adapted to the reality of wartime conditions. The fear of invasion coupled with radical changes in daily living had stiffened the morale of British citizens, and a palpable spirit of people togetherness gathered momentum through the cities, towns and countryside of our threatened Islands. After the festive season the early bloom of that heightened community spirit began to fade as fear of invasion waned and we entered a period known as 'The Phoney War'.

So perhaps my life was not really 'messed up' – only changed and restricted.

Two positive changes were school and choir: the former requires a score in a major key so, first, I will play the choir in A minor. An eccentric segue maybe but my new choirmaster, Dr George Aitken, was a renowned eccentric who reigned over a magnificent parish church choir situated in a community teeming with characters in politics, in commerce, in the arts and show business – many of whom were palpably gifted eccentrics.

Hampstead: even typing the word makes me feel posh!

I was poached from Ivor Richard's excellent choir, St. Mary's-at-Finchley, to sing under the baton of Dr Aitken at St John's Parish Church near the Heath. What do I mean by 'poached'? A neighbour in Manor View attended our family musical evenings in the autumn of 1939, impressed us all with his warm, deep bass voice and evidently took note of my capabilities as a soprano. Unbeknown to me, Mr Harris was a member of the St John's choir and discussed with my parents his belief that my voice could be trained to become a principal soloist. I was duly auditioned, invited and began choir practice in early November. Several facets of my Hampstead experience are worth noting: the choirmaster; the music; the robes and the journey.

Dr George Aitken was appointed organist and choirmaster in 1894, served the St John's Church community for forty-seven years and retired in 1942. A virtuoso organist who revelled in playing an instrument built by a predecessor, the revered Henry Willis in the 1850s, Dr Aitken was prone to temperamental outbursts but respected by the choirboys because of his passion for the music, his ability to enthuse and coach us to a high standard of choral performance – and the sheer entertainment value of his quirky personality.

The music – I so enjoyed the music, especially two legendary choral works I had not sung before: Handel's *Messiah* at Christmas and sections of JS Bach's *St Matthew Passion* at Easter 1940. The robes: I preferred the red cassock with white surplice at St John's but took a while to get used to the lightly starched white ruffle collar which irritated my neck when looking down to read the score. The choirboys were friendly, the tenors less grumpy than at Finchley and the congregation full to overflowing on Sunday mornings. But I remember nothing about the Vicar, Reverend Herbert Carnegie, nor about the one solo I was privileged to perform before evacuation to Yorkshire.

However, memory is often most powerfully sealed into the sub-conscious when associated with a dramatic moment or a series of events that build into a habit. Given that the war was extant – though in the 'Phoney' phase – that I was eleven years old, that I would walk just over half a mile to St Mary's but have to travel an hour each way to St John's – five miles by bus or eight miles by the Tube – I am amazed, on reflection, that Father and Mother felt confident about me joining the Hampstead choir and allowed me to continue regular attendance when the 'war in the sky' began in mid-summer 1940.

I attended choir practice on Thursday evenings, Mattins and Evensong on Sundays – home for lunch in between. I remember several weddings on Saturdays and one funeral during the school holidays at Easter. On a fine day I travelled by bus from Finchley Church End (now Finchley Central), changed at Golders Green and caught another bus to Heath Street in the centre of Hampstead. On wet and cold days I travelled by Tube from Finchley Central to Camden Town, changed to the Edgware line and alighted at Hampstead

Station. Air-raid sirens wailed during the Battle of Britain but the dog fights were rarely enacted as far north as the skies above Hampstead. But just before Mother, Derek and I evacuated to Ripon the Luftwaffe began daylight bombing raids on London – the beginning of the Blitz. Travelling to Hampstead on my last Sunday as a chorister at St.John's I witnessed hundreds of families encamped on the platforms when I changed trains at Camden Town Tube station. Exiting the lift at Hampstead station a policeman prevented me from going into the street: "There's an air raid young man ... can't let you go out there yet."

"But sir, I'm in the choir at St John's ... and ... and I mustn't be late for the service."

Having sung my way through that choirboy adventure I must move the timeline back to September 1939 when we were adjusting to minor irritants such as the blackout, no league football and carrying a gas mask everywhere. But the major issues being talked about were evacuation and the status of my new school.

Evacuation to Australia? The directors of Father's employer, Martin & Savage Ltd, offered a family home in Sydney for Mother, Derek and me – all travelling and living expenses paid by the Australian branch of the company. I remember my parents being engrossed in a serious discussion before deciding not to accept the generous offer. Many years later I understood that a long separation between a couple so closely bonded would have caused unbearable anxieties. I admit to a brief day-dream about playing cricket for a school in Sydney – and, of course, on the famous Sydney Cricket Ground when older. In reality Arden Field and Lord's won my silent debate.

There was no debate about official evacuation from our area in London in the event of war because in 1938 the Government's Office of Works had classified Hendon and Finchley as 'neutral educational districts'. The school premises might be commandeered by the Army but otherwise would not be closed – subject only to the provision of air-raid shelters for staff and pupils. Although the local education authority and school boards must have had contingency plans to revise the management of schools in a war crisis they had not, understandably, built air-raid shelters before September 3rd. Therefore, our parents were anxious and uncertain about sending us to school only a few days after the declaration of war. But those parents who had a telephone received the official line: that Christ's College and Finchley County School had been requisitioned by the Army and were asked to spread the information by word of mouth that all pupils should stay at home until further notice. Information about the emergency plans would be circulated when finalised.

Finchley County School

The school badge with scimitars

My new school was originally opened in 1904 as a Higher Elementary School *'for children between the ages of ten and fifteen years who were likely to benefit from a more advanced course than that provided by an Elementary School.'* Awarded Grammar School Status in 1910, the co-educational community was situated on the Great North Road adjacent to the junction with the North Circular Road, opposite the Lido opened in 1932. During WWII twenty-two members of the teaching staff, under the headmastership of Mr Harold Chalk, taught, protected and cared for an average of 330 pupils. In the third week of September I joined my new classmates and teachers on the school premises for the first time.

What do I remember of my first day at Finchley County School? Well, I got up really early, donned my dressing gown, polished my black shoes, washed and cleaned my teeth, then dressed: underwear, white shirt, knitted school tie and long dark-grey worsted trousers, held by an elasticised school belt with snake clasp. My new smart look was completed by a dark-navy wool blazer with a school badge sewn on to the appropriate pocket – and I recall a feeling of pride when I donned the colourful school cap: cerise and navy circular bands divided by silver pin stripes, fronted with the special shield-shaped school badge. Why proud – why special?

Well, first I was still rather surprised that I had passed the eleven-plus examination and proud that I was actually going to a grammar school that day. Second: the design at the centre of the school badge consisted of three gold scimitars below a gold crown. Three scimitars! Gee ... the Middlesex County Cricket Club caps as worn by two of my heroes, Patsy Hendren and Denis Compton, depicted three scimitars in blue. Gee, I am wearing a cap that has a badge with three scimitars! That was very special to me.

I must have been buzzing with excitement because I am able to visualise myself walking over the railway bridge in Squires Lane to call on Len Pilditch, one of my best pals from Manorside, who was also starting at the County School. The excitement was a mixture of curiosity and uncertainty: what would the new teachers and classmates be like; would attendance at school be cancelled because the Army had taken over most of the premises; were the air-raid shelters going to be built? Questions, questions!

Changes, changes! During those early months in the war there were several changes of school organisation and location, the sequence of which is now unclear to me: I need help – phone a friend.

I phoned Len Pilditch, now in his eighties. Fortunately, my dear friend and team-mate has a remarkable memory. He proceeded to reel off in chronological order the major events and locations of our early wartime schooling.

> During that first wartime term we went to the school premises one morning and one afternoon each week. We were given loads of homework to supplement the ten half-hour lessons we

received. In January 1940 we started normal schooldays and timetabled lessons at Henrietta Barnett School in Hampstead Garden Suburb. Do you remember that long walk, Al ... the snow ... the cold classrooms? By the spring of 1940 there had been no obvious threat of invasion so the Army derequisitioned our school premises. We commenced full-time classes at Finchley County for the summer of 1940, but at the beginning of the Blitz in September a bomb that exploded on the glebe land opposite the school caused sufficient damage for our return to 'Henbarn' until Christmas. But you missed out on that second Hampstead trek because you evacuated to Yorkshire.

Thank you, Len, you have flipped my memory switch, and the pictures begin to roll. During those first wartime weeks, new school felt like no school – a vacuum of peaceful unreality poised to be filled by the anticipated reality of massive air raids by the Luftwaffe. The German bombers did not come – but surely would when the Nazis had completed their occupation of France.

I picture walking home from school during that first term with Len and neighbour Maggie Jones, each of us carrying the essential gas mask, a small suitcase loaded with text books and our satchels full of work set by teachers to occupy us at home. I was not a scholar or a swot and really needed a standard school structure to motivate even moderate study. In many ways I felt I was on holiday during that autumn term and spent more time with friends playing ball games on Arden Field than applying my energies to study. During our chat Len and I agreed that we quickly adjusted to our 'funny school routine' – 'funny' then being the idiom for 'weird'. We both have strong memories of the next adjustment to that 'funny girl's school', three miles away in Hampstead Garden Suburb, where standard full-time classes were organised for pupils of Finchley County at Henrietta Barnett Junior School from January 1940. 'Henbarn' and snow are forever associated in our minds.

The heavy snowfalls and icy pavements hampered our long walk to and from Henbarn – the wintry conditions were so severe that the River Thames froze over for the first time since 1888. Due to inadequate heating in the classroom it became essential to wear thick coats, scarves, mittens and woolly hats. But hey! – it was wartime – heating fuel was rationed so we 'got on with it' – thankful that we did not have to cope with bombs as well. Both the boys and the girls moaned a bit about the lack of soccer and netball matches against other schools but we stretched our lungs and limbs in snowball fights and competitive tobogganing on a variety of home-made contraptions purporting to be sledges.

At Upton Lodge we huddled round the old black range in the family room during week days to conserve fuel consumption. On Sundays Father laid and lit a coal fire in the drawing room – I loved the aroma of burnt toast and roasted chestnuts. As a family we occupied ourselves playing a variety of board games including Monopoly, cards and darts, reading and drawing; we listened to the wireless and sang round the piano. I enjoyed playing with Derek, zooming dinky toys down planks, building castles with large wooden bricks and reading stories. Despite the wintry weather I rarely missed my choirboy duties at St John's in Hampstead, travelling by the Tube because the bus services were unpredictable. Cinemas and the indoor roller-skating rink were warm and popular; shopping was a chilly chore – complicated in January 1940 by the first use of ration books.

Every family had to register with one local butcher and one grocer. For each person the first commodities rationed were: butter 4 ounces (100 grams); sugar 12 ounces; bacon or uncooked ham 4 ounces – and 2 eggs. In March meat was rationed by price: 1 shilling and 2 pence would buy two small pork chops or 8 ounces of mincemeat. Many families combined their meat rations to buy a small joint to roast for Sunday lunch; all the left-overs were saved to serve cold on Monday or minced for Shepherds Pie. Offal, poultry, game and fish were not rationed.

The Ministry of Food originally promoted the food rationing scheme as a means of distributing supplies more efficiently. However, the increasing loss of merchant shipping to German submarines and mines constituted a major threat to essential imports of food; also to supplies of raw materials needed by manufacturing industries for the production of vital armaments. From September 1939 to the end of February 1940 over 140 British merchant ships had been sunk, total tonnage approximately 650,000, in addition to a considerable tonnage of neutral merchant ships destined for ports around the British Isles. Although the war at sea had no defined beginning and end, the first major escalation – declared by Winston Churchill as 'The Battle of the Atlantic' – began several months later when, during the month of April 1941, nearly 700,000 tonnes of merchant shipping were sunk and thousands of crew killed.

Despite the first death of a British civilian in March 1940 during a German air raid on Royal Navy ships in Scapa Flow, Orkneys, the relative normality of everyday life on the mainland encouraged the government to lift the ban on spectator sports and entertainments that attracted large crowds. In March the FA's wartime format for Regional League Soccer kicked off in Birmingham. In the same month the Oxford and Cambridge Boat Race attracted thousands of spectators at Henley-on-Thames.

Long queues snaked round cinemas showing the bumper crop of films made in Hollywood and British studios in 1939. There were so many stellar performances by actors and actresses that deserved Oscars: Robert Donat in *Goodbye Mr Chips*; James Stewart in *Mr Smith Goes To Washington*; Bette Davis in *Dark Victory* and Greta Garbo in *Niniotchka*. *Gone With The Wind* won the Oscar for Best Picture and the English actress, Vivien Leigh, lifted the spirits of British film-goers by winning the 1940 'Best Actress Oscar' for her role as Scarlett O'Hara in that film. Too young for Scarlett but I was in a bubble of happiness as I exited our local Odeon having been bowled over by Judy Garland and her friends in *The Wizard of Oz*. Singing – I couldn't stop singing – '*Somewhere, over ...*' and ... '*We're off the see the Wizard, the jolly old ...*' My own jolliness flowed into joyful hymns on Easter Day as I let rip with my new mates under the eagle eye of the idiosyncratic Doctor at St John's.

Easter heralded the green shoots of Spring: holidays, longer warmer days and the phut-phut sound of the Dennis mower shaving Arden Field's green acres. I was longing to begin cricket practice when the outfield dried after the rains. The aromatic ceremony of applying linseed oil to my precious size-five Jack Hobbs bat highlighted my anticipation of the new season. I was sure I would play for Finchley Juveniles 2nd XI ... but would I be good enough to play for my West House team at school? Might I even squeak into the County School second eleven ... after all, I would be twelve in May.

My cricketing speculations were stimulated by official notification that we were to attend our own school premises from April 1st. The winter sojourn at Henbarn had acquainted members of my class year with new subjects, enabled us to develop new friendships and form personal opinions about the teachers. Reminding myself that all the teachers at Manorside Juniors had been female, I was delighted to experience male teachers for the first time in my life. I did not actually dislike any of the teachers – though a few were rather dull in personality. My favourites were Miss Martin, History; Miss Peeling, English; Mr Howland, Art; Mr Murphy, Physics and Mr Corns, Geography. I also enjoyed Mr Sturdy's classes in Wood and Metalwork – oh, and Biology with Miss Comber. The PE and Sports Master, although efficient, did not inspire me.

On reflection I have the greatest admiration for all the teachers, the caretaker and his wife, the administrative and catering staff, who coped so well with the many changes of venue and wartime regulations during those first five terms, remembering that many had their own family responsibilities to consider. The headmaster had reorganised the daily timetable and general operation of the school to encompass the wartime regulations and conditions. Teachers and senior pupils had helped dig foundation trenches for the air-raid shelters, criss-cross the tall windows with buff-coloured parcel tape, install blackout curtains and prepare 'dig for victory' vegetable plots on the Back Field. Builders had completed the concrete-roofed, brick air-raid shelters.

Male teachers who had been called up for military service were replaced by retired County School veterans, including Mr Murphy, Mr Corns and Mr Quilliam. I already knew 'Potts' Murphy because of my mother's friendship with his wife: Mrs Murphy's intervention when I was in danger of starving at four months saved not only my life but my parents from the agony of that ordeal. I had visited the Murphys' house several times with my mother for afternoon tea when I was at junior school and found Mr Murphy to be an enthusiastic and knowledgeable Middlesex cricket supporter.

The County School's sports ground was just over a mile away, next to the premises of Woodhouse Grammar School. The cricket pitches at Hilton Avenue were well prepared and safe; the outfield on the soccer pitches well mown and rolled. Whereas I have some memory of cricket at Arden Field in 1940 I have no recall of matches for West House or junior FCS teams at Hilton Avenue. Nor can I remember a Sports Day for athletics: perhaps the event was cancelled due to the crisis of Dunkirk and ensuing Battle of Britain.

Despite holding a strong majority of seats in the House of Commons, Neville Chamberlain's Conservative government approached the serious need to re-organise the nation's economy, manufacturing industries and even the military services, with a feeble lack of common sense let alone intelligent awareness. That many historians depict the Phoney War period as a failed opportunity by the Luftwaffe to bomb south-east England in preparation for a German invasion is, in part, true. It is also true that Chamberlain's Cabinet did not face up to the reality of the German threat to our islands. Writing about our nation's un-preparedness in the spring of 1940, the historian AJP Taylor comments:

> *The government were still moving into war backwards, with their eyes tightly closed. Churchill was the one exception, a cuckoo in the nest, as restless against inaction as fertile with proposals ...*

The British public woke up to the government's ineptitude following an aborted military campaign to prevent the Germans occupying Norway and Denmark. A three-day debate in the House of Commons, commencing on May 7th, resulted in the resignation of Neville Chamberlain as Prime Minister and the appointment of Winston Churchill at the head of a National Coalition Government composed of the three main political parties. Clement Attlee, Leader of the Labour Party, became Deputy Prime Minister.

On that same day, May 10th, Hitler's tanks and infantry, supported by the Luftwaffe, poured into Holland and Belgium, swiftly overpowering defending armies. The Phoney War was over: so was the era of the appeasers supporting Chamberlain and Lord Halifax. When the House met on May 13th the new Prime Minister, Winston Churchill, was cheered, paradoxically, by the Labour members – the deposed Neville Chamberlain by the heads-in-the-sands Conservatives. Churchill, a mixture of visionary and pugnacious realist spoke bluntly to the elected Members in the Commons that day: the recorded speech broadcast to the nation that evening reassured the British public with words that thrilled me then and still tingle my nerve-ends in the 21st century:

I have nothing to offer but blood, toil, tears and sweat. You ask, what is our policy? I will say: It is to wage war, by sea, land and air, with all our might and with all the strength that God can give us. You ask, what is our aim? I can answer with one word: Victory – victory at all costs, victory in spite of all terror; victory however long and hard the road may be.

However, the Foreign Secretary Lord Halifax would not let go of his almost paranoid belief that a peaceful settlement could be negotiated with Hitler through the offices of Mussolini, even though that would entail the loss of some peripheral territories, cause rearmament to cease in Britain and the Commonwealth and for our nation to be governed by a puppet administration which Hitler controlled.

Churchill was adamantly opposed to such a notion but, being unpopular with the majority of Conservative MPs – his own party – had to steer his way through a series of serious diplomatic meetings with the inner circle of the War Cabinet between May 25th and 28th in order to retain his position as Prime Minister. Finally, Churchill convened a meeting of the full 25-member Cabinet and spoke openly and unreservedly of his analysis of the critical situation and his conclusions.

At the end of his address to that powerful group of experienced Labour, Liberal and Conservative politicians Churchill stated:

> I am convinced that every one of you would rise up and tear me down from my place if I were for one moment to contemplate parley or surrender. If this long island story of ours is to end at last, let it end when each one of us lies choking in his own blood on the ground.

Churchill was agreeably surprised by the reaction of his decision-making audience:

> There occurred a demonstration which, considering the character of the gathering, surprised me. Quite a number seemed to jump up from the table and come running round to my chair, shouting and patting me on the back. There is no doubt that had I, at this juncture, faltered at all in leading the nation I should have been hurled out of office.

One commentator proposed that by establishing unrivalled leadership that day Churchill saved Britain and perhaps Western Civilisation from the threat of Nazi domination.

The Times reported that on that same day, May 28th, the Belgium armed services, who were fighting side by side with the French and British defending the northern approaches to the French port of Dunkirk, were withdrawn from the conflict on the orders of King Leopold, their Commander-in-Chief. The

Belgium Prime Minister and senior politicians objected, stating that the King's decision was contrary to the constitution but had no power to reverse the decision because their army had already capitulated. Churchill, in a statement to the politicians assembled in the House of Commons noted that they would be aware of the Belgium situation, then added:

> Whatever our feelings may be on the facts so far as they are known to us, we must remember that the sense of brotherhood between the many peoples who have fallen into the power of the aggressor, and those who still confront him, will play its part in better days than those through which we are passing. The situation of the British and French Armies, now engaged in a most severe battle and beset on three sides from the air, is evidently extremely grave ... the House should prepare itself for hard and heavy tidings. I have only to add: that nothing which may happen in this battle can in any way relieve us of our duty to defend the world cause to which we have avowed ourselves; nor should it destroy our confidence in our power to make our way, as on former occasions in our history, through disaster and through grief to the ultimate defeat of our enemies.

The Kid felt reassured, consciously thankful that in the crisis of now and the perilous months ahead we, the British people had a real leader, a man of strong character who was not only not afraid of Hitler's Nazis but believed we would win the war ... "however long and hard the road may be."

That long hard road was just beginning.

CHAPTER 16

DUNKIRK AND THE BATTLE OF BRITAIN

"we shall never ... surrender!"

Winston Churchill, 10 Downing Street, London, 1940

Winston Churchill's broadcast speeches remain among my most powerful and abiding memories of living in London in the 1940s; not the days and nights spent in air-raid shelters; not the rationing, the blackout or the interrupted rhythms of school and family life; not the drone of German bombers nor the occasional bomb exploding nearby, but Churchill's speeches. His unique oratorical style, his sonorous voice tones, clipped phrases and timed pauses – his undoubted passion, transparent determination and utter confidence inspired every man, woman and child during those anxious months of our nation's *Darkest Hour.*

Seventy years later I still get goose bumps on my goose bumps whenever I hear, or read, or write those stirring historic words. Even as my fingers drill this keyboard, Churchillian tones rise from the depths of my being, my pulse races and eyes moisten ... *"we shall not flag or fail."*

We shall not flag or fail. We shall go on to the end. We shall fight in France, we shall fight on the seas and the oceans, we shall fight with growing confidence and growing strength in the air, we shall defend our island, whatever the cost may be. We shall fight on the beaches, we shall fight on the landing grounds, we shall fight in the fields and in the streets, we shall fight in the hills ... we shall never ... surrender!

Churchill addressed the House of Commons with that rousing *'rally to the cause'* speech, broadcast later on BBC radio, the day after the last British and French troops had been evacuated from Dunkirk on June 4th 1940. On that dark day our homeland was isolated and vulnerable – the people anxious. Churchill's speech made clear the spirit and the intent of the British people: to defend our land, our families, our freedom and our democratic way of life ... *at all costs!*

We were on our own.

DUNKIRK

That one word encapsulates the reality of the miraculous evacuation of 338,226 British and 139,097 French soldiers from the small French port and its adjacent beaches in Normandy. I feel a strange personal connection with that historic event because my future father-in-law, RSM Kenneth de Torre, RE, MBE, survived that dramatic retreat and recovered to serve in, and again survive, the Burma campaign and the infamous Battle of Kohima. I was privileged to meet many of Ken's comrades at annual reunions in Eastbourne and, sharing an ale or two, listened to the stories of their harrowing experiences, their humour and their deeply-bonded companionship. Those veterans were forever thankful for the skill and bravery of their rescuers at Dunkirk, especially the men who crewed 'The Little Ships'.

From many ports, little harbours and river moorings in south-east England, 860 fishing boats, river ferries and small leisure craft – some helmed by professional seamen but many by amateur weekend sailors – ferried the English Channel alongside sleek destroyers of the Royal Navy to rescue those British and French soldiers from the carnage experienced in the retreat to, defence of and disembarkation from Dunkirk. To balance the outpouring of heartfelt thanksgiving by the British people for the rescue of so many young men –and some women in uniform – the human casualties need to be remembered. During that two-month campaign in France, 68,111 British military personnel were killed. We also lost all the military equipment of the British Expeditionary Force. During the evacuation six naval destroyers were sunk and nineteen damaged. The RAF lost 474 aircraft. The Miracle of Dunkirk was a narrow beam of light shining in the bleakness of *Our Darkest Hour.*

The Little Ships at Dunkirk, 1940

Six weeks from the commencement of the German Blitzkrieg through Holland, Belgium and northern France, the French leaders capitulated to the Nazi invaders. Sadly, the senior French politicians and generals, divided on policy and tactics, failed to defend their proud homeland and signed an armistice with the invading Nazi leaders on June 22nd. I shudder, even now, as I recall cinema newsreels showing German tanks thundering down the Avenue des Champs-Elysees in Paris ... a sickeningly incongruous experience, even though I was twelve and had never been to Paris.

Also rather sickening was the sycophantic behaviour of the Italian fascist dictator, Mussolini, who had been in power since 1922 and had posed, only three weeks earlier, as a neutral peace-broker between the British Foreign Secretary, Lord Halifax, and the German Chancellor, Herr Hitler. Now that Hitler's hoards were in Paris, Mussolini became fearful that his Italian fascists would miss out on the spoils and declared war on the Allies on June 10th.

Hitler and his henchmen now controlled the western seaboard of Europe from the northern tip of Norway to Biarritz on the French-Spanish border. U-boats, operating from ports along that two-thousand-mile coastline, sank so many merchant ships carrying vital supplies to Britain that they posed as great a threat to our survival as the Luftwaffe. The United States continued to ship essential supplies to Britain but remained politically neutral, sitting on the fence regarding total commitment to 'freedom's cause'.

Britain and the Commonwealth stood alone in that darkest hour.

The feeble pacifism maintained by the United States of America was shattered eighteen months later on December 7th 1941 when thrust into the war by the Japanese air attack on Pearl Harbour, Hawaii. Apparently, in that critical summer of 1940 the majority of politicians and citizens of the United States of America were not seriously concerned that the might of the German war machine was based along the coasts of Belgium and France, poised to cross 21 miles of the English Channel and invade the land of their British forebears, extinguish the foundations of democratic freedoms – to be replaced with totalitarian control and potential genocide.

We were seriously on our own!

Thankfully, we in Britain did have the support of the peoples and resources of the Commonwealth nations, without whom the struggle would have been even harder – maybe impossible. Importantly, despite the odds stacked against us, we displayed the stubbornness and bloody-mindedness of the British psyche that rises to the surface when we find ourselves in a 'backs-to-the wall' situation.

Bolstered by Churchill's declaration of fighting intent and heartened by the escape of so many dads, sons, husbands and boyfriends from France, the British people got busy with schemes large and small which might thwart the Nasty Nazis, should they have the temerity to contaminate our shores. The Home Guard – 'Dad's Army' – recruited over a million men: road signs and street names were removed, booksellers destroyed maps, primitive road blocks were erected, machine-gun pill boxes built and more children evacuated from southern cities to the country. Over 2,600 children from London's East End were shipped overseas.

Fortunately for us, Hitler and his High Command had made no preparations for an invasion and concentrated on completing the campaign in France. On July 2nd, Feldmarchall Wilhelm Keitel noted in his diary: 'the Fuehrer has decided that a landing in England is possible ... *providing air superiority can be attained* ... all preparations to be begun immediately.' The flamboyant Hermann Goering, Commander-in-Chief of the Luftwaffe, believed that the British would surrender following a full-scale blitzkrieg by his bombers, after which a costly invasion would not be necessary because the Germans would be able to cross the English Channel and occupy Britain virtually unopposed. Goering's arrogance and egotistical fantasies caused him to demand several unrealistic goals from the Luftwaffe, decisions that, in part, eventually caused the numerically superior and otherwise well-organised Luftwaffe to lose the key battle of the skies.

Spectating the spectacle of Spitfires and Hurricanes duelling with Messerschmitts in the airspace over London in the late summer of 1940 was an awesome and never-to-be-forgotten experience. My friends and I were enthralled by the vapour trails criss-crossing the skies to the south and east of us as we proudly and uninhibitedly cheered those brave young glamorous RAF pilots who were our heroes – later to be immortalised by Churchill as 'The Few'.

Although my pals and I were still in our first year at grammar school we were well enough informed to be aware that the outcome of 'The Battle of Britain' would determine whether or not Hitler's armies would attempt to invade our country and curtail our freedom. Yes, we were proud, patriotic, optimistic and adventurous. Many of us wished we were eighteen and could join the Forces to fight the Nazi military machine that had swept with such relative ease through the Low Countries and France to command the coastline on the opposite side of the English Channel. Might the Nazi Storm-troopers soon try to ferry 'The Ditch' and land on our shores we wondered? We were all avid listeners to BBC radio, read the newspapers and voraciously absorbed everything portrayed on newsreels in the cinemas. Though young and unworldly we were seriously conscious of the plight of our Nation.

That we 'backs to the wall Brits' not only survived but turned impending defeat into miraculous victory is the story of 'The Battle of Britain'. We held on during the massive German bombing raids on Britain, then turned the tide with the RAF's devastating air raids on their cities and industrial complexes. That is the full story of 'The Blitz'.

THE BATTLE OF BRITAIN

The historic air battles above the counties of south and south-east England are very well documented in print and on film. I would recommend young people to borrow a few books and a film or documentary from the local library in order to taste – maybe begin to feel – a tiny morsel of the reality my generation not only experienced to some degree, but also *knew for sure* that to lose the battle would mean our country would be invaded, the direction of our young lives changed radically and our freedoms eliminated. The danger was real ... really real!

That the Royal Air Force won the historic encounter was, of course, due to a multiplicity of complex factors, the most trenchant being the strategic and tactical brilliance of the RAF High Command combined with the skills, heroism and stamina of our fighter pilots, their ground crews and support services. A major factor in the victory was our newly invented and installed radar system. Air Chief Marshal Sir Hugh Dowding and his senior colleagues out-thought and out-classed the German High command; Spitfire and Hurricane pilots out-fought and out-classed the Luftwaffe aircrews.

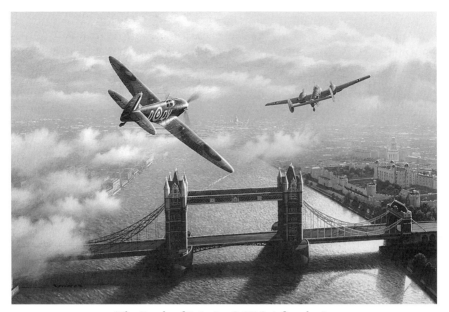

The Battle of Britain: RAF Spitfire chasing
a Luftwaffe Messerschmitt 110 over London's Tower Bridge

The historian AJP Taylor states:

> Dowding had two invaluable assets. The first was radar ... the
> second himself. Like all great commanders he had a clear picture
> of the battle he was about to fight and how he would win it.

Evidently Dowding and his 11 Group Fighter Command Chief, Air Vice-Marshal Park, resisted efforts by chiefs of staff and Churchill himself for more dramatic action. Another historian, James Collier, summarises this important factor in our victory:

> Whereas Dowding and Park proved capable of standing up to
> men who wanted them to do the wrong things, their German
> counterparts proved incapable of standing up to Goering.

Prior to the main aerial battles of 1940, the numerical strength of the Luftwaffe based across the Channel was: 1,131 medium range bombers; 316 dive bombers; 809 single engine fighters; 246 twin engine fighters and 150 reconnaissance aircraft. In addition, a reserve fleet of 130 bombers and 80 fighters were stationed in Denmark and Norway.

The RAF could muster 700 Spitfires and Hurricanes, plus two squadrons of slow out-of-date Boulton Paul Defiants. The 100 twin-engined Blenheim fighter-bombers also proved to be slow and lacking manoeuvrability and were assigned to night defence and light bombing raids. As the Battle of Britain progressed, men and women working day and night shifts in our factories maintained high production levels of aircraft to replace the inevitable losses. Our most serious problem was the lack of trained aircrew to fill the places of so many of 'The Few' killed in action in the defence of the nation.

On July 10th the Luftwaffe stepped up attacks on shipping convoys plying British waters from Aberdeen in Scotland to Cardiff in Wales, bombing many of the ports along that extensive coastline – with Dover being a particular target. The first phase of the anticipated battle for control of Britain's air space had begun. Though heavily outnumbered, our fighter planes successfully defended the convoys against the German bombers and Messerschmidtt 109 escorts. From July 10th to August 10th, the Luftwaffe lost 227 aircraft; the RAF lost 96.

Although Hitler and Stalin had signed a pact of neutrality in August 1939, there was mutual mistrust between the fascist and communist leaders and their respective advisers – each faction suspicious of the motives and territorial ambitions of the other. When Russian forces occupied Estonia and four other Baltic States in June 1940, Hitler's anxieties about Stalin's intentions caused further prevarications about an invasion of England. However, further consultations with his Army and Navy chiefs convinced the Fuehrer that, on condition that the Luftwaffe gained complete air supremacy, an invasion across the English Channel would be successful.

However, being aware of the potential danger of a 'second front' opening up against the Soviet Union, Hitler's Directive No.16 to his High Command on July 16th summarised the Nazi leader's caution:

> As England, in spite of the hopelessness of her situation, has shown herself unwilling to compromise, I have therefore decided to begin to prepare for, and if necessary carry out, an invasion of England.

A further directive on August 1st stated:

> In order to establish the necessary conditions for the final conquest of England the Luftwaffe will proceed to overpower the English air force in the shortest possible time.

The key phase of the battle for air supremacy commenced on the 12th of August when the Luftwaffe launched a full-scale pre-invasion air attack on southern England. Hundreds of twin-engine Dornier and Heinkel bombers, escorted by a full complement of Messerschmitt 109 fighter planes, attacked our airfields, radar stations and communication centres. Aircraft factories and ports in the rest of the country were also heavily bombed. The RAF was stretched to the limit: airfields took a pounding – some became unserviceable – thankfully for very short periods. Mechanics and airfield support staff, including thousands of members of the Women's Auxilliary Air Force, did a magnificent job in maintaining the serviceability of the airfields – all heroes and heroines in their own right. Tragically, so many of the front line heroes – the pilots and aircrews – were killed or seriously injured ... so many others shattered with exhaustion.

Hitler and his cohorts could not understand why we did not capitulate; that we could be cheerful was beyond their understanding. The British people 'carried on as usual' – indefatigable, courageous and cheerful, going about their daily business on farms, in offices, schools and factories. Those living in Essex and Kent, Sussex and Surrey, Hampshire and the Isle of Wight – when not diving for shelter – were partisan spectators of the appalling yet enthralling mayhem in the skies above. Death and damage, loss and sorrow, fear and courage, doggedness and cheerfulness permeated every minute of every day. Battered yet holding on, hoping that we would hold out, the civilians worked and prayed while our gallant armed services fought and prayed – then fought some more. Would we win?

Would our RAF pilots in their Spits and Hurrys out-manoeuvre and out-class the Hun in his surely inferior Messerschmitts? Would 'our boys' shoot down so many German bombers that Hitler would be deterred from his planned invasion? Trained fighter pilots were our most precious and scarcest resource – we were losing too many. Would the very young, newly trained pilots survive their first 'dog fights'? In reluctant desperation the Air Chiefs permitted a small group of Polish, Czech and Israeli pilots serving in the RAF to enter the critical air combat. Their extreme hate of Nazis contributed to a high success rate of 'kills'.

We, the proud British people, knowing the consequences of failure, cheered the victories of the RAF and hoped that our factories were producing enough aircraft to replace the considerable numbers shot down in battle.

We need not have worried.

When Churchill became Prime Minister in May 1940 he immediately appointed the dynamic and controversial Canadian owner of the *Daily Express* newspaper, Lord Beaverbook, as Minister for Aircraft Production. Beaverbrook muscled aside all political obfuscation and bureaucratic procrastination to get the job done. Ernest Bevin, Minister of Labour in Churchill's Coalition Government, was a tough and intelligent socialist politician who had created and led the Transport and General Worker's Union. Bevin teamed up with Beaverbrook to organise the massive recruitment and training of the labour force necessary for the expansion of aircraft production.

In the factories, skilled and unskilled workers rose magnificently to the crisis, setting aside trade disputes and battles with managements to work very long hours. Thousands of new workers, the majority of whom were women, trained in new skills to raise production levels far beyond previous norms and expectations. The production target of Spitfires and Hurricanes for the month of May 1940 was 261 machines. The initiatives taken by Beaverbook and Bevin pushed actual production to 325. In June 446 fighter planes rolled out of the factories and were flown to RAF airfields by the Air Transport Auxiliary, the majority of whose pilots were female. In July and August a total of 972 new aircraft were delivered to the RAF.

The co-operation between Beaverbook and Bevin – two leaders from opposite ends of the deeply embedded class structure – caused one social historian to comment:

> This most spectacular, as well as the most important, single incident in the history of war production was crowned with success.

Another author not only highlights the vital roles played behind the scenes by Beaverbrook and Bevin, but also praises those who 'did the job':

> … justice must also acknowledge Beaverbrook and Bevin were immensely aided by the sudden realisation on the part of the British workforce that the moment indeed cried out for supreme efforts. The end of the dismal Chamberlain regime, the debacle in France, the escape from Dunkirk, Churchill's eloquence and honesty – offering only 'blood, sweat, toil and tears' – created a mood in which, for a time at least, cherished trade union restrictions could be swept aside and a willing labour force work its heart out in long hours of overtime.

Indeed, the mood of the whole country was one of supreme effort and cheerful defiance. The success of the aircraft industry meant that the RAF had more serviceable fighter aircraft after the Battle of Britain than before that crucial engagement began. But there continued to be a critical shortage of trained pilots. Young veterans flew many missions per day until overcome with exhaustion; the even younger, newly trained pilots flew bravely into the aerial conflict without battle training. Too many did not return.

Goering, who had assumed that his Luftwaffe would achieve victory over the RAF in two weeks, was shocked by the success of the RAF in aerial combat, the resilience of the ground defences and the indefatigable spirit of the British people. Angry and determined to destroy the RAF, the petulant Goering ordered heavier and more frequent bombing attacks on the RAF's '11 Group' airfields in late August. Fighter Command's resources were stretched to the absolute limit. The scoreboard count of losses in grounded fighter aircraft was considerable. In the air battles between August 13th and September 6th the RAF lost 400 aircraft; the Luftwaffe 670, plus many that crashed before making it back to German airfields in France. Not all the pressure was on the RAF: interrogation of captured German aircrew indicated nervous exhaustion and a considerable reduction of morale in the Luftwaffe.

Fear probably induced the unconscious human error by a Luftwaffe aircrew that led to profound ramifications of historical proportions and radically changed the military tactics extant in opposing High Commands. In retaliation to an 'own goal' error by a Luftwaffe aircrew, the public morale of the German people received an unexpected and almost unbelievable blow. Berlin was bombed by Britain's Royal Air Force! Berliner's were shocked and their confidence in the Luftwaffe severely shaken:

> How can they do that? Surely we are out of range – we are almost 1,000 kilometres from London. Why didn't our Luftwaffe protect us?'

The fateful chain reaction was sparked by a German Dornier pilot and navigator in a raid on south-east England on August 24th 1940. In order to avoid heavy ack-ack fire the pilot changed course and gained height – then jettisoned his bomb load. But the navigator had made a serious miscalculation and the bombs fell on the City of London – the first since the Gotha bomber raids in 1918. The aircrew were severely reprimanded by their senior officers because Hitler had retained sole authority regarding the bombing of Liverpool and London.

Churchill and his service chiefs ordered a retaliatory raid – immediately! The next night 80 RAF Wellington and Hampden aircraft rained high-explosive bombs down on Berlin. Hitler and his High Command were staggered – their pride and that of the German people severely dented. After the RAF's third bombing raid on Berlin in four nights, a resident American newspaper correspondent wrote:

> The Berliners were stunned. They did not think it could ever happen. Goering had assured them that it couldn't. Their disillusionment today is even greater. You had to see their faces to measure it. (W Shirer)

Hitler met with Goering on August 30th and reversed his ban on the bombing of London. In a Directive on September 5th he ordered:

> ... harassing attacks by day and night on the inhabitants and air defences of large British cities, especially London.

The Fuehrer's vengeful reaction also had a tactical and strategic motive in that the Luftwaffe top brass believed a major bombing attack on London would induce great air battles in which the remnants of RAF fighter command would be destroyed.

The German perspective is succinctly summarised by Hough and Richards:

> ... there was an overall strategic motive to bring about the conditions for invasion or British capitulation. A grand assault on London, it was hoped, would create administrative chaos and terrorise the British into submission.

The date for the invasion, code-named 'Sealion', was now fixed for September 21st.

However, Hitler's air commanders, Goering, Kesselring and Sperrle, had made serious errors in their intelligence gathering and subsequent planning at this critical juncture in the battle for air supremacy. Overall, the arrogant mind-set of their Nazi philosophy often outweighed their undoubted intellectual and organisational brilliance. Three major miscalculations thwarted their egotistical assumptions. First, German opinion of the remaining defensive capabilities of the RAF was warped by highly inaccurate claims by Luftwaffe pilots of the number of aircraft they had shot down, combined with over-estimates of the number of British airfields and aircraft production factories destroyed. Second, the fact that by extending the range of bombing attacks to the London area, the short-range Messcherscmitt 109 fighter escorts would only have ten minutes' combat time over the British capital. Third, the indefatigable spirit and indescribable work ethic of the British leaders, workers and *ordinary* people – all of whom proved to be *extraordinary!*

Meanwhile, the Germans continued intensive preparations for the invasion of England. Hitler remained adamant that before the final orders were given the Luftwaffe had to establish air superiority over the Channel and southern England. In early September Goering and Kesselring still believed that RAF Fighter Command was so depleted and dispirited that it was ripe for a knock-out. On the other hand, Admiral Raeder and the German Naval Staff were less confident that the Luftwaffe would gain sufficient air superiority to support landing craft against the powerful Royal Navy. Doubts about the efficacy of Operation Sealion among the German Army and Navy chiefs were also conditioned by Hitler's remarks in July that it might soon be necessary to take the initiative against Russia.

The turning point in the Battle of Britain occurred on September 7th when the Luftwaffe massed 1,000 aircraft to bomb London in daylight followed by a heavy night raid. The change of target, though calamitous for people and property in London, actually created a reprieve for the RAF's heavily damaged airfields in southern England. The repair and refitting of those airfields proved to be another major factor in staving off near defeat and eventually winning that historic battle in the skies.

History also records that, following the first huge raid on London, the escalation of bombing by the Luftwaffe devastated many British cities and caused thousands of deaths and injuries to their citizens. Over the next eight days thousands of tons of bombs and incendiaries rained down on Southampton, Portsmouth and Merseyside; on major cities in the Midlands and south Wales in addition to the Luftwaffe's main target, London. In that period, the Germans were again surprised at the strength of our resistance, losing 135 of their aircraft against 94 RAF losses. Hitler again postponed the decision to invade England – the revised date now being 27th September. In preparation for their planned invasion of our shores the German Navy had transported thousands of barges to ports in Belgium and northern France, some loaded with tons of military equipment – others ready to carry 500,000 troops across the English Channel. The threat of a land war on British soil was an imminent reality.

On September 15th the Luftwaffe made its last great pre-invasion effort to bomb the British people into submission as wave after wave of bombers unloaded their destructive cargoes on London's dockland. But again, the people responded with immense fortitude and courage, pride and ineffable humour – and the RAF shot down sixty German aircraft while losing less than half that number. Two days later Hitler once again postponed the invasion. On October 12th he cancelled Operation Sealion for the winter. He also ordered that night bombing of British cities be escalated and replace major daylight raids from mid-September.

In his famous speech to salute 'The Few', Winston Churchill expressed the depth and warmth of our nation's gratitude to the pilots and ground crews of the RAF who had, against the odds and with tenacious bravery, won the battle of the skies over southern England – and thus saved our nation from invasion.

The odds were great; our margins small; the stakes infinite. Never in the field of human conflict was so much owed by so many to so few.

CHAPTER 17

EVACUATION, THE BLITZ AND MAYOR'S CUP

Dunkirk, the Battle of Britain and Winston Churchill symbolised the resolve of the British people to defend democracy and their homeland. In the darkest hours of 1940 the waters of the English Channel proved, once again, to be our greatest protector from invasion.

For my parents, Sam and Wyn, the times were particularly worrying and perplexing. The following conversation combines snippets lodged in my memory, augmented by sensitive creative intuition from my clear picture of the occasion:

"Why – oh why, oh why?" exclaimed Wyn, furrowing her brow and shaking her head from side to side, "why, after the terrible lesson we learned – or thought we had – from the last lot ... only twenty and a bit years ago ... why did we let that so-and-so Hitler rearm Germany so quickly? Now we're being bombed again and trying to shoot down their planes, like we did – or you did, Sam – attempt to shoot down those dreaded Zeppelins last time."

"Soft, we've been too soft, Wyn," stated Sam, "too soft, and too late preparing our military for this war because the last one was so terrible ... cost millions of lives ... we thought it could never happen again ... thought it was 'the war to end all wars'. Now this time, after the defeat in France, we're really on our own ... the war is on our doorstep ... well, in our skies. We're in for a tough time from the Luftwaffe, Alan, my boy. Yes, it's all very worrying! But then, when I think about it, in 1915 we had no real air defences at all when the German Zeppelins started dropping bombs on London. Thankfully, no family or friends were hurt, though later I was shell-shocked by one of our own – and the rest is history, my boy."

History! We were actually living through one of Britain's – indeed the world's – most challenging historic crises. Would our democratic way of life survive or be overwhelmed by totalitarian dictatorships? That Hitler's generals had amassed half a million troops and thousands of barges to effect an invasion of British shores was a reality. Thankfully, the Nazi storm-troopers and Panzer tanks never landed on our shores, but the Luftwaffe bombers continued to invade the skies over Britain.

THE BLITZ

The severe night-time bombing of London, the major British ports and provincial industrial cities by the Luftwaffe, lasted from September 1940 through the long winter months to May 1941. London, attacked every night

The Blitz: picture taken from roof of St Paul's Cathedral, London, on December 30th 1940: the dome of the Old Bailey Court survived

The Blitz: Londoners sleep in Piccadilly Tube station during an all-night Nazi bombing raid, September 1940

from September 7th to November 2nd, was devastated by high-explosive and incendiary bombs. In the first week of the Blitz my father's office in the City, close to the Bank of England, was levelled to a heap of rubble, and my school in the suburbs of north London was severely damaged by a parachute mine. Therefore the staff and pupils of Finchley County would return to Henrietta Barnett School in Hampstead. Would I join the Henbarn trek again? My parents, bless them, decided on a wise course of action: evacuate to Ripon in Yorkshire.

Private arrangements were made to stay with close friends of the family with whom we had spent enjoyable holidays before the war. 'Aunt' Rose Taylor and her retired father lived at the end of Canal Road in a delightfully spacious home with extensive gardens. 'Field House' was a welcome and comfortable refuge for Mother, Derek and me from September to late December 1940.

Having helped with the move, Father returned to London to continue his job from offices in Great Portland Street and his duties as a sergeant in the Special Police. Mother's feelings were divided: thankful that her boys were safely out of London, yet understandably anxious that her husband was plying his trade travelling around central London by bus and Tube during the Blitz. As ever, Wenner Rayment 'just got on with it', thankful for the caring support of Rose and her elderly father.

As a twelve-year-old, blond-haired bundle of energy I had to adjust and 'get on with it' too. I missed Father, of course – and Arden Field, St John's choir, my best pals Len, Dave and Dick – also the good-natured banter of my co-ed school mates who were veterans of air raids, dog-fight watching, shelters and shrapnel collecting. In comparison, life in and around the ancient city of Ripon and its grammar school seemed so detached from the war – so quiet at night and unhurried by day.

At first I found it strange to be in an all-boys class in an ancient school that had existed in Saxon times and was re-founded in 1555AD. I was fascinated by the design of the school badge: a quartered shield depicting crossed swords, crossed keys, a portcullis and the Town Crier's horn – not a scimitar in sight. The motto in Old English meant, 'Eager to learn and seek after righteousness'. I didn't want to be righteous, but in general I adjusted, once again, to a new environment. Yes, I was eager to learn, to make friends and play rugby. On the other hand my heart ached for familiar places and faces in Finchley.

This octogenarian begins to chuckle as I recount the few memories retained from that short spell at Yorkshire's Ripon Grammar School. First, the amusing atmosphere created by the language barrier when norf lunnun speak met yorkie dialect ... 'ee lud tha noes ... awlreet.' My musical ear tuned in so rapidly and completely that on my return to Finchley three months later my mates and their parents needed an interpreter. In my first couple of weeks back home I was the butt of much leg-pulling and several jokes: "Ay, mate, yer ain't a bleedin' spy are yer ... lann-ed by parachute, did yer?" ... or: "wat planit did yer visit, Al? ... der one wif der bleedin apes, I rekun." Musical ear soon changed key, and I was back on form with my repertoire of accents from near-cockney to posh BBC, and from Aussie to Irish to Jewish, to which I now added an almost genuine variety of West Riding. I continue to enjoy the distinct sounds and subtle variations of tone within every regional dialect in Britain, and ... but I digress.

Second contrast: no girls. As I may have said before, and will certainly emphasise in a later chapter, girls in the classroom were a norm from day one of my education. They were mates wearing skirts instead of trousers. But girls certainly added variety, colour, character and naturalness to everyday school life. I discovered that an all-boys classroom was more serious and competitive – and less fun. So I was glad to return to the familiar co-ed atmosphere and London humour at Finchley County for the spring term of 1941.

However, I do not want to give the impression that life in Ripon was all dull and dour – it was just different. One important element in our education is absorbing and understanding values, tastes and lifestyles unlike our own. Those months living in Yorkshire were a valuable and happy experience for me, though rather expensive for my parents who had to buy a new school outfit and a complete set of rugby kit. I really enjoyed having a crack at 'that other' winter sport and have a vivid memory of my first outing in the 'third game'.

The Stiffs were a bunch of non-athletic twelve-year-olds, some fat, some unfortunately mildly asthmatic, some spindly, bespectacled bookworms half-blind without their glasses. I was rather miffed that the games master assumed that because I was a soccer player I would be no good at rugby. "Hmm ... a touch of the North-South divide and snobbery about the round ball game. I'll show 'em!" Unfortunately I entered that first game with an unconscious handicap.

I always cycled back to Field House for lunch, and on that particular day Aunt Rose, thinking naively that a sturdy meal would give me extra energy for the afternoon's combat, served up a full roast meal with Yorkshire pudding followed by a generous helping of apple pie and custard. A kind thought – I enjoyed the meal but was not experienced enough to realise the possible consequences.

Ripon GS was rightly proud of its wonderful playing fields – acres of neatly mown grass which I loved, of course – and I was excited that I was about to run around out there to try my ball skills with a leather 'thing' that was not even round. Lots of Yorkie banter in the changing room as I donned my new kit and, while wondering why the boots studs were a funny shape, the booming voice of the master-in-charge silenced the jabbering: "All outside ... thi' know thi' teams an t'positions ... er ... 'cept Rayment. You'll be t'hooker for thi blue team, lud."

"What does a hooker do, Mr Blaithwaite," I queried.

"Ee-e leads t'scrum, lud ... I'll show thi ont' pitch."

Having glimpsed a few rugby scenes on a cinema newsreel I had a vague ideas about a scrum but was surprised to be in the middle of the front row. Non-athletic maybe, but those young Yorkshire lads used the scrum as a licence to have a disorganised scrap ending in a heap of wriggling bodies. After extricating myself from the bottom of the heap for the third time I felt nauseous: bent double I staggered to the touchline and unloaded Aunt Rose's magnanimous offering. Still on my knees I saw the oval ball bouncing towards me ... looked around ... no other players within thirty yards. Instinctively, I crossed the touchline, picked up the ball and ran unchallenged to the goal line. Try!

Rules? Rules and Tries were minimal in the 'third game', so Mr Blaithwaite blew his whistle and said to me, "Well done, lud, thi runs fust so thi'd better go on't wing. By t'way, thee's a soccer player so 'ave a go at t'conversion." He scratched his head when I set up the ball sloping towards me so I could kick it, soccer style, with my instep, but as it sailed between the posts remarked, "Ee lud, thi can kick t'ball reet good, too." From left-wing three-quarter I scored three mores tries – easy really because the opposition were so slow – and converted each one. For the rest of the term I played proper rugby with athletic boys in the 'first game', represented my house in the Under-14 competition and played in three matches against other schools.

Rugby – ah! but what about cricket, especially as I was in Yorkshire where cricket was a religion and Len Hutton the Master. Fortunately, Brian Husband – who was my age and at Ripon GS – and his younger brother, Alan, lived in one of the cottages in Canal Road a few yards from Field House. Both were typically cricket-mad Yorkies, who, incidentally, I was pleased to meet up with again at Headingly eleven years later when I happened to score a few runs against Trueman, Appleyard and Wardle.

But in 1940 the three of us played street cricket in our cul-de-sac next to the canal for hours on end. A lot of the time we played 'wet creeckit', as Brian would say, often carrying on with our game in fine mist-drizzle and spending too much time playing another game – ball fishing. To retrieve tennis balls from the canal we had tied a fisherman's landing net to a roach pole. A 'lost ball' cost the batsman a deduction of ten runs and an apology to Aunt Rose who, having a grass tennis court in her garden, supplied the used balls.

I have fond memories of life at Field House; of happy laughter in the huge kitchen as Mother and Aunt Rose prepared and cooked experimental dishes, combining the meagre rations with abundant winter vegetables from the market; of home-grown fruit and home-made jam secreted away in preserving jars. Both ladies played the piano, a grand piano indeed, which made me fantasise that the Taylors must be very rich when, in fact, they were moderately well off. Mother ensured that I practiced my singing, and our hosts often invited friends to a musical evening when everyone would perform. I would sing *O For The*

Wings of a Dove and try new songs introduced and coached by Mother. Before his bedtime, brother Derek – then three and a half – stood confidently beside the piano, singing nursery rhymes and hymns – the star of the show.

Derek was not only a ball of energy with a blond top but also a gifted ball player, and as soon as he could crawl I played 'throw-and-catch' with him. And, of course, like all small children who discover that a new skill is fun and draws excited praise from adults and siblings, Derek threw everything within reach – toy bricks, Dinky toys and apples. To Derek an apple was a ball; not plums – and there were no oranges in wartime – only apples. Before Derek was three, Father bought a toy cricket set from Woolworths, and I cut down the blade of the bat to fit my talented brother. During our time in Ripon the weather was most often chilly and wet but one sunny Sunday in December Derek joined the big boys in a proper game of cricket on the tarmac beside the canal. The Husband brothers were very impressed with his ability and style; they only regretted that neither Derek nor I could ever play for Yorkshire. They are wonderfully tribal, those Yorkies.

Cricket, rugby, singing, new friends, Rose Taylor's warm hospitality and wonderful food highlight happy memories of our evacuation to Ripon. But Mother, Derek and I had missed Father; we were continually concerned about his safety as the heavy bombing of London continued. Thankfully he had remained safe and well and joined us for a sumptuous Christmas at Field House.

In Ripon Cathedral on Christmas Day 1940 I let rip when singing the familiar hymns, yet felt uncomfortable listening to some of the words in the bible readings and communal prayers. Maybe I really listened because I was not in the choir but sitting with my parents and the Taylors – or maybe because of my experience in Arden Field the day war was declared ... whatever the unfathomable reason ... a few words from the Gospel story of the birth of Jesus lit up in my mind:

> And suddenly there was with the angel a multitude of the heavenly host praising God, and saying: *Glory to God in the highest, and on earth peace, goodwill to all men.*

Though my young mind reached no conclusions I still remember the puzzle I was trying to solve: "If God loves us and wants peace and goodwill among all the people on *His* earth, why doesn't He stop this terrible war?"

A few days later we returned to normal family life in Finchley – normal in that prior to our idyll in Yorkshire we had become accustomed to the dangers and restrictions of life in wartime London. We bade farewell to our Yorkshire hosts on Ripon station and boarded a steam train bound for London – a very slow train diverted from the main route due to bomb damage in the King's Cross area. I remember that we completed our journey to Finchley on a Green Line coach from a station somewhere in Hertfordshire.

Back home – and back under the stairs that same evening we listened to the ack-ack guns during a major incendiary raid by the Luftwaffe that destroyed many as yet undamaged historic buildings in central London. While Father was on police duty or fire watching, Mother, Derek and I spent many unsettled nights under the stairs until the middle of April when our Morrison indoor shelter arrived. Father and a friend erected the monster steel table-cage in the dining room under the stern gaze of *The Monarch of The Glen*. Derek and I were tucked up inside Morrison every night until sometime in the summer of 1941.

Although very few bombs exploded in our area the sirens wailed regularly until the end of May when the Luftwaffe moved most of their bomber squadrons from western France and Belgium to bases in eastern Germany and Poland. The tide of war was changing, moving east to Russia and south-east to North Africa.

Before the final ebb of the Blitz the Luftwaffe bombed Liverpool for eight consecutive nights in May. Hull, Belfast, Clydeside, Birmingham and Manchester were also targeted by large numbers of German bombers. On May 9th over 500 Heinkels and Dorniers rained incendiaries and high explosives on London, crippling the rail networks. The next night London suffered its heaviest air raid of the war: the colossal damage made one-third of all streets in Greater London impassable, killed 1,436 people, seriously injured 1,792 and left 155,000 people without gas, water and electricity. In the previous month a total of 6,065 British people were killed in air raids and 6,926 injured. Those two examples of air-raid casualties in Britain in that critical phase of the war, harrowing in their reality, were fewer than the casualties being inflicted on the populations of German and Nazi occupied industrial cities by our squadrons of long-range RAF bombers.

In January 1941 I began the new term at Finchley County School. The bomb damage had been repaired, the air-raid shelters completed and permission granted to return to the premises beside the Great North Road. No doubt all pupils and staff who had trekked across the suburban streets to Henbarn while I was in Ripon were relieved to begin the Spring term at 'home'. My classmates, twenty boys and seven girls, welcomed me back with reservations about 'that foreign accent'. I relished the sense of belonging and being among familiar faces again – faces that faced each other for too many hours across the narrow dank belly of the air-raid shelter. And gas-mask drill? The fusty rubber smell – stink really – still roams in my sub-conscious as I type. We read a little, sang a lot, made up our own lyrics to a few popular songs – especially *All Over The Place* which became our class signature song: *All Over Two B*. The words were not only topical but expressed our youthful confidence that *'we will win this war'*. I wish I could remember those lyrics.

However, bright is the remembrance of my exuberance when playing soccer that term and, of course, cricket in West House and school teams the following summer. I was also enthusiastic about the gym apparatus attached to the walls and high-cross girders supporting the elliptical glass ceiling of the Assembly Hall: the wooden wall bars, the beam and the ropes – especially the ropes. For PT, gymnastics and sport the boys and girls were separated, though the A and B classes combined each term to play a truly competitive 'boys-v-girls' netball match. Thankfully however, we were not as aggressively competitive in any sport as school children in the 21st century. Different era – different values. Sport was fun and I loved it all – except boxing.

Although at the age of 12 to 13 I was not fully aware of my natural athleticism I revelled in every opportunity to attempt a new sporting skill or enter competitive events on Sports Day – or the next year at the Swimming Gala. Boxing was the exception. Why? Because I hurt one of my best mates. Under the supervision of our sports master, Mr Champion, the boys in our class tied on the gloves to begin instruction in the basic techniques of boxing – beginning with defence. Towards the end of the first session Mr Champion told us to pair up and have a friendly bout: "concentrate boys ... concentrate on keeping up the -guard ... gloves high, boys." Well, it so happened that I had 'quick hands' and, quite unintentionally, I threw a rapid left-right and caught Len Pilditch on the side of his jaw. Down he went, not 'out' but dizzy ... and I felt sick in my stomach. "Len, Len ... are you all right?" "No, I'm not bleedin' all right ... that hurt!" Thankfully, we are still friends.

From disaster in the gym to triumph on the soccer pitch. Len and I were members of the school's Under-14 Soccer Eleven who beat the champion soccer school, Christ's College, in the final of the Mayor's Cup in 1942 at the Finchley Football Club ground in Summers Lane.

Feelings of team triumph – and a few pictures – are still clear in my memory. However, in 2005 I phoned two team-mates to check the validity of those mind-pictures. I had not seen or spoken to my good friend Len Pilditch since the 1970s, or Derek Humberstone since 1944. Not only was it a joy to have a yarn over the phone but also a great bonus that both Cup Final medal winners embellished the story with more background and detail than I had remembered.

First of all, Derek and Len gave good reason as to why that one match is so imprinted in our minds, as indeed it is in the minds of non-playing members of our class year with whom I have spoken more recently. Basically our victory was a David versus Goliath triumph because Christ's College had a population of 500 male pupils compared to the 160 boys at our co-ed school. Christ College's domination on the sports field over other schools in the area was a legend.

In addition, Derek and Len reminded me about the equipment used in those days, which, although the same for both teams, seems laughable today and certainly inhibited our development of the refined skills attained by young players in the modern era. The thick leather boots were chunky and laced high on the ankle – and stiff if not regularly 'dubbed' – the toe caps were thick rock-solid leather akin to metal-capped miner's boots. The ball ... ah ... the all-leather ball with protruding leather thong laces!

If the pitch conditions were wet and muddy – as they were for our Cup Final – even a new ball would absorb water and become swollen and heavy before half-time; dangerous for youngsters to head and difficult to control long passes and corners. And in that particular match, given the wet conditions and Finchley Football Club's steep-sloping, maximum-sized pitch – and the reputation of the opposition – the stamina, character and high level of team spirit in the County School's Under-14 XI proved to be key elements in our victory.

We were a noisy bunch of north London kids, anxious but confident. My nerves evaporated as soon as my studs dug into the soft turf, and I was running rather than chattering. Shouting, waving school scarves and stamping their feet to keep warm, parents, teachers and pupils from both schools formed the largest and noisiest crowd we had experienced – well five hundred anyway.

We lined up in the standard formation of that era: goalkeeper, two full-backs, three half-backs and five forwards. Tom Mackenzie, our captain and best player, was a tall powerful athlete who dominated the defence at centre-half. Len played at right half, Derek outside-right and, being a two-footed player, I roamed around from the inside-left position. Christ's College attacked from the kick-off and almost overwhelmed our defence. But Tom Mackenzie was an excellent leader who skilfully marshalled his colleagues in defence: Ron Lence, Dennis Weaver, Mike Cain and Len Pilditch – our goalkeeper Ron Pick was the youngest player. That we won, eventually, was due to Tom's brave play and leadership in marshalling a superior defence.

Our attack made occasional raids on the College goal, and there was a lot of scrappy play in mid-field until our opponents scored a goal just before half-time. We were a little disconsolate, but Tom kept our spirits up and we levelled the score early in the second half with a poacher's goal from Iky Cowan, our centre forward. Both teams were now attacking, and play swung from end to end – which meant that wing-halves and inside-forwards had to cover a lot of ground. Our defence blunted yet another College attack, and Len bought the ball out of defence to the halfway line, causing the College mid-field to scamper back towards their penalty area expecting a diagonal cross. But Len moved forward with the ball and passed to Derek who took it another twenty yards along the touchline. Meanwhile I held back from the rush into the penalty area, and, unmarked, yelled and yelled "Humby ... Humby!!!" Derek slotted a perfect cross-field pass along the ground into the vacant space just outside the penalty box for me to run on to ... I let the ball pass in front of me to have greater control – then drove it with my left foot.

As I type this story sixty-odd years later, I 'see' the flight of that ball into the top corner beyond the goalie's outstretched right arm as though I am watching a 'slow-mo' replay on television in the twenty-first century. And, as I think about it now, I am only able to recall that sequence of passes from Len to Derek to me ... and the flight of the ball into the net, in very slow motion. Call in the psychologist. I have no picture – no memory at all of what happened next, nor do I remember the Mayor presenting the Cup to the deservedly proud Tom Mackenzie.

One humorous detail came to light when I discussed the event with octogenarians Len and Derek, both of whom exclaimed, "And we are still waiting to receive our medals!" I laughed and asked to be enlightened.

"Well," said Len, "when the Mayor presented the Cup to Tom he made a little speech, congratulated both teams and apologised that due to wartime restrictions there were no medals to present to the winning team. But he promised he would see to it that the Finchley Borough authorities would send each one of us a winner's medal after the war. Before the end of the war we had all left school and forgotten about those medals – but I hadn't." Neither had Derek.

> *Bliss in possession will not last;*
> *Remembered joys are never past.*

James Montgomery, 1825

~ ~ ~ ~ ~ ~ ~ ~ ~ ~

Finchley County School Under-14 Football XI, winners of the Mayor's Cup, 1942
Mr H. Chalk (headmaster); R. Lence; A. Cowen; R. Pick; L. Pilditch;
Mr Champion (sports master). Sitting: M. Cain; A. Rayment; A. Sylvester;
T. Mackenzie (capt); D. Humberstone; D. Weaver; A. Cutting

CHAPTER 18

HAPPY DAYS IN WARTIME

'Remembered joys are never past.'

I love that line by Scottish poet James Montgomery. It resonates within – gives me a warm feeling in a similar way to certain song lyrics – *Somewhere*, for instance: Sondheim's words surrounded by Bernstein's music sung by Streisand turns me into a jelly of joy with droplets of tears.

Unhappily, tears of sorrow abound in wartime among peoples of all nations involved in the conflict. In our local community many friends, and people we knew well, experienced the devastating effects of loved ones killed or injured. The brothers of David Limbert and Dick Nelson – two of my best pals – were 'killed in action'. My dear cousin Tilly waited four years for the release of her fiancé, John, from a German prisoner-of-war camp.

Loss wounds the hearts and souls of those who mourn, of those who care for their injured or wait for news from prisoners-of-war. But although in many families the barometer of human emotions may have been volatile, the down-to-earth day-to-day business of contributing to our nation's war effort continued unabated, whatever one's task or role. Morale continued to be high through 1941 – and lifted higher in 1942 and 1943, as the British, American and Commonwealth forces defeated General Rommel's German and Italian armies in North Africa and followed up with the invasion of Sicily. The tides of war were turning in the Allies' favour: my young friends and I were sharply aware that the direction of our young lives was utterly dependent on the Allies winning the war in Europe.

Happily, we spent much more time on normal everyday activity than serious thinking or friendly discussions about the war. Some of my 'remembered joys' in 1942 and 1943 are from special occasions – a holiday at Elmer Farm in Suffolk for instance – while others popped up during routine events.

Well, perhaps a Sunday lunch in March 1942 was more than a routine event, especially as Mother had saved enough ration-book coupons to buy a good-sized joint of meat. Having consumed succulent roast beef with Yorkshire pudding, vegetables and gravy, followed by apple pie and custard ... yes, the spices too, Father announced to four-year-old Derek and me that we were going to move from 34 Manor View to a house in Briarfield Avenue.

At first I was rather shocked but Father explained that as our lodgers, the Richards family, were moving out, Upton Lodge was now too big for the four of us and too much work for Mother. But shock soon turned to joy when I realised that number Twenty-Three Briarfield Avenue was in line with the cricket table in Arden Field. After lunch I ran up the road about eighty

*Brothers
Alan and Derek,
23 Briarfield Avenue,
Finchley, 1942*

*Brothers Sam and Bert
at 23 Briarfield Avenue,
1942*

yards and stood at the gate of number 23, thrilled to see the heavy-timbered, white sightscreen obscuring my view of the wickets. In fact the location of the sight-screen was close to the spot where I had had my debate with Mr Big on September 3rd 1939: "I know You know, God, that this war is really going to mess up my cricket career."

The move was fun – and hard work clearing out lots of 'stuff' not needed in the smaller house. Number 23 was a neat three-bedroom property in an elegant terrace, with two reception rooms, a decent kitchen and bathroom – oh, and a lean-to conservatory enclosing a coal store and small workshop. The garden led directly on to tennis courts and a bowling green that nestled between the rear gardens of four roads – a private haven for well-behaved children – miscreants banned. Father set up his HQ in the shed, reorganised the garden and let me use the small workshop for woodwork, mending things and experiments. For a while I became interested in chemistry, learned how to make stink-bombs but preferred wood carving and model making. I continued to enjoy reading books from the library, a weekly comic and newspapers – and became keen on drawing with pencil or charcoal ... mostly furniture, street scenes and trees. I loved trees almost as much as grass: was I really a country boy trapped in suburbia? Thinking about that question in the 21st century, my subjective answer is that the suburban environment was balanced by my emotional bonding with nature; also my second home, Arden Cricket Field, was now literally 'over the road'.

Before we moved house, and before the cricket season started, I had won a prize in the County School Eisteddfod for the best soprano voice. I was pleased: I enjoyed singing and winning. I was not so pleased when the music master, Mr Johnson, informed me that I was to perform at an Evening Concert for parents. Whereas I felt comfortable when singing the occasional solo in the ambience of St Mary's Church (I had rejoined that choir on return from Ripon), to be alone up there on the bare stage of the school hall that doubled as the gym would be embarrassing. I was not nervous, just reluctant.

"Oh well, I suppose I'll have to," I said to Mother as we sorted through some sheet music the evening before the concert. We agreed on the *Londonderry Air* and rehearsed for half an hour, but I had difficulty remembering the lyrics of the second verse. I was so unsure that I scribbled all the lyrics on a bit of paper and shoved it in the top pocket of my blazer.

While Father stayed home the next evening to look after Derek, Mother and I walked down Squires Lane to the County School where she joined the chattering adults and I linked up with other performers in a classroom screened from the stage. "Shuuusshh ... keep it down," boomed teacher Jones in an attempt to quell the high-energy buzz bouncing off walls and ceiling, "save it for your act."

"Well," I thought, remembering the humiliation of the disappearing Bunny at Manorside – "at least I don't have to act, only sing." I went over to Mr

Johnson, handed him Mother's rather dog-eared sheet music and had a quick chat about pace and holding the high note in the seventh line of each verse.

Mr Johnson was a popular teacher, respected not only for his abilities and warm personality but also because he had been crippled through polio: he had one leg in irons. When I made my stage entrance he was already seated at the upright piano, ready to accompany my rendition of *Danny Boy*. Mildly nervous yet remembering to project my voice to the back of the hall, I thanked the Eisteddfod judges for awarding me first prize and announced to the audience the title of my song. Mr Johnson played the introduction, I came in came in on cue ... *Oh Danny boy, the pipes, the pipes are cor-or-lling* ... – pitched and held the high note – then took a deep breath after the last phrase of the first verse – *I love you so*. Quick thought, "That went well," as I listened to the interlude before the second verse ... then *calamity*! The sheet music floated through the air and soft-landed on the stage beside me.

Two corners of the dog-eared score had decided to join each other as Mr Johnson turned the first page. He stopped playing. Unable to move from the piano stool he motioned to me to collect the sheets. But first I apologised to the audience and said I would sing the first verse again. I replaced the sheets on the music desk. Mr Johnson smiled and calmly played the introduction. I hit and held the high note, focused on the page turning moment – then blanked – no words in my head. Red-faced and perspiring, I whipped the scruffy bit of paper from my top pocket a split-second before my first bar and sang the words ... the words of the first verse ... *for the third time*. Instantly I was cross with myself ... but inwardly I was chuckling.

Without hurrying I powered my way through the last verse, determined to finish in style. The applause was loud and long: were the adults expressing release from their own embarrassment or expressing support for the beetroot-faced singer? Moments later Mr Johnson was helped down from the stage, smiled and said, "Well done, Alan ... thanks for helping me out." Kind man, Mr Johnson. Mr Jones looked at me and 'huummphed'.

And why was I chuckling? I can't remember. Writing about the event now I feel as though I'm hitting a couple of sixes having been dropped in the slips three times in a row.

From singing to swimming – and larking about at Finchley Lido opposite our school on the Great North Road. Opened by the Duke of York (later King George VI) in 1932, the grand swimming-pool complex provided an inexpensive playground before and during the war. On hot summer days and holidays my pals and I enjoyed diving in and out of the fifty-metre heated pool and chasing each other around the spacious poolside facilities. Hundreds of people flocked to the Lido to swim, socialise and sunbathe – to cool off in the shade of the colonnade or douse under one of the magnificent fountains. By the age of eleven I had plucked up courage to dive from the second highest board and could swim a width under water. On hot days during the later stages of the war the pool was popular with County School pupils during the lunch break. How lucky we were to have such a healthy and inexpensive recreational facility just over the road.

The Lido experience reminds me of another enjoyable outdoor activity during the war that began on my fourteenth birthday. I was surprised when Father came home early from work that Friday and said he wanted to take me shopping. I was more than curious: "Father home early? Shopping at tea time? Must be a birthday cake ... but Mother always bakes the cakes ... she wouldn't forget my birthday cake." We walked at a quick pace up Litchfield Grove, round the corner into Regent's Park Road and through the door of Mr Ames' bicycle shop. "Hello, Sam, I was waiting for you before I locked up ... oh, and happy birthday, young Alan."

"Thank you, Mr Ames." I knew he was a friend of Father's in the 'Specials' but had no idea why we were in his shop.

Mr Ames reached into a row of bikes and released a brand new Raleigh with 24-inch wheels and ... and a Sturmey Archer 3-speed gear in the rear hub!

"I think this is the one you wanted for young Alan, Sam," said Mr Ames as Father, with a twinkle in his eyes, took the handle bars, rang the bell and exclaimed: "Ding-ding ... ding-ding – sold!"

I was speechless ... open-mouthed ... momentarily dumb with excitement: "Daddy, Daddy ... for me ... a brand new Raleigh ... with a three-speed gear ... and a dynamo for the lights ... really for me?"

"Yes, my boy, a special birthday present from your mother and me ... anyway, you are too big now for your old 18-inch bike."

"Thank you, thank you, Daddy!"

Father and I walked the bike home to find Mother waiting, excited and beaming with happiness – we were all beaming with happiness – Derek, too. He immediately asked to be lifted on to the saddle and wheeled down the garden path. I was itching to ride my gleaming posh bike so, with Father in attendance, I ventured along the wide-gravelled pavement of Manor View. I wobbled but did not fall off.

That Raleigh bicycle was the best and most surprising birthday present of my young life. Family and friends reading this in the 21st century may be puzzled by that statement. 'Why so special?' you may ask. For several reasons: first, my parents could not really afford to buy a new bike. I expect that Father arranged some friendly credit with his policeman friend ... but to Sam and Wyn it was a secular sin to be in debt, however small. Second, young people in our neighbourhood did not *expect* to receive expensive birthday presents during the war.

Cycling alone, or with friends, the Raleigh gave me a new freedom – a freedom to adventure around the countryside beyond Totteridge and Mill

Hill, to cycle to school and sports grounds and, best of all, to go fishing with Father. We ventured to ponds at Elstree and the reservoir at Aldenham, caught roach and perch and the occasional eel. Time spent with Father coarse-fishing and angling greatly strengthened the bond between us. He was a countryman, knowledgeable, patient, and a good teacher. Fishing with Father is one of my special *remembered joys.*

In contrast I had not been keen when Father asked me to help with digging or planting on his two allotments early in the war. Any enthusiasm I might have had about the 'Dig For Victory' campaign was deflated when I helped him trench the virgin soil of his new passion. The land commandeered for allotments had been pasture for Deard's lovely shire horses – not really virgin soil but thick tufty grass 'dobbined' with shit. Being eleven years old, the combined plots looked like two acres needing a plough rather than a small spade. After two long sessions Father could see that I was fed up ... really fed up ... and signed me off so that I could join my mates to kick a soccer ball around on Arden Field. On the plus side Father's labours of love produced masses of succulent vegetables throughout the war, benefiting the health of neighbours and friends as well as our small family.

Recent research into healthy eating has highlighted a conclusion that in WWII the majority of the British families enjoyed a healthier diet than in the modern era. Rationing was severe but home-grown vegetables and apples were plentiful. I made a brief mention of rationing in a previous chapter and, though the subject is vast, I will summarise a few of the facts and my experience of rationing. However, to young people living in the twenty-first century, I do recommend a browse on the internet ... you will find statistics of the shortages horrific and some of the foods we ate unbelievable. We were fitter with less available – you are fatter with more.

Rationing of petrol began in September 1939 and lasted until May 1950. By the middle of 1940 all meat (except offal), bacon, butter, sugar, tea and margarine were rationed. In 1941 cheese, eggs, jam, clothes and coal were added to the list. The next year coupons were required for rice and flour, dried fruit, tinned tomatoes and peas, sweets, chocolate and biscuits. Supplies of coal, gas and electricity were rationed by volume or time (hours available in any one day). Many non-rationed foods were in short supply – therefore a 'first come, first served' system often created long queues for fruit and sausages – sometimes for bread.

The Ration Book was as essential on a shopping trip then as a passport at Heathrow Airport today: no coupons – no food. Although the amount of food available varied according to supply a typical average 'per-adult – per week' might be: 6 ounces of meat (150g); one egg; 4 ounces of fats (butter, margarine, lard) 100g; 4 ounces of cheese (100g); 8 ounces of sugar (200g); 2 ounces of tea (50g); 2 ounces of sweets (50g). Bread was not rationed until after the war, and coupons were needed for meat until 1954.

Clothes rationing was more complex: for adults the sixty-six points allowed each year was the equivalent of one complete outfit. A new raincoat or overcoat required 16 points, trousers 8, a shirt or blouse 5, a woman's dress between 7 and 11. Clothes for growing children had a lower-points value to allow for expansion in size and extra shoes. Many women – even some men – made their own clothes from old garments, curtains and even blankets. Knitting needles clacked throughout the country; Mother and I unravelled dozens of old jumpers and rewound the wool for her to knit new garments. Off-ration parachutes were big-game – captured during and hunted down after the war – the white silk or nylon being ideal for making ball gowns, wedding dresses and underwear. The motto 'Make do and mend' is embedded in my psyche; I still hang on to frayed clothes and worn-out shoes for far too long before chucking them into a recycle bin.

Contrasting austerity with abundance, a well-remembered joy in 1942 was the family summer holiday at Elmer Farm in Suffolk. The first memory is of Mother and Father holding long discussions about 'the weather'; that we would have to pack clothes for all seasons – sun, wind, rain and mud – then helping Mother fill a trunk and two heavy suitcases which were forwarded to Finningham by Carter Paterson's parcel service.

Having boarded a Northern Line Tube at Church End, Finchley, I became impatient with being underground for nearly an hour and thankful to breathe fresh air – well half-fresh, half-smoke-laden air under the awning of Liverpool Street Station. "Ah! proper trains!" I exclaimed excitedly: steam engines and soot, carriages with clunking doors, guards whistles, porter's sack trucks and taxis, all backed by an orchestra of steam blasts and hissing pistons ,accompanied by the human hubbub – a choir of a thousand unmatched voices scurrying to and fro. As always, I revelled in the sights, sounds and smells of a railway journey – especially our magnificent Gresley B17 4-6-0 locomotive which Father and I duly inspected before the guards blew whistles and waved flags.

While Gresley chugged slowly but resolutely through inner London and its north-east suburbs, I observed flattened acres of brick-rubble, twisted metal and splintered timbers, overshadowed by precarious tall jagged walls standing guard over the ruins of their one-time functional beauty. I felt sad ... people had lived there, worked in the factories and offices; many were killed, injured, in hospital *now* ... I couldn't look anymore, said I was going down the corridor to the toilet, and cried. I felt better after Chelmsford and began to enjoy the flat farmland and pastoral colours of East Anglia.

"Finningham ... Finningham," boomed the porter from the narrow platform of the Victorian station where Doris, my 26-year-old cousin, greeted us warmly and drove us in her Hillman car to Elmer Farm. More warm greetings from Father's older brother Charles and his wife Kezie – who even gave me a hug.

Their thatched, white-limed cob farmhouse was certainly old and picturesque but rather too olde worlde for this 14-year-old suburbanite as there was no electricity or running water. The infrequently used front door led to a Sunday's only drawing room on the left ... on the right the family's general purpose living room-cum-kitchen dominated by a big open hearth, a long pine table and an enormous old-fashioned water pump beside the stone sink. I was fascinated by the rituals required to start the oil lamps used for lighting and cooking; their aroma, when combined with the wood fire under the wash-boiler and the frying of bacon and eggs, created a distinct country odour which I called 'that Elmer smell'.

Uncle Charles leased the twenty-five acre Elmer Farm and managed an adjacent five-hundred-acre arable and dairy spread owned by Mr Prescott, a wealthy American businessman whose family were the first US citizens I had met. I was fascinated by the strange 'music' of their East Coast accents, their colourful clothes, the beautiful Buick, the battered Jeep. They lived in London but spent occasional weekends and summer holidays at 'The White Lodge', a modest modern country house on the estate.

All the farming operations were directed by uncle Charles. Doris was the capable and somewhat formidable foreman. She was a tough young woman, both physically and in character – and she needed to be to manage a staff of seventeen men in those days of labour intensive farming. Most of the younger male farm workers had been called up into the armed services, except for two dairymen and a tractor driver-engineer whose skills gave them the status of 'reserved occupations'. The majority of the farm workers – whom Doris ordered about like a sergeant major – were a bunch of wizened and wise-cracking older men who jabbered among themselves in unfathomable Suffolk accents.

Elmer Farm focused on breeding and marketing pigs, egg production from hundreds of hens and a squadron of ducks. A dozen or so turkeys were fattened for the Christmas market, an orchard provided saleable apples and plums in a good season and the small fields were sown for hay or barley. Food on the table was scrumptious and sumptuous – eggs, meat, cheese, home-made bread, fruit – but I overdosed on the plums and was allergic to *prunus domestica* for many years.

Doris used to challenge me to wrestling matches, seriously testing my physical strength and fighting skills. At that age – 14 – I had absolutely no knowledge about human sexuality, but in later years when studying psychology, wondered whether my cousin was unconsciously expressing her religiously repressed sexual energies. She owned and controlled two powerful Alsatian dogs ... other animals included a troop of crossbred kitten-breeding cats who dutifully patrolled the barns and sheds to control the over-sexed population of mice. But the rats ... gee, the rats were big: over-fed, over-bred and over-running the feed store barn. Uncle Charles and Doris organised a hunt – with 12-bore shotguns.

Five-year-old Derek stayed in the farmhouse with Mother and Aunt Kezie to cook delicious fruit pies and cakes for tea. Doris ensured that all live stock and domestic animals were safely enclosed in other buildings. The shooting party was led by the Rayment brothers, Charles and Sam, joined by neighbouring farmer friends the Owers and two of the wizened and wise – each stationed in strategically safe locations inside and outside the big barn. Doris, though she was a good shot, took charge of the 'smoke-em-out' operation. I was her assistant, armed with a stout stick to whack a rat if one ran in my direction. No chance. Doris fixed a long fire-hose to the exhaust of the Hillman car, placed the nozzle into a rat-hole, started the engine and revved up: rats, rats and more rats scampered about in all directions. Watching from a safe distance I could see Father Sam and Uncle Charles standing back to back outside the door of the main barn, their 12-bores tracking then firing, followed by staggered volleys from the other guns out of my sight line.

Uncle Charles shouted, "Cease Fire!" A brief silence during re-load – then "free to fire!" – as the procedure was repeated at varying locations until a couple of sacks holding forty or more bloodied rats were soaked in paraffin and thrown onto a crackling bonfire in the far corner of Home Field. Hot tea, cool home-made lemonade and yummy cakes greeted us all in Elmer's kitchen. Revived, the pipe-smoking rat-pack party shared tales of vermin bagged and ones that got away. I listened intently to the accents ranging from mid-posh London through boss-farmer East Anglian to outright local sing-song speak whose sounds I enjoyed but blanked the words.

Apart from the activity emanating from nearby airfields the war seemed remote. Here we were in the quiet beauty of the Suffolk countryside, experiencing the natural flow of everyday country life at the height of the harvest season. But war's harsh reality announced itself every evening when voices hushed at the sound of the six pips and the solemn voice of Alvar Lidell intoned: 'This Is The BBC'. News that the RAF and the American Army Air Force were bombing targets in Germany almost every night was, in general, old news. The fresh experience for me was actually seeing RAF Lancasters and US B17 Flying Fortresses at low altitude as they took-off and landed at several nearby airfields. By 1944 there were nineteen active airbases in Suffolk alone.

Although I was not an expert plane spotter like my classmate George Cull, I was a keen member of the Air Training Corps and thrilled by everything connected with flying. I was certainly excited when, one cloudy day whilst stooking sheaves of barley in the harvest field, I heard the drone of a powerful aircraft, thrust my pitchfork into the soil and, gripping the handle, gawped at an American B17 Flying Fortress flying very low overhead. The next morning Doris had to drive to the market in Diss and invited me along for company, knowing I would see American air and ground crew personnel. And there they were, in small groups strolling through the market, some wearing leather flying jackets and fleece lined boots, forage and peaked caps at jaunty angles, some smoking – but most were chewing gum. I was fascinated but shocked, shocked that they were talking so loudly and uninhibitedly *in public*. So un-British – *so American* ... so unreal I felt as though I was walking through a Hollywood film set.

That experience kick-started a lifetime double-think about American people and their culture; an unresolved niggling mental tug-of war between admiration for their landmark achievements, their go-getting positive attitudes and, in general, their warm hearted hospitality and openness in person to person communications. On the other hand ... but those thoughts must wait for my next book – if I have enough years left to write about living in Malibu and Honolulu. However, during that enjoyable time 'down on the farm' in 1942, I first became aware, dimly, of something that linked with later experiences both in England and America: Bible Christians ... or Fundamentalists.

My uncle, aunt and cousin were stalwart members of a strict Baptist Church in Stoke Ash. I was accustomed to going to church and naturally accompanied my uncle's family to the Sunday morning services. Mother did not go, partly to look after Derek who was five, but also, as I discovered many years later because, although she believed in God in a general and practical sort of way, she disliked the hypocrisies endemic in religions. "All those different churches and all the other religions ... all they do is squabble between each other about who is right and who is wrong. Why can't they get together and agree that God is God and have done with it? Lot of nonsense in my opinion – but you'll have to find out these things for yourself, Alan dear." Wise mother.

At the Baptist Church I enjoyed singing the hymns – though some I had not sung before – but felt really uncomfortable during the long, long sermon about all the things God did not approve of in the human race and the ways of the world; our daily lives ... and nights too ... because we were all such terrible sinners. I had never felt uncomfortable during the sermons at St Mary's or St John's – which we choirboys hardly ever listened to – and in any case only lasted ten minutes. Now, at the age of fourteen, I felt confused because, according to the Baptist preacher that morning, God didn't seem to like any of us, whereas in my church at home I had learnt that God loved everybody. Why didn't God like these people in Suffolk?

I wondered too, why, after the service everybody was so friendly with each other: even that sin-preaching man smiled at me when Doris introduced me to 'our Pastor'. The mood inside the church had been solemn, dour and a bit frightening; outside, those same people were smilingly polite to each other; some were even laughing ... *even joking!* Puzzled? Yes I was puzzled ... so puzzled, in fact, that although I rarely said my prayers at bedtime I did endeavour to have a chat with God ... or was it Jesus ... or was it Mary ... that night, saying that I didn't like that long sermon – or Baptist churches.

But ... ah ... But! The Good Lord – or Whoever He-She-It maybe – has The Source Book of the best jokes.

Thirty years later I was appointed to the South London Circuit of the Baptist Church – as a Lay Preacher. That, dear reader, is a story with a very long introduction that may get written one day in the distant future – if I am still on this planet.

By early breakfast the next morning my puzzled thoughts had disappeared and I ran off across the farm to join the reapers, the stookers and the stackers in a good day of hard work and banter with the natives – even though I did not understand half of what they said. Yes, I loved the earthy life: The Good Life.

When my voice broke in early summer of 1942 my Sunday morning routine changed from processing in cassock and surplus at St Mary's to parading in uniform with 393 Squadron of the Air Training Corps. If, in four years' time the wars in Europe and the Pacific had not been concluded, and therefore conscription was still in place, my ambition was to train as a Spitfire pilot.

The surprise bombing by the Japanese of the American Pacific Fleet in Pearl Harbour, Hawaii, on December 7th 1941 had shocked the isolationist United States into joining Britain, the Commonwealth nations and Russia in the war with Germany and Italy. Reluctance to engage in the war in Europe was trumped when Hitler declared war on the United States on December 11th 1941. World War II was now seriously global.

Churchill and his entourage of senior political and military chiefs of staff flew to Washington DC to meet with Roosevelt and his staff to discuss strategy to win the war. Roosevelt and his advisers concurred that the primary objective was to defeat Nazi Germany and to focus the Allies' main resources on achieving that goal. The military manpower and industrial productive capacity of the United States greatly strengthened the British and Commonwealth resources in North Africa and Europe. In the Far East Japanese armed forces quickly occupied territories in the Pacific and South-East Asia held by the United States and Britain. The greatest capitulation in British history occurred in February 1942 when General Perceval surrendered sixty thousand British troops to the Japanese at Singapore.

Although nothing was really predictable, the war in the Pacific had only just begun and, given the geographical spread of island and mainland territories, seemed likely to go on for years. As the pendulum of military power in Europe swung in favour of the Allies it became apparent to me and my fellow cadets in the ATC that although Germany and Italy would be defeated before we were eighteen years of age we would probably be conscripted for service in the Pacific war. For many of us our ambition to train in the RAF as pilots and aircrew remained undiminished.

In February 1942 the appointment of Air Marshal AT Harris as Commander-in-Chief of the RAF's Bomber Command coincided with the introduction of the new four-engine Lancaster bomber. The British chiefs of staff resisted 'Bomber' Harris's plans to launch a major air offensive on German industrial complexes and populous cities, arguing that Britain's military industrial production, including aircraft and munitions, should be focused on supplying the current land war in North Africa, the vital need to bomb German submarine bases and to build-up military resources for future land operations on French and German soil. Harris's passion countered those rational calculations by pointing out that if the RAF and USAF did not carry out a continuous large scale bombing offensive, the Allies would be doing nothing to attack German industry and morale until an invasion of western Europe was possible. Harris won: Lancasters, Wellingtons and US B17's rained bombs on German targets until the end of the European war in May 1945. Two years later I witnessed the unbelievable (a concept I rarely use) results in Hanover, Hamburg and Berlin. Horrific devastation!

After three years of hard fought and costly see-sawing battles in North Africa the German and Italian armies surrendered to General Montgomery and US General Bradley in May 1943. On July 9th British and American paratroopers made an overnight drop in Sicily to prepare beachheads for 160,000 men and 600 tanks of the British Eighth and US Seventh Armies. Two weeks later Mussolini was deposed by the Fascist Grand Council; the new leadership under Marshal Badoglio dissolved the Fascist Party after Italian forces had suffered heavy casualties in Sicily. The new Italian government signed a secret armistice with the Allies on September 3rd: that treaty enabled Allied troops to cross the Straits of Messina to the Italian mainland without resistance. Meanwhile Hitler, furious that his enemy was winning ground on European soil, ordered several heavily armed divisions and Luftwaffe squadrons into southern Italy, annexed Rome and took control of the defence of Italy.

News ... news about most aspects of the war, as I have mentioned before, was followed avidly by everyone around me. I became as addicted to the BBC radio news as Father and devoured every newspaper at home and in friends' houses. Newsprint rationing drastically reduced column inches. Recent research produced a sample from random dates in July 1943: *The Times* printed 10 pages; the *News of the World* 8 pages and the *Daily Mail* 4 pages – all broadsheets. Tom Hopkinson, wartime editor of the popular weekly magazine *Picture Post* (28 pages) said his photographers were thoroughbreds: if the pictures were not good enough he and his writers had nothing to write about. The photographs and supporting texts were beyond good; the magazine presented a panorama of the vicissitudes of war, an education in the paradoxical horrors and triumphs inherent in military conflicts born out of incompatible socio-economic and political ideologies.

Whilst I understood the basic incompatibilities between fascism and democracy I could not, at the age of 15, really get my head around the war between Germany and Russia. I enjoyed history, was clued up about the geography of Western Europe and the Mediterranean, but relatively clueless about Eastern Europe and Russia. The Germans had invaded Russia in June 1941, made deep incursions into Soviet territory, were held at Leningrad and the outskirts of Moscow and finally lost the long epic battle of Stalingrad (now Volgograd) towards the end of harsh winter of 1942-43. In July '43 the Germans launched their last major offensive on the 200-mile Russian front. The opposing forces constituted the largest concentration of military power ever assembled in history. By winning the long, bitter and costly battle for Kursk the Russians nullified German offensive operations and began their advance westwards to recover lost territory. The momentum of those powerful Soviet military resources slowly but surely overwhelmed all German resistance on the eastern front. The Russians won the race to Berlin.

But I am getting ahead of myself ... enough of war on the cold Eastern Front – what about warm happy days in 1943 – and *remembered joys*? As always the most fun for me was taking part in any sport or physical activity; the social spin-off from being involved in organised team games extended my network of friends and acquaintances – be they all-male at that period of my life. In small ad hoc groups we would cycle to a hill above Hendon aerodrome to spot planes; to Totteridge ponds with fishing gear and optimism; to Whitestone Pond by Hampstead Heath with model yachts and competitive pride. Always a ball to hand – throwing, catching, hitting, kicking – no, not each other – the ball!

One bright day at the end of summer a few of us played 'one bounce only' with a soccer ball in front of the cricket pavilion in Arden Field. In a moment of frustration I kicked the ball high in the air – then watched it bounce around the angles of the pavilion roof and settle on the flat surface above the clock. After much ribbing I climbed up on the roof, retrieved the ball and began my descent – easier up than down. Attempting to jump from steeply angled asphalted roof to the flat concrete top of the men's toilets I trusted one foot on the cast iron gutter – pushed off ... dropped and bounced between two walls – and landed on the narrow path beside a piece of broken gutter. "That bloody hurt," I shouted to myself ... then felt something wet under my right sleeve: blood.

Two of my mates picked me up – another rushed into the pavilion bar, grabbed a laundered teacloth and wrapped the folded bandage tightly round the deep gash in my right forearm. I then walked home across the road where

Mother was busily treadling her Singer machine. Without fuss, she inspected the blood-gushing gash, bathed it gently and bandaged a thick wad of liniment over the wound.

"Now, Alan, you get on your bike and ride to Dr Holmes' surgery as quickly as possible – he'll probably stitch it up and apply sterile dressings." Result – five stitches, a sore arm – and proof of my mother's swift, calm, no-fuss reaction.

A triumphant chuckle rises up from within as I recall racing along on my bike with something wet in my right hand ... not blood this time but paint. One Friday in the autumn term the art master Mr Howland set the homework subject: 'A Storm' – in watercolour. Cycling home for lunch with neighbour Maggie Jones a week later she startled me by saying, "It's art this afternoon ... what scene did you paint, Alan?"

"Paint, what do you mean ... oh heck ... art homework, I haven't done it, Maggie."

My very organised classmate commented, "Nothing unusual, Beryl and I call you 'last minute Al'."

I gulped down the shepherd's pie Mother had prepared, grabbed a glass of milk and rushed upstairs to my room: cartridge paper – water in a cup – brushes – dab at colour blocks in a Windsor Newton box ... hurry – hurry! Thatched cottage – garden path – picket fence – hedges – grass – tall trees swaying – autumn colours. Twenty minutes ... rushed past Mother, mumbling "Late, I'm late."

Holding my 'wet art' at arm's length with the finger tips of my right hand I jumped on bike, zoomed down Briarfield Avenue, turned into Manor View by our old house ... over the bridge in Squires Lane ... Great North Road ... school ... fit but panting. Up the stairs two at a time, entered the art room five minutes late, peeked at my offering as I lay it on the pile of returned homework and muttered: "Gee, it's dry ... but squiffy."

Result? Full marks (20/20) – and a comment to the class by Mr Howland as he held up my quick-splash painting. "Alan has somehow captured the energy of the storm ... look at those tree tops being driven by the wind ... even some leaves torn from the branches and flying through the air ... wonderful technique, young Alan ... wonderful."

I didn't reveal my 'technique' to Mr Howland, but after being interrogated by Maggie Jones, 'Kipper's Technique' became the class joke of the week.

Kipper ... who was Kipper? When experimenting with Kipp's apparatus in the chemistry lab my classmates associated the aroma of my farts with hydrogen sulphide. I was addressed by the nicknames 'Kipper' (crudely funny) or 'Skipper' (respect as team captain) for three years of my school life until superseded by 'Ginger' (blushingly embarrassed). What made me blush and cop the name 'Ginger?'

Ballroom Dancing!

In November 1943 the boys and girls in both fifth forms were informed that in preparation for a school dance at Christmas a ballroom dance teacher had been hired to teach us the basic steps. A few of my bolder male friends had girlfriends and were keen to learn; most were reluctant. Now fifteen, I was scared and confused: my clear thinking about female mates clashed with a newly discovered shyness in the company of some – but not all – girls. My subconscious was battling with my sexual development – about which I knew absolutely nothing.

The dreaded moment arrived when, under the supervision of Miss Martin our history teacher, members of both classes gathered in the School Hall to be introduced to the ballroom dance teacher, Miss Kathleen Hughes. When the hubbub of nervous chatter eventually faded, the confident and youthful-looking Miss Hughes directed the boys and girls to form separate circles; the boys, being more numerous, on the outside. The teacher demonstrated the forward change step in the waltz, beginning with the left foot, then showed and instructed us how to change weight after the 'close' on the third step in order to progress to the second change step beginning with the right foot. The resulting shambles caused an outbreak of nervous chatter and giggling until Miss Hughes quietly insisted that we all start again ... and again ... and again. After twenty minutes' practice came the challenge to repeat the two 'change steps' – and again – until both circles progressed with reasonable success. Ah but! – the next movement was to repeat the 'change steps' backwards, beginning with the right foot. Mayhem!

With saintly patience and charming smile the determined Miss Hughes encouraged and cajoled the high-spirited but well-behaved fifteen-year-olds through the drill until the two circles were able to progress in both directions. "Well done, everybody! Now we will try to keep time with the music of a slow waltz."

Cue pianist – chaos!

Well! ... learning dance steps in the familiar form of a new PE drill was relatively easy: performing dance steps to a waltz played on the school piano produced much kicking of ankles, treading on toes – and more giggly laughter. But the best, or the worst, and certainly the most embarrassing aspect of this first dance lesson, was about to be revealed by Miss Hughes. 'The Hold'.

Released from the circles we gathered in random groups whilst our charming teacher gave a short talk on dance etiquette and explained The Hold. My mind had drifted away to thoughts of our next soccer match against Woodhouse Grammar School – then jumped back to reality when Grant Stanley jabbed me in the ribs and said: "She's talking to you, Al."

"Me, Miss?" "Yes you, blondy ... wearing the ginger jacket ... I would like you to join me to demonstrate The Hold ... and you dear, the dark girl in the navy jumper ... please come and help me ... thank you ... you both did the steps so well ... natural dancers, I'm sure."

Dancer? ... Me? ... I was rooted to the floor, perspiring buckets and certain my face was beetroot in colour. As Grant and Tom Mackenzie pushed me to the front of our casual group my eyes took in the scene: Miss Hughes alone in acres of unoccupied floor – and Shirley Bagrit gliding across that space to join Miss Hughes.

Although my face must have been fire-engine red by now I knew instinctively that I could cope with the embarrassing ordeal confronting me: a matter of pride because I was the school cricket captain and, as a successful sportsman and latterly a solo singer, I was used to the limelight. However, I was not used to being face to face with, and having one arm around, a beautiful girl. And Shirley Bagrit really was a darkly beautiful young girl: in today's terminology 'sexy looking' – in old money, 'a smasher'.

Because Shirley was in the brainy class 5A I hardly knew her, but we both seemed to know instinctively that we *must not* make a mess of this performance. Focusing primarily on Miss Hughes and her instructions, rather than the dark beauty in my arms, enabled me to learn and apply The Hold without further embarrassment. Shirley and I then proceeded to demonstrate a series of 'change steps' in a basic manner – without rise and fall – and no damage to toes.

Easy actually, when concentrating on the task and being encouraged and congratulated by Miss Hughes. But as I parted from Shirley Bagrit and walked across the floor to rejoin my classmates I experienced a dizzy array of feelings: success in the task akin to going out to bat and scoring fifty – but in partnership with a girl?

A first experience of holding a girl's hand and placing the other on her back – and standing face to face in such close proximity and sensing her feminine vitality renewed the debate in my head about sport and girls – that they don't mix – but I might like dancing – and that meant keeping social company with girls – and that meant dancing ... which before today I had always thought was sissy. "Oh boy! ... growing up is confusing."

I remember little about the following 'rite of passage', the Christmas Dance, except the girls sat on benches on one side of the hall – the boys on the opposite side. Ah yes, I picture a radiogram playing records of dance music – Victor Sylvester and Joe Loss – whose bands were familiar through the radio, oh – and the energetic Miss Hughes eventually coaxing some of us on to the floor by organising a Paul Jones, several snowball dances and the Lambeth Walk – a shambles but fun. My sporting mates and I thought the two hours at that dance was a more scary experience than being in the shelters during an air raid. We were fifteen, growing up in an era of very little information about ... well ... growing up. By the next summer some of my school pals had serious girl friends: I remained a cricket bachelor.

Meanwhile, enter the Doodlebugs!

CHAPTER 19

D-DAY AND DOODLEBUG SUMMER 1944

*I failed to fail the School Certificate exams and
thereby failed to achieve an important goal.*

Why the desire to fail? Ambition!

I had had the privilege of being school cricket captain for two seasons. Tom Mackenzie, good friend and commanding centre-half, skippered the soccer team. Tom was definitely leaving school at the end of term and, if I passed the exams, I had to leave school and find a job. But ... but if I failed I could stay on at school to retake the papers at Christmas and, in the autumn term, almost certainly fulfil my ambition to be captain of Finchley County School's soccer eleven. Logical – or stupid? Well, not illogical in the mind of a confident sixteen-year-old to whom sport was life. But, dammit, I did not fail. I will tell this tale at the end of this chapter under the sub-heading: *'thwarted by examiner and diddled by doodlebugs'.*

'What was a doodlebug?' my grandchildren may ask. Answer: a pilot-less flying bomb. Some historical background and personal stories may help to colour the realities of everyday life in that happy summer of '44.

Happy summer? ... when V1 flying bombs were liable to intrude on everyday life and even kill or maim? Well, happiness is relative to circumstance, and whilst not detracting from the tragic effect the flying bombs had on many lives and communities in the south-east of England that summer, the spirit of the nation was upbeat because we, the Allies, had the Hun on the run.

On the eastern front in the harsh winter of 1943 the Russians, after eighteen months of bitter fighting, had, at great cost in lives and equipment, reversed the German siege of Stalingrad and won the biggest land battle of the war at Kursk. In the summer of that year German U-boats withdrew from the Atlantic. In North Africa General Rommel's army had been routed and the subsequent Allied invasion of Italy had caused Mussolini's forces to surrender. From the autumn of 1943 into the spring of 1944 British, Commonwealth and American forces prepared for the planned invasion of German occupied territory across the English Channel. The American General, Dwight Eisenhower, headed the overall operation: General Montgomery commanded the British army units that were to land on the beaches of Normandy.

'D-Day' on June 6th both mirrored and magnified in reverse our retreat and disembarkation from Dunkirk four years earlier. Magnified? Yes, I have to pause for my mind to contemplate the colossal numbers of men, ships, aircraft and equipment that the Allies had assembled: more than three and a half million men, twelve hundred fighting ships, four thousand assault craft, sixteen hundred merchant vessels, thirteen thousand aircraft and too many tanks, artillery weapons, trucks and jeeps to count.

Dunkirk in reverse: D Day, June 6th 1944,
British commandos landing on a Normandy beach

But to deliver that vast number of men, machines and equipment onto beaches in Normandy, and maintain supplies over months, required daring inventiveness and innovative engineering on an enormous scale. The two Mulberry Harbours are an epic story in their own right and a worthwhile research study for students of the history of WWII. In essence, construction of the two Mulberries absorbed over 40,000 personnel working for 300 companies around the country to create 212 caissons in concrete and steel, each weighing between 1,672 and 6,044 tons, plus 23 pier-heads and 10 miles of floating roadway. They were towed across the English Channel by tugs at 4.3 knots and arrived at Arromanches and Omoha beaches three days after the initial landings by British, Commonwealth and American troops. Unfortunately, due to violent storms from June 19th to 22nd, the Mulberry deployed by the American Services at Omaha beach was destroyed.

The newspapers, radio and cinema newsreels had kept us well informed of Allied successes and German losses in Russia, North Africa, Italy and the North Atlantic, but of necessity there was a news blackout regarding preparations for D-Day. However, such was the scale of the military movements around the country that the general population knew 'somethin's up'. It was not difficult to guess what – the question was 'when?' I recall my own mixed emotions of pride and concern when hearing news of the D-Day landings on the wireless. My mind raced with a mixture of excited and sombre thoughts: how quickly would the Allied forces establish successful bridgeheads? How organised and effective were the German defences? Would our casualties be high? Was this historic event the beginning of the end of the war? Well, this horrible war was now 'over there' and the Luftwaffe would surely be much too busy to bomb London and our major cities.

Yes, the Luftwaffe were too busy but not Hitler's scientists and engineers who had developed two secret weapons, the first of which was about to be launched against south-east England from sites in occupied France and Belgium. Early in 1943 Intelligence Headquarters in London had received reports from their agents that the Germans were secretly testing new types of rocket weapons at Peenemunde on the German Baltic coast. In May 1943 a young WAAF officer, Miss Constance Babbington-Smith, was analysing aerial reconnaissance photographs at the Photographic Interpretation Unit near Henley when she identified what appeared to be a small aircraft on a launch ramp. Further aerial reconnaissance and photographic analysis led to the discovery of similar combinations of aircraft and ramps on other sites nearby. Immediately after this discovery the RAF severely disrupted the operational use of that site in a massive raid on Peenemunde, dropping 2,000 tons of bombs which not only devastated laboratories and engineering installations but also killed over 2,200 scientists, technicians and workers.

Now aware of the potential danger of the German V weapons, Churchill set up 'The Flying Bomb Countermeasures Committee' under cabinet minister Duncan Sandys, to gather further intelligence, organise home defences and increase the bombing raids on launch sites. Although we, the British public, had known little or nothing of the dangers posed by the German's secret weapons, Winston Churchill spoke openly of the new threat in one of his regular 'State of the War' speeches in Parliament on February 22nd 1944.

> There is no doubt that the Germans are preparing on the French shore new means of attack on this country, either by pilotless aircraft, or possibly rockets, or both on a considerable scale. We have long been watching this with the utmost vigilance.

Imagine the lively discussions with pals at school following release of this news on the wireless and in the papers. Little did we then realise the direct affect that the V1 Doodlebugs would have on our daily lives that coming summer, nor the serious yet amusing drama that would unfold when we sat for our examinations – but I'm getting ahead of myself in unfolding this story of the Doodlebug Summer.

During the winter of 1943-44 German factories manufactured thousands of Veggeltungswaffe 1 (Revenge Weapon No.1), pilot-less flying bombs, which were then distributed to dozens of launch sites in northern France. Hitler was impatient to launch his last desperate assault against Britain, his expectation being that the V1 and V2 would terrify the Brits into submission ... who were you kidding, Adolf? The scale of the new threat was thwarted by the continual bombing of the launch sites by both the RAF and USAF until, ironically, the first V1's were launched one week after the successful D-Day landings on the Normandy coast.

According to official records the first 'Vergeltungwaffe 1' to fall in England burbled across the English Channel in the early hours of June 13th and exploded at 4.13am in Swanscombe, near Gravesend in Kent. Within the hour three more fiery-tailed Doodlebugs crossed our shores, causing some members of the Royal Observer Corps to report, "crippled plane with engine on fire," while others reported to Headquarters that they had spotted a 'Diver' – code name for a V1. The second 'Diver' exploded at Cuckfield in Sussex; the third devastated an area in Bow, City of London; the fourth landed in the countryside near Sevenoaks in Kent. That salvo of four in mid-June signalled the start of the Doodlebug menace. But were they the first to explode on English soil? What of the 'Mystery of Sarisbury Green?'

For me the name and place of Sarisbury Green evokes romantic post-war memories of village cricket on 'The Green atop the Hill', but in the reality of war that romantic venue east of the river Hamble fielded a mysterious lethal missile. As the warm evening of the Spring Bank Holiday faded to dusk on May 29th, two Civil Defence wardens on night-watch duty near The Green were alerted by a strange burbling roar in the sky. Peering into the darkness in the direction of the Isle of Wight they saw the outline of an aircraft spewing fire from its tail – then the roar stopped. Seconds later the eerie silence was shattered by an explosion in a line of trees beside The Green camouflaging army tanks awaiting shipment to the Normandy beaches.

The military authorities took immediate action to delete all written reports of the incident by eye-witnesses in the local Civil Defence units. However, thirty years later a Civil Defence operator, who had been on duty in the control room in Fareham that night, wrote a statement verifying his own eye-witness account and those of fellow Wardens on duty at Sarisbury Green. Whilst Mr BW Rands acknowledged that the military and political authorities were right to organise a cover-up of the facts a few days before D-Day, he confirmed that a V1 had exploded among the tanks at Sarisbury Green and that there had been casualties. It is commendable that the civilians in the surrounding area remained tight-lipped and held to the wartime mantra, 'Careless Talk Costs Lives'. But sadly, the V1 onslaught that followed on June 13th did cost many lives.

Doodlebugs killed 450 people in the first week of the raids, over 2,000 injured and approximately 100,000 properties were destroyed or seriously damaged in London and the south-east of England. A direct hit on the Royal Military Chapel in London during a Sunday morning service killed 119 and seriously injured 102 servicemen and civilians. How random and tragically ironic is the encounter between religion and war.

The Doodlebug war had begun: the people in south-eastern England had to reproduce their defiant Blitz spirit, their tough physical efforts and selfless communal support to overcome hardships that were unexpected at that phase of the war. The sirens wailed again, drowned by the cheerfulness exhibited by Brits in hard times, twinned with total belief that we would overcome the hardships and revel in victory when the time came.

I know: I was there and I shall never forget.

Nor shall I forget the cinema newsreels, the BBC news bulletins, the speeches by Churchill, Bevin and Morrison – or the newspaper headlines. The headline in the *London Evening Standard* on June 16th 1944 read:

PILOTLESS PLANES NOW RAID BRITAIN
announces Mr Herbert Morrison, Home Secretary, in the House of Commons.

Mr Morrison said: "It has been known for some time that the enemy was making preparations for the use of pilotless aircraft against this country. He has now started to use this much vaunted weapon. The enemy's preparations have, of course, not passed unnoticed, and counter-measures have already, and will continue to be, applied with full vigour. It is, however, probable that attacks will continue. Subject to experience the usual siren warning will be given for such attacks.

While I thought it right to give the House, at the earliest opportunity, information about the use of this weapon by the enemy, available information does not suggest that exaggerated importance need be given to the development. Meanwhile, the nation should carry on with its normal business."

(Cheers from Members in The House).

The Doodlebug threat prompted a new evacuation from London in mid-June and by the end of July 1944 over 1,500,000 women and children had exited the capital. On July 6th, three weeks after the Home Secretary's speech, Winston Churchill addressed the House of Commons on the subject of casualties caused by the V1s:

Up to 6am today, 2,752 people have been killed by flying bombs and about 8,000 have been injured and detained in hospital. The number of flying bombs launched up to 6am today was 2,754.

The Prime Minister then spoke to the House about our bombing raids of V1 launch sites. His conclusion, in typical Churchillian style, made reference to another weapon planned by the enemy – a 'rocket bomb':

> The House will ask – what of the future? Is this attack going to get worse? Will the rocket bomb come? Will more destructive explosions come? Will there be greater ranges? I can give no guarantee that any of these evils will be finally prevented before the time comes when the soil from which these attacks come has finally been liberated.
>
> I must make it perfectly plain. I don't want any misunderstandings. We shall not allow the battle in Normandy – nor the attacks we are making on specific targets in Germany to suffer. They come first.
>
> We will fit in our on domestic arrangements in the general scheme. There is no question of the slightest weakening of the battle. It may be a comfort to some that they are sharing in no small way the burdens of our soldiers overseas. London will never be conquered – and we shall never fail.

Failure was not on the agenda for the inhabitants of London and her neighbouring counties. Except for a minority of people who were seriously affected, the Doodlebug menace in the summer of 1944 was certainly of less consequence than the important news of Allied successes in France following on from D-Day. We were winning the war; Hitler's armies were in retreat; our morale was high. We accepted that the Doodlebugs were a temporary nuisance, that they sometimes interrupted the busy rhythms of daily life in factory and office, in homes and schools, in theatres, dance halls and fields of play. The ingrained habit remained: 'we just got on with it.'

Interruptions on the field of play? Ah, a personal story comes to mind that gives colour to the picture of our young lives in the summer of '44 ... a picture which in turn triggers a chain reaction of memories: two contributed by school friends; the last my excuse for failing to fail the School Certificate examinations.

One calm sunny July evening I was captaining Finchley Colts on Arden Field in a home match against our main rivals, Southgate. We were a confident, successful and enthusiastic bunch of young cricketers – even now I can sense the energy of that enthusiasm and picture the team's brilliant fielding and catching. I had won the toss and, batting first, we notched up a winning score at a fast rate. Now in the field, we had achieved a commanding position by taking five Southgate wickets for seventy-seven runs.

Finchley Cricket Club Colts, 1945

from left, standing: E.Hughes; B.Hanley; D.Graham; A.Clayton; P.Sutherland; J.Ridley. Seated: R.Robins; P.Harwood; A.Rayment (capt); I.Bedford; M.Shipman

We had heard a few Doodlebugs groaning in the distance earlier that evening – the faint growl of their engines culminating in a soft 'cruuuump' as the bombs exploded several miles away in central or north-east London. The V1 raids had quickly become part of everyday life: the likelihood of becoming a victim of those indiscriminate weapons was so small that scant attention was paid to air-raid warnings – people of every age and in every walk of life 'carried on as usual' ... unless. Unless the distant growl grew into a raucous spluttering roar and continued to increase in volume to a deafening cacophony of discordant sound – as was happening *NOW* – just as Ian Bedford commenced his short run-up.

"EVERYONE TO THE DITCH," I yelled in my loudest sergeant major voice ... "THE DITCH ... NOW!!"

All the young players and the two adult umpires sprinted at top speed toward the chestnut trees lining the boundary adjacent to Deard's stable yard – where the Middlesex indoor cricket school is now situated. The Doodlebug's raucous engine cut out as we hurdled the two rows of low wooden bench-seats and flattened ourselves in the dry ditch alongside a few female school-friends who had been watching the game. Hands covered heads as silent seconds ticked by ... then a deafening cruuummp!! The bomb hit and destroyed some houses in Ossultan Way, less than half a mile from the cricket ground.

Silence! ... a long, long silence ... then a babble of excited chatter among the players as nervous tensions were released – though a few recovered more slowly due to shock. As we untangled ourselves and slapped the dust from our cricket whites, I called out: "OK, everyone, let's get back to the game." Five minutes after the explosion Ian Bedford resumed his over and bowled the unsettled batsman with an unplayable googly. The Southgate boys lost – but we all won – in that defiant spirit of Brits in wartime to *'carry on regardless'* ... though we were not regardless of the pain and loss suffered by our neighbours in Ossultan Way.

Two memorable cameos emerge from that dramatic evening. First, the adult umpire standing at the bowler's end removed the bails from the wicket before scampering to the ditch – and ceremoniously replaced them before we could resume play. How British was that?

Second, a young County School girl, then aged fifteen, still has a vivid memory of diving into the huddle in the ditch, the explosion and the immediate resumption of the game. A year later, Betty Griffin became my girl friend and dance partner. We often joked about the fictional 'cuddle in the huddle in the ditch' in the Doodlebug Summer of '44.

Doodlebug over London rooftops: the German V1 Flying Bomb

233

Another huddle caused by a Doodlebug was 'The Huddle in The Hut' at the County School where our School Certificate Examinations were held. Three days before the commencement of those exams, a V1 flying bomb dived into the glebe land opposite our school, blowing out all the glass, many window frames and plaster from the ceilings. This event occurred, fortunately, out of school hours. Some of the teachers and senior students cleared up the debris while we collected our books to swat up at home. I read a little – but not a lot – and swatted more balls in the cricket nets across the road than book pages in my bedroom.

I find it interesting to read accounts of that summer written by three contemporaries at Finchley County School: George Cull, Dickie Seymour and Brian Cross. First, in the Old Fincunians' magazine, *The Scimitar*, George Cull wrote about a hobby, a dangerous duty and an eye witness account of bomb damage to our school:

> To boys like me who were obsessed with making aviation models, the war was a fascinating time and attendance at FCS was felt to be a grave interruption to the pursuit of several hobbies. For instance, in addition to model making, there was a School Flight attached to the 393 Squadron of the Air Training Corps; also the School Aero Spotters Club: No.228 of the National Association of Spotters Clubs.
>
> We were all expert at aircraft recognition and were entitled to become fire-watchers at school when we were sixteen. This meant that two boy spotters would return to the school at 8pm and sleep on camp beds in the boy's cloakroom. Of course there was a Master in attendance too, but since most were no longer young and didn't fancy the camp beds in the draughty cloakroom they did not always turn up – much to our delight.
>
> Other adult officials – Air Raid Wardens and sometimes off-duty police – would often arrive late for the night shift, stay half an hour and then, if the sirens had not wailed their mournful warning, would say, "You'll be alright, lads," then give us half-a-crown each and vanish. Therefore we were often left in sole command at FCS and would get out gym mats from under the stage and have a highly gymnastic time.
>
> We were trained to extinguish any incendiary bombs that penetrated the school's roofs. We were equipped with stirrup pumps, buckets of water and sand; we could also operate the main fire hoses. No incendiary bombs fell on the school premises but the V1 Doodlebugs often kept us awake. Off duty at 7am, we would cycle home, clean up and eat a hearty breakfast before returning to school for lessons at nine.

One sad yet exciting event was the blast damage caused by the doodlebug that exploded opposite the school in June 1944. Most of the window frames were either blown in or splintered and all the glass shattered except, I think, the Hall's elliptical glass roof. The windows of the Art Room were all blown in and I had the enviable job of poking out the jagged remains, nudging chunks of glass out of their frames to crash and smash on the floor. No supervision, no safety helmet or protective clothing, just a good long window pole was all that was required to 'do my bit' as a member of the team of volunteers who willingly cleared up the debris.

Classmates Dickie Seymour and Arthur Clayton were actually on fire-watch duty that night when the Doodlebug's blast damaged our school. Dickie recounted his tale of good fortune:

Alerted by the wail of the sirens, Arthur and I were outside in the school grounds late that evening listening to the familiar muted growl of distant Doodlebugs – and occasionally spotting a fire-red glow traversing the skies to the east before silence ... then thud. Suddenly, from a different direction, a disconcerting roar grew louder and louder – then cut out – causing us to sprint across the playground into the school, hit the deck and sprawl on the stone steps just inside the boy's entrance. A huge explosion rocked the building, shattering windows and covering us with plaster ripped from the ceilings. Recovering from the shock, Arthur and I picked our way through the debris to inspect Room A where our camp beds and overnight kit were located. Had we been asleep, or sheltering in that room, we would have probably been injured by flying glass ... we were lucky! The next day we returned to inspect the damage and I particularly remember the banter and effusive spirit among teachers and senior pupils as we got stuck in to clearing up the debris – and the news that our exams would have to be taken in The Hut.

Exams in The Hut are remembered by another classmate, the Reverend Brian Cross, in an article entitled 'An Extra Subject', written for *The Scimitar* in 2002. Having noted the major events of the war and our chequered attendance at school, Brian made the following interesting observation:

Throughout the war it was 'Business As Usual' at school, in the home and in the workplace. It was business as usual at the swimming baths – the Lido opposite the school and the indoor baths in Squires Lane and all the local cinemas. It was business as usual at White Hart Lane where Tottenham Hotspur shared their ground with Arsenal, so that in addition to seeing all the Spurs stars and guest players we could watch Bastin, Hapgood and Drake. There were very big attendances at all matches and at very low entrance costs. It was business as usual with the 609 trolley-bus, though sometimes I was late for school due to the necessity of repairs to the overhead electric cables after a bombing raid. And it was business as usual for our teachers, who, like the rest of us, had many disturbed nights but were always on teaching duty the next day, putting on a brave face and leading by example.

More 'business as usual' when soon after D-Day the wretched V1 Doddlebugs began to arrive and one exploded on the Rough Lots opposite the school a few days before our School Certificate Examinations. We sat our exams in The Hut. Air raid precautions were now rudimentary so we ducked under our desks when the roar of the missile's jet engine was deemed too close for comfort. Over the two-week examination period there were very many such occasions – as many as six in one examination. Marking, we were told would allow for this – but our attitude to this latest 'blitz' was now blasé indeed. I was in the sixth form in September 1944 when indifference became the norm again during the V2 rocket attack; over 500 landed in the London Civil Defence region in the next few months. The war ended suddenly in May 1945. Six long years of not entirely happy schooling – but I do know that many of us now value the experience of that 'Extra Subject'. (*Edited AR*)

I take the liberty to quote again a passage from Churchill's speech in the House of Commons on July 6th 1944 following the first Doodlebug raids:

> I must make it perfectly plain. I don't want any misunderstandings. We shall not allow the battle in Normandy nor the attacks we are making on specific targets in Germany to suffer. They must come first. We must fit-in our own domestic arrangements in the general scheme. **London will never be conquered – and we shall never fail.**

'thwarted by doodlebugs and diddled by examiner'

We, the sixteen-year-old examinees, did 'fit in our domestic arrangements', sitting in The Hut and scribbling away between doodlebug emergencies. 'We shall never fail.' We completed all the exam papers and, if memory serves me correctly, none of us failed. The memories of old class-mates contacted more than sixty years after we last met have given me a clearer picture of those eventful weeks.

Travelling to and from school was simple: bike or walk or a red London bus that stopped outside the school in the Great North Road. I cycled, sometimes walked, occasionally having to shelter behind a front garden wall and hedge because one of those 'noisy buggers' sounded too close for comfort. Passing through the school gates into the playground on the first day of the exams my mates and I enjoyed some respectful banter with the old carpenters repairing damaged window frames, and skilful glaziers cutting sheets of glass to fix new panes in hundreds of vacant apertures.

Leaving behind our bomb-damaged school we strolled towards The Hut on the soft grass of the small 'back field' past the half-buried, very damp and unusable brick air-raid shelters. The Hut, a gable-roofed, army-surplus hut purchased and erected in 1919, was surprisingly undamaged. Many generations of Fincunians retain a whimsical affection for The Botany Lab, but probably none more so than The Class of '39 who sat within for today's equivalent of their GCSE exams at the height of the Doodlebug air raids in 1944.

I am surprised that after all the intervening years I am so vividly recalling scenes and sounds as I write: writing stirs all the senses at times ... the mind video rolls ... my inner commentary is in the now ...

> I see myself walking towards The Hut chatting about sport with Charlie King and Jean Birrell – both of whom excel in sports. We skip up the wooden steps into the lobby and are immediately sucked into the vibrant energies and buzz of excited-nervous chatter emanating from fifty youthful examinees. I stop for a moment to take in the scene and decide which little group to join; some crammed into the narrow rows between desks, others congregating around the confined area adjacent to the teacher-invigilator's throne beside the portable blackboard. Hush descends as our popular and respected history teacher begins to thread her way through the throng to her seat of authority. Before I'm able to join my closest friends it is time to bag a seat on one of the uncomfortable wooden chairs paired with a small, unstable oak-wooden desk.
>
> Miss Martin, serious but often humorous and occasionally coquettish, begins to address us in a cheerful manner regarding the standard rules of examinations, then adds a solemn footnote on procedures in the event of imminent danger from an approaching flying bomb. "I will blow my whistle ... you will take cover under your desks ... *no talking*! I will blow my whistle

again to recommence the examination. You may now begin the history paper. Good luck to you all."

History is one of my stronger subjects ... Hmm ... questions not too bad ... should be all right, I mutter to myself. A quiet half-hour of undisturbed concentrated writing, then the distant unmistakable drone ... getting louder and louder ... oops ... getting serious. Miss Martin blows her whistle, chair legs squeak and bodies thump to the floor as we take cover. Cover? The proverbial Big Bad Wolf had enough 'huff and puff to blow The Hut down', let alone the blast from a really Big Bad Doodlebug exploding within five hundred yards. Thankfully, this one splut-roars on, cuts out and cruuuumps a couple of miles away. Miss Martin blows her whistle again, chair legs squeak and muted murmurings reverberate around room, initiating a stern rebuke from our soft natured teacher: "Next time there is to be absolutely NO TALKING!"

I admit that some of us did share clues to answers when scrabbling on the dusty floor under our wobbly antique desks – yes – more than a score of times during that unforgettable fortnight.

Before recounting the reasons why I failed to fail those examinations in the Doodlebug summer of 1944, I am reminded of a cricket story connected with the school that underlines my priorities at that time and clarifies my lack of ambition for scholastic achievement. As I mentioned at the beginning of this chapter, I was already captain of the school cricket eleven but had a burning desire to lead the school soccer team in the autumn term of that year. However, success and ambition may sometimes obscure wise choices.

When I was voted in as captain of Finchley Colts first eleven one evening in April 1944, I immediately foresaw a conflict of interest when the Colts would play the County School. A dilemma: a difficult decision about priorities and my prime loyalty. "Well," I thought to myself, perhaps rather selfishly, "last season I scored a hundred for the School against the Colts so it would be interesting to see if I could score a few runs against the School. In any case, I may be leaving school this term and ... and??" Illogical logic toured my brain for days. I do not remember how I persuaded the sports master, Mr Cleghorn, to leave me out of the County School team, but I captained the Colts and scored a hundred.

Announcing the result at school assembly the next morning our begowned Headmaster with apt name, academic stoop and unappealing voice paused in mid-sentence: "Yesterday evening the first eleven lost to Finchley Colts by seven wickets and ..." Mr Chalk frowned, looked up from his script to scan the silent faces looking up at him, then pointing to the back rows, commanded:

"Rayment. Stand up. Do I understand this correctly, Rayment, that you played for the Colts ... and scored a century ... against the School?"

Muted murmurs reverberated around the hall, and dark admonitory stares from cricket playing teachers, Jones and Howland, deepened the hue of my blushes. I felt like a naughty five-year-old at infant school. My dry vocal chords croaked, "Yes, Sir."

"Report to me in my study after assembly, Rayment. We will sing hymn 107: *Awake my soul, and with the sun ...*"

Well, I was awake – and awash with trepidation as I waited outside the door of the Headmaster's study, then knocked. "Come in." I entered, stood in front of Mr Chalk's imposing desk, feeling small and somewhat guilty.

"I am very disappointed that you were disloyal to the school, Rayment. After all, you have the honour and responsibility of being captain of the team ... er ... I cannot understand how you could let down the other players in the school team, after all, they are your friends, too. I know you also play for Finchley Colts, but surely your first loyalty is to the school? What do you have you to say?"

"Sir, I don't know what to say really. I am proud of the school and that I am cricket captain. But I am also captain of the Colts so I ..."

"So ... I see ... I didn't know that, Rayment ... so you had to make a choice and you chose to play against the school, yes I understand that you had a difficult choice to make ... hmmm ... even so, to my mind the school comes first. I will speak with the sports master about this ... you may go now ... er ... but before you do, did any other members of our school team play for the Colts?"

"No, sir, Charlie King and Arthur Clayton played for the school, sir."

"Hmmm ... they open the bowling, don't they, and you scored a hundred against them ... hmmm. Well, congratulations on your hundred, Rayment, but I still think that while you are here the honour of the County School is paramount. You may go now."

Duty and service, honour and loyalty were paramount principles of that era; principles which I had imbibed and in which I too believed. The headmaster, who had played cricket in his younger years, was fair and understood my dilemma to a degree. I did not receive the severe reprimand that I had expected – maybe I had learnt an important lesson. From my choir-boy days I recalled words from the Gospel reading: *No man can serve two masters ...*

Trapped by twin loyalties! Dammed by success! Would I succeed in failure?

A pass mark in five subjects was required to achieve a School Certificate. Even though I had made little preparation for the examinations – after all, it was a busy cricket season – I was surprised that I eased through the two compulsory subjects, English Language and Mathematics, which included arithmetic, algebra and geometry. I felt I had done well in History and Art. In the three Sciences I struggled to complete the papers and had already failed French in mock exams. I approached my final subject with confidence and breezed through the first sections of the Geography paper. But as I read and re-read the alternative questions in the last section about Australia I was stumped. I knew nothing – or very little about Australia – except cricket. Nothing? No panic – I felt challenged, looked out of the window, doodled on a notepad and day-dreamed about playing at the Sydney Cricket Ground.

My musings roamed through oft-read tales of Bradman and Hammond, of Jardine, Larwood and Voce and the infamous Bodyline Test Series in 1932-33. Ah! Inspiration! The romantic within dreamed up a whimsical way to answer one of the questions: 'Discuss the Distribution of Population in Australia.' After all, I didn't want to pass so I might as well have fun.

My Conway Stewart pen raced over the paper, concocting an essay based on my knowledge of the large numbers of people who attended the England versus Australia Test matches in the 1930s, played in the major cities located on the south-eastern seaboard of that vast island-continent. Over 90,000 spectators filled the Melbourne Cricket Ground each day of the Bodyline Test; similarly there were sell-out crowds at Adelaide, Brisbane and Sydney.

I made mention of Australia's economic dependence on exports of grain, timber, meat and wool; of vast agricultural stations and isolated mining communities. I remembered from geography lessons with Mr Corns that the Australians had built a new capital city, Canberra, situated about 150 miles inland from Sydney; the opening ceremony had been conducted by the Duke of York as recently as 1927. In conclusion I reiterated that the majority of the country's population lived and worked in and around the four great commercial-industrial cities of the south-east where thousands of Australians paid homage to Don Bradman and his famous team-mates who wore their 'baggy green' caps with enormous pride.

I recall how much I enjoyed writing that essay, even though I was mindful that the content was cheekily irrelevant and that I would certainly fail in one of my favourite subjects. But that was my aim – to fail the exams. When the results dropped through *that* letterbox, I was shocked to discover that I had passed! How could I have passed?! I was unlucky – the examiner must have been a cricket aficionado!

The other factor that defeated my intention to fail was the Examination Board's decision to lower the bar of the pass mark in each subject. They were evidently concerned that interruptions during the exams caused by the German Doodlebug flying bombs had had an adverse effect on the examinees.

Adverse effect? On us? We were confident, Blitz-hardened, tough-minded and high-spirited – you might even say 'cocky' young Londoners. We felt challenged, not affected – or even effected. By 1944 my male and female classmates had evolved a cheerful and special togetherness that reflected the very real community spirit prevalent in wartime Britain. We were winning the war. British, American and Commonwealth troops had landed on the Normandy beaches two weeks before our exams. Our morale was high.

We had imbibed the Churchillian spirit resulting in a visible determination to overcome all hardships that enabled the people of our nation, young and old, to survive the darkest days and nights of the Blitz, the rationing and austerity, and hardest of all, the sad loss of friends and members of family. Living through those times had caused my generation to grow up prematurely; toughened adults before our time.

So what adverse effect? The Examination Board's compassionate intention was therefore, in a sense, reversed: not the intended make-weight for nervous tendencies supposedly caused by the Doodlebugs but an unexpected bonus for the examinees at Finchley County and other schools – a prize for our up-beat morale and gung-ho spirit.

It is of no matter to me now, in the 21st century, that I failed to fail the exams in '44 and so became an Old Fincunian without achieving my ambition to lead our talented soccer team in the battles against arch-rivals Woodhouse and Christ's College. But in reviving memories of the teachers and my young colleagues at FCS during those war years – and that Doodlebug summer in particular – I am proud in every respect to be an Old Fincunian.

I am also proud to have been cricket captain of the school's successful first eleven, yet remain puzzled as to how I passed the geography exam by presenting an irrelevant essay on Australian cricket.

And so, remembering our wartime adventures, I salute my friends from 'The Old School'.

Cricket: writing this chapter has reminded me that I need to retrace my development in the sport from the first summer of the war in 1940. Living in and through those wartime experiences and conditions tempered my character and firmly established personal values learned from my parents, significant adults and communities of influence: family, schools, church and music, sport and friends, our neighbourhood and the national psyche. I'm very proud to be British!

~~~~~~~~~~~

CHAPTER 20

WARTIME CRICKET 1940 – 1944

Who do you think you are kidding Mr Hitler,
if you think Old England's done ...
'cos you should have known we'd never give up cricket,
that is why you lost – we won!

The rhythm of my fingers on the keyboard induced a chuckle within as I hummed the first line the *Dad's Army* song – then added a new line of my own.

So I apologise to you, patient reader, both for the corn and that in writing about cricket in the wartime years I shall be overlapping some of the stories in adjacent chapters – a necessity in order to retain some fluency and comprehension in these memoirs.

As far as I remember, cricket at school continued normally during the summer term of 1940 but from mid-July Finchley's matches on Arden Field were sometimes interrupted by the serious dramas being enacted in the skies above during the Battle of Britain. How quintessentially British that men and boys, bedecked in whites, ducked in and out of dark air raid shelters or crouched in ditches to ensure that 'the game goes on' – in a similar spirit to the legendary tradition of London's Windmill Theatre: 'We never closed!'

To ensure continuity of Finchley Cricket Club Colts during the war the enlightened committee of the men's club decided to delegate the administrative responsibilities to the boys themselves and appointed two senior members to be available for advice and assistance if needed.

From 1940 our young committee arranged the fixtures, public transport for away games, prepared the wickets, selected the teams and adult umpires. On home match days we played host to the visiting teams and set up a rota of parents to provide sandwiches and cakes, tea and lemonade. We were also responsible for tidying up and cleaning the dressing rooms after the game, and importantly, checking the black-out curtains when the lights were on during dull evenings in late summer. These responsibilities at the club, as in so many other aspects of living in wartime conditions, prepared my young pals and I for practical adulthood while still young teenagers – but teenagers full of energy, confidence and fun, serious about the chores and duties involved to organise and play the sport we loved.

I was particularly keen on preparing the wickets and, as I lived opposite the ground, spent many happy hours alone removing plantains, repairing damaged turf caused by the bowler's footmarks, watering the pitch – and from my mid-teens, mowing the wicket with the club's valuable sharp-bladed, eighteen-inch Ransome hand-mower – another 'grass' story. Heavier duties required a small gang of boys – some less keen than others – to push and pull the heavy horse-shafted roller. Even fewer were enthusiastic about mixing and applying 'the gunge'.

Way back in the history of the club a local blacksmith had created the ancient mixer cart from heavy forged iron. The strange-looking vehicle had a wide self-balancing half-drum suspended between two huge iron wheels on a frame with long shafts to enable manual manoeuvring. The ingredients for 'the gunge' were cow dung and marl stirred into measures of water by trial and error in order to obtain the consistency of brown milk (apologies to all cows). Dick Nelson and I really enjoyed the messy earthy task of mixing, splattering each other's shirts with smelly brown spots as we stirred and stirred – then uncontrollably splashed some of the liquid as we grappled the monster tank from dung hut to wicket. Dunking large watering cans into 'the gunge' we proceeded to treat our precious cricket pitches with the organic fertiliser and binding marl. Later, after several inspections to ensure that the turf was damp – not wet – we applied the smaller roller.

Growing up between the ages of twelve and seventeen our group of keen young cricketers enjoyed the freedom and responsibilities of running our own show. We became budding administrators and produced excellent pitches on which we developed and honed our cricketing skills. Aged 13 in the summer of 1941, I played my first matches for the Finchley Club men's 2nd XI and the County School 1st XI, scored my first century for the Colts against Clarke's College and was always on the look-out for the opportunity to play in a men's match if, as happened often in wartime, a Finchley team or their opponents were short of a player or two. Though small in stature I was physically well developed, and my athletic fielding contributed to the team's performance even if I was placed too low in the order to get an innings.

The next season I was higher in the batting order, scored my first century in men's cricket and took a few wickets with medium-paced in-swingers. I have a cutting from the *Finchley Press*, dated 1942, which reads:

> Finchley 2nd XI visited Parkhill Sports, a strong side, who after amassing a good total (212) proceeded to skittle the Finchley batsmen out. However, a good knock (42) by 14-year-old Alan Rayment who, with rather enviable energy, is turning out for the 1st and 2nd teams and Colts as occasion demands, made the score reach reasonable proportions (105) although still a long way behind Parkhill's.

Before that season began – and still aged thirteen – I was voted in as captain of the Colts 1st XI by our young committee of active players, some of whom were aged seventeen and would soon be called up into the armed services.

Looking back I think my appointment was a political accident in that two older boy candidates had fallen out with each other, and I was either the peacemaker or the safer option. Even though I was too young to be helmsman of such a lively older crew, there was no mutiny and we won most matches. However, given that I had no understanding of such matters in 1942, I now realise that the process stretched my personal growth and leadership skills at a very young age. Above all I enjoyed the opportunity to orchestrate team tactics and encourage individual players – as though I was an ardent musician training to be a conductor of his own orchestra in his favourite auditorium, Arden Field. Whoops ... I have just realised the connotation between 'ardent' and Arden.

Individual skill and enthusiasm melded with fair-minded relationships and insightful leadership produces a synergy we identify as team spirit. From the inception of my sporting life at junior school and cricket club – and continuing throughout my youthful years – I was blessed with peers who were not only keen to practice together to develop individual skills, but also, on match days, to play as a team – to play for each other. On reflection I realise that we imbibed the co-operative spirit of that period of British history; the 'spirit of community' so evident during and after the war – a cheerful 'backs to the wall' and 'pulling together' spirit which sadly, yet inevitably, dissipated from the late 1950s onwards. Given that our formative social environment coincided with those wartime years I am thankful that we survived the dangers, grasped unexpected opportunities and developed strong bonds of comradeship.

But I digress – because in writing of individual skill, enthusiasm and team spirit – I was about to introduce the emergence, in 1942, of the twelve-year-old cricketing prodigy Ian Bedford. Already a star at Woodhouse Grammar School, Ian bamboozled men and boys alike with his leg breaks and googlies at the Finchley Club's early season net practice. Small for his age and rather frail looking, Ian's control of beautifully flighted leg breaks combined with a top-spinner and alternative googlies – one the batsman could read, the other not – mystified us all. Ian came into the Colt's first eleven under my captaincy, took scores of wickets and fielded competently. His batting improved – so did mine – as Ian and I spent countless hours practising in the nets together over the next few years. Later, in county cricket, I was more confident when batting against wrist-spinners than any other type of bowler – for which I have my highly skilled and enthusiastic friend to thank. During those early formative years we played hundreds of matches together for the Finchley Club at junior and senior level as well as representative games at Lord's. Honours were probably even in the hard-fought rivalries between our respective grammar schools.

Later to become a star cricketer at the County School and the Finchley Club, my brother Derek displayed exceptional cricketing talent from a very early age. I recall that during the tea interval of a charity match at Finchley in 1942 when Alex James, the Arsenal and Scotland soccer legend, led a star-studded

XI that included Denis and Leslie Compton, I introduced five-year-old Derek to the Compton brothers. Well ... being only 14 myself I was too star struck to ask them myself, but I persuaded the Finchley skipper Josh Levy – who was friendly with Denis and Leslie – to ask the brothers to watch Derek bat on the outfield in front of the old wooden pavilion. Denis and Leslie were impressed, encouraged Derek and chatted to him after I had under-armed a dozen or more balls to show off his classic off-drives and back-foot defence. At that very young age Derek displayed prodigious talent and enthusiasm. I was very proud of my young brother's cricketing progress: in hindsight I may have hindered his later development by over-coaching him in those formative years.

I find it interesting that I have so little recall about cricket at school during the war compared with vibrant memories of events connected with Finchley Cricket Club. Even so, it was only when I delved into a few tan-faded press cuttings saved by my mother that my subconscious archive was awakened by printed fact that, in the summer of 1943, at age 15, I had played *with* cricket stars!

The highlight of the season at Arden Field was a charity match in aid of the Merchant Navy Comforts Fund. The visiting team was led by Archie Fowler, a former Middlesex player and MCC Head Coach at Lord's. His team included two Test players, Laurie Fishlock of Surrey and Jim Sims of Middlesex, plus two other county professionals: Eric Bedser of Surrey and George Lambert of Gloucestershire. Finchley batted first and declared at 224 for 7. Nearing the winning target but with time running out, Archie Fowler's team lost two quick wickets, bringing the wily Jim Sims to the crease to join 17-year-old Highgate schoolboy, David Cairns. The *Finchley Press* reporter wrote rather flatly about what must have been, for the players and the many spectators, a nail biting finale:

> CLOSE FINISH. The largest crowd of the season saw AJ Fowler's
> XII beat Finchley on Sunday off the last ball of the match. In
> the last over Cairns repeatedly attempted the required single and
> was sent scuttling back by Davison at point. From the last ball
> of the match he succeeded in driving to the boundary.

The young hero of the hour who scored 26 not out later went up to Oxford to study for a medical degree and play for the University. Laurie Fishlock top scored with 67; Eric Bedser made 62 runs and took 3 wickets – one being Finchley's top scorer Jack Vaughan on 59. Jim Sims' leg breaks and googlies foiled two home batsmen including Peter Nelson whose powerful driving took him to 46; George Lambert bowled opener George Wood for 2. Reading the tattered cutting I suddenly exclaimed to myself and the keyboard: "But what is this ... what on earth is THIS?"

> Did not bat:
> JJHanley, AJ Fowler, G Lambert, AW Rayment, H McIndue.

"So I played ... well, I fielded anyway ... in *that* game! ... it's coming back ... the visiting team was short of two players – the Compton brothers! So Finchley's old man Hanley – a lovely Australian guy – and AWH made-up the numbers. But I was only fifteen ... fifteen!! ... and I was in the dressing room ... and on the field ... and round the table at tea comfortably chatting away with five county players ... and two had played for England ... minor gods!"

Talk about 'tales of the unexpected' ... and 'close encounters of a cricket kind' ... about which I had no initial recollection in the twenty-first century. "Well!" I said to myself, "I would not have believed then, when fifteen, that in two years' time I would be playing with and against Jim Sims at Lord's – and against Laurie Fishlock, the Bedser twins and George Lambert in 1949 and 1950 during my first two seasons with Hampshire. But then ... some dreams do come true!"

In 2006 I surprised Dr David Cairns when I wrote to him in Toronto, enclosing a photocopy of the press cutting. David delved into his archives, found the 1943 match scorecard of 'Archie Fowlers XII versus Finchley CC XII' and sent me a copy together with a lovely note in which he confirmed that Jim Hanley and I replaced Denis and Leslie Compton.

According to my small collection of cuttings from the *Finchley Press* I had another dream game that season, scoring 106 and taking 5 for 40 for the men's 2nd XI against Parkhill Sports – who won by 53 runs. Before the season began the young members of the Colts committee, on which I sat, appointed Dick Nelson as first-team captain. Though disappointed at losing that role, I had realised during the previous season I was too young to be in that position of leadership. I was, however, appointed captain of the County School first eleven for whom I scored a hundred against the Finchley Colts – a notable triumph, considering the strength of their bowling line-up which included my friend Ian Bedford.

I was now fifteen, able to bowl faster and hit the ball harder because I was physically stronger – so too were my contemporaries. Sixteen-year-old Peter Marshall of Christ's College had grown tall and developed a good physique. In previous seasons I had played his medium-pacers with ease, but he was now much quicker and bowled in-swingers when there was shine on the ball. Batting for Finchley Colts one evening at Arden Field, Marshall bowled one that rose and swung into me as I attempted a pull shot – I missed and the ball hit me high on my right cheek by the nose and eyebrow ridge of my forehead. Blood, swollen face, headache and first-aid – but no visit to a doctor. You can imagine the questions and the jokes when I arrived at school the next day all bandaged up as though I had been in a serious fight – worse a few days later when the bandages were off and the bruises looked horrendous. No PE or cricket for the next two weeks ... and for the rest of my life a pinched vein on my bottom-right eyelid that looks like a blue scar or a birthmark. The incident was my most serious sports injury, and I am thankful that my eyesight was not affected, neither was my nose broken.

I did, however, break two bats that season and therefore became a regular visitor to the local cricket bat factory in Church Lane, East Finchley. Summers & Browne crafted 'Force' bats bearing the branded signature of Jack Hobbs, known throughout the cricket world as The Master. Sir Jack, as he became in 1953, was a prolific opening batsman who scored 61,760 runs and an unsurpassed 199 centuries in his thirty-year career for Surrey and England.

The manager of the factory was a very kind man who, realising that I was a keen, ambitious and chatty young cricketer, took me on a tour of the workshops to witness the amazing skills of the craftsmen who fashioned beautiful blades with hand tools from matured wood clefts of a species of willow tree – 'salix alba var.caeulea'. Because one of my hobbies was 'making things from bits of wood', I was in awe of the skill of the craftsmen, drawn in by their friendliness, the ambience of the small factory and the distinctive aroma of willow shavings and sawdust. "Come and see us again, young nipper ... there's a lot more to show you if you're interested," said Mr Kind Manager. And I did visit again, several times that year, and, with typical Gemini imagination, thought I might like to learn the trade when I left school next year.

Before the next year arrived our family had to move from 23 Briarfield Avenue because the owner and his family were returning to Finchley following their private evacuation. Father and Mother were fortunate to find a semi-detached 1930s house that had similar accommodation and a longer garden – which pleased Father. Rosemary Avenue was a pleasant residential street that ran parallel to Briarfield and backed on to the railway line; I had to accept that I would no longer have a view of Arden Field. But I was pleased that my pals were still close by, in fact Dick Nelson, David Limbert, Norman Lake and young Peter Robinson all lived in Rosemary Avenue. Although the soft rattle of the Tube trains running on the open line disturbed me at first in late evenings there were no changes to daily routines – anyway I led such a busy life so I 'just got on with it'!

I was certainly busy, occasionally in danger of double bookings when the next cricket season started which was also my last term at school – including the School v Colts game described in the last chapter. Finchley Colts played their home and away games on Friday evenings, Finchley County School on Saturday mornings and the Finchley men's elevens on Saturday afternoons and Sundays. Until I left school I often had a tight timetable when travelling to an away game for Finchley men's first or second elevens on Saturday afternoon. On Sundays we occasionally played an all-day match, one in 1945 being particularly memorable against the All Star Women's XI.

The *Finchley Press* reporter must have enjoyed writing up the match of the day:

The honour of making the season's biggest hits on the Finchley ground has gone to a lady, much to the consternation of 'the ancients'. The fair Jessop in question is Miss D McEvoy (Surrey and England), who in Sunday's match succeeded in lifting two balls well over the pavilion roof. Finchley batted first and amassed a good total, with Greenaway (90) as the main contributor *(yours truly scored 34)*. The bowling was surprisingly good, but with only three bowlers in the side fell away at the close of the innings. The fielding too was excellent, save in one important department – the catching. The ladies could not force the pace enough when batting, but bright efforts came from Miss McEvoy and another England player, Miss A Brown. Altogether their team included six England players and three other county representatives.

The game attracted a large crowd, most of whom had never witnessed women's cricket of a high standard. I was very impressed and respected the skill and enthusiasm of the players. I particularly remember being surprised at the pace of the opening bowler, Miss Wheelan, and being pinned down by the accurate slow left-arm spin of Miss Aline Brown, who took four for 81. Aline's brother was FR Brown, the famous Surrey all-rounder who captained England after the war.

Although there were no first-class county or Test matches during the war, the game thrived in local clubs throughout the country. Famous players in the armed forces stationed near village, town or northern league clubs were invited to play when available and attracted even larger crowds of enthusiastic spectators. Also, the majority of the top players in the armed services or civil defence units were given leave to play in special one or two day matches. Many of the county grounds, and Lord's in particular, were filled with thousands of spectators when the Army played the Royal Navy, or the RAF fielded a star team against an equally strong Civil Defence (personnel in police, fire-brigade, ambulance). In 1944/45 the Royal Australian Air Force fielded a team of Test match strength against an All England XI. With some of my pals I watched several fascinating matches at Lord's in 1943 and 1944, including Middlesex & Essex versus Kent & Surrey; also 'An England XI versus The Dominions'.

Imagine, dear reader, how excited we all were on the bus going to Lord's in 1943 – yours truly especially so at the prospect of watching my two heroes, Denis Compton and Learie Constantine, play against each other. England batted first: Denis faced Learie's varied paced seamers but was run out for 58 ... maybe by his brother Leslie – I'll have to check. Leslie Ames, the great England keeper-batsman, scored a magnificent 133. England declared on 324 for 9 at the tea interval.

The powerful veteran New Zealand and Leicestershire batsman, CS Dempster, opened with Keith Carmody for the Dominions, followed by the charismatic Aussie Keith Miller – a great buddy of Denis Compton. Keith was batting well until he reached 32 when one ball from Denis scripted a scorebook entry that created competitive banter between those two iconic cricketers for the rest of their lives:

KR Miller caught LH Compton bowled DCS Compton.

Denis, serious whilst appearing nonchalant trundling his chinamen and googlies, took six wickets in eight overs for fifteen runs: the Dominions all out for 115. The England skipper RWV Robins, having belted a rapid 69 not out, declared the England second innings closed on 150 for 6, leaving the Dominions to score 359 to win.

Dempster batted as magnificently as Hammond in scoring 113: the Aussies Carmody and Sismey kept up the run rate and, surprisingly, the West Indies Test player, Dr CB Clarke, batting at No.10, notched 52 before missing another Compton chinaman. Tension, excitement, even comedy as occasional off-spinner Jack Robertson bowled his first over and the last of the match with the Dominions requiring 14 to win and 2 wickets in hand. Sismey hit out and was caught in the deep by Alec Bedser; MacDonald scampered three and the last man Roper nicked two before he was caught by Bailey. The England XI won by eight runs and Jack-the-Gentleman Robertson bagged two wickets for six runs in one over.

Thrilling cricket – forever memorable for the thousands of spectators taking time out from wartime conditions and duties and forever memorable for the impressionable fifteen-year-old now reliving the experience in the 21st century. Most of all, I enjoyed the all-round performance of the dynamic West Indian, Learie Constantine, whose energy, skill and stamina belied his 42 years.

By the summer of 1944 the tide of war had turned in the Allies' favour as our combined armed services fought hard and costly battles against the retreating Germans in France. There were now fewer interruptions to daily living in Britain except for the Doodlebug menace which had little effect on the continuity of the nation's daily life at work or play. Dancing and girl friends were not on my agenda that summer: in fact I considered both to be unnecessary distractions from my only passion, playing cricket. The School Certificate examinations diverted my attention for two weeks in June, and a holiday on my uncle's farm in Suffolk ate up two precious weeks in August. Other than those necessary duties I played in every cricket match available to me in any team at whatever level, travelling to faraway places around London by bus or Tube, occasionally taking shelter when one of those 'noisy buggers' sounded too close for comfort.

From the age of twelve in 1940 to sixteen in 1944 I had grown in physical stature and agility, gained a lot of experience through the adult environment at home and in the cricket world – and, of course, from the actuality of living through every day in wartime conditions.

I was Learning to Live and Laugh and Care about other people – but I had not yet experienced romantic Love.

~~~~~~~~~~~

CHAPTER 21

WORK BEGINS – WAR ENDS

Dunkirk, The Blitz, we Brits survived,
our Spitfires won that Battle in our Skies,
in shelters long we thronged as fires above
destroyed our cities and friends we loved.

Then Doodlebugs with fart and flame
blazed oe'er Dover's cliffs new bombs to rain
on London, Sussex, Kent – more modern war
– the last dice throw of Hitler's broken claw

Or so we thought – until The Silent Terror struck,
tough luck you Nazi sods, Brits grit and pluck
has overcome all this before,
so stuff your rockets, 'cause you've lost!
We've won this bloody war!

Paradoxically, I was anxious because I wanted to fail.

Envelopes were my worry: one brown envelope through the letter box at 34 Manor View had signalled my entry into wartime education at Finchley County School. Now in July 1944 a second important brown envelope was due to arrive that would reveal whether I had passed or failed the School Certificate examinations.

It arrived ... I had passed.

I was half pleased – half annoyed: surprised by success; annoyed to have failed in my ambition to be my school's football captain.

Quite naturally, Mother and Father were delighted and proud.

Reality knocked out my internal debate – "how come I passed ..." ... and ... "I'm not going to ..." when Father came home from work, shook my hand and said, "Well done, my boy, well done ... I didn't think you had it in you" ... whatever *it* was that he thought I did or did not have. Then the unwelcome reality, the punch-line that prefaced fact with imponderable question: "You'll have to get a job now, my boy. What do you want to do until you are called up for conscription – I suppose you'll be going into the RAF?"

"I don't know," I replied. "I would like to be a professional cricketer – maybe soccer too – but the war makes that impossible. Do you think it will be over soon, Father, now that our troops – and the Americans – have got a foothold in France?" ... avoiding the real issue about a job.

"Too soon to say, but I don't suppose it will be over until you have to sign on for National Service in two years' time, young Alan," observed Father, who followed every detail and comment about the war through the press and radio.

"So you can forget about earning a living from sport and get down to the business of earning a real living. Anyway, whatever happens in the future you need a normal job to fall back on even if you do get signed on for Middlesex one day, my boy. I expect you could get a job in the City ... er ... in banking or insurance – seeing you have passed the School Certificate." I felt a little sick, remained silent and excused myself: "Got to go to the toilet, Father."

The thought of being stuck indoors in a boring bank truly horrified me. I had never been through the doors of any business institution except that of Martin & Savage, Father's small firm in the City. As I write this in 2009 I am reminded of my experience on September 3rd 1939 when I was 'having a think' and doodling with that pile of mown grass behind the boundary line at Finchley Cricket Club:

> God, you understand why I'm so cross ... this war is really going to mess-up my cricket career!

Some prophecy! Metaphoric too: thwarted 'behind the boundary line' of war; men, women and children 'mown down like grass'; careers lost in the undergrowth of man's inhumanity to man. And that prophetic statement addressed to – or debated with – a Divine Presence was now biting into the reality of my immediate future.

I really did not know what sort of job to apply for, nor do I remember any constructive discussion with my parents. They knew I would obtain employment quite easily; that in two years I would be conscripted and that my true ambition lay beyond their say-so or influence. "You were always such an independent child," my mother often reminded me in later years. Now sixteen, that independence was being challenged with the responsibility of making choices based on little or no information about jobs or careers – other than cricket or the Royal Air Force.

Given the psycho-social, cultural and practical wartime conditions of the day, my generation grew up very quickly. There was no middle ground of teenage culture to buffer the gap between leaving school, going to work and joining the armed forces. Yes, there was the Saturday night hop at the local Drill Hall, the cinema, serious hobbies and sport – but no teenage clothes, music or, for the majority, sex. Except for the few entering sixth form we jumped from being a schoolboy-schoolgirl to becoming a responsible young man-young woman – from schoolbooks to ledgers, filing cabinets and typewriters; from maths and art to factory lathe or commercial drawing board. If my memory serves me correctly only seven of my fifty contemporaries at FCS entered the sixth form and double that number left school to become apprenticed to practical trades.

The remainder entered offices in central London; some of the girls attended a secretarial course – a few became student nurses at the appropriate age. The war conditioned our response to every aspect of living. We had to be grown-ups before we were grown up.

I hear you thinking, dear reader, 'Surely you were advised by the Local Authority Advisory Service regarding possible career paths.' Respectfully: "Are you kidding ... in 1944?!" I do have a vague remembrance of conversations with our highly respected English Master, Mr TS Jones, who tried his able best to steer me towards training as a surveyor – a most suitable choice. An appointment was made for an interview with a recruiting official attached to the Coal Commission. A most unsuitable choice! I would have enjoyed surveying land and buildings, but coal mines – certainly not. In any case, the geographical location of coal mines would cut me off from my home turf – those beloved acres of Arden Field and Lord's Cricket Ground.

In the here and now of the 21st century I can claim the wisdom of hindsight and, given those same circumstances in 1944, it would have been sensible to apply to the BBC, or the sports editor of a newspaper, or to seek a trainee position with a chartered surveyor in London. How I ended up at Unilever House at Blackfriars on Monday 25th of September 1944 remains a mystery. Desperation probably – anything to earn £2.00 per week until I reached eighteen and was called up. Mother hinted (on audio tape): "We thought that maybe ... maybe by joining a diverse organisation like Lever Brothers you might find a niche that would suit you."

Suit me? In the bowels of that vast curved edifice dominating the Embankment at Blackfriars Bridge there was a poorly lit, ballroom-sized dungeon with low ceiling – The Post Room. Inappropriately dressed in a smart new suit, semi-stiff collared shirt and cricket club tie, I was dispatched aloft by the Post Boss with batches of letters in a big canvas shoulder bag, only to lose my way in the labyrinth of corridors and offices within that battleship of commerce. Always late, I was mercilessly harangued by the pretty young secretaries who received the mail. The School and Colts cricket captain had become a red-faced post boy. I survived for less than one week.

Dressed appropriately in a tan-brown greengrocer's smock-coat – a la Ronnie Barker – the good-natured, heavy-jowled Boss of the Post Room thought I was a 'bit posh' for his crew of boy-runners. On the third day he released me from his dungeon and sent me upstairs to the Personnel Department where a pleasant matronly lady (PML) ticked boxes on a foolscap questionnaire as she frisked my mind for personal information. She took note of my School Certificate subjects and initiated a 'going nowhere' dialogue.

"We have so many departments where I could place you, Alan. What would you like to learn? Accounts, or sales – or maybe transport?" queried PML in a kindly manner.

"I don't really want to work in an office," I replied. "Are there any jobs where I could travel, where I could be outside in the fresh air some of the time?"

"Well, to become a sales representative calling on grocery stores you would have to have to work as a clerk in the order department of one of our companies, at least until you are called up. Then perhaps another two years after you are demobbed before you would become old enough to 'go on the road'. I see that your father is a commercial traveller in the textile business ... does he enjoy his job ... and do you aim to follow him in a similar occupation?"

"Hmmm ... I'm not sure that Father likes his job ... and I am certain that I would hate it," I replied confidently, realising that I was engaged in a discussion and was not before the headmaster for some misdemeanour. Emboldened, I blushed as I confessed: "My ambition is to be a professional cricketer – but I have to wait until I come out of the Forces – and then it will depend whether I'm good enough to be signed on for Middlesex."

"Ah, hmmm ... a cricketer ... that's interesting," replied PML, her eyes lighting up as she laid down her pen and eased back into her comfortable swivel chair: "I've been a Surrey supporter for years – watched Len Hutton at the Oval in 1938 when he scored that wonderful 364 against the Australians," she continued enthusiastically.

"Did you really?" I exclaimed, open-mouthed in awe ... then in polite hushed tones ... "you *really* saw Len Hutton break Don Bradman's record Test score ... oh boy!" My heart was racing as PML and I shared a long silent moment of glorious memory broken only by whispered sighs involuntarily escaping my lips: "You saw Hutton ... the great Len score ..."... then suddenly snapped out of my semi-trance and realised that I was being interviewed for a job. And that I was sixteen.

Strange magic – cricket! In seconds our relationship was transformed from that of office boss interviewing office boy to a bond beyond definition. Silence stilled the air between us as we communicated with broad smiles and we became, momentarily, maiden aunt and young nephew sharing a passion. How often, in future years, that strange magic broke the ice and opened doors at interviews and business meetings; triggered friendships and listening-in counselling sessions through coincidental meetings on planes, trains and in pubs. Amusingly, living in faraway places such as California my passion for 'cricket' usually provoked short-lived discussions on entomology. Even then, explaining to Americans that cricket is a *sport,* moved anthills. How often? Many many times!

Back to 1944.

PML refocused, sat forward, eyes down and shuffling papers, picked up her pen: "Well, Alan, we'd better find something to occupy you for the next two years or so ... I've been thinking ... you are good at art ... so how about trying our commercial art department? I know it means being indoors but you might find it interesting."

Warmed by her caring thought and tone I found myself answering, "Yes, I am quite good at drawing, and yes, I would like to be among some arty people," – thinking that they would be more lively than stuffy accountants.

"If you come to see me here first thing on Monday morning, I will introduce you to the manager of the Commercial Art Department, Alan."

And so, with firm handshake and cheerful words we parted. I thanked PML for her help and returned to the Post Room dungeon in high spirits. Mr Brown Smock seemed really pleased that I was going 'upstairs', in part no doubt because he would receive fewer internal phone calls from angry managers asking why the so-and-so mail had not arrived. On Friday I received my first pay packet. What a week: first two days of gloom in the bowels of Unilever House, released by the sensitive Mr Brown Smock and cheered up by PML on the third day, first pay packet on the fifth day and brighter prospects for my second week.

The Art Department had to be brighter than 'the dungeon' – there were windows. The people, too, were brighter and welcomed the blond kid in a suit, especially the young ladies. However, although I gave a nod to work and art I gave none to the girls in a flirtatious way – and certainly not a wink: polite and friendly yes, but girl friends? Not interested! I was married to cricket and soccer. 'Going out' with a girl did not enter my experience for another ten months ... by the way, the term 'date' was not in our vocabulary. I settled in to the duties of office boy and advertising apprentice, attended after-hours art classes paid for by the company and enjoyed the work environment – up to a point.

The point was – it was all rather pointless. My ambition was singular. My affinities were with grass, with ball and bat, the skills of my sporting heroes. But there was a war going on, with all its attendant restrictions affecting everyday life. Even if the war ended next year I would not be free to test my singular professional ambition for another four years – at least. And two and a half years of that delay would be spent in the RAF. Understandably, I was mildly frustrated but understood why and got to grips with day-to-day living – and surviving.

As I write this, and with a little more understanding of life than when I was sixteen, I am thankful that my frustrations were tempered by three factors. First, the values inherent in my upbringing: 'duty, loyalty and service to others'. Second, ironically, by the war itself and those restrictive wartime conditions which were, to a modern idiom, 'in yer face' – every moment of every day – and every night too. Third: probably the fact that I had been starved during the first four months of my life yet survived, had, I think, deepened psychological roots and strengthened response mechanisms with an unconscious ability to 'wait and trust'.

Delayed gratification has always been natural for me, though, as I am 'many several persons' — as we all are — my contrary inner drives to initiate, to be resourceful and *to get things done* have caused countless inner conflicts and not a few disasters. But overall, and through all the years 'til now, the angels – or whoever – of 'delayed gratification' have proved their point. Experience is never pointless.

My experience in the Art Department was not without value but was short in duration. Not sure why – maybe a Geminian pattern of frequent change was in play or maybe PML, my friendly cricket fan, received a divine nudge to shunt me across the Thames to another tentacle of the multi-national company? Without interview or job description PML informed me that I was to report to a Mr Tom Lacey at Gravel House off Southwark Street on January 8th 1945. My new post of Junior Clerk in the office of the Director of Engineering of SPD proved to be a blessing regarding my ambitions in sport.

'Speedy Prompt Delivery Company Limited' looks, on paper, like a crazy lyric seeking a bouncy tune. Well, the lorries were bouncy – hundreds of 1930s vintage Bedfords, Dennises and a few old Thornycrofts trundled all over the nation delivering soap, toothpaste, ice-cream and sausages to bombed cities and pristine villages. The huge maintenance garage was in Battersea, but the two directors and the chief engineer ran the operation from a tiny suite of offices on the second floor of a grey Victorian building in which the stair-wells and corridors occupied as much space as the offices. As junior clerk I was to assist the chief administrator, Mr Tom Lacey, and the Chairman's secretary, Miss Hall. The latter was a glamorous drama-queen-cum-drill-sergeant whom I nicknamed, for my ears only, 'Boris'.

Tom Lacey, then in his 50s, had played non-professional soccer to a high level including a trial for England's amateur international team. We soon discovered our mutual love of sport ... ah! ... but did he already know that my ambition was to be a professional cricketer and that I was quite a good soccer player too? I have often thought that the honourable PML knew Tom Lacey was a distinguished amateur sportsman and that they arranged my quiet transfer from Unilever House so that he could take me under his wing. If they did, I am eternally thankful. And the Chairman, Colonel Jameson, was a sporting type who must have endorsed my appointment. Dear Tom Lacey – a very kind man – ensured that I not only kept on top of my job but also arranged with the directors to allow me time off, with pay, to play cricket and soccer – a story for a later chapter.

But now a little Gravel House story – therefore probably a long one: a story about tin hats, typists, confectionary and rocket bombs. By February 1945 the SPD Director's office boy was humming along in his new status as junior clerk and beginning to master the long-carriage, high-standing Underwood typewriter – virtually a miniature organ if there had been pipes to hoot a tune.

Also, importantly, I was getting on well with the five members of the office team. But unbeknown to me there was a sixth senior member of our staff in Gravel House – a nationalised Belgian gentleman named Légère to whom I was introduced one Monday morning by Mr Lacey. No wonder I had not met this mysterious character – whose craggy face and French accent triggered filmic images of foreign spies – because his office was in a semi-basement at the rear of the building. Access was through the typing pool, and I had never dared to venture beyond the first desk to deliver files because some of the young typists had already embarrassed me at lunch in the canteen. Flirts – I didn't trust flirts – they caused me to blush.

Mr Lacey explained the reason for the introduction: "Alan, Mr Légère has been in charge of our Civil Defence Section since 1940, but we are now closing down that operation. For the next two weeks I would like you to assist Mr Légère in moving stock out of his store and clearing out his three offices."

"Yes, certainly, Mr Lacey," I replied, already thinking how I could avoid going through the typing pool ... ah, yes, I can go outside the building, round the block and in through the double doors of the store. "Blast! – bound to be locked."

"I'll leave you with Mr Légère now, Alan. But do come upstairs after lunch to check your other work."

Gemini – two jobs – normal.

I grew to like Mr Légère. He had been wounded by shrapnel in the Great War and moved to England in 1936 because of the growing Nazi menace in Europe. Now, in 1945, we were fast approaching the denouement of the second devastating war in Europe in twenty-one years and, thankfully, the end of Hitler's destructive fantasies. However, as far as London was concerned, 'it was not all over!'

I asked Mr Légère: "Why are we throwing out or selling off this emergency equipment when London is being bombed by those awful V2 rockets?"

"I know not why, young man – but is it ours to reason?" responded the Belgian gent who was inclined to show off bits of mangled Shakespeare at the drop of a tin hat. And tin hats, stirrup pumps, shovels, first-aid kits and thick brown scratchy blankets were the reason for our labours: out of the store, into a van and over the river to some dodgy dealer in the East End.

Our labours ... and I did most of the labouring ... included moving all the furniture into one room, burning hundreds of files in the basement furnace, emptying out desk drawers and setting aside personal items hiding within: fountain pens, earrings and lipsticks, an old pipe, a silver cigarette case and some chocolate ... an eight-ounce bar of chocolate. Due to rationing I had not bought such a big bar of chocolate for several years ... and I loved chocolate.

Clearing my throat, 'Aghuggmm' – feeling guilty about asking yet driven by an overwhelming desire I ventured the question, "Erhmm, Mr Légère, would it be all right if I took the chocolate?"

In a manner akin to that of his country's famed fictional detective Poirot, my Belgian associate picked up the brightly wrapped bar to examine it closely, first with spectacles on – then off – then on again.

"Hmmm, zee choc-o-late … is zee rare huh … and you like zee choc-o-late to eat, Al-lain … huh?"

"Oh yes, Mr Légère … as long as you say I can have it … and you don't think it would be stealing … because you say your staff were transferred to another department last month … and … " … rabbiting on, trying to sell the idea on the one hand and assuage my guilt feelings on the other.

"Hmmm, yes, Al-lain, it is o-kay for you to have zee choc-o-late," concluded Mr Légère, picking up the luscious bar and handing it to me, his squinty eyes looking deep into mine – an almost lascivious grin stretching his thin-lipped mouth. "Here you are, zee choc-o-late is yours, but don't eat it all at once … huh."

Sitting in the canteen as far away from the flirty girls as possible, I wolfed down my lunch, rushed back to my desk upstairs, ripped off the outer wrapping and some of the thin crisp silver foil to reveal the dark brown lusciousness beneath. I broke off two pieces, muttering to myself, "Yummee … two more … hmmm, it's special chocolate, has an almond flavour … hmmm two more bits then back to work in the basement … no … I'll have another couple of squares later with my tea." I ran downstairs, zoomed through the typing pool menagerie and got busy, sweeping the rubbish-strewn floor of an office in the semi-basement.

Allow me to move the story into a present tense narrative:

Half an hour later Mr Légère and I are struggling to move a heavy desk through a narrow door … ooops … I feel unwell … worse … I need to shit … now … before I have an accident. Leaving my boss and desk half-jammed in the doorway, I mutter, "Gotta to go to the … " … zoom up the mezzanine stairs, fly past the flirts clattering their typewriters and crash through the heavy door of the ground floor toilet. "Phweew … just in time." But it's a long time before I feel safe to leave the loo.

I must have a red face, or something, because as I walk back through the typing the clattering stops and three of the typists call out, "You awl rite young-un?" … "don't look well, do yer, mate" … "wot yer in such a bleedin' 'urry fer?" … in lively cockney tones. Innocent, I have no clue why I'm the target of this banter.

Mr Légère, having extricated himself from the desk jammed in the doorway, is sitting at his own desk, puffing his curly briar. He appears to be in an unusually humorous mood.

"Now … zit down, young Al-lain, I have something to tell you. You know that …"

"Excuse me I've got to … " … jump up before either of us can finish a sentence, rush down the corridor, up the stairs, and, holding the buckle of my belt to the accompaniment of cheers from the typists, crash through the door of the toilet again. Agony – I feel as though my guts are falling out. Twenty minutes pass before I wash my hands, sluice my perspiring face, comb my hair and breathe deeply to give myself courage to face the mocking female mob.

I'm talking to myself – out loud: "What is going on ... why am I so ill ... and why are the typists taking the micky?"

Gritting my teeth I swing open the door of the typing pool to be confronted with hand clapping and cheering. The brassy blond – leader of the pack – yells out, "We're countin', mate ... betyer make it five – at least."

Silently: "What is going on – this is *so* embarrassing," I mutter under my panting breath.

"What is going on, Mr Légère," I enquire, as once again, I approach the spare chair in his office and slowly, very slowly, ease my backside onto the hard seat. Demeanour changed, he now seems genuinely concerned. "I think you should go and see Mrs Morant, the Welfare Officer upstairs. She is zee nurse, you know."

Innocent yes – daft no! "Look, Mr Légère, I know I'm unwell – I've got 'the runs', but why are those silly girls in the typing pool cheering me as I run through their office? It is so humiliating ... why are they taking the micky so? Have you said something to them, Mr Légère?"

"Ah, my boy," exclaims the Belgian, unable to restrain his laughter, "it is zee choc-o-late."

"What about the chocolate?"

Laughing, hands holding in his stomach, he eventually manages to get out the words, "Zee choc-o-late ... it is zee Exlax," ... bending forward, guffawing, tears rolling down his cheeks.

"What ... what is Exlax?" I reply, frowning. Yes, innocent and ignorant.

"Zee Exlax is for when you are const-stat-iptated ... when you can't go," he announces in Belgian speak.

"You mean that that chocolate was not really chocolate ... that it's ... it's some sort of medicine?" I reply, feeling even more stupid. "And you told those girls that if I ate some of it they would see me visiting the toilet, regularly?".

"Yes, Al-lain, I am zee sorry, but I thought zaay would be ... how you zay ... amused?"

"Hmmm ... well, I'm not," I reply ... then mutter to myself, "Bloody continental humour."

Three more encores. On the last occasion I was sick. The maternal instincts of the young girls had tempered the earlier response after I had been upstairs to visit Mrs Morant. Most of them realised that I was truly unwell. Compassion elicited kind words ... "Is yer all right now, Alan?" ... and ... "I 'ope yer feel better tomorrow, lovey." Next day I stayed at home, feeling really unwell. Mother did not think the incident was at all funny – but, of course, Father laughed and laughed: "Serves you right for being such a glutton for chocolate, my boy."

On my return to work at Gravel House I was immediately aware of a change of attitude from the girls in the pool. Some enquired, politely, whether I had fully recovered; others nodded and smiled in a friendly and non-flirtatious way. Two nineteen-year-olds, Mary and Molly, became friends in a matey sort of way and we used to lunch together, sharing dreams and problems and tales about their romances. But they could not get their heads around the fact that I didn't want a girlfriend because, as they failed to fathom, sport was my only love at that time. However, before I left SPD to go into the RAF, I was engaged. But again, that is another story.

On reflection, the Exlax incident provoked a 'rite of passage' – an acceptance by my peer group in the workplace – all young females – there being no other young males working for SPD in Gravel House. I was already comfortable in my relationships with the bosses – with a slight reservation about Boris. In retrospect, I am thankful that my Belgian mentor allowed me to take that 'choc-o-late' even though, at the time, I thought it was a bloody unfair trick.

A new bloody unfair trick had been invented by German scientists: 'The Silent Terror'.

Is 'all fair in love and war'? We Londoners more or less accepted as fair-play the attack by V1 flying bombs from June 1944, which my schoolmates and I rationalised as a new era of jet propulsion. At least we could hear them coming and sometimes watch them flying above our heads. "If you can see 'em, you're safe, mate." But V2 rockets, which obviously we could neither see nor hear coming, were considered to be 'not cricket' – really unsporting, given our deeply ingrained values. Our only logical moral conclusion at the time was: *'They are Nazis – thankfully we are typically British.'*

By the time the last Doodle-bug exploded on English soil on March 1st 1945, over 6,000 people had been killed and thousands more injured – which was terrible. The first V2 rockets hit London on September 8th 1944; the last on Orpington on March 27th 1945. Over eleven hundred rockets killed 2,754 people and seriously injured 6,523.

MARCH 8th 1945, 11.10am. I was sitting at my desk next to a large sash window on the first floor of Gravel House, happily typing away on the Wurlitzer Underwood when my body and mind was suddenly jerked into acute awareness by the unmistakable long-loud kruuummmp!!!! of a V2 rocket. Before I could duck under the desk all the windows of the four-storey buildings on the opposite side of the street were sucked out, glass crashing on the street below accompanied by shock waves vibrating through our building. Everything shook, nerves stirred but not shaken. Even Boris herself displayed an uncharacteristic nonchalance. "Would you go and make us all some tea, please Alan?" Gee, she said please!

I boiled the much-dented aluminium kettle on the ancient gas ring in the cubby-hole apologising for a kitchen. I made tea in the large enamel pot and distributed to the five incumbents, all busily engaged with paper work at their own desks. I returned to mine to tackle a job I hated ... marrying hundreds of yellow dockets from the Battersea garage with their office copy counterfoils. We were all back to work within seven minutes of that thunderous explosion. Normal!

But life was not normal a mile away across the Thames. Smithfield meat market off Farringdon Road had been crowded with traders and a number of women and children who were shopping for off-ration rabbit to supplement the family meat ration. The V2 rocket plunged through the huge Victorian building to explode on the railway below, destroying the market, killing 110 and seriously injuring 366 men, women and children.

When I arrived home at 6.30pm Mother told me that Father had phoned her at mid-day to assure her he was safe but would be late home due to the disruption of bus and Tube services. He arrived just in time for the all-important 9 o'clock BBC News on the radio. As we listened intently to the BBC announcer recounting details of the Smithfield disaster, Mother, in an agonised tone kept repeating, "Dreadful ... so dreadful ... oh my ... Sam, it's so so dreadful ... and you were so near ... I was so worried."

Father switched off the radio to share his story of the day: "I was on top of a bus in High Holborn, travelling from Great Portland Street to the City, when suddenly there was a terrible explosion. From the top of the bus I saw lots of debris flying through the air followed by clouds of smoke and dust."

For a few seconds Mother and I looked at each other, wide-eyed and questioning, then at Sam – the silence pregnant with a dozen thoughts and thankfulness that he was alive.

"How near were you Sam ... were you all right ... did it shake you up?" said a worried Wyn, remembering that her husband had experienced shell shock on Hampstead Heath in 1917.

"No, we were not that close, Wyn, although we did feel the shock waves. Everybody started talking at once but nobody got off the bus."

"Did the traffic stop, Father ... and ... and did you see the ambulances and fire engines?" I enquired, partly in excitement and partly sadness, knowing that there had been a lot of casualties.

"Well no, my boy. Although the traffic stopped for about five minutes the police quickly got it flowing again and the bus continued on a different route into the City. I was only a little bit late for my appointment."

"Oh! Sam, I'm so glad you are alright Sam ... you know I've always worried, terribly, every day since this dreadful war started, when you've gone off to work in the City. Surely it will all be over soon and these dreadful rockets will stop. Our boys and those Americans are doing so well in Germany ... they crossed the Rhine yesterday ... surely it can't be long ... can't be long ... "

Father interrupted to calm Mother down and reassure her: "No, Mother, it won't be long now: we've got the Hun on the run, and it'll be all over when we get to Berlin. The Russians are nearly there already, but I don't trust those Russians, neither does Mr Churchill. But don't worry so, my dear, we'll soon be drinking a glass of sherry to celebrate victory and the end to all these horrors."

Russian armoured and infantry units reached the outskirts of Berlin on April 20th and overran German opposition to reach the centre of the capital on April 30th. Earlier that day Hitler had committed suicide – his legal wife Eva Braun too – in the Fuhrerbunker beneath the Reich Chancellery gardens. On May 7th Hitler's chosen successor, Admiral Karl Donitz, surrendered Germany's remaining forces in the west to General Eisenhower at Reims in France; German forces in Berlin and to the east under General Keitel surrendered to Russian General Zuchov on May 8th.

Victory in Europe! VE Day was celebrated on the 8th of May throughout Europe – and in Russia the next day.

In Finchley we ripped down the black-out curtains, turned on all the lights and went out into our street to shake hands with our neighbours – some even hugged each other. Thousands of joyful people gathered in front of Buckingham Palace to cheer the King and Queen – then lifted their voices to even greater volume when His Majesty invited Winston Churchill to join his wife Elizabeth and their daughter Princesses, Elizabeth and Margaret. In London's Trafalgar Square thousands danced and cavorted in the fountains to the backdrop of searchlights and church bells accompanied by a cacophony of hooters, trumpets, tambourines and firework crackers ... alcohol and laughter ... cheering and singing and snogging ... wonderful, joyful, uninhibited craziness.

> *Tis Forty-Five: peace now – those bombs survived,*
> *'Remember Them!' – We Do! – who gave their lives*
> *that Freedom's spree enjoyed on Island Wight*
> *back Thirty-Nine returns – to Brits delight.*

Sam and Wyn opened a bottle of Jerez and I joined in the ' Toast to Victory' with a bottle of Watney's Light Ale – Derek with a Tizer – before I escaped adult company to join my mates in the pavilion at Finchley Cricket Club. We celebrated with ginger beer and cavorted uninhibitedly all over the field – being silly and acting as though we were pissed. We were sixteen. We were Brits delighted!

While millions of people in Britain, Europe, the Mediterranean and Russia celebrated Peace and adjusted to new realities, throughout the Far East the horrors of war continued: humans killing and wounding each other in their thousands; thousands too, both men and women, incarcerated in prisoner of war camps – and more thousands of mum and dads, wives, children and friends waiting at home for news of their loved ones and dreading the arrival of The Telegram.

Winston Churchill, his inner cabinet and heads of the Armed Services remained focused on the conduct of the Pacific war in close liaison with the

President of the United States, Harry Truman, and his team of political and military advisers. However, the British parliamentary parties agreed to hold a General Election in July. Churchill resigned on May 23rd, the National Coalition government broke up but Churchill retained the premiership of a weak Conservative government until the election but focused his time and energies more on the Pacific war than winning votes.

Was our war hero Premier unbeatable in the coming election or politically vulnerable? Although opinion polls were an unproven novelty at the time they indicated that Labour were leading the race by a considerable margin – even as much as 20%. The Labour Party were campaigning strongly for social reform founded on the principles and plans set out in the acclaimed Beveridge Report in 1942. William Beveridge, a Liberal economist, social reformer and former Director of The London School of Economics, advocated wide-reaching reform in housing and employment, social security, transport and medical services. The Labour Party won the General Election by a landslide majority of 145 seats, the percentage of votes being Labour 49.7%; Conservatives 36.2% and the Liberals 9.0%. The new Prime Minister, Clement Attlee moved into No.10 Downing Street and together with his cabinet ministers began a programme of social reforms that led to the National Health Service, the nationalisation of the Bank of England, the railways, the coal and steel industries, a new social security system and a bold programme for new housing.

The euphoria of Peace and the hopes for radical social reform were tempered with the fact that the war had almost bankrupted the nation. When the new government took office the Treasury announced that without substantial financial aid from the USA the country faced a financial Dunkirk. A few days later the Americans cut off their Lend-Lease life-line – our nation was virtually broke. But we rescued ourselves from that financial Dunkirk as well: the war effort had created a new and larger labour force working in new and progressive industries that created a rise in exports which in turn slowly improved our financial stability through the 1940s into the 1950s.

For me – and many millions of people of many nations who lived through those dangerous and disruptive years of war – Winston Churchill is not only a hero but in the highest sense, the saviour of human freedoms. And, as Churchill acknowledged in a typically gracious manner, he was so ably supported by his family and staff – from ministers and service chiefs to secretaries and drivers and cooks. Writing of Churchill at the time of his humiliating election defeat, the historian AJP Taylor wrote:

> On May 28th Churchill entertained the leading members of the former government at 10 Downing Street and said: **"The light of history will shine on all your helmets."**

~~~~~~~~~~~

CHAPTER 22

OPPORTUNITY

Sixteen – I need to slide back the doors of time a little to glimpse moments of opportunity that encouraged my dreams of a sporting career – opportunities that were unforeseen, unexpected, serendipitous – a combination of favourable circumstances.

In the early 1940s the cream of football talent from Finchley's four grammar schools had voluntarily joined '393 Squadron' of the Air Training Corps because one of the officers, Mr Marr, was known to be a gifted and enthusiastic coach. By the autumn of 1944 Mr Marr had developed a tactically brilliant and competitive team with a terrific team spirit. We were all very fit and quick thinking; I was fast, powerful with both feet, a left-winger who could drift inside and shoot with my right foot. Trained and encouraged by our excellent coach we became the most successful young soccer team in North London. I remember all but two of the player's names in a photograph of the team taken in April 1945: Roberts, Graham, Clayton, Robins, Scutt, Rayment, Cowan, Fox, Pearce, Wilson, Shipman (eight of whom were gifted cricketers playing for Finchley Colts). The photograph depicts four players holding silver-plated trophies and a display board resting against skipper Pearce's knees portrays our successes:

Winners of the North Middlesex League Cup: The Challenge Cup: The Six-a-Side Cup. Finalists in the Middlesex Cup and Finchley Six-a Side Cup.

"Wotta-lotta-socca!" But now, as I read that list more than sixty years later, I am amazed at the number of games we must have played that season. The sad irony is that I remember only one match in early April 1945 – a Six-a-Side Final – a game which opened up an opportunity beyond my expectations.

The North Middlesex Six-a-Side Knock-Out Tournament was held on the numerous pitches at North London Playing Fields. The final was refereed by Mr Joe Hulme, the pre-war Arsenal and England outside right and Middlesex cricketer who was now the manager of Tottenham Hotspur. We won, I scored three goals, and after the presentation of the cup and medals, Mr Hulme came into our dressing room to congratulate the team members and our coach. As he was leaving Mr Hulme took me aside and, to my great surprise, asked me to take a walk outside with him.

When we were clear of the racket being made by my mates in celebration of victory, Mr Hulme said: "Well played today, young man ... your team deserved to win ... you out-thought and out-ran them ... you have to be very fit to get through to a final in a six-a-side tournament. By the way, I've heard that you are a promising cricketer, too ... an all-rounder, cricket and soccer."

393 Squadron ATC Cup Winning Football Team 1945
from left, standing: F/O Marr (coach); P.Dale; D.Graham; A.Clayton;
R.Robins; D.Scutt; A.Rayment; Sqr.Ldr. Fuller, CO.
Seated: A.Cowam; E.Fox; T.Pearce; R.Wilson; M.Shipman

Tottenham Hotspur Juniors, White Hart Lane, 1945

"Yes sir," I replied hoarsely, being rather in awe of his fame.

"Are you still at school?"

"No sir, I work for Unilever in an office off Southwark Street."

"I see – so how old are you now, Alan, and when will you be called up?"

"I'm sixteen ... seventeen next month, sir. I expect I'll go into the RAF next year."

"Hmmm. so you'll be playing for your ATC team next season ... hmmm ... well ... would you like to play for my junior team at Tottenham and come to our training sessions at White Hart Lane? If so, you may have to ask your boss for time off ... to leave work early ... do you think he would agree to that?"

"I expect so, sir ... my immediate boss, Mr Lacey, was a good soccer player ... I think he had a trial for the England amateur team in the 1920s."

"So, Alan, think about my offer and when you have decided, come and ... "

Interrupting, I blurted out, "I have decided, sir, I'd love to train with 'The Juniors' next season ... and ... and ... I hope I'll be good enough to play in the team ... thank you very much, sir."

"Good ... you are a decisive young man. Can you come to my office next Wednesday evening at about six o'clock to sign some forms ... and I'll introduce you to the Juniors' coach.

"Yes Mr Hulme, I'll be at your office next Wednesday ... thank you very much, sir!"

As we parted, Mr Hulme smiled, shook my hand and said: "You'll be changing boots and getting into the nets soon, Alan ... have a good cricket season."

"Thank you, Mr Hulme ... thank you very much!"

Opportunity! Shock! ... head swimming with thoughts ... in a daze ... I remember absolutely nothing of the remainder of that day. Nothing about the questions my team mates must have asked – nothing about the journey home on an ordinary London bus – nothing about what I said to my parents or Mr Lacey and Colonel Jameson at the office on the Monday. But I do have a vague memory of checking my cricket gear a few days later in preparation for something even more exciting than signing forms for Spurs Juniors: I was booked to attend the Easter Coaching Classes at Lord's!

Although my parents had become keen followers of my soccer and cricket adventures, the world of professional sport and how to further my promising abilities was a closed book to them. However, as honorary members of the Finchley Cricket Club, they had become friends with knowledgeable grey-haired veterans whose own sons had benefited from the coaching at Lord's before the war. With the encouragement of Tom Birkin and Lionel Bishop, Sam and Wyn sent an application by post to Lord's and paid the fees by cheque when I had been accepted. Given that my parents worked so hard for little money I shall be forever grateful that they set aside a few precious pounds to send me to the Easter coaching classes at Lord's in 1945. I was granted leave from my job, bought a new bat and gloves and paid my bus fares to and from St John's Wood.

On a warm bright Monday morning in mid-April, dressed smartly in grey suit, white shirt and Finchley club tie, I walked with light step and brimming heart along tree-lined Litchfield Grove, carrying my long leather cricket bag to the bus stop at Church End. The No.2 red double-decker eased through light traffic up the hill through Temple Fortune to Golders Green where we waited while the female clippy had a lengthy 'barney' with a much older male inspector – a man of military bearing and stern countenance. She pulled the bell cord 'ding-ding' and addressed the passengers: "Cor blimey, don't arf go awn that one, thinks he's still in the 'bleedin' army."

My feelings were mixed: calm yet excited, impatient at the delay, yet apprehensive about arriving at St. John's Wood. What would it be like at Lord's ... *Lord's*! ... I'm going to bat and bowl at Lord's – even if it only on the Nursery Ground. I wonder who will be my coach – who I will meet – what will the other boys be like – mostly from public schools, I expect. Thankfully, I was a socially confident teenager, used to mixing with men and boys from posh backgrounds in the middle-class environment of London club cricket. Most of my excitement was focussed on what I might learn – how much I could improve my skills – and again, which famous county players I would meet at the nets.

As I entered the North Gate from Wellington Road a cheerful cockney steward directed me towards the changing rooms under the Mound Stand: "Good luck nipper – d'yer bat or bowl?"

"A bit of both," I replied with embarrassed modesty, "but I'm a pretty good fielder, too."

"Well, you enjoy it – I hope to see yer play in the middle one day, young blondy."

"What a kind man," I thought, not realising until later that evening how much his cheerful words had washed away my nervousness and made me feel immediately welcome and comfortable in the hallowed environs of 'The Mecca of Cricket'. Lord's was to become 'home' to me as much as Arden Field: I still get goose-bumps on entering both grounds and become charged with the vibrant energies at the sight of their green green acres.

> As Lord's I enter thru' memorial gates,
> Graced by bearded one of ancient fame,
> I pause, reflect the triumphs, fates
> Of white and coloured heroes, flannelled same
> In white to fight fair cricket's glorious game,
> On white man's hallowed verdant sward.

Oh Constantine, my hero first in '39,
In awe I watched at Lord's with envious mind,
Black gifted clown, yet serious gifted man
Who graced that other House of Lords in ermine gown
To fight fair politics of race and kind,
In white man's hallowed halls of history's time.

Walking from the North Gate round the Nursery Ground behind what is now the Compton-Edrich Stand, I was joined by two chatty younger boys also eagerly anticipating their first coaching sessions at Lord's. As we entered the excited buzz and distinctive aroma of the changing rooms under the Mound Stand an MCC official handed us a revised programme. Due the uncertainties of daily life in wartime, and the possibility that coaching staff involved in civil defence may have been on duty during an air raid, the daily schedule had to be updated. I was to meet my coach, Mr Frank Lee, at 9.50am in net number five, bowl to other boys in that net under the direction of the coach until 11.15 then pad-up and bat from 11.30 until 12 mid-day.

From reading the sports press before the war and a friend's *Wisden*, I knew that 'Lee F.S.' was a capped Somerset professional, batted left-handed and scored over two thousand runs in 1938. I was surprised and pleased to learn from a chat with the friendly official that Mr Lee had played a couple of games for Middlesex earlier in his career, having been on the ground staff at Lord's from the age of sixteen. I quickly changed into cricket attire, gathered up my pads, bat, gloves and box, then walked to the nets alone in order to 'have a think' about this moment and about my coach ... "Hmmm ... Frank Lee must be a Londoner then ... not a west countryman ... hmmm ... and he was on the ground staff here as a boy ... ah, so he's a man of Lord's – I expect we'll get on OK." I 'got on' with nearly everybody I met, even so, I was still a bit nervous as I walked towards No.5 net and spotted Mr Lee, wearing a Somerset cap, surrounded by half a dozen lively boys of varying ages all trying to talk at once.

Mr Lee caught my eye and moved out of the group towards me, his warm handshake and soft-eyed smile seemed, for a few seconds, to mesmerise me and freeze my vocal chords. "And you are ...?" "Oh ... er ... er ... Mr Lee," clearing my throat, "I'm Alan Rayment from Finchley."

"Ah yes, Alan ... I'm very pleased to meet you – welcome to my net. I have heard about you from Archie Fowler who said he'd seen you bat and ... er yes ... said that a few years ago you fielded for him in a charity match – goodness, how old were you then may I ask?"

"Fourteen, I think, Mr Lee," I replied.

"You're keen then ... now let's see ... you bat later, at eleven thirty, so do join in and bowl ... what do you bowl by the way, Alan?"

Frank Lee, my warm-hearted coach and shamanic guide

"Quickish seamers ... in-swingers if there's some shine, Mr Lee," I replied, regaining my confidence.

"Well, have a bowl at Christopher ... he's a pretty good player from Oundle School ... a bit older than you ... see if you can bowl him out."

Picking up a ball I took a short run and bowled a low full-toss which Christopher dispatched high out of the net. The resultant chase across the Nursery ground limbered up my muscles and mental faculties. As I ran back to the nets I woke-up to the reality that I was in action at Lord's ... "Gee whiz, I'm bowling at Lord's ... and that Mr Lee is a really nice man and made me feel so welcome. Yes, I'm going to enjoy myself this week."

More than any of the high points of my life up to April 1945, that week in the nets at Lord's was the mountain peak – and Mr Lee my shamanic guide. Under his wise, quiet-mannered tutelage, my batting technique improved enormously. I was a hard-hitting young batsman with an attacking temperament, blessed with quick footwork and fast hands. I scored most of my runs by powerful front-foot drives on both sides of the wicket, square cuts and pulls. But my defence was weak, especially on the back foot. Frank Lee transformed my back-foot play, both defence and attack, drilling into me the mantra, "back and across – back and across – eyes in line with the ball – watch the ball all the way!" By the middle of the week my defensive play was tighter, though still vulnerable due to my attacking temperament and desire to hit the ball out of the net – which I did – often. More than one pulled drive disappeared over the groundsman's sheds and beyond the wall into Wellington Road. I became aware that the head coach, Archie Fowler, was having a chat with Frank Lee at the bowler's end, after which Mr Lee strolled down the wicket to have a quiet word in my ear: "Hit 'em hard but keep 'em down, young Alan." Wonderful coach, wonderful man, Frank Lee: always patient, soft voiced and wise, never discouraging ... the best!

I was further encouraged later in the week by the increasing numbers of spectators who gathered behind my net when I was batting. I was still only sixteen and somewhat naïve about the significance of this development until Frank Lee took me aside and said: "Some of the 'big wigs' were watching you yesterday, and again today, Alan."

"What do you mean, Mr Lee ... what are 'big wigs?'"

"Now don't let this go to your head young man, but Sir Pelham and Mr Robins – and even the Colonel – were all watching you today. Mr Robins came round the nets to ask me who you were and where you are from – and if you become good enough to play first-class cricket when you are older, whether you would play as an amateur or a professional."

"Did he really?" I replied, surprised and embarrassed, knowing that Mr RWV Robins had captained Middlesex before the war – and had played for England. "I don't know what to say, Mr Lee ... and who is the Colonel?"

"The Secretary of the MCC, Colonel Rait-Kerr," was the reply, "and we don't often see him out here ... you go off now to eat your sandwiches and I'll talk to you again this afternoon" ... leaving me in suspense with lots of questions racing around in my mind.

I bowled to other boys most of the afternoon, breaking off for a while to dive around with three boys enjoying the novelty of the slip cradle. At the end of the session I waited for Mr Lee to be free and walked with him round to our changing rooms. For a moment there was silence between us until I burst out with the question: "Mr Lee, do you think I might be good enough to be a professional one day?"

"Well, you might be – but cricket is a 'funny game' ... as they say ... and life even stranger. And the way things are going, you'll have to go into the services even if the war is over, so it will be another four years before you could play first-class cricket regularly, even if you continue to develop ... so it is much too early to tell. I think you will enjoy a lot of good cricket as an amateur, so it is best to think of a career which pays well – cricket professionals get very little money, you know."

"Hmmm, I don't know, Mr Lee ... I don't know what I want to do ... I've only ever dreamed of playing cricket every day – dreamed of playing for Middlesex."

"Well, if you did become a professional you'd still have to find work in the winter you know – and that is never easy – unless you have a qualification of some sort or a little business ... or, say, you're good at painting and decorating.

Anyway, you'll have to see how life works out – and you have a lot of growing-up to do yet, so be patient. Oh, by the way, Alan, I've asked a friend of mine to have a bowl at you tomorrow, Squadron-Leader Alec Mackenzie, who played for Hampshire as a leg spinner."

As we parted and I entered the changing rooms my head was spinning and my heart pounding – but I also had a naughty chuckle inside me: "I'll bet that war hero's bowling arm is a bit rusty, and anyway, he can't be as good a leg spinner as my young mate, Ian Bedford." Ah, loyalty and self-confidence – a heady mix.

The coaching session the next day was my last – six days in which I had grown significantly in skill and self-belief as a batsman due to the immeasurable all-round skills of Frank Lee as a tutor – plus a little boost to my self-esteem from the attention of the 'big wigs'. A danger there, of course, of getting a swollen head, but my upbringing under the wise elders at the Finchley Club had conditioned me in the mores of understatement and modesty – perhaps too much modesty? In any case the game itself is a great leveller: failure is a constant companion – though an impostor just the same – because there may be triumph in the next match.

Entering Frank Lee's net for the last time I felt not only confident but determined to bat really aggressively ... well, anyway, when the other boys bowled to me. But when I was introduced to Alec Mackenzie I had a brief touch of the 'awesomes', thinking, "Gee whiz, a war hero, RAF pilot *and* Hampshire county player!" But only a touch because I was in great form, bounding with energy and his bowling arm really was rusty. At first I belted so many balls out of the net – including one from Alec Mackenzie into Wellington Road – that the bowling rate slowed down to about two-per-minute. Mr Lee, his unique lop-sided grin expressing his thoughts from afar, walked down the net and said: "Ration 'em, young Alan ... remember there's a war on ... those bowlers need their ammunition."

A dry wry wit, our coach. I got the message and thus drove and pulled more balls into the netting – only a few went aerial and some rattled the wickets. I was having so much fun, bursting with confidence and energy, learning lots, being thankful for and taking full advantage of this very special opportunity.

I could not know, at that moment in time, that my unforeseen opportunity would bloom and grow into fulfilling the dreams and desires of the ten-year-old who longed 'to play cricket every day' ... and the eleven-year-old who told Mr Big that the war would mess up his cricket career. Nor could I have foreseen that in a few weeks time I would play cricket in Wales with Mr Joe Hulme, and later in the season at Lord's under the captaincy of Mr RWV Robins.

Thank you, Lord's ... and, above all, a big thank you to the wonderful Mr Frank Lee.

〃〃〃〃〃〃〃〃〃〃

CHAPTER 23

DREAMS COME TRUE

My childhood dream unfolds and leads to destinies beyond the dream.

On the Monday morning after saying goodbye to Mr Lee at Lord's I joined City commuters on a packed smoke-filled Tube train at Finchley Central, breathed in the Thames' refreshing tang as I walked Blackfriars Bridge, entered my office-boy's cubby-hole and opened wide the sash window. I sat down to clear my head and 'have a think' ...

"Has it all been a dream then, or had I – only two days ago – really been running round the Nursery Ground at Lord's, whacking balls out of the nets, chatting with famous cricketers and absorbing the wise words of Mr Lee? And had I really, the week before, been listening to Mr Hulme in his manager's office at White Hart Lane as he outlined the training schedules and introduced me to the Junior's coach? If not a dream come true then a taste – a taste of what is possible if I work hard to develop my talent – to improve and improve until I prove I am good enough to play county cricket ... maybe league soccer too. "I know what I really want ... to be running around on grass applying my mind to improving my cricket skills alongside experienced county players. And I know what I don't want: to be sitting on this office chair, thumping these typewriter keys and *trying* to apply my mind to matching those bloody yellow garage dockets. But I'll have to wait ... wait another four summers ... another four summers!"

Suddenly, I woke from my reverie and muttered out loud: "I'd better make some tea for the bosses."

Mr Lacey looked up from his papers, thanked me for the cup of tea, then added, "Too busy now, Alan, but we'll have a chat at lunch time about your week at Lord's ... no doubt you enjoyed it?"

"Yes, thank you, Mr Lacey, I had a wonderful time ... Frank Lee was my coach."

Next, I delivered teas for the directors to Mrs Hall's office. She ... Boris ... actually looked up from her typewriter and actually said 'thank you' ... then actually beamed a smile and said, "I expect you wish you were at Lord's again this week – I love Lord's ... er ... and I hope you did well!"

"Yes, thank you, Miss Hall."

I blushed because I was flabbergasted that Boris had spoken to me at all ... and "I hope you did well" was beyond belief. My-oh-my, cricket, and especially Lord's, seems to have a strange power over some people – like a song that awakens a happy memory.

I found it hard to resume the routine of commuting and clerking and longed for the weekend. Awake early on a bright yet chilly Saturday morning, I dressed in soccer shorts and plimsolls to dribble a ball round Arden Field: I needed to wash away the City's dross in the freshness of nature's morning calm. Spring's awakening shone sharp-green from the chestnut trees framing the glistening dew-sprinkled grass of the field that birthed my dreams. I felt at home, at peace, at one with self and life.

My inner musings were not disturbed during a quiet breakfast and chat with Mother, but on returning to my haven in mid-morning the harsh putt-putt-putt of the outfield mower and the fine-tuned muffled whirr emitted by the wicket-shaver blemished the stillness and softness of the early hour. Regimented mounds of new-cut grass lay at ease beyond the Briarfield boundary line now being refreshed by liquid chalk flowing from the broad iron wheel rotating in its hand-pushed reservoir on mini-wheels. I joined the club's members happily preparing the five-acre stage and rustic auditorium for the season's opening rehearsal – a practice match between teams selected by two veteran players, Bay Bishop and Cecil Parkin.

On joining senior members and fellow colts in the old timbered pavilion I found myself answering so many questions about my recent experience at Lord's: who had coached me; what did I learn; who did I meet and did I enjoy myself? That I enjoyed myself was obvious from my effusive answers; that my batting technique had improved was obvious to the bowlers against whom I scored forty-odd that afternoon – and to my friendly mentors including George Wood, the Woodhouse schoolmaster and prolific opening batsman, who complimented me on my defensive play off the back foot.

Before I reached seventeen at the end of May I was batting high in the order and scoring runs in the men's first team and, surprisingly, taking wickets as a first-change medium-paced seam bowler. I say surprising because while Mr Lee's skilled and encouraging tuition had rectified flaws in my batting techniques, my over-zealous bowling had evoked grinning caution:

"Alan, you are not going to be a Larwood – or even a Maurice Tate. Bowl a bit slower ... within yourself ... pitch it up and keep saying to yourself ... off stump ... off stump ... off stump."

But my growing physical strength, mental stamina and boundless youthful enthusiasm produced more speed – and many 'off-days' when I would 'spray it about' and take nought for plenty. On the other hand, I bowled more accurately when captaining Finchley Colts due, I expect, to a greater sense of responsibility for the result of the match.

Finchley Cricket Club Colts had attracted and developed the cream of local cricketing talent during the war years, paralleling the magnetic pull of 393 Squadron Air Training Corps for soccer players. As I mentioned in the last chapter, eight members of that cup-winning soccer team played cricket for the

Colts before being called up for National Service. Woodhousians Ray Robins and Martin Shipman were prolific opening batsmen followed by six gifted players whom I had to juggle in the batting order so they had a knock in the middle now then. Bowlers ... we bowled out most teams so cheaply that many gifted bowling all-rounders would neither bat nor bowl: two defected to other teams the next season. Our bowling star was the youngest and the smallest, Ian Bedford, age 15, who was to make his first-class debut for Middlesex two years later. To skipper Finchley Colts that season was a joy: enthusiasm was high, the fielding exceptional and team spirit superb.

Colts matches were played on Friday evenings. On Saturdays and Sundays we played for Finchley first or second elevens, except one of the Colts who played for his Old Boys team and two who were loyal to 393 Squadron. I must have played an occasional game for '393' because in July I received an invitation to play for the Air Training Corps against the Royal Naval College, Dartmouth ... in a two-day game ... at Lord's!

Lord's again ... breathless with excitement my imagination filmed the scene in technicolour: I was going to enter that historic pavilion, mount the wide staircase to one of the famous dressing rooms, walk through the legendary Long Room, then down the gentle steps onto the lush outfield of the most iconic cricket theatre in the world.

But hold on – I'm getting ahead of myself because in June, ten days after my seventeenth birthday, I experienced an adventure beyond my dreams at that time: my first invitation to play in a team with well known county players. The adventure would involve my first long-distance train journey to play cricket, my first stay in a hotel and my first game on a ground where county cricket had been played. Thanks to Mr Frank Lee I was selected to play for London Counties against a Glamorgan XI on the Rodney Parade Ground, Newport, Monmouthshire. And who was our captain? The Tottenham Hotspur soccer manager I had met only three months earlier: Mr JHA Hulme, Arsenal and England footballer and Middlesex cricketer.

It will be difficult for young people in the 21st century to understand what a momentous event that was for me in 1945. Even though Britain and her Allies had celebrated 'Victory in Europe Day' only a month earlier, the war in the Pacific was serious daily news. Rationing was tight, travel restricted and wages low. The prospect of a seventeen-year-old travelling with seasoned professional cricketers and veteran amateurs from London to Newport to play in a cricket match was, at that moment, beyond my comprehension.

Bearing in mind that staying in a team hotel was totally new to me, I can now chuckle at the memory of sharing a room with the huge and boisterous Spurs centre-half, Jack Chisholm. At first I was a bit scared because the 20-year-old giant was a boozer-bruiser, but evidently his manager had instructed him 'to look after the young-un'. And I remember the easy acceptance and friendship of characters like Jack Young, Vic Evans and Bertie Buse as we travelled on from Newport to play a match at Pontypridd. In the one-day match at Newport, London Counties won a low scoring contest against a weak Glamorgan side skippered by legendary Johnny Clay. I managed to break my duck, just. Jack Chisholm belted 31 not out before Joe Hulme declared at 150 for 8 wickets. On a turning wicket the opposition scraped 72: Vic Evans of Essex taking 7 for 35 and Jack Young of Middlesex 3 for 21.

Looking back I now recognise my experience with London Counties as 'a right of passage'. My first taste of playing 'on tour' with – and being accepted by – seasoned County cricketers no doubt notched up my inner self-belief and outward status. As mentioned in the last chapter, I was fortunate that my upbringing at home and at the Finchley Club conditioned a cheerful modesty, a balanced ego. But in the 1940s I was certainly not aware of self-analysis so I conclude that for the rest of the season I sailed along in a breeze of naive self belief combined with the sunshine of enjoyment. I truly loved playing, improving, meeting new people and climbing the lower rungs of the ladder of success.

The next big step was that first game at Lord's – of which I retain but three feelings and few facts. Reports in *The Times* of August 16th and 17th prove I had little success with bat or ball, that the Royal Naval College beat the Air Training Corps and that my good friend, Ian Bedford, was not well served by our fielders – as expressed by *The Times* cricket correspondent:

> ... if only PI Bedford had been served more appropriately behind the stumps they well might have lost a great deal of their advantage. Off three consecutive balls Bedford, who without doubt is a young bowler of exceptional merit, had a batsman a yard out of his crease without being stumped, had a catch dropped at square leg, and yet another catch missed at second slip.

My first reaction on selection was one of disappointment: the ATC cricket selectors had not appointed me as captain – but then I was not a public school boy. The second memory is of the Visitors Dressing Room: spacious old fashioned luxury, opulent leather settees and chairs, the cheerful dressing room attendant ... and, above all, the panoramic view of the historic arena from the balcony. Hundreds of truly great players had sat on those balcony seats calmly watching the progress of their team mates – or nervously smoking – even biting their nails while watching and waiting ... waiting to go into bat in the middle of that almost holy amphitheatre below. The third, most tangible and lasting feeling, was to tread the turf one step beyond the pavilion's white-painted gate, held open by a steward redolent with Lord's tradition. I had always loved grass ... as I surveyed the green expanse and cultured stands from cover point I fell in love with Lord's again – on a higher level – as a player.

The joy I felt that day when taking my first romantic step 'beyond the pavilion's white-painted gate' was *infinitesimal* when compared to the millions of people around the world who were celebrating 'Victory in Japan Day'. The use of atomic bombs to affect surrender was in itself horrendous: deaths of human beings at Hiroshima and Nagasaki were eventually above 200,000. Debate covering every aspect of the use of atomic weapons rages on into the 21st century. However, it was purported at the time that the planned invasion of Japan in October would cost over one million Allied lives and several million Japanese, especially in light of their tradition and avowed practice of Kamikaze tactics. Whatever the pros and cons, the moral, ethical and scientific debates, the war was over.

WORLD WAR II ENDED ON AUGUST 15TH 1945

Church bells rang, factory sirens blared, ship's horns blasted and car hooters ... well ... hooted. In huge typefaces the newspaper headlines blazed ... VICTORY! ... and ... IT'S ALL OVER!!

Celebrating VE Day, May 8th 1945 – Winston Churchill invited by King George VI and Queen Mary to join them on the balcony of Buckingham Palace with their daughters, Princess Elizabeth and Princess Margaret

Having missed out on London's 'Victory in Europe Day' celebrations in May I was determined to be in Trafalgar Square that evening with my girl-friend Betty. Following the post-match social pleasantries of my debut at Lord's we hopped on a bus and headed for Piccadilly Circus, but due to the congestion of traffic and people we had to alight in Oxford Street to join the thousands of people who were jostling joyfully down Regent's Street and the Haymarket towards 'The Square' dominated by Nelson's column. The pubs were overflowing so we squeezed into a crowded café for spam sandwiches and tea, followed later by sausage rolls, lemonade and lots of ice cream from roadside stalls. Above all I remember the exuberant atmosphere, the unique sound created by that mass of happy people, singing, laughing, hugging, waving flags and letting off fireworks. As darkness fell there were lights everywhere – some buildings were floodlit – a truly uplifting sight after six years of the blackout regulations.

We were young – we were happy – we were fit ... and we walked the seven miles home to Finchley. The next morning I caught the No.2 bus that covered the return route of that long long walk, to arrive in the dressing room at Lord's by 10.15am. No wonder I have no memory of the second day of my first match at Lord's.

Until recently I could neither remember nor trace a match record of my second game at Lord's. But since August 1945 I have kept a valued team photograph which, to me, symbolised my respectful acceptance of the amateur-professional tradition of the era and, given the status and age range of the photographer's subjects, reminds me of the relaxed and friendly flow of conversation between all present.

Taken in the Harris Memorial Garden the photograph shows the captain of the team, Mr Ronald Aird, seated in the middle of the front row – the legendary Sir Pelham Warner to his right and Archie Fowler to his left. Mr Fowler, a long-serving professional at Lord's was the MCC's Head Coach. Ronald Aird, Cambridge and Hampshire batsman, had been assistant secretary of the MCC from 1926 to 1939. As a tank commander in the North African Desert Campaign, Major R Aird won a Military Cross. Recently demobbed, he was about to resume his duties at Lord's, replacing Sir Pelham who had deputised for him during the war.

The 72-year-old Sir Pelham – once captain of Middlesex and England, a selector, journalist, controversial manager of the England team in Australia during the highly contentious Bodyline Series, and a leading cricket administrator for many years – had invited a disparate set of individuals to represent his Lord's XI. He was a kindly man who was especially encouraging to young players. I thought of him as 'The Archbishop of Lord's'.

The symbolism continues at either end of the front row: two playing professionals steeped in the Lord's traditions since boyhood, Bill Wignall and Jim Sims – both faithful, one famous. Behind the Lord's quintet stands the Cambridge University double centurion Alan Ratcliffe and six amateurs from London Club Cricket, including three Finchley Colts: John Stacey, Ian Bedford and myself.

But against whom did this team play – and when? My memory had led me to assume that this particular match was against Surrey Colts but when searching *The Times* online I discovered that another, and stronger Lord's XI that included yours truly played that fixture on September 10th. I was still sure

Sir Pelham Warner's Lord's XI, 1945
from left, standing: ?; I.Bedford; A.Ratcliffe; D.O'Shea;
M.Fitzgerald; E.Murphy; J.Stacey; A.Rayment
seated: W.Wignell; Sir P.Warner; R.Aird; A.Fowler; J.Sims

that the team in the photo had played at Lord's between my first match and the unforgettable England v Dominions game at the end of August.

Really sure? No – so phone a friend. Peter Jenkins, a member of MCC who lives nearby, has a gallery of *Wisdens*, including those oh-so-slim volumes from the early to mid-1940s. Peter found it ... 'it' being one-and-a-half lines in minute print stating that the game between a Lord's XI and the Forty Club on August 22nd was abandoned due to rain when the Forty Club had scored 118 for 4: RWV Robins 51 not out. Ah! – washed from my memory. But my little grey cells are tingling with excitement as they recall my next experience as a spectator of a historic game, followed the next day, at Lord's, by a personal life-changing experience.

Keith Miller, the Australian Air Force night-fighter pilot, was tall, athletic and sun tanned. Keith's exceptional all-round cricketing talent and swashbuckling style as a fast bowler, attacking batsman and dynamic fielder thrilled every spectator, young and old, male and female wherever he played. Also, his film star good looks and mane of dark hair – tossed back with nonchalant confidence – stirred even the hearts of ladies who knew nothing about cricket.

In 1945 he starred in a series of 'Victory Tests' organised by the MCC to celebrate the end of the war in Europe. Huge crowds attended three-day matches played between England and the Australian Services at Lord's, Sheffield and Old Trafford. The highlight of the season was an encounter between England and the Dominions on August 25/27/28th that attracted over 80,000 spectators to Lord's. I was determined to be there for the thrilling prospect of seeing Keith Miller, Martin Donnelly and Wally Hammond bat – and, most importantly, to join with the multitude of fans who would be saying farewell to the forty-three-year-old Learie Constantine playing his last first-class match. Yes, so determined that I sacrificed playing for my own club on the Saturday and negotiated three days' holiday time from work. I was not to be disappointed; nor was Betty who was watching Test cricket stars for the first time on the Saturday. Ever practical, Betty insisted on taking an umbrella when we set out from Finchley on a dull, rain-threatening morning.

From the moment we settled in our seats high in the Mound Stand I realised that beyond the buzz of excited anticipation reverberating around the half packed arena I was experiencing something 'other'; something beyond my love of cricket and of Lord's itself, beyond my coltish love of my sporting girl friend: something beyond my understanding. But I felt *it* strongly and remember *it* distinctly.

Was that mysterious other 'something' simply post-war euphoria? Or was the sensation a more complex cocktail of thoughts, emotions and energies – an invisible collective consciousness created by an expectant crowd of cricket aficionados who, after long years of war-time hardship and severely rationed sporting festivals, were anticipating a feast at high table with cricket royalty? Were they longing to experience again the athletic poetry in motion displayed by the game's greatest artists and entertainers – Hammond and Donnelly; Wright, Miller and Constantine – longing to refresh the bygone memory of the ineffable beauty and excitement created by thirteen men in white apparel playing a game with bat and ball at the highest level, set on a stage of luscious turf in the historic theatre of Lord's Cricket Ground?

Waves of joyful anticipation were released with cheering and clapping when a special announcement was made over the tannoy:

> Due to the absence through illness of Lindsay Hassett, the Dominions players have chosen Learie Constantine as their captain for this match.

How wonderfully appropriate that in his last first-class game – and at Lord's – the great West Indian cricketer was voted in as captain by his international colleagues. Yes, truly appropriate to be so honoured because Constantine the cricketer was also a lawyer and politician who was knighted in 1962 and later appointed to the British House of Lords. In 1969 Sir Learie Nicholas Constantine, MBE, was created Baron Constantine of Maraval in Trinidad and of Nelson in Lancashire.

Writing about these preliminary events to the match lights up my visual memory and powerful emotional imprint. The sight of the barrel-chested Walter Hammond, resplendent in a full-sleeved MCC touring sweater, leading his team through the pavilion gate on to the lush-green outfield is a picture I have retained in my mind for over sixty years. Maybe the Hammond Presence radiated a distinct aura fused with the enthusiasm of people around me who, in this new peacetime era, were really thrilled to welcome back to Lord's England's greatest player of his generation.

Constantine had won the toss and England won the opening encounter, taking five Dominion wickets for 109 including, much to the disappointment of the majority, those of Miller and Constantine himself. Then Mr Pugnacious, the Australian Cec Pepper, joined master artist Martin Donnelly to rebuild the innings with a stand of 120 before Pepper succumbed to a fast leg-break from Doug Wright. But the New Zealander continued to enthrall us all with his elegant stroke play until he was caught and bowled by Hollies for 133 – an innings of beauty that remains memorable to this day. The Dominions innings closed on 307.

Expectation was high among England fans as the in-form Laurie Fishlock and jaunty Jack Robertson walked to the wicket to face the moderately quick Australian Robert Williams and Learie Constantine – past his prime but still dynamic. By close of play England had lost the openers and Phillipson for 36: disappointing for the partisan but a satisfying day's play for the connoisseur.

A beautiful summer's morning attracted a full house on Monday. The palpable energy of excited anticipation reminded me of the concert at the Queen's Hall when the orchestra tuned up while we waited for Sir Henry Wood to mount the podium. I had borrowed father's binoculars and now focused on the pavilion gate where stone meets turf, awaiting the appearance of Mr Constantine as he led his team on to the green acres, holding him in view until the first ball was bowled. England's night-watchman Billy Griffith hung on for a while with James Langridge before caught at the wicket for 15. Enter Captain Hammond: would he save his fast sinking team? I could hardly look at the scoreboard when Hammond lost partners Langridge and Gimblett to the quickish leg-spinner Cristophani: England 96 for 6.

Some of the England supporters sitting near me expressed feelings of disappointment and anxiety as their expectations of a competitive first innings total faded. Betty stayed home so being on my own I joined the discussion and offered positive and hopeful comments. Hope was revived by the combative Middlesex and England star – and RAF pilot – Bill Edrich, DFC, who patiently supported Hammond as he began to dominate the four main bowlers. I was mesmerised by the classic skill and controlled power of Wally Hammond throughout his innings of 121, and thrilled to take in the smooth run-up and bowling action of the wonderful Learie Constantine, now less than fast but causing even the great Hammond to be wary of his subtle changes of pace. From *The Times* I quote:

> Hammond was particularly severe on DR Cristofani, and there were times when no place in the pavilion was safe from the fury of his off-drives, the luncheon interval arriving with the score at 152, of which Hammond had made 57. No sooner were they out again than Hammond drove another ball into the pavilion, with Edrich still modestly curtailing his own hitting powers. Hammond's selection of the suitable ball to hit – and hit it he did terrifically hard – and his perfectly shaped defensive strokes which, with his sense of timing, often found runs were those of the man who can make all other batsmen look second class.

When Hammond reached his century, and a short while later when he was stumped on 121, the applause was thunderous and prolonged. The partnership that raised all our hopes had reached 177 and Edrich, 65, soon followed his captain when the total had reached 278 for 8. The last two wickets failed to raise that total. With a lead of twenty runs the Dominion's openers Craig and Fell succumbed to Jack Davies and Pettiford to Doug Wright – the total being 93 for 3 when, ominously for the home side though thrilling for true cricket lovers, Martin Donnelly joined Keith Miller on centre stage at Lord's. I could hardly sit still on the bus home and immediately found friends in Finchley's pavilion on whom I poured out stories of the day's events at Lord's – also my excitement about tomorrow's play because those two truly great antipodeans were not out at the close with the total at 145 for three wickets.

The magnificent cricket at Lord's on Tuesday 28th August 1945 is indelibly etched in my psyche – and no doubt in the memories of every spectator and every scribe fortunate enough to witness that historic last day of the Victory Tests. Keith Miller dominated the morning's play with a display of aggressive batting acknowledged by cricket historians to be in the top echelon of the great innings of all time. His power and placement off the back foot equalled that of Hammond at his best, but of all the great batting that I have witnessed, none surpass the awesome and graceful power of Miller's straight driving off the front foot along the green carpet and over-the-top – so over-the-top that one of his seven sixes almost cleared the pavilion roof, the ball landing atop the broadcaster's box high above the England dressing room. As cricketers know, only Albert Trott, an Australian, has driven a ball over the pavilion roof, when, ironically, he played for the MCC against the Australians in 1899.

Keith Miller, facing his first over of the morning on his overnight score of 61, made his intentions clear, cutting a swathe through the England attack with a brace of glorious cover drives. England quickly dismissed Donnelly and Pepper which set the stage for high drama. Enter the cavalier Constantine, cheered all the way to the wicket to join the rampant Miller – both legends intent on hitting the bowling out of sight.

Entertainment? Unbelievable and unforgettable! The two swashbuckling heroes drove, cut or pulled almost every ball for four or six ... the scoreboard could hardly keep up and we, the spectators, developed hoarse throats and sore hands. When Laurie caught Learie on the boundary, the great West Indian had scored 40 and the partnership had amassed 117 runs in only 45 minutes. But the incredible Australian glamour-boy pilot pumped the throttle yet again and was finally out for 185, having that morning scored 124 in 90 minutes. Electric! The standing ovation for Keith Miller continued until he reached the dressing room atop the many flights of stairs in the Victorian pavilion. A Star already, Miller had now joined the Immortals of Cricketing Fame.

Despite that batting hurricane England had its own hero. Doug Wright, the Kent and England leg- spinner with the long bounding run-up, took 5 wickets for 105 in thirty overs in that second innings to give him a match analysis of 10 for 190 from 60 overs. Another star performance! Was that it – was there to be a disappointing anti-climax when England batted again in the forlorn hope of scoring 357 in the remaining 270 minutes? Or was there more excitement to come?

Hammond came – and conquered once again! The captain of England commanded the Lord's stage as Olivier commanded the historic Old Vic theatre and hammered his second magnificent century in the match. Yet, when Walter ... our own 'Wally' ... was out, and our cup was full and brimming over with the majesty of his art, I doubt that many spectators cared who won or lost that final Victory Test. Surely we were already satiated at this Feast – this Victory Festival! Could we, the hoarse voiced audience with reddened hands, cope with any more drama?

We would have to, because in the denouement before the final curtain the game's script-writers introduced another plot twist to get us on the edge of our seats again. Jack Davies and Billy Griffith attacked the bowling in cavalier fashion, thumped a few boundaries, edged a few twos, pushed and ran a few singles, scampering up and down the wicket like schoolboys to add 83 in the next hour. Griffith, caught for 36, left Davies and the tail-enders to score 74 in forty-five minutes. We, the spectators, were literally on the edge of our seats, some biting nails, some chain-smoking, many perspiring, all jabbering and clapping – then silence as the bowler got into his run to delivered the next ball.

Agile fielding by the ageless Constantine ran out Phillipson, then Pepper bowled Davies, leaving our leg-spinners Wright and Hollies to hang on for fifteen minutes to draw the match. The Dominions fielders crowded the bat – the spinners survived two maidens – then Constantine brought back Christofani who immediately bowled Wright. The Dominions had won. The crowd stood to applaud the Dominions players all the way back to the pavilion ... my hero ... our hero Learie Constantine for the last time.

That final Victory Test, played in the heavily bombed capital city of Britain and the Commonwealth, not only symbolised the end of a long and terribly destructive war but also celebrated new hope, new freedoms and new beginnings. Speaking personally, and reflecting on all my visits to Lord's both as a spectator and player, no gathering of cricket lovers ever created an atmosphere more uniquely celebratory, no spectacle of the skills inherent in the noble game displayed and enjoyed more appreciatively, and for me, in a historical perspective, no sporting occasion signified such a positive hope for the future way of life in our nation after six years of war. I conclude that, as a spectator, the England v Dominions game at Lord's when I was seventeen was *the greatest cricket match I have ever witnessed!*

I felt both exhilarated and exhausted as I queued for the bus back to Finchley where I overwhelmed my parents, during and after supper, with dramatic stories of the day. Tired and happy I went to bed early knowing I would be returning to Lord's the next day. Having experienced cricketing paradise, what gifts – sweet or sour – would the morrow bring?

The triumvirate of Middlesex and England captains – Sir Pelham Warner, GO 'Gubby' Allen and RWV 'Walter' Robins – headed the hierarchy of the Middlesex County Cricket Club and were in the top echelon of influential big-wigs in the Marylebone Cricket Club from the mid-1930s through to the 1960s. Evidently, according to my coach Frank Lee, all three had watched me bat in the nets at the Easter coaching classes in April 1945. Mr Allen had spoken with me when playing for Sir Pelham's Lords XI but I had not met Mr Walter Robins until I arrived at Lord's on the morning of August 29th. An all-rounder who bowled leg-spinners and fielded brilliantly at cover point, Mr Robins was to captain the recently formed Middlesex Colts, four of whom were from Finchley Colts. Our opponents in the one-day game were 'The Cross Arrows,' a historic cricket club formed at Lord's in 1880, whose teams were drawn from MCC members and staff – and selected guest players many of whom had played for their country.

Although bouncing with confident energy I was more than a little apprehensive about meeting our captain as I entered the pavilion and mounted the grand sweeping staircase to enter the Home Dressing Room. Mr Walter Robins had a reputation as a martinet; a highly knowledgeable and enthusiastic cricketer who promoted attacking cricket and was a strict disciplinarian. He greeted me with a strong handshake and penetrating eyes, as though he were reading my mind and character, followed by positive and complimentary words: "Welcome to my team, young Rayment ... I've heard of your reputation as captain of Finchley Colts ... and know you can play attacking shots because I saw you in the nets at Easter. Good luck – but you won't be fielding at cover," he chuckled – then turned to greet Ian Bedford who had just arrived.

Ian, then aged fifteen-and-a-half, was already known to the Middlesex hierarchy as a leg-spin bowler with exceptional talent, and our skipper for the day was particularly interested in the development of Ian's skills. Two other close friends from Finchley Colts were John Stacey, a sixth-former at Christ's College, who bowled accurate fast-medium left-arm seamers, and Brian Hanley, an all-rounder from Australia whose father was a diplomat based in London.

Led by our legendary and dynamic captain my young colleagues and I walked proudly through the Long Room and down the slope through that special white wicket gate on to the green of all our dreams. As Mr Robins set the field for John Stacey I became aware that Mr GO Allen was one of the umpires: "Gee-whizz, we're like actors performing at an audition," I thought to myself. John and Ian bowled well, we were all sharp in the field and restricted the Cross Arrows total to 174, of which Alan Ratcliffe scored 62 not out. John Stacey was outstanding, taking five wickets and finishing off our opponents innings with a hat-trick; a hat-trick at Lord's when you're eighteen is something I'm sure my modest friend always remembered.

Back in the dressing room Mr Robins gave his young hopefuls a pep talk, saying he was pleased with the bowlers and that we had fielded quite well but lacked awareness of his silent signals: "You must glance towards your captain every time the bowler walks back to his mark ... just one subtle field change – a yard or two sideways or up or back – can win a match. And we must win this match ... we have time to score 175 if we don't dawdle! Top order batsmen – play yourself in for ten minutes, then aim at five runs an over."

Our opening pair played themselves in against the Middlesex fast bowler Laurie Gray and the medium pace of the veteran Lord's pro Bill Wignall – then played themselves in again against accurate spin bowlers, skilfully protecting their wickets but adding so few runs to the total ... a definite 'dawdle'. Next to bat at No.3, I was sitting on the balcony watching the action – or inaction – when I became aware that Mr Robins was pacing up and down in the dressing room, firing off questions to members of the team: "Do those batsmen always score so slowly ... we need runs on the board ... do they think we're playing for a draw?" Seconds later Walter Robins, small in stature but bristling with the energy of frustration, is standing next to me on the balcony – hands cupped around his mouth and shouting:

"*HIT OUT OR BLOODY WELL GET OUT!!. ... DO YOU HEAR ME BATSMEN ... HIT OUT OR BLOODY WELL GET OUT!!*"

His angry energy reverberated through my body, firing off my own adrenaline ... because, silently, I agreed with him. "Well, I'll soon be in," I thought to myself as I returned to the dressing room to gather my gloves and bat, swing my arms and legs to warm-up – and to do something with the nervous energy that was pulsing through my body and brain. "I'll attack the bowling, pinch singles ... yes, I'll have a go ... and if I get out quickly, Mr Robins will see that I tried to move the score along."

My team-mates at the wicket were trying but failing, another four overs producing only eleven runs. Our angry captain went out on the balcony again: "BATSMEN ... ONE OF YOU GET OUT ... GET RUN OUT ... WE NEED SEVEN AN OVER!"

About three hundred boozers and sober aficionados standing around the concourse in front of the old Tavern could hear every word, especially as the wicket was close to the Tavern boundary. The most inebriated took their cue from the famous England player and began to barrack the batsmen. A sardonic cheer greeted a desperate slog resulting in splayed stumps: I was in! Walter Robins placed his hand on my shoulder: "I don't mind if you get out quickly Rayment – I do mind if you and the other batsmen do not make a big effort to win this match. Good luck."

I nudged my first ball from Bill Wignall behind square-leg for two, then pushed a single wide of cover to keep the bowling. Oh jeeps! Their skipper is setting the field for Laurie Gray's second spell – down the slope from the pavilion end. Thankfully his first ball was short outside the off stump which I square-cut for four to the long boundary by the Grand Stand. The next was short – I flashed and nicked four past second slip. The fifth I played defensively off the back foot into the mid-wicket area for a single. Batting against Laurie Gray had caused me to raise my concentration above normal levels; we knew nothing of 'the zone' in those days but for the rest of that innings I experienced 'that otherness' for the first time– therefore recall only a few scenes in my video memory.

First, I constantly chasséd up the wicket to the spinners and medium pacers to drive off the front foot or 'up and back' to cut or pull. I lofted an off-drive one bounce into the pavilion and pulled a six over the short boundary into the Tavern boozers ... now chanting, "let the blondy nipper bat on, get his bleedin' 'undred," followed by the winning pull shot for four to the same boundary. Eighty not out – game won with time to spare. Then I woke up!

Laurie Gray and his team mates congratulated me as we walked towards the pavilion gate; Taverners clapped and cheered; a sprinkling of MCC members nodded and muttered 'well done' as I walked up the steps and through the Long Room where I was met by a beaming Walter Robins: "You won the game for me – and your team, young Rayment ... splendid innings ... one you'll always remember. Thank you – well played!" Praise indeed.

The *London Evening News* reported:

COLTS HAT-TRICK AND SPLENDID BATTING

Possible Middlesex cricketers of the future played at Lord's yesterday and won with a degree of comfort which surprised their Cross Arrows opponents. Without noticeable help from GO Allen, according to his own confession "a bad and biased umpire", they dismissed a strong batting side for 174 and lost only two wickets while knocking off the runs. Of particular promise were two members of the Finchley Colts team, Rayment and Bedford, while John Stacey, the quickish left-arm bowler, who had previously played at Lord's, polished off the Cross Arrows innings with a hat-trick.

Bedford, aged 15½, and little more than knee-high to a grasshopper, bowled leg-breaks and googlies very well. Rayment, a sturdily built, fair-haired youth of 17, scored 80 not out, and that against an attack that included Gray and Wignall

At Lord's when seventeen I played one of the best innings of my life – an innings that opened the door to all that was to follow in my cricket career – a career that began so promisingly but in which I failed to develop my talents to their full potential. But, again, that is another story.

The doors of my dream had opened. I had played at Lord's, scored runs and revelled in every aspect of the experience – but the summer was ebbing away. The end-of-season show was enacted in that same glorious theatre of cricket where tradition and legend have ever been the backdrop to new history being created in the 'now of today'. In April I had entered the North Gate to be coached by veteran Frank Lee; in August passed through the Grace Memorial Gates to enter the pavilion and play my first match on the historic green stage; witnessed one of the Great Matches in the euphoric atmosphere of The Peace, and the next day, batted with focus and skill beyond my own expectations. But the mountain-top experience in the 'now of today' becomes the 'now of start again' on the morrow. Some heights are seldom, even never, scaled again, but there is always more to learn, more to experience, more to fulfil. In September I consolidated my potential with an innings of value in gloomy autumn conditions. The *Times* cricket correspondent wrote:

A great season at Lord's came to an end on Saturday with a game in which a team from Surrey Colts beat a Lord's XI by four wickets. The Lord's XI, batting first after they had won the toss, lost a wicket with only two runs on the board. A good partnership between D Roberts and AWH Rayment then added 72 runs before Roberts ran himself out. With G Smith and PS Russell keeping a good length, and a slow outfield, runs were never easy to get, but the score was 146 when the fifth wicket fell, CH Palmer again playing an innings of class. After that there was a disastrous collapse, the remaining wickets providing only 14 scratchy runs.

I enjoyed observing the technique of Charlie Palmer while batting with him in a second-wicket stand following my partnership with David Roberts. Geoffrey Smith shattered my stumps on 46 while Charlie Palmer went on to score 49. I also have a vague memory of facing a red-haired, sixteen-year-old left-arm spinner named Tony Lock. Considering that Sir Pelham's XI included three Middlesex and England spin bowlers: the veteran Ian Peebles, Jim Sims and Jack Young – also my young friend and prodigy Ian Bedford – Surrey's young Colts batted with commendable skill to win the match. The *Times* correspondent wrote a fitting conclusion to his piece:

> J Sims offered some perplexity with his tweakers and CM Wheatley was bowling steadily and straight but the Colts had a solid foundation in Whitworth (82) and when Beet and Fowler – those noble servants of cricket – put the bails in their pockets for the last time at Lord's this year the match had been comfortably won and there still remained a comfortable three-quarters of an hour for play. *And so through the WG Memorial Gates – and the end – until next May.*

In forty-five, so young and free,
coached at Lord's by veteran Lee,
while big wigs noted, 'just a boy
with promise – does enjoy
the game – but will he shine
in later years: maybe in time.'

In forty-five, naïve but full
of life, enjoying drive and pull,
while others strived and died for peace
till Victory celebrated, joy released
by heroes past on Lord's green sward
thrilled thankful hearts with one accord.

~ ~ ~ ~ ~ ~ ~ ~ ~ ~

CHAPTER 24

DANCING AND COURTING

From walking home we progressed to walking out
- dating was not in our vocabulary.

Girls at school, girls playing sport, girls in the neighbourhood were mates: now that I was sixteen there were girls at work – flirty and embarrassing.

I had grown up in an extended family and surrounding community that held to the traditional middle-class values of that era: respect and good manners were of paramount importance in all relationships. Sex was something to look forward to on the wedding night after a long courtship and an engagement of several months. Thus conditioned, I dealt with my own hormonal changes, fantasy dreams and increasingly strong sexual urges through masturbation, thereby separating those powerful natural feelings from the daily reality of live female proximity and unconsciously sublimating my sexual drive into my passion for sport.

In my last year at Finchley County School I was so passionate about soccer and cricket that even the summer exams were a nuisance, diverting my attention from important duties as cricket captain and improving my own performances on the field of play. I did not even think about walking out with a female schoolmate: after all, they were mates!

Although inwardly confusing in psychological and sexual terms, growing up in the mid 1940s for boys in our social category was deemed outwardly simple: be polite and well behaved, do your best at school, then leave, go to work and await conscription into the armed services. Relatively few entered university. Similar for girls except there was no conscription. We were expected to be mature and responsible and community minded during and after the war: then peace heralded greater freedoms, and greater freedoms eventually heralded artistic licence and rebellious experimentation. As a 16-17-year-old the only collective noun applied to young people that I can remember was 'The Youth'. The war had programmed my generation to be adult before the normal biological time. 'The Teenager' and 'Adolescent Behaviour' were gestating in the next generation of young people.

Even when I left school and started work in the late summer of 1944 I still held on to my strong opinion that 'girls and sport did not mix' – until! Until three months before my seventeenth birthday I walked Iris Cramphorn home from a Saturday dance. We progressed to 'walking out' – dancing and football matches twice, the cinema once and one kiss. A slim, good-looking brunette with a gorgeous smile, Iris was one of a small group of girls from my old school who watched the boys play soccer and cricket. She was in the fifth form at the County School – a classmate of Betty Griffin who lived less than one hundred yards from my house. One of my best cricketing mates, Peter Sutherland, was walking out with Betty, and we made up a foursome to go dancing one evening in the spring of that year.

Dancing? Me? ... the young athlete who lived only for cricket and football – how come I went dancing? Well, that is another story – but I'll tell it anyway.

One warm and peaceful evening during the previous cricket season I was assisting the kindly grey-haired club legend Mr Tom Birkin in the preparation of a wicket at Arden Field. Chatting about footwork as we knelt on the turf removing plantains with our pocket knives my mentor remarked: "Ah footwork, Alan, yes nimble footwork to get into line with the ball is very important – or even to chassé up the wicket to the pitch of the ball when facing spin bowlers. You have naturally quick footwork, but you could improve if you learned ballroom dancing. Jack Hobbs and Charles Fry, both great batsmen, were also accomplished ballroom dancers."

Although impressed by the credentials of Hobbs and Fry I blushed, remembering my acute embarrassment when the dance teacher visiting the County School paired me with Shirley Bagrit.

"You really think so, Mr Birkin ... and ... and what is a chassé?" The wise veteran cricketer and businessman had sown a seed in my mind whilst we tended the grass I loved at Arden Field – a seed that was to produce much good fruit and happiness, though eventually not a little sadness.

Having shared Tom Birkin's wise opinions with my cricket pals, the adventurous Pete Sutherland and I dared each other to attend a ballroom dance class. Pete, tall and athletic with a mop of curly black hair, had been educated at a boarding school and was, like me, embarrassed and not a little scared about dancing, up close and personal, with nubile young females. On the other hand ballroom dancing was hugely popular – and what was the point of going to a dance if we couldn't dance properly?

Debate and uncertainty prevailed until one dark wet Thursday evening in January 1945 we boarded a No.2 bus from Finchley to Golders Green and bravely entered the forbidding domain of an old balletomane and ballroom teacher, Miss Helen Wills. Taking our time to wipe our shoes on the doormat, Pete and I paused to exchange anxious frowns as we surveyed the unfamiliar scene within the long, narrow shop-cum-dance studio. Then, drawing a deep breath to summon-up adolescent courage, we skirted past three couples performing a waltz to approach the unnerving apparition of the Proprietress.

Miss Helen Wills was chain smoking scented Passing Cloud cigarettes whilst reclining in a Lloyd Loom armchair surrounded by cats. She seemed so old – her dark wrinkled features caked with cracked make-up and her frazzled black bobbed hair fringed over her eyes caused my filmic imagination to leap to opium dens in China. First impression? Helen Wills and her cats gave me the creeps and srange involuntary shivers.

Pete and I felt very uncomfortable. This milieu was in complete contrast to the familiar sports pavilion resounding with confident male banter and healthy odours of sweat and Sloane's liniment. In these unfamiliar arty and strange-smelling surroundings all confidence drained down through our legs into the sprung maple dance floor. Neither of us could speak; then, without turning her head, Miss Wills addressed us in a smoker's low croak, "You boys come for the beginners class?" We nodded. With one arm embracing a cat she waved the other in a graceful balletic manner towards the changing room. Changing room? Was this cramped little kitchen with fish heads boiling in a saucepan on a gas ring and well-licked saucers decorating the floor really a changing room? Holding our breath, we hung up our raincoats and rapidly exchanged day shoes for black patent evening pumps – mine, belonging to my father, were two sizes too big.

Two smartly suited elderly gentlemen, the brothers Joe and Andy Andrews (probably fifty), taught the waltz to a class of fifteen beginners, mostly young females. Miss Wills made an occasional observation from her clouded throne. We learned the change step, the natural and reverse turns, finally succeeding in linking the three in sequence and reaching the safety of the far end of the studio. I say 'safety' because embarrassment turned to relief as we disentangled outstretched arms from those of our attractive female partners. The brothers Andrew dismissed the class with suitable encouraging comments as Pete and I headed for the kitchen, passing the still seated Dame who received our half-crowns and deigned to remark, huskily: "Thank you boys, I hope you will come again next week."

Pete and I exchanged glances and silently mouthed 'maybe'. But I had enjoyed the unexpected success of learning the steps and fitting them to the metronomic tones of a Victor Sylvester waltz.

From metronomic to catatonic – well that is a misuse: a catachresis – but certainly everything to do with cats. One of the blighters had heaved half-digested fish-heads into my walking shoes, bones and all! Yuk! I swore, Pete laughed. "Nothing to laugh about Pete," I exploded, as another male waltzer quickly removed his nose from the doorway, "well have to walk home ... and in these thin pumps, 'cos we can't get on a bus ... the stink ... those stinking bloody cats!" I rarely swore in those innocent days, but the cats received everything in my limited vocabulary. We walked home. Fortunately it had stopped raining, but Pete did not cease from raining cat jokes upon me – when he was not doubled up with laughter.

We decided to risk the dance class the next week, but after that Pete gave up and I continued, shyly at first but strongly motivated by Mr Birkin's tales of Hobbs and Fry. And though distant – seemingly living in the clouds of her long-passed heyday – Miss Wills turned out to be a sad but kindly soul who occasionally deigned to offer an encouraging remark to regular students like myself. My attitude to female dance partners changed, embarrassment faded, confidence increased and skills developed until I was able to complete a circuit of the dance floor in the waltz and quickstep, even mastering the natural spin turn in both dances. In those few weeks I discovered that I really enjoyed this dancing lark – this moving to big band music by Joe Loss and Ted Heath – even to the thinner sounds of Strict Tempo Sylvester.

From the time I first wound up my precious gramophone in early childhood I had absorbed a love for music through singing, through listening to my mother playing the piano and from records and radio. During the choirboy days my eclectic taste broadened to include choral oratorios and classical concertos. From wartime radio and films I soaked up songs from the famous musical shows and the big band sound. I was now beginning to enjoy traditional jazz.

Looking back, I realise how much I needed to express myself musically in adolescence. I had not learned to play an instrument, and now that my voice had broken I seldom went to church, nor was I able to let rip during our family evenings around the piano. However, in March 1945, Pete and I began to attend the Saturday night hop at Gordon Hall in West Finchley. To my surprise I discovered that I enjoyed the music played by a seven-piece band and general social atmosphere generated by a good MC. Also it was fun meeting up again with several old school friends, boys and girls, but there was not a thought or a whiff of romance for many weeks. I danced with Iris Cramphorn – even dared to hold hands as I walked her home – but there was no real romance in my life ... until. Here comes *until* again!

Until in April 1945 Pete Sutherland enlisted voluntarily and reported for training as a Naval Cadet at Chatham. He had been 'walking out' on a regular basis with the lithesome brunette, Betty Griffin. Pete asked me to look after Betty until he came home on his first leave. Two weeks later Iris and I decided to meet at Betty's house and chaperone her to the Saturday dance. I do not remember why, but a heated argument ensued which resulted in Iris storming off home and Betty and I going on to the dance. In that brief moment of time a dramatic and unexpected change of partners determined our future pathways for a long time – a lifetime, in fact.

When writing this piece sixty-five years later I telephoned Betty to corroborate the story of 'changing partners' that led to our dance partnership, our romance and long courtship. Betty agreed that we not only clicked as dance partners but reminded me that she was keen on all sports and was already a supporter of Finchley Colts: "Don't you remember that I was one of the girls who dived into the ditch in 1944 when that doodlebug interrupted the Colts game at Arden Field?"

Betty Griffin and Iris Cramphorn
Arden Field, 1945

Peter Sutherland with Alan
Arden Field, 1945

Betty also reminded me that she had an impressive sporting pedigree. Her parents, Ben and Tricie Griffin, both achieved considerable prowess in North London sporting circles in the 1920s: Tricie as a competitive tennis player who was good enough to play friendly doubles with Suzanne Lenglen; Ben, an all-round cricketer with the prestigious North Middlesex Club also played for the Bank of England and the Middlesex county second eleven.

In that summer of '45 Betty was a student in the fifth form at Finchley County School and sat for the School Certificate Examinations a few weeks after the joyful national celebrations of Victory in Europe Day on May 8th. She represented the school at tennis, swimming and athletics and passed her School Certificate exams with flying colours, gaining a distinction in Art, credits in English and Geography and passes in Maths and French. She then stayed on in the sixth form to take a commercial course in shorthand, typing and business administration, finally leaving the County School at Easter in 1946 a few weeks before her seventeenth birthday on April 29th.

Betty began her working life as a filing clerk in the Transport Department of Unilever at Blackfriars. For the next year we travelled to work together on the Tube from Finchley Central to Charing Cross. Dancing was our main joint recreation but we also enjoyed cycling, weather permitting, into the Hertfordshire countryside and train journeys to explore Box Hill in Surrey, the Thames at Maidenhead

*Betty Griffin wearing Finchley
County School blazer, 1942*

*Betty's mother Tricie,
circa 1914*

Betty Griffin, age 16

Alan Rayment, age 17

and Brighton's pier and pebble beach. Betty and I were habitual film-goers: in the autumn and winter cinemas were a haven from cold and damp evenings. I remember most of the great films of that era but few of the poor B movies; the rear seats in cinemas were, and probably still are, ideal places for a cuddle and a snog.

On reflection I am both amused and amazed that at the time we 'walked out' to our first dance Betty and I were both sixteen: after Betty's birthday and before my seventeenth on May 29th 1945. Although naïve regarding romantic relationships, we had matured beyond our years in several aspects of our individual characters and personalities because we had grown up in the environment of wartime conditions. We were certainly aware of the preciousness of life and thankful that we, and our families, had survived the Blitz and the Doodlebugs. We had also absorbed the ineffable wartime spirit that had pervaded our community; an amalgam of determination, responsibility, hope and humour which, in general among our known contemporaries, manifested in a perky spirit of self-belief. All those immeasurable influences, later mixed with the national euphoria and celebrations of Peace due to the Allied victories in Europe and the Pacific, undoubtedly contributed to the uplifting social climate in which Betty and I began our twenty-three year journey together.

My Golden Journey through 1945 overflowed with positive change, abundant opportunity and exciting new experiences. In *January,* ballroom dancing classes; *March,* a girl friend; *April,* signed for Spurs Juniors; also *April,* cricket coaching at Lord's; *June,* cricket for London Counties in Wales; *August,* played three matches at Lord's and watched the historic England v Dominions game; *September,* played in the last match of the season at Lord's; *October,* played football for Spurs Juniors at White Hart Lane.

During the 1945-46 soccer season I played about a dozen games for the Juniors, including two in mid-week at White Hart Lane, but because I was under contract at Tottenham I only played for 393 Squadron ATC when one of their regular forwards was not available or injured. I certainly enjoyed playing football but not nearly as much as cricket; my passion for the summer game was growing, and the winter sport now had two competitors, dancing and girl friend. The wisdom of hindsight suggests to me that the new experience of having a girl friend to watch me play cricket and football boosted my healthy confidence and, combined with new opportunities, certainly notched up my cricketing ambitions for the future.

I am forever thankful that my progress in sport was generously encouraged by my bosses at SPD Ltd: the Colonel and Mr Tom Lacey willingly gave me days off with pay to play in some of those matches at Lord's and allowed me to leave early for soccer training at White Hart Lane. There was also a cheerful interest expressed by the chief automobile engineer, Mr Cyril Reid – and even Boris herself. And two of the girls in the typing pool supported Spurs – another interested in cricket had seen my name in the *London Evening News* – so their attitude towards me changed to one of respect – even admiration. In the canteen at lunch times the 'flirts' no longer teased the red-faced office boy but asked questions about well known sports people I had met. However, I determinedly refused to satisfy their curiosity about my girl friend and dancing by stating: "I'm a very private person."

In the spring of 1946 I booked six coaching sessions at the Sandham, Strudwick and Gover Indoor Cricket School. Mr Lacey allowed me to leave the Wapping office at 4pm for the Tube and bus journey to East Hill, Wandsworth. At first I was rather overwhelmed by the atmosphere – cricket legends and current stars everywhere I looked – but the quietly spoken Mr Andrew Sandham walked me away from the noisy banter at the bowling end of the several nets to have a chat with me at the wicket. The Surrey and England opening batsman – who had scored 107 centuries in first-class cricket and partnered Jack Hobbs in 63 opening stands of a hundred or more – concentrated on my back-foot play much as Mr Lee had done. On one occasion I was tested by some 'quick stuff' from Mr Alf Gover and later overheard the inimitable tones of his deep voice in conversation with Mr Sandham: "He's got good footwork ... quick hands too, Andrew ... but I think he's too nice a young chap to be a pro ... too amiable." Some years later I met Alf Gover at the Oval and joked about his assessment of me when I was seventeen.

In May 1946 Betty was awarded her bronze medal in ballroom dancing by Josephine Bradley, famous examiner for the Imperial Society of Teachers of Dancing. I failed that day but retook the test with the National Association a week before I joined the RAF – and passed. The examiner was Miss Gwen Sylvester. As I note that achievement I reckon my venerable mentor 'on the other side' must be chuckling with delight.

Thank you, Mr Tom Birkin.

～～～～～～～～～～～

*Alan and Derek,
1945*

CHAPTER 25

RELUCTANT CONSCRIPT

I laugh at myself now – or more accurately – not at this overweight octogenarian but at the slim, fit and possibly handsome me way back in 1946.

I was cross: how dare they – those myopic fool clerks at the Air Ministry – how dare they issue my call-up papers instructing me to report to RAF Padgate on July 25. Didn't they know that that date was in the middle of the cricket week at the Finchley Club? I would miss four matches!

And surely those ministry pen-pushers had read that I had made my debut for Middlesex second eleven earlier that summer and would not be eligible for selection for the rest of the season due to leave restrictions when square bashing. Couldn't they have waited until the end of the season to post that horrible letter in that repulsive buff coloured envelope? Nasty bureaucrats!

However, before I change out of civvies into uniform, I feel a need to identify 'probable cause' of my pique – actually multifarious rather than singular because I was experiencing an all-round full and happy life. Betty and I were in love, enjoying life in general and social dances with friends at Gordon Hall. We were also training in a our serious quest for Silver Medals. Though marking time in our rather mundane jobs we happily joined the crush on the Tube every day but now parted at Euston because I had to change trains twice to get to Wapping in the East End where SPD Ltd had moved into better offices combined with large garage workshops. Sitting quietly at my Wapping desk one day in March 1946 Mr Lacey told me that I was to be introduced to a famous sportsman who would be accompanying a Director of the Marsham Tyre Company to a meeting with Colonel Jameson and Cyril Reid. "Who, Mr Lacey ... who is it ... who is coming today to meet the Colonel?"

"Oh, you wait and see, Alan ... I don't want to spoil the surprise."

Surprised? I was astonished ... and speechless for some long seconds when ushered into the presence of England's master batsman, cricket captain and legend, whom I had revered from the Mound Stand at Lord's the previous August as he held a full house enthralled powering his way to two majestic hundreds in the England versus Dominions match. I was more than enthralled as I shook hands with Mr Walter R Hammond, and not a little embarrassed as my boss, the Colonel, sang my praises as a very promising batsman who had scored eighty not out at Lord's under the captaincy of Walter Robins. I was too awe-struck to remember Mr Hammond's encouraging words as he wished me good luck in my cricket career. Shaking my hand again ... gee, a powerful grip ... he then rejoined his business colleagues to discuss a bulk order for lorry tyres. I returned to our new kitchen to make a cup of tea to calm my excitement.

The process of moving SPD's huge vehicle maintenance operation from Battersea to London's heavily bombed docklands took several months because much of the large property was either under repair or being rebuilt, surrounded by Wapping's acres of bomb-site rubble. In contrast the acres I loved best were green of course, inhabited by men in whites rather than suits, tapping the crease with bat rather than typewriter keys with fingers, and shouting for an LBW rather than asking Boris if she would like me to make tea. Yes, I was happy enough with the daily routine but doubly blessed with opportunities to test my development as a cricketer in two special matches before donning that RAF uniform.

The first was my debut for Middlesex second eleven against Sussex at Hove on June 10th and 11th, two weeks after my eighteenth birthday. I have no memory of the travel or hotel arrangements, but I do recall my excitement when viewing the panorama of the famous county ground in sight of the sea, and have forever remembered a certain fast bowler approaching the crease from the Sea End. Commentary in the present tense:

> The scene opens as I drop my bat to shake and rub my right thumb, now swelling with a bruise inflicted by Jack Nye who is the fastest bowler I have faced in my brief career. Is his opening partner John Duffield as quick or quicker? Playing in my first match for Middlesex 2nd XI I am beginning to understand the jump from good club cricket to the standards of county second eleven games. I have managed to achieve the second top score of 18 in our first innings – the cheery professional Harry Sharp reached 39 in our total of 116. Our skipper, Mr HJ Enthoven, is pleased with my bowling, especially as I removed the veteran professional all-rounder, HE Hammond, in both innings. I love fielding at cover on this smooth turf and am enjoying every minute of playing cricket in this 'county' atmosphere. In our second innings we need 199 to win but are six wickets down for 28; I scrape four when John Duffield bowls me before I have lifted my bat. Reg Routledge, the chirpy Middlesex pro with typical Cockney style humour, goes into bat at number eight and attacks every ball on a 'shit or bust' basis to score 93 out of 138. On the train back to London I am 'having a think': "Yes, this game at Hove does signify another step up the ladder of my hoped-for career, but I am becoming more aware how tall the ladder and how steep the climb."

The second special match was one of the most memorable experiences recorded in these memoirs. On the Sunday following the game against Sussex at Hove I was selected to play in a team organised by Mr GO Allen against Southgate Cricket Club. Harry Sharp and Reg Routledge, whom I had met at Lord's the previous season, had become friends and kindly looked after this greenhorn young amateur at Hove. They said they would see me next Sunday at Southgate.

Thankfully, Harry saw me arrive on the ground, broke off from a small group by the pavilion, walked towards me, shook hands and said: "Hello Alan, good to see you again ... thought I'd better let you know that you'll be meeting Patsy Hendren who is skippering the team ... and Denis ... who is needing some middle practice because he is out of form. I know they are your heroes but don't be embarrassed ... they are both friendly blokes ... like me," expressed with his characteristic wide gentle grin. For a moment I was in mild shock – then thanked Harry as he took one handle of my cricket bag and chatted as we walked across the outfield to the pavilion. As soon as we entered the dressing room Harry introduced me to Mr Hendren – a very special moment – which was interrupted when Mr Allen entered and announced, "We are batting, chaps – but as Denis has not arrived the order will be flexible. He will bat at four ... Alex at five ... and Alan, you'll go in after Alex."

If, dear reader, you are a cricket enthusiast you may well be asking, 'Why was Denis Compton playing in a club game on a Sunday in the middle of a championship match against Yorkshire at Lord's?' When Harry Sharp had made the remark about Denis being out of form I responded by saying that I had read various accounts in the press which indicated he might not be selected for the Test Match against India at Lord's next Saturday. The background to the situation is worth a little research.

Having served in the Army in India during the war Denis Compton returned to England in February 1946 to be demobbed and resume his professional soccer career with Arsenal. On April 13th Denis played at outside-left for England in the Victory International against Scotland at Hampden Park, Glasgow in front of 139,468 wildly enthusiastic spectators – then back to Lord's for net practice in preparation for the resumption of first-class cricket. In India Denis had played a lot of cricket on hard surfaces, including matting, and now had to adjust to the ball turning and lifting on uncovered wickets often affected by rain. In his first game, MCC v Surrey at Lord's, Denis scored 0 and 20 but then flowed into a purple patch of ten innings in which he scored 675 runs, two not-outs, averaging 84.37. His three centuries included two in the match against Lancashire at Old Trafford.

But from May 29th Denis scored only eighteen runs in four innings, all at Lord's. However, in the next first-class game on the beautiful Fenner's pitch Compton scored a double century against a weak Cambridge University attack. Surely the indications of loss of form had been reversed – or had they? To answer the question I will refer to Denis's own words from his book, *Playing for England*, published in May 1948.

Never shall I forget the ups and downs of that first post-war season of English cricket. I started off with a real bang. Runs flowed easily from my bat, and I felt in wonderful form ... then, as if a gremlin had perched itself on the handle of my bat and did everything to prevent me getting runs, my luck departed. I tried every possible thing to overcome this lack of success, but nothing, it seemed, would bring me back to run getting. I will confess, too, it occurred to me that my place in the England Test team might be in jeopardy, for the five innings preceding the first test against India were 0 - 0 - 8 - 0 - 1! Hardly, you will agree, the kind of form expected from a player filling the Number Three position in the England team.

Back to the Southgate ground on June 16th. By this date Denis had succumbed to the first two zeros in the above sequence. Rain had washed out most of the play at Lord's on the previous day, but now the sun was shining and we, GO Allen's XI, had lost our first wicket for two runs. Still no sign of Denis. Bill Harrington joined Harry Sharp, and the two Middlesex professionals built a century stand before Harry was caught and bowled by Dr Rowland Shaddick on forty-nine. Denis had arrived but was not changed so Alex Thompson proceeded to the wicket, only to return after two balls and two runs. I was padded up, went into bat and got off the mark before Bill was out for 61. As he walked back to the pavilion excited mutterings increased in volume among the sizeable crowd of spectators, uncertain whether or not to believe the rumours that Denis Compton had arrived on the ground and might even change into cricket gear to have a bit of batting practice.

While waiting out in the middle I was chatting with a group of Southgate players whom I knew quite well because we had played against each other many times in club matches. Naturally, most of my attention was focused on the pavilion. I would be thrilled, and respectfully in awe whoever emerged, because I was about to partner either Denis Charles Scott Compton or Elias Henry (Patsy) Hendren. I remember that my heart beat faster and the back of my neck felt prickly when the hero with the inimitable athletic waddle appeared through a bunch of camera clicking spectators, swinging his arms and twirling his bat as he neared the wicket and took guard. Moving back and across to his first ball, Denis Compton nudged Dr Shaddick's off-spinner wide of mid-on and called for an easy single. No duck this innings.

For a few overs I pushed for one to make sure that Denis faced most of the bowling, and of course he was adept at taking a single from the fifth or sixth ball. But when he had settled and had overtaken my score of fifteen I refocused on my own batting and began using my feet to chassé up the wicket to Doc Shaddick's quickish off spinners – or step back again to cut or pull. My normal way of playing. However, I sensed that Denis thought I was copying him ... either as an experiment or 'taking the micky'. So, at the next opportunity I stayed in my crease and drove a full half-volley back over the Doc's head for four.

I then had a naughty thought, a temptation I suppose ... "If Denis gets out, Patsy Hendren will come into bat next ... me batting with Patsy as well as Denis ... gee whiz ... but the tea interval is only fifteen minutes away and we will probably declare ... hmmm ... I could run Denis out ... not difficult ... but would I even dare?" I cut the thought – felt guilty and shocked at my imagination – but I knew about Denis's reputation regarding run-outs. Many have laid claim to the famous line: 'When Compo calls for a run he is only opening negotiations', but it probably originates with Jim Sims, nodding his head from side to side and delivering his mumbled bon-mot through the side of his mouth.

What did I learn whilst batting with one of the greatest cricketers of all time? First, that he got in line with the flight of the ball so unhurriedly, yet always had plenty of time to execute his defensive or attacking shot. Second, bearing in mind that there were no really quick bowlers, Denis seemed to play every ball off the pitch ... that is, he often adjusted his stroke very late ... so much time to play the ball and place it between fielders. Third, that although I had talent, was 'promising', and might one day reach the batting standards of Bill or Harry, I would never be in the same league as Denis Compton. But I thoroughly enjoyed the experience and remember chatting amicably with my hero as we walked off the field, both undefeated and having put on an unbroken stand of fifty-nine.

After tea I again felt as proud as Punch as I followed Patsy Hendren onto the field of play ... and remember his chirpy voice saying, "Out to the covers, young Alan ... I expect a couple of run-outs from you." Although the Southgate captain, FC Hawker played really well for sixty-one, his team were all out for 120. Bill Harrington claimed four wickets with his seamers and Denis Compton cheekily bagged three wickets for one run in four overs. I remember nothing of the social scene in the bar after the match, but avidly followed the 'Compton Crisis' in the press over the next two weeks, almost praying that Denis would score a hundred in his next innings ... and the next. Ho Hum ... on the Monday following the excitement at Southgate, he scored 8 and 0 against Yorkshire; only 1 against Glamorgan at Swansea ... then another duck in the Test Match at Lord's. Crisis indeed!

Relief: the siege was over when Middlesex played Warwickshire at Lord's on June 26,27,28. Denis Compton played himself out of the fog of despair into the sunlight of new found confidence when he scored 122 against bowling that included his England colleague, leg-spinner Eric Hollies, who bowled 53 overs in one innings to take 4 for 125. Crisis overcome!

When researching material for this chapter I phoned the Secretary of Southgate CC who put me in touch with a member who kept the club's records. Ricky Gunn phoned me, "I've had a look in the archives in my garage ... found the scorecard and will gladly post it to you Alan. What is your address?"

Thank you, Ken – here is a copy of that scorecard:

Southgate C.C. vs G.O. Allen's XI

Played at the Walker Ground, Southgate, Sunday 16th June, 1946

G.O. Allen's XI

N.A. Robinson	b Burton	2	*Bowling*	*O*	*M*	*R*	*W*
H. Sharp	c&b Shaddick	49	Burton	10	1	27	1
W. Harrington	c Edwards b Walker	61	Bodkin	17	2	56	0
A. Thompson	lbw b Shaddick	2	Shaddick	20	3	58	2
A.W. Rayment	not out	28	Walker	12	1	37	1
D.C.S. Compton	not out	36					
*E.H. Hendren							
#G.A. Turner							
B. Pearson							
J. Marshall							
W. Ashmore			1-2, 2-112, 3-122, 4-122.				
	Extras (b 7, lb 2, nb 4)	13					
	(for 4 wkts, declared)	**191**					

Southgate C.C.

*F.C. Hawker	b Harrington	61	*Bowling*	*O*	*M*	*R*	*W*
T. Crabtree	lbw b Harrington	4	Ashmore	4	2	6	0
#M.S. Glennie	lbw b Harrington	0	Harrington	17	4	34	4
P.E. Bodkin	st Turner b Pearson	33	Thompson	11	1	33	0
J.F.H. Tyler	lbw b Marshall	4	Robinson	3	1	8	0
J.I. Wilmore	hit wkt b Compton	6	Marshall	6	2	14	1
G.J. Fish	b Compton	0	Pearson	4	1	17	1
H.W.F. Edwards	b Compton	1	Compton	4	3	1	3
T.J.D. Walker	c Ashmore b Harrington	0					
R.A. Shaddick	not out	4	1-11, 2-11, 3-80, 4-87, 5-113,				
W.R. Burton	not out	0	6-113, 7-113, 8-115, 9-115.				
	Extras (b 7)	7					
	(for 9 wkts)	**120**					

Umpires: F.W. Canham and G.O. Allen

Match drawn

Crisis loomed and temporarily lowered my spirits as I faced up to the reality that next month I would have to travel 'up north' to Lancashire – always cold and wet in my imagination – and go through the charade of marching about imprisoned in a uniform until demobbed in the unforeseeable future. Although I was still peeved with those 'nasty bureaucrats' about the timing of my call-up, National Service was compulsory for all medically fit eighteen-year-old males unless engaged in a 'reserved occupation'. My friends and I had long accepted that even though the wars in Europe and the Pacific had ended in 1945 we would leave parents, homes, jobs and girl friends for two years, be trained in skills most of us would never use again and be posted to military units anywhere in Great Britain or abroad. The future was uncertain though adventurous, probably filled with opportunities to meet interesting people and visit interesting places, but likely to strain established relationships and prove to be a waste of valuable time regarding career development.

With only one real career ambition I felt I had already idled away two years as a clerk with Unilever and was about to waste another two in the RAF unless ... unless I was accepted for training as a pilot, or at least air-crew. However, even that worthy ambition was shredded when, in April, I had attended a recruiting office in central London. Armed with a full set of Air Training Corps certificates, an excellent testimonial from the Commanding Officer – including confirmation that I had flown in an Avro Anson and a Westland Lysander – and already graded A1 at my medical examination, I was confident that I would be recommended for interview with the Air Crew Selection Board. On entering the dingy brown bureaucratic gloom of the recruiting centre in North London I was given a number, sat on a wobbly bench and waited. Eventually called to one the many trestle tables I was confronted by a balding civil servant nearing retirement age who seemed preoccupied with thoughts beyond his day job – probably dreaming about moving to a bungalow in Bexhill-on-Sea.

"Sit down, Rayment ... er ... please sit down. Now let me see ... er ... oh yes, first of all, which Service would you prefer to join?"

"The Royal Air Force, sir ... I've been in the ATC for four years and I ..."

"Ah, I see you have some papers – let me have a look. Hmm ... I see that your Commanding Officer recommends you for air-crew training, Rayment ... is that right?"

"Yes sir, I would very much like to ..."

"Well, you do realise, young man, that there are hundreds of trained aircrew still waiting to be demobbed ... so you see, the RAF will only consider candidates who agree to sign on for a seven-year service commission."

"Seven years!" I exclaimed ... "but I hope to play county cricket ... I couldn't possibly sign on for seven years ... so ... uhmm ... could I train to be a PT Instructor instead?"

"Well, you could, but the same conditions apply – too many PTIs hanging about waiting to be demobbed ... so, again, you would have to sign on for seven years."

Seven years ... seven years, I murmured to myself repeatedly, my brain temporarily frozen with disappointment.

Recovering my thoughts and speaking in a low tone from a dry throat I ventured a question: "Well sir, what could I do for two years as a conscript in the RAF ... er ... something interesting and not too boring?"

"Yes, Rayment, from the notes I have in front of me ... and seeing that you are keen to learn something useful both to you and the Service ... I suggest training to become a radar plotter. After you have completed initial training at Padgate you would be posted to a radar station or a similar facility in the defence network. Although the war with Germany is over, the three services maintain a full alert system due to political uncertainties about the territorial ambitions of the Soviet Union in this new era of the atomic weapons. If you agree with my recommendation you will be involved in the national air defence network. On the other hand, there are openings in motor transport and the RAF Military Police."

"No sir, not the Military Police. So, of those three possibilities I would prefer to train as a radar plotter. And you mentioned initial training at Padgate. Excuse me, sir, but where is Padgate?"

"Padgate is near Warrington, between Manchester and Liverpool. I need to remind you, Rayment, that everything to do with our radar network comes under the Official Secrets Act, which I will now ask you to sign, and that you must not discuss your job with anyone not involved with that section of the RAF. Officially, your job is titled as 'Clerk, Special Duties' ... do you understand Rayment?" "Yes sir."

"You will receive your call-up date from the Air Ministry in a few weeks time. I wish you good luck, Rayment ... and I expect you will get plenty of cricket in the RAF."

I was surprised by that comment, delivered with a cheerful smile and firm handshake by my balding interviewer. "I'll be watching out to see if you make it in county cricket."

"Thank you very much, sir."

Maybe he had been day-dreaming about batting, not bungalows. At least the few words we exchanged about cricket had cheered him up.

I felt anything but cheerful as I passed through the platform barrier at Euston station on a bright summer day in July. As I waved my buff-coloured travel warrant at the tough looking, pint-sized LMS ticket collector I took note of his oversize peaked hat resting on large cauliflower ears – a sight that tweaked my imagination to picture him as a bantam-weight boxer. That brief encounter provoked a vision of the heavyweight drill sergeants I would no doubt encounter on the parade ground at Padgate, and, for a fleeting moment, I felt dazed and angry, as though I had been punched to the ground – my mind in a whirl: "This is unfair ... I did not choose to waste two years of my life in the RAF ... I should be playing cricket ... pro or amateur, trying to get into a county team ... there is no war now ... why am I here?" ... mutter ... mutter ... mutter.

My confusion matched that of my immediate environment: the random pattern of hundreds of people scurrying about the great terminus intent on catching their train or hurrying towards their destined appointment in the great city; the intrusive cacophony of human hub-bub ... of 'goodbye darlings', of slamming doors and guard's whistles set to a backdrop of hissing steam engines and clouds of smut-filled smoke billowing beneath the bomb damaged platform canopy. All noise, bustle and dirt. I felt dirty and disoriented, alone and angry. I felt better when I reached the relative sanctuary of a corner seat in a clean eight-person compartment, stowed my small brown suitcase on the luggage rack and washed my face with cold water in a commendably spotless cloakroom at the end of the corridor. Refreshed, I returned to my compartment where I discovered two fellow conscripts en route to Padgate – obviously East End cockneys – cheerfully ribbing each other about haircuts and bloody uniforms:

"Wotcher, mate ... yer goin' up ter bleedin' Padgate too ... 'ere, 'ave a fag mate."

Their cheerful banter quickly dissipated my rebellious self-pity and contracted the journey into one of seemingly short duration. Such merriment, I mused, was a welcome prelude to the stern realities ahead of us. I had enjoyed dabbling with military life in the Air Training Corps, but how would I cope with the real thing every day of every week? I felt dismayed at the thought of living in a Nissen hut for eight long weeks ... not allowed out of camp for six ... hmmm ... thoughts breed thoughts ... no girl friend, no dancing ... marching about on a hard parade ground every day instead of playing cricket at Finchley and Lord's – more than dismayed ... I was appalled. And yes ... when my new mates and I alighted from the train at Warrington it poured ... *it* being vintage Lancashire rain. I had left behind a familiar way of life and was now entering a new unknown world with foreboding and not a little dread.

But Life Loves to Laugh! An unexpected plot twist was soon to open up a seriously amusing episode in my new life as a reluctant conscript.

~~~~~~~~~~~

CHAPTER 26

CALLED UP AND CALLED OUT

INITIAL TRAINING CAMP, R.A.F. PADGATE, WARRINGTON

Cockroaches invade my first memory picture of the square-bashing camp: to snapshots of cockroaches infesting the kitchen of the Airmen's Mess add the horrible taste of bromide in the tea, the prickly woollen underwear, a sore neck from the barber's clippers, our fascist hut corporal – and you will gather, dear reader, that we were not at a Butlin's holiday camp. And SHINE! – everything had to shine to perfection and beam a reflection to shave by ... be polished, scrubbed, pressed, immaculately folded and stacked before inspection – or painted white. So there was some truth in the old joke: 'If it moves, salute it; if it don't, paint it.'

Being supremely fit the physical essentials of drill and PT were easy for me; the food was plentiful and nasty – some of the NCOs even nastier. My hut mates were a bunch of colourful young characters enunciating a wide range of regional accents that rapidly unified into a chorus of rebellion against our lack of freedom, the food and the corporal in charge of our hut. After a few days we settled down and adjusted to the frugal realities of our enforced military service, bonded by invisible traces of the ineffable community spirit and humour that, through six years of the recent war, had conditioned us to survive and overcome hardships during our childhood and youth.

That we were incarcerated in the camp for six weeks was our biggest moan, causing some of the lads to long for home comforts and mum's cooking, others their habitual social life in the pub or dance hall and for female company in general. A few suffered from an unbearable curtailment to their virulent sexual activities which even the bromide did little to subdue, occasionally causing tempers to flare. Consequently, tougher discipline was imposed, cold showers enforced, drill and PT increased and distance running within the camp lengthened. Three weeks into our training most of us were very fit, a few knackered and two in hospital – exhausted.

At the end of the third week a dramatic plot twist dispersed the gloom in our hut. A telegram.

Naturally there was a regular flow of letters and postcards between conscripts and their parents, siblings and girl friends. Betty and I wrote to each other two or three times a week. But telegrams, normally bearing grave news, were totally unexpected by eighteen-year-olds at square-bashing camp.

Before breakfast one morning my hut mates and I were on 'bull duty' – I was buffing the highly polished linoleum floor – when Mr Two Stripes, our infamous corporal, burst through the door and bellowed: "Rayment, come 'ere ... NAHW! ... stand to attention!"

Activity ceased, a hush descended. Everyone sensed trouble afoot. I propped the handle of the heavy buffer against one of the black heating stoves, walked the length of the hut and stood to attention in front of a red-faced Mr Two Stripes, noticing that he was confused – part angry and part apprehensive.

"Yer've gotta telegram, Rayment. I 'ope it's not bad news, but in case it is I want yer to open it an' tell me who sent it and what it says."

"Yes, corporal," thinking he had a bloody cheek to demand knowledge of something that was obviously a private matter. I slit open the small buff envelope and read the following:

SELECTED MIDDX II V SURREY II OVAL AUG 24/26 STOP ALSO CAPTAIN MIDDX YA V SURREY YA OVAL AUG 31/SEPT 2 STOP CONFIRM AVAILABILITY STOP SIGNED G.O ALLEN LORD'S STOP

Two Stripes, staring intensely into my eyes saw my face light up with surprised excitement rather than sadness as expected. He shouted, "Well, no-one 'as died then ... tell me what it bloody says, Rayment."

"I think you'd better read the telegram, corporal."

An eternity of silent seconds passed before the explosion. Shaking with anger, he waved the telegram in front of my face, exclaiming: "What the fuckin' 'ell do you think this place is ... a bloody holiday camp ... cricket ... bleedin' ponces' game ... you're confined to camp for six weeks, Rayment ... tell this bloody Allen bloke that ..."

"Excuse me, corporal, but Mr Allen is a famous captain of England, and I think the commanding officer should see this telegram ... should I put in a written request for an interview with the CO?"

My calm response and mention of 'written request' to the CO stunned Two Stripes into open-mouthed speechlessness, until, realising he needed to 'save face' in front of his charges, he gulped and turned towards the door, exclaiming:

"I'll 'ave to talk to the sergeant about this bleedin' telegram, Rayment" ... then glancing back, jabbed his right arm and index finger at our silent groups, yelling ... "and yer lot of pale-faced wankers ... get on with the bloody bull!"

From a convenient window, my best mate Ken Allen watched the corporal striding across the parade ground to the Sergeant's Mess. "He's gone," announced Ken ... then twenty-odd blokes surrounded me like a pack of news hounds, all asking questions at once and speculating on the odds of breaking the six-week confinement to camp rule – a subject of greater interest to most of them than cricket at the Oval. However, of immediate interest and necessity were the tasks of completing chores and preparing for drill on the parade ground.

Two hours later while practising the slow march on the parade ground, a messenger approached the drill sergeant and handed him a note, whereupon the sergeant yelled: "Squad halt ... left turn ... right dress ... 'eads up, 'eads up now ... stan-agh-eeez! 3085365 Rayment ... ahttinn-shun ... fhaaal out ... report to Warrant Officer Davies over there," he commanded, pointing his cane to the far corner of the square: "look lively look lively lad!"

Look lively? I nearly fell over as I fell-out because ... because I thought I must be in trouble and the shock made me dizzy and feel faint. Marching briskly for seventy yards re-circulated my blood and cleared my head – which was now buzzing with anxious questions to myself: "What's the trouble ... am I on a fizzer for something ... has Two Stripes reported me for insolence about that telegram ... or something?" Banging down my right heel to stand to attention in front of the short, dark-haired, obviously Welsh Warrant Officer, I whipped up a smart salute: "Sir."

He grinned: "Rayment, you do not salute Warrant Officers ... only commissioned officers ... got it?"

"Yes, sir".

"I have been instructed to take you to the Commanding Officer, Squadron Leader Pearson, to discuss your telegram."

"Sir, am I in trouble?"

"I don't think so, Rayment ... now, when you enter his office, make sure you give the C.O. a really smart salute."

There was a musical lilt and smile in his voice. I was confused: was he, or was he not, amused by knowledge of my hapless situation?

Knock knock ... "Enter," replied a plummy voice. The Warrant Officer opened the door – I followed and whipped up a smart salute to Squadron Leader Pearson. A cinematic apparition emerged slowly through a cloud of cigar smoke: a bushy handle-bar moustache attached to a smiling face, golden wings and barred medal ribbons glinting from an unbuttoned blouson jacket. As the smoke rose the scene became clearer to reveal the antithesis of my preconceptions: the Camp Commandant laying back in his sprung office chair, left foot on desk puffing contentedly. Squadron Leader Pearson unfurled himself, stood up, stretched across the desk with arm extended, indicating a hand-shake.

"Do let me congratulate you, old boy ... jolly good show ... playing at the Oval, ay-what."

"Thank you, sir," I responded, hesitating for a second or two before reaching for his hand – confused thoughts rushing through my brain because the Squadron Leader's surprisingly warm welcome was at variance with my expectations and diametrically opposed to the behaviour of Two Stripes earlier that morning.

"Warrant Officer, would you mind stepping outside for a moment while I have a chat with our budding cricketer?"

"Sir, I'll wait to escort him back to his duties."

"Thank you, Davies ... oh, and Davies ... I want you to arrange a leave pass for ten days, travel warrant, ration card and expenses ... er ... say five pounds ... to cover incidentals on his journey to London."

"Yes, sir."

"Now, please sit down Rayment, and tell me about your cricketing exploits ... which club you play for and how you came to be associated with Middlesex ... have you played at Lord's yet?"

For twenty minutes the C.O, a decorated wartime bomber pilot, talked animatedly with this raw recruit about the sport they both loved and played, the relaxed discussion culminating in a surprise directive by the Squadron Leader.

"Oh, by the way, Rayment, I want you to bring along your cricket gear when you return ... you will captain the station team for the rest of your time with us at Padgate. Very best of luck at the Oval ... oh, and I will send a telegram to Gubby Allen confirming I've given you ten days leave to cover the two matches. I shall look out for the scores in the *Telegraph*."

He then shook my hand, flicked the switch on his intercom and called for Warrant Officer Davies who, as we marched back to the parade ground, told me – in his delightful Welsh accent – that he had played a bit of cricket in Swansea. He then added, "You're lucky our C.O is keen on cricket; he's quite a character you know ... but you'd better look out for yourself, you might get some stick from the other lads confined to camp ... and your corporal won't like it a bit that you've been given leave ... I'll have to have a word with him."

The gossip about some young cricketer who had been given ten days' leave spread round the camp like wildfire. At lunch in the airmen's mess the comments directed at me were mostly supportive, if somewhat course. One burly Glaswegian hurled unintelligible invective from the next table ... something to do with cricketers being poofters and upper-class twits. Among my hut mates, the fact that I had bucked the regulations caused a buzz – although many had wagered an odd shilling and lost. Only Ken Allen and a couple of others wanted to talk about cricket and Ken, a Lancashire fan, talked of little else and insisted that I bring back scorecards and a souvenir or two from the Oval.

As I re-entered the bustle of the civilian world at Warrington Station on Friday 23rd August, I felt a little uneasy dressed in my new RAF uniform and carrying a duffle bag. I seemed to be out of character, out of time and place – as though I was an actor on a film set playing the role of a lonely airman travelling in a foreign country. Once settled in my seat, however, I soon returned to the 'real' world as I read the county cricket reports in the *Daily Telegraph*. The fascinating county championship race was being fought out between Yorkshire, Lancashire and Middlesex. Naturally, I was eager for my county to finish top of the table, and they were doing well on the second day at Worcester having bowled out the home team for 128 ... Bill Edrich taking 7 for 48. In their first innings Middlesex were currently 233 for 5; Jack Robertson had scored a century and Bill Edrich, a player I greatly admired, notched 52. Thankfully, the Norfolk-born England all-rounder had survived the war as bomber pilot, been awarded the Distinguished Flying Cross, and was now revelling in a streak of excellent form on the playing fields of England.

Back in the familiar environment of London's bomb-scarred streets I felt light-hearted and free: so pleased to see those cheery red buses, the busy black taxis – and to experience again the distinctive amalgam of odours and sounds echoing in the underworld of the Tube. Betty greeted me with a demure kiss at Finchley Central, but once in Station Road we cavorted like a couple of kids let out of school, arriving breathless and laughing at my parent's terraced house in Rosemary Avenue. After a token half-embrace from my deeply caring mother – her warmth and affection were never expressed by clinging hugs but through her sparkling eyes and cheerful voice – the three of us enjoyed tea and chat in the garden. The subject of square-bashing at Padgate was of minor interest to both mother and girl friend compared to the reason for my unexpected leave; the story of the telegram and the prospect of watching me play cricket at The Oval. When Father returned from the West End he greeted me with a long warm handshake and a couple of hefty thumps on my shoulder:

"Well done, my boy, well done ... we'll all come to watch you next weekend ... hope you get a big score tomorrow ... fancy getting a telegram from Mr GO Allen, no less. You said in a letter that you were surprised to be given leave ... "
So, once again I recounted the story, realising that slight embellishments were creeping into an already colourful tale.

The Kennington Oval and its environs were anything but colourful in 1946. Feeling bright and cheerful when I left home – and pleased to be travelling in civvies again – my mood darkened as I emerged from the Oval Tube station into the post-war gloom and grime of inner London. I was struck by the contrast with leafy St John's Wood and, noting the sad jagged silhouettes of bombed buildings and the soot-blackened outer walls of the Oval's perimeter, wished I was Lord's. However, my spirits lifted again as I strolled through the Hobbs Gates and into the Pavilion. I stood in awe after entering Long Room – the atmosphere impregnated with cricket history and ghosts of the Greats; their images, hanging in oils, looked down on me from high walls as though they were inspecting my credentials and potential. I was early, the first of our team to reach the old visitors' dressing room. I placed my long leather cricket bag on a bench locker, opened the door to the balcony and surveyed the brown marled wicket and patchwork square surrounded by the dull green outfield.

Given that there was so much restorative work to be done following several years of military occupation, I thought that The Oval was almost beautiful ...

except? Except that my romantic notions were tarnished by the giant gasholders towering over the field of play like malevolent ogres. Oh! that ugly five-headed industrial hydra, juxtaposed against my imagined panorama of men in whites disporting on the green sward playing the beautiful game in front of thousands enthusiastic spectators, was as abhorrent to me as the fairground on Southsea's Clarence Pier.

But ... but *this was the historic theatre* upon whose stage legendary cricketers had found fame, if little fortune: the home of Surrey's ten championship-winning teams; the domain of the Master, Jack Hobbs, who scored 199 centuries; the venue of final Test matches; the scene of the Bradman-Ponsford partnership of 471 in 1934; the backdrop to Len Hutton's record Test innings of 364, accumulated in thirteen and a half hours against the Australians in 1938. Having read the 1938 edition of Altham's *History of Cricket*, I also recalled that the Kennington Oval had hosted the very first Test match in 1880. Then at the Oval on August 29th 1882, in a low-scoring match, Frederick 'The Demon' Spofforth bowled Australia to a seven-run victory. Victorian England's pride was shaken. On September 2nd, the *Sporting Times* published a satirical obituary:

In Affectionate Remembrance

of

ENGLISH CRICKET

which died at the Oval

on

29th August, 1882.

Deeply lamented by a large circle of sorrowing

friends and acquaintances

R.I.P.

N.B. – The body will be cremated, and the

ashes taken to Australia.

Thus were sown the seeds of a legendary competition and an iconic sporting trophy.

Challenged to restore England's honour a wealthy cricketing aristocrat, the Honourable Ivo Bligh, immediately recruited an unofficial team to tour Australia with intent to recover the mythical Ashes. Three Australia v England matches were played, Australia winning the first in Melbourne; England the second and third. England had regained the Ashes. Later, a fourth four-day match was arranged in Sydney: Australia won this game played, experimentally, on a different pitch each day. Several years later the MCC classified all four games as Test natches.

The advent of 'The Ashes Urn' is a romantic tale, at once both whimsical and controversial. Probably the truest version is that, when in Melbourne, Ivo Bligh's fiancé and her Australian women friends ceremoniously 'cremated' a pair of bails, funnelled the ashes into the iconic six-inch brown terracotta perfume jar and presented 'The Trophy' to England's cricket captain.

The Oval: was I dreaming, standing here on the visiting players balcony quietly musing on cricket's legendary players and historic events, musing on the unlikely reality that a tongue-in-cheek obituary provoked a group of high-spirited Australian ladies to create a significant trophy from an insignificant perfume pot in 1883, that had, from that day, symbolised the skill, passion and hard-fought pride vibrating in both nations in every subsequent Test match between England and Australia? And in the now, sixty-four years since the Demon Spofforth was carried shoulder high from the field in celebration of his magnificent bowling and the Australian victory, I was romancing about the scene that took place 'down there' in the green-grey amphitheatre guarded by those proud ugly gasholders. Suddenly, waking from my reverie, I saw those gasholders in a different light; they were, after all, part and parcel of the image and the history of this celebrated cricket ground and of all the great athletic feats of heroes past whose feet had trodden those hallowed acres. That I would soon be treading that same turf humbled me. Some dreams do come true – and I would try not to feel intimidated by the legends or the gasholders.

Hearing the chatter of new arrivals, I turned back into the dressing room to meet my fellow players: two good friends from Finchley Colts, John Stacey and Ian Bedford, and two Middlesex professionals who were respected new friends, Bill Harrington and Harry Sharp. A hush descended when our revered captain, Mr GO Allen, entered the room and proceeded to greet us all with a firm handshake and cheery word. "Good morning, everyone ... good to see you all here at London's 'other' famous ground. Hope the bowlers are in good form because I've lost the toss and we're in the field."

We changed, heard the umpire's bell, followed the famous England captain down the stairs and pavilion steps, metal studs crunching the stone paving followed by a soft silence as my boots touched the turf I had been day-dreaming about moments earlier. We were on stage, and I was playing for Middlesex 2nd eleven at The Oval. Another of my dreams had become a reality.

The Surrey team were stronger and beat us in the two-day match by 138 runs. Surrey's Bernie Constable scored a hundred in the second innings and Tony Lock bowled fifteen overs but took only one wicket. For Middlesex, Mr Allen scored the most runs ... 47 and 23 not out. Ian Bedford took five wickets and John Stacey two. In the first innings I did not bother the scorers – a duck – but managed to accumulate twenty- seven in the second before falling to the wiles of Bernie Constable's leg-spinners. I thoroughly enjoyed my first experience of playing at The Oval, particularly fielding at cover. But the most memorable of memories is the enthusiastic leadership of our skipper Gubby Allen, especially the personal encouragement he gave to the young greenhorns in the team – the sixteen-year-old Ian Bedford, John Stacey and myself.

Ian and I took full advantage of Mr Allen's suggestion that we spend some time in the nets at Lord's before the next game at The Oval in three days' time. At home, Mother's tasty cooking was a delightful contrast to the stodge dished up in the Cockroach Cafe. Father relished my tales of square bashing at Padgate and cricket at the Oval; no doubt recounted with embellishments to his colleagues at Martin and Savage. Betty and I danced at Hammersmith Palais and met up with friends from our old school at a local dance on Friday. Sam, Wyn and Betty were looking forward to watching the Young Amateurs match on Saturday and Monday.

Catching an early Tube train from Finchley Central, the four of us arrived at the Oval just after ten o'clock and found seats in the empty Members and Friends Stand. I took Father into the Long Room and left him there to enjoy the paintings and photographs while I went up to the dressing room to meet with the Middlesex players as they arrived in ones and twos. From the team list given me by our manager and mentor, Mr Allen, I was pleased to note that there were two other lads from North London grammar schools in addition to our trio from Finchley; the rest of our team were from five public schools, one of whom was Brian Boobbyer of Uppingham, a rising rugby star. The players representing the Young Amateurs of Surrey were all from public schools.

I won the toss and decided to bat. We reached a total of 179 with DC Kingsley scoring 58, Brian Boobbyer 28 and yours truly 33. Surrey's opening bowler, ID Coutts took five wickets, and a small rotund boy aged thirteen-and-a-half from Tonbridge School bowled high-flighted leg spinners – expensively – and was listed to bat at No.4. His name was Colin Cowdrey. The Surrey innings collapsed to 79, John Stacey taking three wickets. On the second day I declared at 192 for 3; DC Kingsley scoring an excellent 81 not out; JR Tozer 32; P.A. de Zulueta and I scored 25 apiece. Our spinners won the match for us on the Monday, bowling out the Surrey team for 143. Ian Bedford bowled fourteen overs for three wickets and our 'man of the match', DC Kingsley, took 4 for 17 bowling off-spinners. One of his victims was the young Colin Cowdrey for five.

Mr Allen was delighted with the result and made particular comment on the excellent fielding of our team. Certainly his presence and charming manner was an inspiration to us all and manifested in the team spirit engendered among a group of young men who met and played together for the first and last time. To skipper such a team at the Oval was an honour and is remembered as a particularly enjoyable cameo of those halcyon days of innocent youth and post-war euphoria.

My 'Ode To Joy' at The Oval was over. I had to change into uniform and head straight to Euston Station. Mother and Father bade farewell, saying how much they had enjoyed the match and, carrying my civvies and washing in a suitcase, returned to Finchley. Betty came with me to the station for a fond farewell and a long kiss. Delayed by having to change trains at Manchester, I

311

arrived at Warrington station at one-thirty in the morning and, after further delay, eventually found a taxi willing to take me to RAF Padgate. Presenting myself at the locked gate in the hush of a very dark night, carrying a duffle bag and my long leather cricket portmanteau, I called out to the RAF MPs playing cards in the guard-house: "Hello! Could you let me in ... please?"

Shocked by the faint apparition peering through the wire gates I was aggressively challenged by two hefty military police holding Lee Enfield rifles and ordered to put both pieces of equipment on the ground.

"Don't move ... what are you doing here this time of night ... and who are you?"

"Sir, I am 3085365 A.C.2 Rayment."

"What's that long thing you were carrying, AC2?"

"A cricket bag, sir. The Commanding Officer instructed me to bring my cricket gear when I returned from leave ... sir."

Bewildered, and thinking I was either drunk, mad, or intended to smuggle something illegal into the camp, I was ordered to present my papers and to push the leather object and my duffle bag through the gate with my foot. One of them unlocked the gate and opened it just enough for me to obey the order while the other pointed his rifle directly at me.

"Don't move!" he ordered.

My papers were inspected, bags unstrapped and searched. The guards murmured debate resulted in acceptance of my credentials.

"Where have you come from, Rayment?"

"From London, sir ... playing cricket at the Oval ... with permission of the C.O. – sir."

"Playing cricket ... the Commanding Officer gave you leave to play cricket ... while on initial training?"

"Yes, sir."

They were flabbergasted, but held their composure and let me pass on into eerie vastness of the dark silent camp. The time was 3.10am.

Facing away from the brightly lit guardhouse my eyes took a while to adjust to the darkness. Eventually I spotted a few low wattage lights on the path to the distant Nissen huts and progressed, very slowly, towards the door of my own billet. Very tired, but glad there was a bed awaiting me, I pushed gently at the squeaky door and placed my two bags inside, entered, then closed the door quietly, intent on carrying the heavier portmanteau directly to my bed located about half way down the left hand row. The absolute silence, broken only by a snuffled snore, made me acutely aware that I must not wake anyone up ... as for disturbing Two Stripes the thought was unthinkable. It was so dark that I had to navigate by instinct, slowly tip-toeing over the slippery floor, clutching the weighty cricket bag to my bosom like a lover.

My left knee nudged a bed frame causing me to change direction, slip, start to fall and ... whoops ... crash into the stove ... cut my wrist on the corner of the white painted brick surround before ending up in a heap on the floor – lover on top. Mortified, I lay still for eternal seconds, hurting ... waiting for mumbled questions and a roaring Two Stripes. Stirrings and murmurings – but no uproar. Relieved beyond belief, I crawled along the floor, found my bed, stowed Miss Bag and duffle underneath, pulled back the bedding, slipped off my shoes and went straight to sleep – fully dressed.

Shaken – and definitely stirred – I opened my heavy-lidded eyes to see the purple face and bulging eyes of Two Stripes, ranting and pulling me out of bed. Hut mates, dressing and agog with curiosity, kept their distance.

Spewing a stream of unprintable invective, Two Stripes yanked me to my feet and pointed towards the stove. Horrors! Once perpendicular, both stove and stack pipe presented different angles, their disconnection having released copious amounts of soot, which, on closer inspection, had scattered in all directions over the polished floor. The trail of soot leading to my bed appeared to be mixed with blood.

Two Stripes' rage and vehement threats are beyond my powers of description. He was apoplectic. I was standing there in socks and a crumpled uniform, my pillow and bed sheets (yes, we had sheets) streaked with blood and soot – the stove in *his hut* was broken and soot splayed all over *his floor*. Of course, I had to clear up the mess, miss breakfast and PT, not speak to anyone and report to him when finished. He would inspect the result and, if satisfactory, march me to be interviewed by the duty sergeant, whom, he was sure, would put me on a charge for damage to property and negligence of duty.

To say that I was anxious is to belittle my fear – I was shit-scared of the unknown consequences of the sooty calamity that had befallen me – or I had fallen into – in the middle of the night. Yet at the same time I gave a moment's thought to the ironic fact that only twenty-four hours earlier I was seated on a London Tube train next to my girl friend and parents on my way to play cricket at The Oval. Oh the highs and lows of Life: did I want the ground to swallow me up – or to raise the roof with exultant laughter?

I stood beside Two Stripes as he raised the proverbial roof bellowing his accusations to Sergeant Mills. He clearly expected me to be dishonourably discharged from the RAF. "I wish," I thought. Sergeant Mills took notes and said he would present a written report to Warrant Officer Davies. "Hope yet!"

Before being dismissed, the sergeant asked me if I had any questions.

"No, sergeant – but I would like to have some breakfast and a cup of tea."

There ensued a discussion between Mills and Two Stripes as to why I had not had any breakfast that morning – a discussion that became heated – and unpleasant for the latter. The sergeant wrote a chit to authorise a meal in the airmen's mess and told me to report back to him at mid-day. "Dia ... smissed!"

As I closed the door I heard the senior NCO tearing off one hell of a strip to his subordinate. "Yes!"

As with the weather, sport permeates the British psyche and thus has a power to ease communication and influence lives. Certainly, among its aficionados, the quintessentially English game of cricket has the power to win friends and influence people – as I was beginning to discover. Full of uncertainty and not a little anxiety, I reported back to Sergeant Mills, who, to my surprise, addressed me in a conciliatory manner and even apologised for the behaviour of Two Stripes.

"Rayment, I am taking you over to see Warrant Officer Davies ... he has read my report and wishes to take the matter further with the Commanding Officer."

Somewhat relieved, but still unsure as to whether or not I was to be put on a fizzer, the sergeant and I marched around the parade ground where my mates were hard at drill – and no doubt bursting with curiosity as to the outcome of the early morning drama. Warrant Officer Davies dismissed Sergeant Mills and proceeded to question me in a kindly manner about the incident with the stove, assuring me that he considered it an unfortunate accident – was I badly hurt? Having dealt with the formalities he asked how I got on at The Oval and informed me that the CO was impatient to hear the story of my Oval experience.

I had always disliked fun fairs and roller-coaster rides – but I could not help thinking I was riding one of my own making and that, in some ways, this was fun. The Warrant Officer marched me over to the officer's quarters, checked the battledress uniform I had changed into and reminded me to stand at attention and salute when I entered Squadron Leader Pearson's office. Knock – knock. "Enter." I saluted.

"Rayment, my dear chap, I hear you have had an unfortunate accident ... something to do with your cricket bag and a stove. Are you all right?"

"Yes, sir, a couple of cuts on my wrist which bled a bit."

"Well, rather amusing, what? Cricket bag splays stove ... as with ball splays stumps ... ha ha ... most amusing... I hope you are all right to play tomorrow?"

"Yes, sir, I'll be fine, thank you sir."

"Now tell me – what it was like playing at The Oval ... I read that you scored a few for the Young Amateurs ... and that Gubby Allen himself captained your second eleven ... that must have been an honour in itself ... ah, the great Gubby ... saw him play quite a bit before the war you know ... wonderful fast bowler – good all-rounder, actually!"

Thirty minutes later I left the CO's office having recounted details of both matches, the players involved and the 'feel' of playing at The Oval. As I was going through the door the CO called out: "Oh, by the way, Rayment, we're having net practice this evening ... do come over and join us ... meet the chaps – get to know them – because, as I said, you'll be skippering the team tomorrow."

"Yes sir, I'll be glad to ... thank you, sir."

Chuckling within myself at the paradoxes I had experienced since batting at The Oval yesterday – and the variety of personalities I had encountered during that twenty-four hour saga – I repaired to Cockroach Cafe for lunch, filled my hungry stomach and faced the storm of questions hurled at me from over-excited pals.

"What happened ... why ... how was it ... are you in trouble ... did you win ... score any runs ... you had to report to the CO ... what is he like ... you're not on a charge are you ...", etc etc.

"You're a reet looky bougger, Al," observed Ken Allen, "an' ter top it all, you, a bleedin' AC plonk, are goin' ter captain t'station team tomorrow ... 'ob-nob with them bleedin' officers ... what a reet blooudy turn-up, me ol' mate."

Others expressed their thoughts and feelings with ribald affection tinged with a little envy, but for my new friends the best was yet to come – a happening that raised my popularity to the rafters. On returning to our billet we were surprised to encounter Sergeant Mills accompanied by a tall, winsome corporal.

"Stand in two lines, at ease and listen to me," ordered Sergeant Mills, who proceeded to give us a lecture on discipline and respectful behaviour.

"Corporal Hardy is now in charge of this hut, and I expect you all to sharpen up and do your very best for him. Dia ... smiss!"

We heard later that our bête noir, Two Stripes, had been demoted and posted to a maintenance crew on another RAF station. For the remaining weeks of our initial training the upbeat spirit in our billet was palpable; the cricket was fun and the CO delighted – he even scored a fifty in one of the matches.

"Jolly good show – ay what!"

Well, it's not what you know but ...! Yet unbeknown to me the 'jolly good show' Commanding Officer had been in direct communication with Mr GO Allen to arrange a posting to Fighter Command Headquarters at Bentley Priory, Stanmore, Middlesex. Stanmore was a cyclable eight miles from Finchley and a dozen Tube stations from Lord's. Although I was innocently naïve at the time I realised much later that my posting was arranged by the 'big wigs' at Middlesex to keep a close eye on a promising youngster. More promise than fulfilment as it turned out in those vital years between 18 and 20, even though I played – and very much enjoyed – a tremendous amount of cricket while I was in the RAF.

'Di-as-missed' from our last parade at Padgate one early morning in September 1946, our intake group expressed relief and expectancy with noisy and ribald high-jinks in the renamed 'Old Cockroach Canteen'. Marshalled into Bedford coaches we cheered as we exited the camp gates and sang all the way to Warrington station. No longer raw recruits, we had bonded as mates through the Padgate ordeal – though onlookers may have mistaken us as inmates just released from prison – in some senses true. We were scattering to all parts of the UK on a mysterious adventure not knowing what exciting, boring or bloody awful experiences awaited us at our first posting. I was one of a handful among those high-spirited uniformed youths awaiting trains on Warrington's grimy platforms classified as 'Clerk Special Duties'; a category that would involve jobs in radar and air defence. When I boarded the train to London I had no idea what type work I would be involved in at Bentley Priory.

Arriving at Stanmore Park, I was directed by a corporal to my billet and shown the transport office where I was to report the next morning at 8.00am. There I was joined by two male conscripts, a sergeant and a newly signed-on WAAF. We were driven in a Bedford truck through the village, up Stanmore Hill, alighted in the grounds of Bentley Priory, were led through a small door and down many steps to the Filter Room, deep underground. Our induction programme and further training involved an overview of the air defence and radar network of the south-east of England, plotting skills and special sessions on listening, remembering and annunciation skills. I was allocated the role of a 'teller' and placed on the duty rota. If I remember correctly there were three shifts of eight hours for five days, followed by two free days before returning to a different time slot in the shift rota.

During WWII the Filter Room at Bentley Priory and the Operations Room at Hillingdon House, Uxbridge had been highly secret elements of Britain's air defence system. Several post-war films – including *The Battle of Britain* starring Lawrence Olivier, Kenneth Moore and Susannah York – depicted the Filter and Operations Rooms at 11 Group HQ as the vital nerve centres of our WWII radar air defence system. Receiving map reference coordinates in earphones from radar operators at coastal stations, male and female personnel in the Filter Room plotted aircraft movements on large map-tables. From a balcony overlooking the map-table at Stanmore, 'tellers' communicated with plotters on the big 'operations table' at Uxbridge through telephone headsets, reading off the map-grid references and identity tags of attacking hostile aircraft and defending RAF fighter planes.

From the Ops-Room balcony senior officers had a commanding view of the evolving aerial attack below them. They then had the great responsibility of deciding where and when to deploy diminishing numbers of RAF Hurricanes and Spitfires to attack increasing numbers of German bombers protected by Messerschmidt fighter aircraft. After WWII the radar defence network was maintained at high level due to uncertainties surrounding the intentions of the Soviet leaders and the stability of European nations. The vibrant team spirit within Fighter Command and commendable pride for their major contribution in deterring a Nazi invasion of our shores six years earlier was still evident in 1946. To me and my young RAF colleagues memories of the Battle of Britain remained a powerful reality. However, another powerful reality was evolving in 1946-47: The Cold War.

The work of a 'teller' required alertness and concentration when active – a lot of patience when inactive – and clear precise diction when operating. The overall experience proved to be a formative one for many of us. My adult speech patterns and diction that had evolved as a 'Norf Lunnuner' were refined by singing in church choirs, well-spoken members of family, educated middle-class people at work and in the cricket world, then later programmed in the Filter Room at Stanmore. However, from early childhood my sensitivity to sound caused me to adopt – not always unconsciously – some audio variations within local dialects wherever I happened to reside. My new colleagues at Stanmore came from an interesting mixture of locations and social backgrounds – a small number were required to adjust their vowel sounds in order to be clearly intelligible over the air waves.

Concentration and good team work were essential when on duty, but in general there was lots of friendly banter and youthful high spirits. Male and female team members melded into disparate groups through mutual interests in music, dancing, sport or obscure hobbies; the unattached naturally inclined towards romantic adventures. It is interesting to reflect that about one third of the young men and women conscripts were engaged to be married or committed in a relationship – as I was to Betty. However, I was tempted to change strongly established thoughts about my future career.

New experiences in the RAF had opened my eyes to the reality of Life beyond the confines of cricket and football and began to draw me towards flying as a career – to train as a pilot. For several weeks either side of Christmas that year the debate raging within me was about opportunity, risk and commitment. I now had an opportunity to commit myself to the RAF by signing on for seven years and, as I believed, succeed in my ambition to become a pilot. But was my greater ambition to fulfil that childhood dream: 'to play cricket every day of the week'. If true, would I be good enough to play – as an amateur or professional – in a county team in two or three years' time? Risky!

But now, early in 1947, I could commit myself to a more certain pathway; sign on and immediately move into an interesting career that offered economic security. I prevaricated – then decided to wait until the end of the coming cricket season before making up my mind. Meanwhile I became proficient at my duties in the Filter Room, played soccer for RAF Stanmore, Fighter Command and Finchley FC Reserves. Because I had been granted permission to sleep at my parents' home when not on duty, Betty and I saw a lot of each other and our ballroom dancing improved through lessons, lots of serious practice – and fun at the Saturday night 'hop'.

However, from late January 1947 I was mostly confined to barracks when off duty – not for a misdemeanour – but because almost the whole of Britain came to a standstill in the Big Freeze.

~~~~~~~~~~~

CHAPTER 27

ROMANCE AND LORD'S IN 1947

The longest, warmest and most enjoyable summer I had experienced in my eighteen years was preceded by the longest, coldest, most unenjoyable winter of my eighty-plus years on this planet.

The bitter weather in the first months of 1947 symbolised, for me, an awareness that six years of horrendous war had not culminated in true peace but in another, and increasingly dangerous, ideological-territorial divide that had its roots in Russian-European history prior to the Great War of 1914-18.

The Cold War now evolving could develop into an atomic arms race: a third world war would annihilate a high percentage of the population of the planet. In terms of daily living I prayed that the weather would warm up and in metaphorical terms that the East-West power struggle would remain cold.

'Cold' was a constant reality affecting the body, the mind and essential mobility. COLD and FROZEN were daily headlines in national newspapers reduced to four pages. In February 1947 one front page proclaimed:

FROZEN BRITAIN WORKS BY CANDLELIGHT

Snow fell every day from January 24th to March 16th. Between February 2nd and 22nd the observatory at Kew recorded no sunshine – none at all. In many areas of the country snowdrifts of ten feet and higher transformed the landscape, cutting off supply routes to isolated communities who were indebted to the RAF for food supplied by parachute.

One of the bleakest winters in the 20th Century caused the River Thames to freeze over, and raging blizzards blockaded many shipping ports for weeks. Rail and road transport systems were often inoperable, prolonged power cuts affected every home and work-place in the land, factories closed and supplies of fuel, already severely rationed, became seriously scarce in some areas. In an adventure of necessity Betty and I dragged a home-made trolley through trampled icy snow and occasional drifts on a five-mile round trip to the Gas Works at Mill Hill to collect two sacks of coke – one for each household. The Ideal boiler in the kitchen was the only source of heat during extensive power cuts.

Raging storms heralded the great thaw, creating serious floodwaters in thirty counties and serious disruptions to the flow of daily living for weeks on end in many cities, towns and villages. The farming community worked bravely to maintain their contribution to the food supply chain but suffered tragic losses: two million sheep, thousands of cattle and damage to half a million acres sown with wheat. The harsh winter damaged the nation's fragile economy and adversely affected people with fragile health, especially the elderly. But life was not all gloom, the ineffable

British spirit moaned and joked its way through 'the war with the weather' and came up smiling, singing and dancing into the bright warm days of spring.

April In Paris ... is a romantic song and a most beautiful dance tune. And dance we did, though not in romantic Paris but in the ballroom of the Royal York Hotel on the wind-swept Isle of Wight. Betty and I had chosen a modest ring in London's Burlington Arcade, celebrated our engagement with a modest meal at the Trocadero near Piccadilly, then 'travelled abroad' by paddle-steamer over the Solent to the familiar pier-head at Ryde. No, we did not stay with my Uncle Jack over his butcher's shop but booked in at separate boarding houses in George Street – the 'proper thing' to do in 1947.

We met each morning after breakfast and headed for the Esplanade railway station. For five shillings each (25p) we purchased weekly season tickets and viewed the island scenery from smoky wooden carriages pulled by the green and black 'Puffin' Billy' steam engines I had adored as a child. On successive days we alighted at the coastal extremities of several branch lines: Freshwater, Cowes, Ventnor and Bembridge; strolled the sandy beaches, walked along the cliff tops and over the rolling hills of Tennyson Downs – often having to shelter from the rain in seaside cafés. One sunny day we ventured south from Newport to Ventnor West on a branch line I had not experienced before the war. Betty and I had now passed through or alighted at all thirty-five stations on the island. In the evenings we ate inexpensively in cafes, poshed up to go dancing or to the cinema, then enjoyed a long snog before parting and entering our respective B&Bs. A succulent roast beef dinner with Uncle Jack, cousin Tilly and her husband John rounded off a memorable week – a week that flew by because we were in love and so enjoyed uninterrupted time together. No constraints of work or family – only restraints on our powerful sexual drives. But, given the values inherent in our family and social background that was the norm in 1947 ... NSBM!

A spell of bright spring days welcomed us home to Finchley; suburban trees and shrubs were shrouded in a haze of baby green leaves, some proudly budding, others ablaze with blossom full and glorious. In Arden Field the mower's phut-phut and the whiff of new mown grass chimed with the sound of leather on willow from the nets to charm away dark winter's gloom. Spring! No war, new cricket season, good friends at work and play, romance and dancing. Life was good ... so good!

Refreshed from our holiday Betty happily returned to work at Unilever House and Aircraftsman Rayment cycled to Bentley Priory for duty in the Filter Room and banter with his mates in the canteen. But on arrival the happy nineteen-year-old was told by the duty sergeant to report to Flight Lieutenant Dutton, the officer in charge of personnel and staff duty rotas. Promotion?

Dutton was an efficient young officer with red hair and a pleasant enough manner – with the emphasis on efficient. I saluted – he motioned me to the chair opposite his desk and commenced the interview with complimentary remarks about my duties as a 'teller' and general good behaviour. Did these positive affirmations suggest that promotion was a possibility – or, on the other hand, the sugar pill before a dose of syrup of figs. The latter.

"Rayment, I understand from some senior officers who seem to have a link with the secretariat at Lord's, that you are to be given carte blanche leave this summer to play cricket for a number of teams, including Middlesex second eleven and, of course, the RAF and possibly the Combined Services. This will mean that I will not be able to include your name in the regular duty rotas. I have therefore arranged for you to be posted to the Training Centre at Bawdsey as an instructor with the rank of 'acting corporal'. The Commanding Officer there has hinted that your duties will be flexible enough to allow authorised leave for sporting events. It seems you have support from high-ranking officers in Fighter Command, but they also agree with me that due to the increasingly unstable relations with Russia our air defence systems have to be fully manned and efficient. You will report to the duty officer at RAF Bawdsey by sixteen hundred hours on the fifteenth of May."

"Yes, sir – thank you, sir." Dismissed and in shock I had to start my shift in the Filter Room, did not reveal the news to my mates and held on for a much needed 'think' until I was cycling the eight miles back to Finchley. So many thoughts!

> Hmmm, I realise I would probably be a part-time member of Flt Lt Dutton's unit this summer, but why post me so far away? I realise too that tension is growing between East and West and yes, we are now in a Cold War that is creating uncertainty and anxiety about what may happen in the near future ... and yes, I get it ... even if I were to be posted to the Operations Room at Uxbridge or a radar station on the South Coast I would not be available for full-time duties this summer. Ah, I get it, the training school at Bawdsey is not an operational unit. Although I am looking forward to the adventure of a new challenge and making new friends in a new place I shall miss the familiarity of living at home and working at Stanmore. Of course I'll miss my parents and friends but most of all Betty's company and our joint dance lessons and practice sessions.

Betty expressed her disappointment but was thankful I had not been posted abroad and pleased that I expected to be in London playing cricket during the summer. The prospect of our first major parting brought us even closer together ... we would really miss each other. I was given a cheery send-off by colleagues at Bentley Priory, some of whom had trained at Bawdsey Manor Radar School: "You lucky thing, Al ... it's a posting like no other in Britain ... it's a bleedin' holiday camp by the sea, mate."

On the due date I boarded a train at Liverpool Street Station, alighted at Felixstowe, caught a bus to the ferry and crossed the River Deben in an open

RAF launch. My first sighting of the Manor's south wing was impressive enough but later, when I had an opportunity to view the front elevation from the trees screening the beach, I was stunned by the size, the strange architecture, the sheer grandeur of the building and seascape environment. The many ancillary buildings, some original and decorative, others erected to serve the wartime operational needs of the radar station or the pre-war experiments of radar pioneer Robert Watson-Watt, diminished Bawdsey Manor's natural charm.

It was at Bawdsey Manor in 1937 that the pragmatic British scientist-engineer and his team began experiments with radio waves to provide 'long-range detection of aircraft' later known as RADAR – a US Navy acronym for 'radio detection and ranging'. Considering the critical importance of radar as an early-warning system during the Battle of Britain and the Blitz, it is worth noting that, unlike the jet engine pioneer Frank Whittle, Watson-Watt was fully supported and financed by the Air Ministry. Due to the impending war a relatively primitive radar system called Chain Home had been rushed into production. Twenty radar stations built on the east and south coasts of England were operational a few months before September 1939. Throughout the Battle of Britain and the Blitz, Chain Home proved to be the world's first effective aircraft-detecting defence system.

In my early days at Bentley Priory I had been seconded to Ventnor radar station for two weeks as part of my training. And again, here at Bawdsey, I was impressed by the structures dominating the skyline: four 110-metre steel towers holding the array of wires that pulsed out powerful radio waves in a fan-shape of 100 degrees, initially to a range of 120 miles. When an aircraft interrupted the signal, a blip appeared on the operator's screen having been received by adjustable antennas on the four 73-meter wooden towers.

At first I missed home comforts and mates at the Filter Room but soon adjusted to communal living again: the Nissan hut dormitory, the bathhouse and the fairly decent airmen's mess. The officer of the Training school was affable, my new job easy, the location inspiring – even North Sea gales that lashed East Anglia's flat and vulnerable coastline were energising. On sunny days the beach became the playground for off-duty personnel – in so many ways this really was a dream posting – a relaxed military holiday camp that inspired many romances and a freedom for sexual experimentation among those who were away from the strictures of their home community for the first time. Groups of friends formed quickly and would board the ferry to enjoy an evening at a pub or dance hall in Felixstowe but ... but the last return ferry left the quay at 22.30hrs, weather permitting. Not for me: I was engaged, was not a drinker and hoped to pal up with some blokes who kicked a soccer ball around or played darts while having half-a-pint and a chat. Those thoughts had surprising results.

Bawdsey Manor, cricket field on the left

*RAF Bawdsey Manor: The Chain Home Towers
shot from south bank of River Deben*

As I entered the airmen's mess for breakfast on my third morning at Bawdsey I was amazed to see Ken Allen, my best mate from Padgate days, sitting at a table chatting to another chap and a couple of WAAFS. Before I picked up a tray to join the queue I crept up behind Ken, slapped him on the back and in a bad imitation of his Lancashire accent, said: "Ee lud, 'av thee oiled t'bat ready fer t'season?' He turned his head, eyes and mouth wide open, and spluttered, "Eee ... Al ... is it reely thee lud ... where t'bloody 'ell 'as thee cumfrum?"

Ken, who had been at Bawdsey for three months, was a fully paid-up instructor corporal. He understood why I had been shunted from the Filter Room at Stanmore and guessed I would be mostly off-duty during the cricket season that had already started. "Do'st remember t'stir thee caused at Padgate, Al ... I'll never forget it, lud ... an' we all cheered when tha' bleedin' corp'ral got 'is cumupunce. Now then, lud, d'st thee know tha'top man 'ere ... CO of t'whole outfit ... is a bleedin' cricket fan?"

"No, Ken, I'd no idea."

"I'll bet he calls thee in't 'is office when he finds out thee's played at Lord's." Sure enough, a couple of days later the sergeant instructor heading our team called me aside and told me I was to report to Squadron Leader Colquhoun after duty: "I don't know why, Rayment, you can't be in trouble 'cause you only arrived last Monday."

"Cricket, sergeant, I expect it's about cricket." He looked neither surprised nor impressed but smiled, shrugged his shoulders and walked towards the Sergeant's Mess.

The CO was broad in face and beam, rather rumpled of dress and casual in manner – nevertheless a personality that exuded dynamic energy in his movements and humour through his twinkling eyes. And yes, he was a cricket enthusiast, a wicket-keeper who could bat (in fact in the following season he played for Suffolk in the Minor Counties Championship). I was in his office for over an hour, the CO and the acting corporal sharing tall tales and pet theories about the complex game: for those few ethereal moments we escaped the world of radar, duty and the Cold War – then returned to immediate tasks according to our disparate responsibilities. A few days later I was summoned to the CO's office again. He had decided on a plan of action.

"Rayment, do you know anything about preparing wickets?"

"No, sir ... that is, I have no real knowledge but during the war we had no official groundsman at the Finchley Club and I was one of the Colts who was keen on preparing the best wickets for our matches."

He asked me for more detail so I recounted the routine of the weeding, the dung cart, the rolling and mowing – but whilst doing so I wondered why the CO was asking me these questions.

"Right, Rayment, good show ... I will arrange with the Training School to reduce your duties so that you can work to improve our rather rough wickets. I'm hoping we'll get some decent cricket this summer ... more runs, less injuries. Now, the outfield will be mown regularly as usual ... er ... but you will probably need some assistance because there's a lot of work to do out there on our table, you know."

Ken Allen volunteered to be my assistant in the task of stabilising an area equivalent to four wickets on the rather sandy soil of the table. The CO arranged a delivery of friable clay soil and cow dung from a local farmer; he also sent the Ransome hand mower to be cleaned and the blades sharpened. The roller was adequate, the water hoses repairable and the hand tools plentiful. Well equipped, Ken and I worked during periods of fine weather to produce four pitches that were firm, level and safe. Squadron Leader Colquhoun was delighted; he also proved to be a really good wicket-keeper when, under his captaincy, Ken and I played in two matches for the Bawdsey team in that delightful 'country house' setting beside the sea.

In mid-June the CO granted me leave to play for the Combined Services XI, and for the rest of that summer I spent very few days at Bawdsey. In writing this piece I have concluded that the cricketing CO was complicit in the arrangements to free me from service duties in order to play and develop my promising cricket talent. At that time I was rather naive and unaware of those 'arrangements', but I now know that I did not truly fulfil that talent nor the hopes and expectations of those silent mentors at Lord's and in the RAF.

However, there is some truth in the saying: 'Be careful what you ask for – you may get it.' My dream of 'playing cricket every day' came true and overflowed without having to think about joining a county staff because His Majesty's Government were paying me to play cricket, not only for RAF teams but also Middlesex 2nd XI and Club and Ground, for the Air Ministry, the Adastrians, Ariel CC and Cross Arrows – as well as a few games squeezed in for Finchley. Apart from matches recorded in *Wisden* or available on the internet I am unable to recall details of play in the majority of those matches. I remember the teams, some of the locations and a few of the characters –- but very little else. So, with the aid of published scorecards and newspaper accounts to get the facts right, I will have fun as I visualise a few scenes on and off the field when playing at Lord's, Northampton, Finchley – even in Germany – more than sixty years ago.

In the present tense, flash-back style, my mind film begins to roll at the top of the escalator as I emerge from the bowels of London's Tube into Euston main-line station in the mid afternoon of Friday 20th June.

It is around lunchtime. I'm now 19, dressed in civvies: dark blue blazer, grey flannels and white shirt with Finchley CC tie. In my right hand a crumpled suitcase; on my left shoulder a heavy leather cricket bag. I walk briskly across the concourse, purchase a return ticket to Northampton and make my way to Platform 5. I'm enveloped in the smells and sounds of hissing steam engines, the crump of carriage doors closing and guard's whistles piercing the deafening hubbub of people, hundreds of us, hurrying somewhere near or far. I'm in-between: excited, confident, naïve – and a little confused. On the one hand I'm thrilled that I am going to play in my first three-day match against a county team but, on the other, I have no idea that I'm about to make my first-class debut. My natural confidence combined with innocent naivety will cope easily with the fact that I have never met with, or played against, any members of the Combined Services team. Ahead of me on Platform 5 I spot a small pile of cricket bags, a couple of men in naval officer's uniforms and two more sporty looking chaps dressed in civvies, one of whom turns to greet me: "I say, old boy, are you Rayment?" ... I nod as my hand is shaken vigorously ... "I'm Skipper ... Alan Shirreff ... so good to meet you, old boy ... let me introduce you to the others ... by the way, old boy ... no officer-ranks stuff in my teams ... all for one – and all that sort of thing, old boy."

I take note that the Skipper has a warm and energetic personality – the type of wartime, wizard-prang RAF pilot I had seen in films produced at Pinewood Studios. F/O Roland Parker is the other RAF chap in civvies and the two naval officers are Geoffrey Vavasour and Barry Pryer. They are all older than me, but very friendly in the familiar manner of club cricketers. In contrast however, a rather frosty Sub-Lt John Dewes enters our compartment as we leave Euston. I realise that I am the youngest and the greenest member of the team, but Alan Shirreff takes me under his wing and introduces me to the rest of the players at the hotel bar before dinner. During the meal I quickly make friends with George Dawkes of Derbyshire, and over the weekend have long chats with Peter Hearn who had made his debut first-class hundred for Kent earlier in the month. Listening to their tales of experience and success I begin to wonder why I have been selected to play for Combined Services when I have not yet played for a county – nor even for the RAF.

Royal Air Force versus The Army, Lord's, 1947
from left: ?; R.Mills; G.Dawkes; A.Rayment; R.Wilson;
R.Smith; J.Roberts; A.Shirreff, (capt); D.Cockle

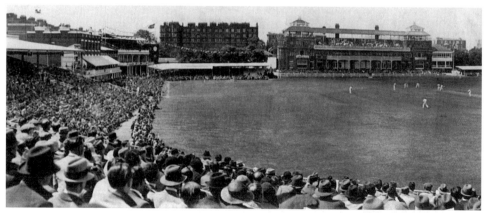

Lord's in 1935: as it was from Alan's first visit in 1937, his debut
in 1945 and through most of his playing career with Hampshire

My few conscious memories of the actual match include my disappointment that the county cricket ground at Wantage Road spilled into the Northampton Town soccer pitch, that the spectator stands were few and drab but that the players were skilful and friendly; that our opening bowler, Yorkshire's Johnny Whitehead, was extremely fast and that Alan Shirreff was not only an excellent skipper but also a really good all-rounder. Fielding in the covers while Denis Brookes scored a big hundred was an education – so technically correct and elegantly beautiful.

When drafting this chapter I recalled that I had enjoyed the new experience of playing at a higher level, had made some new friends but failed in my performance. The records show that I made five runs batting at number four in a first innings total of 401 and bowled three overs for eleven runs and no wickets.

In early July I fulfilled some duties at Bawdsey, passed an instructor's exam and scored fifty-plus on the wickets that Ken and I had nurtured. Once again I boarded the ferry across the Deben – on leave to play cricket until the end of the season.

O how I loved being in the special atmosphere of the Visitors' Dressing Room at Lord's again: the unique aromatic mix, the leather settees, the muted sounds of mowers and traffic wafting through the open doors to the balcony – the panoramic view of the historic arena and an eerie sense of heroes past who had padded up 'over there … in that corner'.

Whilst changing in another corner on August 4th, I was presented with my Royal Air Force cap by the ebullient captain Alan Shirreff who emphasised to our high spirited bunch of regular officers and other rank conscripts, "We're cricketers, old boy … all for one … to have fun, win or lose." Well, the Skipper had the most fun while scoring 120 not out in our first innings total of 200 against the Army. Batting at number five I was bowled for nought by Johnny Whitehead, the fast bowler who had impressed me at Northampton. On this sunny day and on a good wicket we would have to bowl and field really well to contain the Army batsmen.

We followed the Skipper down the wide staircase, through the Long Room and the white gate onto the grass carpeted stage of the greatest cricketing theatre in the world. I felt 'at home' – then was surprised! Before we reached the wicket the Skipper walked over to this nineteen-year-old and said, "You open with the new cherry, old boy – which end would you like?"

"Er … er … the pavilion end, please, Skipper … thank you for the honour."

Alan the Aircraftsman opened the bowling for the Royal Air Force at Lord's, bowled 27 overs, took one wicket for 75. Alan the Squadron Leader, Cambridge Blue and Hampshire county player opened at the Nursery end, bowled 28 overs, took two wickets for 89. In retrospect I realise that Alan Shirreff epitomised the highest and best traditions of amateur leadership, giving great encouragement to his young players and leading from the front in a cheerful spirit. Our Skipper put heart, mind and soul into winning a game, yet was philosophical when losing: to him cricket was the greatest of sports and the greatest fun. Peter Hearn scored 106 out of 311 in the Army's first innings: in our second innings I squeezed a single before falling to the wiles of left-arm spinner John Bartlett. We lost the two-day match by nine wickets. My debut for the RAF was a failure in terms of figures, but a great success in terms of bowling tight through an unexpected number of overs, fielding at cover and enjoying the convivial spirit of my new team-mates.

The morning after the Army match I boarded a No.2 bus at Church End, Finchley and once again alighted opposite the high brick wall defending the Nursery from the noisy traffic in Wellington Road. Instead of my leather cricket bag I was carrying a canvas hold-all containing essential equipment for a day of spectating: fish-paste sandwiches, an apple, a straw hat and my father's binoculars – oh, and a big bottle of Tizer. Southern Schools versus The Rest was a trial match to select the Public Schools XI to play against the Combined Services at Lord's five days hence. Not only was my talented friend Ian Bedford playing, but also two young batsmen much talked about on the cricketing grapevine: David Sheppard of Sherborne School and Peter May of Charterhouse.

I had arrived early enough to enjoy watching the skilful routines carried out by the head groundsman and his staff making final preparations to the wicket located on the Tavern side of the table. At ten-thirty the sun was hot and I was thirsty: I placed my hired green cushion on one of the long, white-painted bench seats by the picket fence in front of the Old Tavern and refreshed myself with Tizer poured into an enamelled tin mug. Looking to the pavilion on my left I spotted a couple of young players chatting on the home team balcony, sipping real lemonade and pointing to the wicket.

I chuckled within myself, thinking: Yesterday I was 'up there' – and fielding at cover a few yards the other side of this fence. Today I'm a paying spectator. I shall be 'up there' again in two days' time in that sumptuous Victorian dressing room, chasing balls 'out there' on the sloping grass carpet ... and then again next week, playing against the talented schoolboys selected from this trial. "Life is sumptuous," I chuckled to myself.

Even though I chatted to a few people settling in adjacent seats, the inner chuckle continued and I drifted, briefly, into a happy day-dream linking my current joy with that special moment in Arden field the day the war began: "God ... this war is really going to mess up my cricket career!" Now, almost eight years later, at Lord's, I was experiencing the silent answer: my heart overflowed with a poetic energy too beautiful to describe – cocooned in a silent reverie of thankfulness. Ding-ding ... ding-ding ... ding-ding – the unique tone of the Lord's 'five-minute bell' called me back to the buzz of anticipation among the

Tavernites and, inexplicably, my eyes noted a beam of sunlight reflecting from a set of stumps bare of bails.

Opening the batting for The Rest, JA Tobin quickly made *that* daunting walk back to *that* Pavilion, bare of runs. His partner, Philip Whitcombe anchored the innings to enable John Riley of Wellingborough to achieve the honour of a century at Lord's before being bowled by Ian Bedford. Ian bowled the most overs in each innings for Southern Schools to bag a total of six wickets for 106. However, Ian was not selected for the Public Schools XI because another leg-spinner, G.P. Esdale from Malvern College, took nine wickets in the match for 112 runs, including the prized scalps of Sheppard and May.

From the moment the 17-year-old Peter May opened his score with a glorious back-foot drive that sent the ball whistling past cover's left hand to crunch into the picket fence by my feet, I sensed he possessed an exceptional talent. In scoring 148 runs out of a total of 278 he also proved his physical stamina and powers of concentration. Peter May was a majestic batsman, unique in style – and if a comparison is required, Walter Hammond comes to mind as similar though different. In those two glorious summer days at 'The Home of Cricket' I was privileged to glimpse the budding talent of two future England cricket captains – May and Sheppard. In his second innings David Sheppard showed skill and determination in scoring a backs-to-the-wall 63. *Wisden* records: 'Sheppard saved Southern Schools from complete breakdown before the leg-breaks and googlies of Esdale when set 229 to win.'

The heat wave continued – 70°F at 8.30am the next morning August 8th – as I walked the half a mile to the bus stop in Regent's Park Road carrying my heavy cricket bag. I cooled off atop the No.2. bus and arrived at Lord's before 10.00am to have plenty of time for a net. In the dressing room my cheerful RAF colleagues were confident we could beat the Royal Navy – and, of course, we were all excited at the prospect of playing at Lord's *again*! Alan Shirreff introduced me to Luke White, a team member I had not met before. When they were both eighteen, the Honourable Luke and John Dewes – opening batsman for the Navy – had played for an England XI against The Australian Services XI in the third 'Victory Test' at Lord's. Luke played only six first-class cricket matches, whereas John Dewes was to play in 137, including five Tests, before focusing his all-round talents and energies on school-teaching, eventually becoming a headmaster in Australia.

The Navy won the toss, batted, and were all out for 157. I was pleased to take two wickets in ten overs, bowling medium-fast in-swingers; then failed with the bat at number eight, being one of leg-spinner Barry Pryer's eight victims. My friend George Dawkes batted soundly for a century to establish a first-innings lead of 62. On day two I excelled myself in the Navy's second innings, taking 5 for 42 in 21 overs, including the wicket of John Dewes, lbw for 3. We beat the Royal Navy by seven wickets.

The next day, Betty and I joined our families and friends in the lively community atmosphere of the Finchley club, occasionally watching the play but mostly chatting about the Test matches against the touring South Africans and the amazing exploits of the 'Middlesex Twins'. Blue skies and hot sun embraced the tranquil scene of peacetime cricket on our local green, a picture etched in my memory as symbolising a significant phase of my growth from club roots to the county circuit. I remember saying to myself: "Tomorrow I catch the bus to Lord's again ... to play for Combined Services against Public Schools. I wonder if I'll ever catch the bus to play for Middlesex?"

Squadron Leader Alan Shirreff captained a team of nine other officers and yours truly – an AC plonk. Combined Services batted first and reached 305 all out, mainly due to a sound 75 by opener Geoffrey Vavasour and a last-wicket stand of 92 by John Deighton (89) and John Bartlett (24 not out). The latter John followed his gritty batting with a brilliant display of orthodox left-arm spin bowling, taking the early wicket of David Sheppard for nine in a tally of 6 for 65, including the prize of Peter May's wicket. However – a wonderful however – before being caught and bowled the seventeen-year-old Peter May had scored 146 for his Public Schools team in a total of 239 all out. A truly memorable innings: technique, control and power beyond his years, and yes, many of Peter's 23 fours fizzed past my outstretched arms at cover point.

Our cheerful and talented skipper enjoyed an opening stand of 162 with Roland Parker, then declared when John Manners was out for a duck, leaving Public Schools a target of 228 to win the match. Aircraftman Rayment took 2 for 13 in the second innings and our match-winning spinner, John Bartlett, bagged another six wickets: 12 for 126 in the match. Combined Services won comfortably by 81 runs.

At that time I was not alone in believing that John Bartlett possessed the talent and character to develop into an England player. John was seventeen when he made his first-class debut for Oxford University: in fact, in that first post-war season of 1946, John was just eighteen when he was selected for the Gentlemen versus the Players at Lord's. Writing this chapter in 2009 I became curious about his subsequent cricket career and researched the Sussex archives. My enquiries led me to discover that, by happy coincidence, John and I lived in the same coastal village in Hampshire. We met at his yacht club and reminisced, among other memories, about his 'twelve for' at Lord's sixty-one years ago. John played little first-class cricket after coming down from Oxford but later, as an educator who was principal of a preparatory school, he enthused and coached hundreds of boys in the game he graced at premier level for so few years.

Two legendary cricketers who graced the game of cricket at the highest level for many years are the subject of my next chapter: therefore the chronology of my personal journey and my first and only cricket tour abroad will have to wait awhile – with pads on.

✓✓✓✓✓✓✓✓✓✓

Finchley Cricket Club players on the old pavilion at Arden Field, 1947
from left, on balcony: F.Hobbs; E.Morgan; A.Rayment; I.Bedford;
J.Prideaux; ?; ?; ?; A.Bryant; R.Davison; J.Norris; G.Wood
middle row standing: J.McKissack; J.Lawrence; ?; J.Hanley; ?; ?; J.Winchester; ?;
front row sitting: G.Davidson; J.Levy; R.Phillips; ? J.Vaughan

Alan, Betty and Sam
at Arden Field, 1947

Alan, Wyn, Sam and Derek
at Arden Field, 1947

CHAPTER 28

CRICKET'S GOLDEN SUMMER

THE CAVALIER AND THE KANGAROO

Cardus, Arlott and Kilburn – imagine dear reader, especially cricket enthusiasts, the bumper harvest reaped by those truly great cricket writers in the Golden Summer of 1947.

Add Swanton and Robertson-Glasgow, Melford and Wellings, Crawford White and Denzil Batchelor – others too who contributed to the bookshelves of aficionados that still groan with weighty tomes and austerity paperbacks. Add news cuttings in bulging scrapbooks bursting with literary masterpieces, mundane daily reports and precious scorecards chronicling so many exceptional deeds on the Test and county grounds of England. A collector's feast!

Leaving the war and the harsh winter behind, our sporting nation went out to play in the sun – to walk the hills, cavort on the beaches and play in the fields that Churchill implored us to fight for in 1940:

... we shall defend our Island, whatever the cost may be
... we shall never surrender!

We had not surrendered: we had rejoiced on VE and VJ days and now needed a national tonic to lift our spirits and give cause for more celebration. Successive weeks of predictable sunshine induced young and old to enjoy all manner of outdoor activity, and cricket, that quintessentially English game, thrived on all manner of treasured acres from village green to lordly estate, from city park to factory field, from picturesque county ground to the grand amphitheatres of Test match dramas. Runs piled high but wickets still tumbled, as did many records concerning bat and ball; spectators too as turnstiles ceased to turn when closed to the dismay of fans. Writer's delight ... how about the statisticians!

While newspaper sub-editors ran out of headline superlatives to portray the run hungry 'Middlesex Twins' Compton and Edrich, it needs to be remembered that fifteen other Test and county batsmen scored over 2,000 runs, including England's famous opening pair Hutton and Washbrook. Bowlers old and young toiled for hours in the heat on hard wickets – though for many a veteran the warmth must have lubricated creaking joints – especially those of Gloucestershire's forty-seven-year old Tom Goddard. The tall, broad-shouldered off-spinner with huge hands bowled 1,450 overs to bag 238 wickets. His nearest competitor was thirty-three-year-old Doug Wright of Kent and England, the quickest of all leg-spinners, whose long bounding run-up sired his nick-name 'The Kangaroo'. Wright relished the heat and hard wickets to claim 177 victims in 1,176 overs. Jack Young, the thirty-four-year-old Middlesex left-arm spinner with the jaunty sailor-like run-up, took 159 wickets and Lancashire's 35-year-old, red-faced fast bowler, Dick Pollard, perspired through 1,218 overs to claim 144 batsmen's scalps.

Another veteran fast bowler, 39-year-old Alf Gover, repeated his long military-style run-up to deliver 5,904 balls and prise-out 121 batsmen. His Surrey colleague and regular England opening bowler, Alec Bedser, 30, lion-heartedly bowled 1,219 overs for county and country to bag 130 wickets. As a rough estimate, and taking an average playing season of eighteen weeks, Alec Bedser and Dick Pollard bowled 68 overs week in and week out – and Tom Goddard 80.

Fitness and stamina? Reflecting on the achievements of batsmen and bowlers alike during that long hot summer, I opine that the players were very fit, and interestingly, given the workloads involved, injury free to a high degree. In those far-off days there were no fitness regimes or physical jerks before a day's play; bowlers and batsmen alike played themselves into, and maintained, high levels of fitness and stamina. Another factor to be borne in mind about fitness levels of first-class cricketers is that up to the age of 35 a high percentage played soccer in the winter, many professionally, even up to international standard.

I will take a moment to reflect on some of the other background issues affecting the everyday lives of the high achievers mentioned above, and of course their team mates, many of whom enjoyed one of the best seasons of their careers in 1947. First, the majority of players over the age of 24 had had first-hand experience of the horrors of war in one of the armed services: a few had been incarcerated for several years in prisoner-of-war camps, some had been injured and several had contracted tropical diseases when overseas.

At home, house building was licensed and building materials in short supply: in many city and town centres, acres of bomb-site rubble were to remain uncleared for years. Food, clothing and petrol were rationed; many household items we take for granted today were either not invented, unobtainable or in short supply. The wages paid to professional cricketers were ridiculously low and sponsorship was unheard of – except Brylcream, who paid Denis Compton a moderate sum to front their national advertising campaign. Players lived on tight budgets, bought their own cricket equipment and managed to dress smartly on and off the field – often thanks to mothers and wives practising their skills with needle and iron.

As with the majority of the national populace, cricketers were used to public transport and conditioned to the habit of walking everywhere: the few who owned cars were subject to the restrictions of petrol rationing. Travel to away matches was by rail or motor coach – no motorways – and many teams arrived at their destination after midnight. Consecutive matches were – well – consecutive. Play ended at 6.30pm on a Tuesday or Friday – the next game commenced at 11.30am the next day. For example, travelling from Southampton to Hull, or Blackpool to Swansea, or Canterbury to Worcester was often, quite literally, a nightmare.

However, writing this chapter in the 21st century, I remind myself that the conditions outlined above were 'the norm', were accepted, were the realistic backdrop to early post-war euphoria that pervaded the national psyche. Both the backdrop and the euphoria were lit up by the sparkling performances of two legendary cricketers who took centre stage that season, Denis Compton and Bill Edrich of Middlesex and England.

Compton and Edrich had graced the noble game at the highest level just before the war that voided six Test-playing years served in the armed forces. In 1947 their performances as artists, entertainers and record-breakers scaled heights beyond compare, inspiring writers and broadcasters to wax lyrical in their praises and to lift the spirits of spectators from winter's gloom into the sunny uplands of breathless adoration. Indeed, the cavalier exploits of the cricketer-footballer with film star looks, combined with the hard-jawed determination of the ex-bomber-pilot hero, created a groundswell of public interest that spread beyond the confines of the sport into the psyche of the whole nation – and beyond that into the hearts and minds of cricket lovers around the world.

The sporting South African touring team bowled valiantly in their attempt to stem the flood as their fielders chased over 2,000 runs from willows deftly and thunderously wielded by Denis and Bill to the delight of capacity crowds around the country. In all first-class matches the Middlesex Twins, batting at three and four, revelled in the joyful expression of their prime form to create 7,355 runs and 30 centuries: Denis a record 18 hundreds with a top score of 246; including a second double and three centuries in the Test matches.

How fit do you have to be, or become, to maintain scoring at that level for nineteen continuous weeks? But more – when fielding Denis and Bill did not stroll restfully from slips to slips – they bowled, too. Bill, who was very quick in short spells, bowled 562 overs, took 67 wickets but bruised a few ribs in the process until, in early August, he suffered a back strain that prevented him from bowling but not from scoring more hundreds. Denis, the Geminian magician flighting left-arm orthodox spin – or when his intuition and astute cricket brain whispered 'chinamen and googlies' – bowled 635 overs to bag 73 wickets.

Despite the absence of the Twins for the five four-day Test matches, their prodigious feats with bat and ball for Middlesex were major factors in their county winning the championship in a close race against Gloucestershire. The county's gifted opening pair Jack Robertson and Sid Brown also entertained magnanimously, scoring 4,838 runs between them – the elegant Jack stroking twelve centuries and Sam the craftsman four. In addition to the wickets taken by Compton and Edrich, the left-arm orthodox spinner Jack Young bowled 1,294 overs for his 159 wickets, veteran leg-spinner Jim Sims trundled 1,045 overs for 124 wickets, and in a season of hard pitches thirty-one-year-old medium-fast opener Laurie Gray pounded his run-up to bowl 953 overs and claim 98 victims. Youth blossomed, too, when my close friend and Finchley Club colleague Ian Bedford made his debut for Middlesex while still attending the sixth form at Woodhouse Grammar School. In 168 overs of well-flighted leg-breaks and googlies Ian took 25 wickets, including five in an innings at Lord's against Surrey, followed by another five against Lancashire, sending their first four batsmen – Washbrook, Place, Ikin, and Geoff Edrich – back to the pavilion – a golden debut season, indeed.

Ian Bedford
Middlesex CCC debut 1947
Middlesex captain 1961 – 1962

Though I can offer but a few humble lines from clear memory of one of the greatest contests between bat and bat that I ever witnessed, I wish to do so in honour of Denis Charles Scott Compton and Douglas Vivian Parson Wright, cricketing artists who inspired poetic eulogies from the pens of those premier writers I referred to at the head of this chapter. In previous chapters of these memoirs I have written personal accounts of witnessing great innings at Lord's that inspired me: Patsy Hendren in 1937; Hammond and Miller in 1945; also, actually darting about at cover myself attempting to keep down the runs flowing from the bat of schoolboy Peter May in that summer of summers. And from that privileged ringside position at cover-point I will recall, in a second book of memoirs, the brilliance, the fortitude and the grace of a dozen or more legends who stroked or thumped the ball past me: Cowdrey, Hutton, Barrington, Dexter ... Harvey, Morris, McGlew, Reid ... the list is long.

Long too my memory of the aforementioned duel in the sun at Lord's between cricketing legends Compton and Wright, filmed in my mind as I remained transfixed on my perch behind the bowler's arm at the Nursery End. So with inadequate skill I will attempt to scribe the scenes of cricketing drama that unfolded on that unforgettable day, Friday August 15th 1947.

First I will quote the *Times* cricket correspondent:

> The whole summer will offer no better game of cricket than that which Kent won over Middlesex at Lord's yesterday, with but five minutes to spare, by 75 runs. Nor will there be a grander innings than that played by D.Compton. This indeed was county cricket at its very best ... it would be a poor heart and a broken voice that did not respond to the excitement of the last half-hour's play ...

To set the scene: when play commenced on the last day Kent continued their second innings aiming to increase their lead of 298 runs with five wickets in hand. Cambridge student Geoffrey Anson and England wicket-keeper Godfrey Evans were principal contributors to the 99 runs added in just over an hour, enabling the Kent captain, Brian Valentine, to declare and leave Middlesex a target of 397 runs at 100 runs per hour. Valentine made an astute and well-balanced declaration, knowing that Middlesex were neck and neck with Gloucestershire in the championship race and would chase the big total – his calculation of the odds evened out by the high-scoring quartet of Robertson, Brown, Edrich and Compton.

Kent's red-haired fast bowler Norman Harding accounted for the Middlesex openers either side of luncheon; Sid Brown for five and Jack Robertson for twelve. Twenty eight for two. The Twins responded to the challenge amid the palpable buzz of expectation emanating from more than fifteen thousand fans. My mental film library now reels off the first cameo: Harding versus Compton:

Norman Harding starts his very long run-up high on the slope at the pavilion end as Denis taps the toe of his bat in the dust of the popping crease area – the aura around his athletic frame and beautifully balanced half-open stance suggestive of assured confidence and cheeky command. As Harding strides on towards the bowling crease Denis begins a side-step-side shuffle towards his charging opponent until he is six feet down the wicket ... Harding keeps his head, adjusts his length and Denis pats the ball into the mid-wicket gap for two. Game on!

Denis repeats his foxtrot shuffle almost every ball during Norman Harding's next three overs, sometimes continuing the advance and driving, at other times darting back towards the crease to pull or cut ... oh those deliciously delicate late cuts! Harding loses his control as boundary follows boundary ... then a single on the sixth ball. Harding takes his cap from umpire Coleman and retreats to mid-off. Bill Edrich succumbs to Wright, and Middlesex are in trouble at 88 for 3. Skipper Walter Robins, always a passionate and aggressive cricketer, revels in a stand of thirty-seven with the brilliant Brylcream Boy before being bowled by the Kent amateur Jack Davies. Although Kent are in the ascendancy many of the Middlesex supporters are relieved to see the skipper returning to the pavilion. Why? Because Walter Robins is very quick between the wickets, and therefore the odds were increased of inducing a mid-wicket discussion with Denis when the ball was in play, a possibility that I mentioned in chapter twenty-five ... "when Denis calls for a run he is only opening negotiations."

Kent are in the ascendancy with the score at 135 for 4: the debate around me is loudly partisan as next season's captain, Francis George Mann, enters the arena to join Denis Compton. "Is he good enough to hold up one end while Compo gets the runs?" declaims my neighbour, a solicitor having time out from his office in Baker Street. "Bloody well got to," states his legal companion – same office.

The next phase of the nail-biting drama was encapsulated by *The Times*:

There followed a partnership between F.G. Mann and Compton which first stemmed Kent's hopes and then actually offered Middlesex some prospect of victory. Compton played every manner of stroke least expected by the bowler. With three men close in on the leg side and three more spread on the boundary he yet found every manner of means, moving his feet even as the ball left the bowler's hand, to place or strike the ball to every part of the field. It was a truly great performance against so adept a bowler as Wright and, with Mann equally ready to accept the challenge, there was every possibility of Middlesex winning the game, for such a rate of scoring cannot be reckoned by so many runs in so many minutes. Middlesex have a measure of time quite of their own.

My second cameo reel now rolls, triggered by a mental picture of Doug Wright's leg side field as described by the *Times* correspondent. Wright versus Compton – team-mates in the England Test side now in high form playing for the counties in which they were born – Denis from Hendon, Doug Wright from Sidcup – the latter a uniquely gifted leg-break and googly bowler – really quick through the air – a prodigious spinner of the ball who often produced one with seam-up at the pace of Norman Harding. Wicket-keeper Godfrey Evans proved his brilliance and his courage in 'standing up' to Doug Wright.

As I reflect on the unfolding drama in cricket's greatest theatre on that particularly bright summer's day, I am once again inspired by the consummate skill and confidence of the principle actors, Compton and Wright, who were duelling for personal supremacy and team victory loudly encouraged by partisan supporters among an audience of thousands high on hope yet mollified by anxiety. My commentary may not be adequate to describe the noisy, colourful and dramatic scene revolving in my mind-film – but I will make an attempt:

Wright from the pavilion end to Compton: field set with one slip, a regular third man, cover square and deep for Compton – to tempt the single – similarly mid-off wide and deep. On the leg side three men on the Mound Stand fence to save fours from Compton's variety of sweeps; one square of fine, one behind square, one square of mid-wicket. The two remaining fielders patrolling the half-way area between wicket and boundary – one around mid-wicket, the other at wide mid-on – adjusting their positions in attempts to stem the run flow – and the flow from Compton is akin to a tidal surge.

From his marker Wright bounds through his long run-up past umpire Harry Baldwin to deliver a fast leg-break that turns and lifts, beats Compton's back and across defence and thumps into Godfrey's gloves at shoulder height. Concerted gasp from the mouths of all eyes. Denis inspects the guilty spot on a length, gently taps the toe of his bat on three other suspect spots of the wearing pitch, twirls his blade three times and calmly returns to stance and concentration. Again the Kangaroo bounds down the slight slope as Compton's feet suggest a dancing drive, but on delivery his right foot slides back inside the crease, the knee of his right pad touches the grassless soil – the resultant sweep dissects the two boundary guards either side of square leg. Four ... thunderous applause!

Wright continues to bowl magnificently – length, spin and occasional lift: the brilliant Compton seems to develop into a magician as he drives, cuts and sweeps his way beyond his century, beyond 130. The duel between master bowler and genius batsman enthrals the audience – every ball a potential wicket taker – the grace and power of every stroke a work of art eliciting a communal gasp rolling into applause. Our hands are sore, our voices hoarse. I take the liberty to transpose that most apt phrase written of Patsy Hendren by the *Times* Correspondent in 1937: *'Compton is The Master On His Heath!'*

The brightest jewels in my last cameo are a series of Compton sweeps off Wright's magnificent bowling – bowling that is almost unplayable to all but a batsman of consummate genius:

Brian Valentine moves his slip to increase the Mound Stand boundary guards to four, but Compton's wand conjures the ball past outstretched limbs and umpire Baldwin's tired right arm signals another four runs. Wright's superb bowling tests Compton's inventive artistry to the extent that he displays three varieties of stroke under the general heading of the Sweep: the paddle, the swat and the classic – all executed with an extension of the front leg towards the line of flight but with lateral and vertical adjustment of his bat to account for the line and pitch of the ball, the type of spin and placement required. Compton's speed of thought and physical adjustment are phenomenal.

Denis plays 'the paddle' from an almost upright position with the bat about ten degrees from vertical to balls of varying length destined to miss the leg stump – usually googlies. His wrist action raises and turns the face of the bat to follow the ball and caress it on its way to the fine leg area. To balls pitched just short of a length – on or outside the off stump – usually leg breaks, Compton stretches his left leg outside the line of the ball, adjusts the angle of the bat according to need and executes a short arm jab to 'swat' the ball between mid-wicket and long leg. He plays the classic sweep, or 'grass cutter', by stretching the left leg towards the line and pitch of the ball, collapses the right knee to the soil to bring a near horizontal blade across the line of an over-pitched ball and place it to split the leg-side field with amazing accuracy. Always, always – Denis rolls his wrists to carpet the ball from blade to boundary ... and his timing ... oh such exquisite timing!

Denis Compton
The Cavalier plays 'the swat'

Douglas Wright,
the inimitable Kangeroo

But even Compton's timing is not infallible and Doug Wright deserves his moment of triumph when spin and lift induce a catch at cover from a classic front foot drive: Compton caught Davies bowled Wright, 168. Five seconds of involuntary silence ... followed by tumultuous applause as the multitude stand to honour the duelling champions. The Kent players clap as Denis departs; he raises his bat high in acknowledgment to the crowd who cheer him all the way to pavilion gate until he is engulfed by MCC members in full costume lining the steps – then disappears into the half-light of the historic Long Room. Meanwhile, the Kent captain and players surround Doug Wright – as worthy as Compton of their highest praise for his graceful skill and immense stamina.

Leslie Compton replaces his younger brother to join George Mann, unbeaten and unbowed after his stand of 161 in ninety-seven minutes with the departed hero. Middlesex are now 296 for 5 and require another 99 for victory ... there is hope, we feel, if gifted amateur and seasoned professional can keep up with the clock without losing their wickets. We know that of the remaining four batsmen only the veteran Jim Sims is capable of holding up one end – or slogging a few boundaries to maintain the already dramatic tension. Mann is bowled by Wright for a valiant 57 – our hopes sink while those of Kent fans sitting nearby are expressed in a surge of confident chatter.

More nails are bitten, hands wrung and cigarettes lit while only nineteen runs are added before the Middlesex number eleven, the young quick bowler Norman Hever, walks forlornly to centre stage, snicks two runs and is bowled by Jack Davies. Middlesex have failed to hold-on for a draw; Kent have won by 75 runs with only five minutes remaining of extra time.

Kent's hero Douglas Wright has bowled 57 overs in the match to account for 11 Middlesex batsmen for 194 runs – yet even those figures fail to record the poetry, the skill and the thrill of the Kangaroo in top form vying for supremacy against the incomparable Compton.

I remain in my seat, elated yet exhausted: chat with my neighbours ... so much to share – nothing partisan –– all of us overwhelmed by the breathtaking, unscripted dramatic spectacle that has unfolded before our eyes – and toyed with our emotions – on that never-to-be-repeated day in the Home Of Cricket: Lord's, St. John's Wood, London, NW8.

Again however, I realise that my words are inadequate to portray all that I sense as my memory rolls the 'film' of those cameos again and again. For not only are the pictures clear but the colours, the sounds, the heightened emotions – and the joyful exuberance shared with thousands of cricket loving men, women and children – fill my heart and mind with awe and thankfulness ...

... that I was there, on that day, in that Golden Summer to experience that unrepeatable reality sixty-five years ago.

~~~~~~~~~~~

*Footnote:

In 2009 some friends and I visited the Surrey and England keeper, Arthur MacIntye, who lived near me in Hordle, Hampshire. His stories were gems of experience and cricket wisdom; one such jewel was in praise of Doug Wright. Arthur reminded us that he often 'stood up' to the medium fast bowling of his Surrey colleague, Alec Bedser. However, Arthur had toured Australia in 1950/51 with Alec and Doug Wright and confirmed that Doug Wright was the most challenging of all bowlers to keep wicket to: first, because of his speed and spin – and fast ball; second, because matches were played on uncovered wickets.

CHAPTER 29

FLYING CRICKETERS

With due respect to Noel Coward I find myself singing his
famous lyrics – plus my own extension:
'Mad dogs and Englishmen go out in the midday sun' ...
dressed in white with ball 'n' bat to play and run
for fun in Hitler's old Olympic Stadium.

An unrepeatable anomaly and an unrepeatable reality – though real *it* was – *it* being twenty-two cricketers clothed in whites performing their eccentric rituals against the stark grey-concrete backdrop of Hitler's 1936 Olympic Stadium in Berlin – two years after the Allies had defeated Germany and WWII ended in Europe.

Why Berlin? One of the peculiar facts of my life journey is that my first trip abroad was the only overseas cricket tour I ever embarked upon. In late August 1947 I was a member of the Royal Air Force team that crossed the English Channel to play against teams drawn from Allied Forces stationed in Bad Eindhoven, Bad Eilsen, Hanover, Hamburg and Berlin. I have no records to check results and performances, but I do have a few photographs which remind me that in Hamburg I kept wicket and scored a hundred.

However, recorded in – or rather burned into my memory – are awful scenes of destruction and pungent smells of decayed bodies and raw sewage witnessed from the safety of the RAF's Bedford coach as we approached Hamburg. Hundreds of men, women and children were hunting through vast areas of bomb-site rubble for anything to salvage and sell, or materials to build primitive shacks as temporary homes ... two years after the end of the war! As a Londoner I had sat in shelters and ducked behind garden walls during the Blitz and doodlebug bombings; I had worked in offices in Southwark and Wapping surrounded by acres of bomb-site rubble, but the immensity of the war-scarred ruins in Hanover, Hamburg and Berlin impacted my senses and temporarily deflated my spirit.

When leaving Hamburg our high-spirited amalgam of officers and rankers, regulars and conscripts, were warned not to exit the coach until we reached the safety of the British Sector of Berlin. We were to travel some 200 kilometres through the Russian Zone along one of the autobahns designated as Corridors. During the journey the coach would make two stops on the hard shoulder so that we could, if needed, pee from the step above the opened door. If we stepped out of the coach, we might be shot at!

In Berlin we actually played cricket in one of the secondary stadia of the 1936 Olympic Games: a strange emotive experience because we all remembered the dark history of those Games through print journalism and newsreel footage. Hitler had exploited the international event to glorify himself and his Nazi regime through controversial speeches and displays of political and military power. The Nazi's blatant glorification of the Aryan race as superior to all others was particularly challenged by the success of the black Afro-American sprinter, Jesse Owens, who won four gold medals.

Eleven years after the symbolic Olympic flame was dowsed, an athletic cricketer, Flying Officer Robert Mills, performed a headstand atop the torch bowl high on the main stadium. With F/O Roland Parker in the frame as witness I took a photograph of our friend's daring feat. For me the picture represents 'victory' on several philosophical levels: the most light-hearted being the British sense of humour created by an officer of His Majesty's armed services enacting an upside down V sign, or an 'up yours', on the torch bowl high above the podium where Hitler's highly controversial speeches had claimed superiority for his Fascist philosophy and efficient regime.

The grim human consequences of that regime were sickeningly evident in every devastated town and city we passed through. The bright lights and night life in the centre of West Berlin were the antithesis of the sub-human existence reported above. I was not interested in night clubs, nor was I a serious drinker. Roland Parker and I were unimpressed when we made a brief attempt to extend our cultural experience in a very noisy, smoke-clouded beer-keller. However, an organised daytime excursion through Check Point Charlie into the twilight zone of Communist East Berlin was of greater cultural interest; the experience proved to be of stark contrast to the vibrancy of human life in the Allied sectors of the city.

Accompanied and protected by official military guides we walked through drab streets in the Russian Sector, past bombed ruins and dark unkempt buildings, past a few large shops displaying very little stock in their windows – and grim-faced people averting eye contact. My sensitivities tuned in to a general atmosphere of negative stillness tinged with fear.

Having thoroughly enjoyed the cricketing and social aspects of the RAF tour we were looking forward to meeting up with wives, fiancées and girl friends on our return to England. However, a political storm that had been brewing between the Allies and Stalin's communist government suddenly developed into crisis. In a display of power the Russians closed the 200km road-and-rail corridors through which essential supplies of food and fuel were transported to the Allied forces and German civilian population residing in the British, American and French sectors of Berlin.

Flying Officer Robert
Mills performing
headstand on torch
base of the 1936 Berlin
Olympic Stadium

Alan keeping wicket on
RAF tour, Hamburg, 1947

The crisis meant that we had to remain inside an RAF base, a situation that provoked much debate among the junior officers and rankers in our team: "How long are we likely to be stuck here in Berlin?" Meanwhile, the officer in charge of RAF cricket, Air Commodore ACH Sharpe, made a decision to commandeer a Lancaster bomber to fly the team back to RAF Northolt. We raced across the tarmac to bag one of the few seats ... I was the quickest and funnelled my way down the fuselage to sit in the rear-gun turret for the 580-mile flight to Northolt. An unforgettable though somewhat cold and lonely experience contrasted by the welcome sights below – the patchwork of fields in East Anglia, the snaking curves and reflecting light of the River Thames, the grey buildings and dark tarmac of the landing strip at Northolt. Having extricated myself from the cramped rear gunner's pod, I relished the hot August sun that eased my stiff muscles and a hot cup of tea that warmed me up from the inside. Still on leave, those muscles were soon dancing quicksteps with Betty, scoring runs and bowling a lot of overs. In my last match of the season I scored a big hundred for the Air Ministry.

The longest, warmest and most enjoyable summer I had experienced thus far in life was over. I returned to duties and communal living at RAF Bawdsey, played a few games of soccer for the station team and enjoyed swimming and relaxing on the beach with friends from the Training School. On October 15th I was posted back to the Filter Room at Bentley Priory and resumed my home-billeting arrangements except when on night duty. Betty and I were delighted because we could now resume regular ballroom dancing lessons and practice in preparation for our Gold Medal tests. Soon after my return we were surprised by an unexpected event that meant we would be living in the same house – though not 'together' as such.

Unbeknown to either of us our parents had, out of necessity, been plotting a property coup. Betty's mother, Tricie, had been given notice that her landlord planned to sell number 27, Dudley Road: my parents had been given notice by their landlord that he wished to re-occupy 54 Rosemary Avenue, about one hundred yards from Tricie's house. Father negotiated the purchase of Tricie Griffin's rented house on the basis of her status as the sitting tenant. When the contracts were exchanged Betty and I were told the surprising news and how the four-bedroom accommodation would be divided: Betty and her mother were to share one of the double bedrooms while Derek and I each had a small single room; Sam and Wyn to occupy the other double bedroom. Each family would have sole use of a reception room – the kitchen and scullery to be shared.

The new arrangement worked well, mainly because our respective mothers were calm and easy-going, had known each other informally for many years and had worked together as volunteers in the cricket club's tea kiosk a long time before Betty and I began 'walking out' in 1945. And though tempted, Betty and I had been brought up with such strong family and moral values that the expression of our sexual drives was limited to fully dressed snogging. How innocent we were – and disciplined, too – between the ages of eighteen and twenty-something.

Due to my innate need 'to understand', I was asking myself a multitude of imponderable questions. I was beginning to realise that change is constant, opportunity transient and disappointment capricious:

> When shall we get married? ... what will I do when I am demobbed? Does my potential as a cricketer warrant the risk of seeking a contract with another county club? My dream of playing for Middlesex seems impossible because I now see that Middlesex have capped players, like my friend Harry Sharp, who only get a game when the stars are playing in Test matches. And professional cricketers earn very little money. But I cannot think of anything else I want to do as a career. O my, life is getting complicated.

I had not yet learned to play one ball at a time let alone to live one day at a time – the latter would take more than half a lifetime. But at nineteen this energetic and at times impetuous Gemini Kid could at least try to steer a course, one month at a time, through the rapidly unfolding changes in his personal life. However, as always, the personal journey is often influenced by socio-political and economic events in the home nation and abroad, creating uncertainties and negating natural self-confidence.

In Britain we continued to experience the economics of survival during 1947: greater all-round austerity and longer queues as the food rationing crisis deepened. Strikes by road haulage workers and coal miners increased the strain on food and electricity supplies and many other basic needs for families. Paradoxically, the Parisian fashion designer, Christian Dior, introduced the 'New Look' – a fashion that swept through Britain and strained clothing production due to rationing and the shortage of fabrics – although rayon and other man-made fibres became increasingly available.

In India Lord Louis Mountbatten was appointed Viceroy, the last, with the brief that he was to preside over the peaceful transfer of administrative power from the British government to the people of that country. In reality the disparate aims and beliefs of India's political and religious leaders led to violence that was often mishandled by government forces controlled by the British, leading to Partition – the creation of Pakistan as a separate nation for Muslims. Back in Britain, Lord Louis' nephew, the Greek Prince and Royal Navy Lieutenant Philip Mountbatten, married Princess Elizabeth, heir to the British Throne and Head of the Commonwealth.

While America's economy began to flourish, the implementation of their Marshall Aid Plan for economic and industrial aid for European nations progressed at an uneven pace. A US Navy test pilot, flying a jet propelled aircraft, became the first to break the sound barrier. In Washington Senator Joseph McCarthy created huge controversy about the Constitutional Rights of individual citizens in a paranoid campaign to name and shame people alleged to be communists, including many in the Hollywood film industry. In the Mediterranean thousands of Jewish people from many countries boarded ships in the Mediterranean in an attempt to create a new home nation, Israel, by landing in Haifa to occupy Palestinian territory. In Japan, the American General MacArthur continued to lead the Allied Council's campaign to eradicate traditional militarism, to effect radical changes to democratise the system of government and rebuild a new style economy.

I continued to debate with myself:

> While millions of people on the planet are trying to re-establish their lives after the devastating losses of WWII – and millions more are attempting to establish new national and economic structures – I am simply and singularly trying to 'think through what to do' in Civvy Street after demob. And, sooner or later, I will shoulder the responsibilities of a married man – maybe even a father. Life is not simple!

And yet, when compared with my dear cousin Beryl, my life during and after the war had been simple. Beryl met her future husband, Ronald Barker, at a North London tennis club in the mid 1930s, but their responsibilities during the war delayed their wedding plans until November 1947. Ronald had seen active service as a tank commander and Beryl as a nursing officer in the Women's Royal Air Force. From the age of thirty Beryl gave birth to seven wonderful children.

In the months leading up to Christmas 1947 I played regular soccer matches on the left-wing for RAF Stanmore and a couple of games for Fighter Command. I kept fit by cycling from Finchley to duties at Uxbridge – also hours of dance practice as Betty and I approached, and passed, the Gold Medal test in December. We met old friends at the Christmas Eve dance at Gordon Hall including several cricketing mates of mine who were on leave from their service units. Betty and I attended St Mary's for the Christmas morning service followed by a combined family lunch at Dudley Road, completed in time for silence during the King's Speech on BBC radio at 3 o'clock. Happy times!

In January 1948 Betty and I decided to train as teachers of ballroom dancing and began the long process of learning technical theory for the examinations conducted by the Imperial Society of Dancing (Ballroom Division). We also had to learn to dance in the opposite role and expound the theory of all the standard steps, male and female, up to gold medal standard. Our hobby became a serious and satisfying study as we stretched our minds as well as our limbs to achieve new goals. We also enjoyed regular visits to the cinema and to major London theatres, courtesy of Nuffield Centre which issued free tickets to service personnel for undersold performances and matinees. Betty was sometimes working, but the shows included *The Crazy Gang* and *The Black and White Minstrels* at Victoria Palace Theatre; Danny Kaye at the Palladium, the amazing Katherine Dunham Dance Troupe at the Prince of Wales Theatre and several serious plays, including *Rebecca* at the Theatre Royal.

Net practice at Finchley, dance practice at Golders Green and the rest of my off-duty time spent with Betty meant little time for reading; however, I started reading novelists of the nineteenth century such as Hardy, Barrow and Dickens when I had to stay over at the RAF camp on night duty. As always I kept abreast of current affairs and sport through the newspapers and radio.

The 1948 cricket season opened with games for Finchley, RAF Fighter Command and Middlesex Club and Ground XI. On May 18th I travelled with the RAF team to play a three-day match against a full Worcester county eleven, took the wickets of Don Kenyon and Martin Young and was twice a victim of Roly Jenkins for 0 and 18. Interestingly, the MCC ruled that this match was not first-class, even though the same fixture in 1946 was awarded that status. Playing on Worcestershire's beautiful ground with a view of the cathedral across the River Severn was inspiring, the grass a lush green carpet, the pavilion homely in a Victorian manner and the people most hospitable. I was so impressed that I clearly remember thinking, "That was a real taste of what county cricket will be like if I'm ever good enough to become a professional." Three weeks later destiny gave me a friendly shove towards the fulfilment of that long held dream.

Of course I was proud to be playing for my county second eleven, yet on meeting my team mates at Waterloo Station I was disappointed that we were all amateurs – no Harry Sharp, Bill Harrington or Reg Routledge. We were scheduled to play Hampshire 2nd XI in Bournemouth, but stayed in a pleasant, moderately priced family hotel at Purewell, Christchurch. After dinner Tommy Dewhurst and I took a stroll to find the River Avon. We were surprised by the quaint bridges and adjoining ruins of the ancient monastery. Always sensitive to new environments, I felt strangely at home – as I did the next morning when we arrived at Dean Park cricket ground in the heart of the coastal resort of Bournemouth. The beautiful playing area was almost circular in shape, surrounded by pine trees and large Victorian residences with a cosy pavilion built in a similar style to the houses. I noticed a strange low level building twenty yards from the pavilion – a long shed with a rounded roofed rather like a railway carriage. On enquiry I was told that the shed had been the professional's changing rooms before the war when only the amateurs used the pavilion dressing rooms.

Royal Air Force versus Royal Navy at Lord's, 1948
from left, standing: G.Senior; A.Rayment; I.Lumsden;
P.Fitzgerald; F.Parr; T.Dewhurst; B.Hedges
Sitting: E.Murphy; W.Payton; A.Shirreff (capt); D.Cockle; R.Wilson

Middlesex 2nd XI versus Hampshire 2nd XI at Ealing CC, 1948
rear: D.Carty; G.Hebden; R.Dare; R.Hawkey; W.Harrington; ?; M.Fitzgerald;
J.Taylor; ?; ?; J.Gray; T.Dean; A.Holt; G.Heath; M.Burden; R.Prouton
Front: A.Rayment; R.Cooper; D.Newman; T.Dewhurst; H.Sharp; R.Routledge

Our skipper was the renowned seam bowler from the Ealing club, Leslie Thomson. He won the toss on a grey damp morning and decided to bat. Hampshire's Basil Bowyer led his team of three amateurs and eight professionals on to the beautiful playing area of Dean Park; veteran George Heath and newcomer Derek Shackleton opened the bowling and took an early wicket apiece before Robert Felton and Rusi Cooper took the score to 62. Major Alan Waldron had Felton caught at slip by the Hampshire skipper but, as I took guard to face 'the galloping major', rain threatened and washed out the day's play.

On a rather tricky drying wicket the next morning I played a mainly defensive innings while the tall burly Mike Fitzgerald attacked with great success and had scored 86 not out when we declared at 220 for six. After quite a long innings and a memorable duel with left-arm spinner Reg Dare I was caught at slip by Jimmy Gray. In June 1948 I had not the vaguest notion that that innings of forty runs on a turning wicket at Dean Park was to create such significant change in the direction of Life Journey.

Basil Bowyer's innings of 56 not out on a bowler's wicket saved the Hampshire professionals from embarrassment, though Jimmy Gray defended well in an innings of 28 from a total of 168. Fielding at cover I ran out opener Arthur Holt with a direct hit – of no special significance to me at the time but probably noted by Arthur and the retiring coach, Sam Staples. Due to time lost on the first day Middlesex had less than an hour to bat in the second innings, scored 46 for three – yours truly returned to the cosy pavilion with three not out: match drawn.

After a quick half pint and a chat with the friendly Hampshire professionals we were taxied to the station and arrived in London at about ten o'clock. On the train I remember thinking how much I had enjoyed my first trip to Bournemouth. Although there had not been time to have a peek at the sea, the pier or the beach I had been impressed by the historic sites in Christchurch and the colourful ambience of Dean Park cricket ground.

Back in the relative grey hubbub of North London I was pleased to see Betty, enjoyed some advanced dance lessons and played a lot of cricket with Finchley, the Adastrians, the Air Ministry – also a few Middlesex Club and Ground matches with Harry, Reg and Bill. Apart from occasional duties at Stanmore I played cricket all through the summer of 1948, a season renowned for the high standards of the Australian touring team who did not lose one of their 32 first-class matches. 'The Invincibles' were captained by the legendary Donald Bradman.

Traditionally, the Australian tourists opened the season at Worcester, and on all three pre-war Australian tours Bradman had scored a double century on the beautiful, if chilly, New Road county ground. On this, his last tour of England, he disappointed the press and statisticians by notching up a mere

107, but celebrated his 40th birthday during a match at Lord's against the Gentlemen of England in which he scored 150. The Don scored two centuries in the five-match Ashes Series and completed the tour with 2,428 runs in 31 innings for an average of 89.93.

I was determined to see The Don bat in a Test match but, due to my own playing commitments, managed only the first day at Lord's. Having joined the queue at eight o'clock I was disappointed when he was out for 38, caught Hutton bowled Bedser. I have few clear memories of that innings except that I noted his compact style, a controlled sweep off Doug Wright and a magnificent square cut off Yorkshire's quick bowler Alex Coxon. Alec Bedser bowled magnificently – in long spells. I do remember thinking, "When will captain Norman Yardley give Bedser a rest?" The Australians batted into the second day for a total of 350 from 129 overs, of which Alec Bedser bowled 43 for 100 runs and 4 wickets. I find it interesting that I have retained a stronger impression of Bedser's bowling than of Bradman's batting.

Playing at Lord's in late July was a sunny delight – in early August a grey washout. Conscription had changed both the Royal Navy and RAF team lists: Peter May graced the Senior Service eleven but scored few runs; Bernard Hedges, Tommy Dewhurst, Frank Parr and Scotland's Ian Lumsden enjoyed the enthusiasm of the RAF team led by the ebullient Alan Shirreff. Centuries in the first innings contest by Ian Lumsden and the Navy's John Manners resulted in an eleven-run lead for the Navy. Alan Shirreff declared our second innings at 188 for eight – Doc Murphy scored 38 and yours truly 40 – leaving the Navy a target of 177 in 140 minutes. Our brilliant Lancashire wicket-keeper, Frank 'The Rascal' Parr, stumped John Manners on 21 and Peter May for 12, thereby slowing the Navy's run rate and lowering their morale. We expected to win but two Navy Commanders, Vavasour and Martin, clung on with eight wickets down and fifty short of their target.

Three days later we boarded a Douglas DC-3 Dakota at RAF Northolt and were flown to an airfield near Newcastle to play a three-day match at the delightful Jesmond ground against a representative Minor Counties XI. Our opponents notched up 438 mainly due to a sound century by Freddie Jakeman. Our reply was led by Bernie Hedges who played beautifully for 143, backed by the Rev WEG Payton's 60 and four other scores around 30 (AWH 29). Unfortunately the Minor Counties dour Yorkshire captain, Mr J Raper, ruined the game as a sporting contest by a declaration that, given the good third-day wicket, made it impossible for either side to win. The unpopular Raper set the RAF to score 355 in two and a half hours (approximately 53 overs): our openers batted out time with the Reverend scoring 51 and Doc Murphy 101. Our much loved skipper, Alan Shirreff – an enthusiastic upholder of 'the spirit of the game' was outraged ... and I remember how pissed off we all were with *that* Yorkshireman.

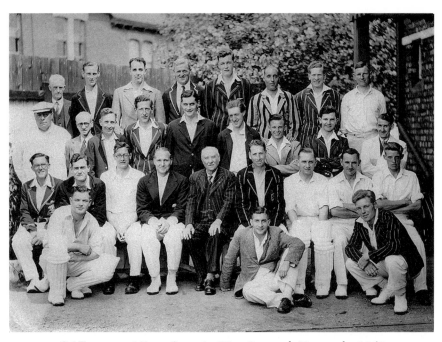

RAF versus a Minor Counties XI at Jesmond, Newcastle, 1948
from left, rear: ?; ?; I.Lumsden; J.Deighton; ? E.Senior; W.Payton; ?
niddle: ? ? D.Cockle; E.Murphy; R.Wilson; F.Parr; B.Hedges; T.Dewhurst; ?
front, sitting: ?; ?; C.Foord; J.Raper; ?; A.Shirreff; C.Walker; J.Firth; M.Hilton;
squatting: F.Jakeman; ?; A.Rayment

More expletives by senior officers when we alighted from our Bedford coach at the airfield. Due to Bank Holiday leave there no pilots available to fly the Dakota. The dynamic Air Commodore Sharpe was furious and disappeared into the air-control premises all verbal guns blazing. I joined Bernie and Tommy in a canteen for a cuppa and a fag with Frank Parr. We discussed the plight about the flight and the fact that we were due to play in a charity match, organised by the Air Commodore himself, the next day in Somerset. We reckoned that 'Sharpy' was giving hell to the officer who had granted leave to the aircrew who were on standby orders for our flight booked to Somerset. Half an hour later we were told to muster on the tarmac outside the control tower. Almost bursting with merriment Squadron Leader Alan Shirreff announced:

"Well, chaps, Air Commodore Sharpe has commandeered a Royal plane and aircrew – a Vickers VC-1 of the King's Flight ... jolly good show, don't you think?!"

The King's Flight!? We were abuzz with questions ... mainly: "How on earth did our team manger commandeer one of the three, relatively new, VC-1s of the King's Flight? But here it comes ... taxiing towards us" ... our group of varying ranks all open-mouthed in amazement! Air Commodore Sharpe marched briskly towards our group – officers and men alike straightened up; our captain, though not in uniform, reflexed a smart salute. "Thank you, sir!"

"Now look here, chaps ... sorry about this bloody mess-up ... but we'll soon get down to Yeovilton, get a good night's sleep down there and be fresh for tomorrow's game. Now I must make this very clear: you know this is a special aircraft – used by the Royal family – please respect both plane and crew. Make sure there is no mud on your shoes ... that your hands have been washed ... no sticky sweets or cigarettes ... and do not touch any dials knobs or switches. All your luggage is being loaded into the hold by ground crew. Enjoy your flight."

One by one we stepped cautiously into the luxurious interior of the VC-1, sunk into spacious, cream-coloured, forward-facing leather arm chairs and fastened our seat belts. As the twin engine Viking taxied down the runway a sense of non-reality overtook me that rolled into blissful excitement as we lifted off, banked and headed south-south west. I was also aware that I was itching with curiosity about all the knobs and switches within an arms length ... but *'must not touch'*. Lots of banter of course ... but even our high spirits were expressed *sotto voce* in unconscious respect to an invisible royal presence.

We were soon descending over the West Country's glorious patchwork of undulating green and golden fields. From my starboard window I revelled in the scenery: some brown and stubbled fields already harvested – or dotted with stooks awaiting a ride to the stack. Woods, fields and farmhouse barns rushed by – then noisy revs, flaps and wheels down as we approached the runway ... down down ... touchdown any second now ... then R O A R ... throttle open wide ... flaps and undercarriage up ... rapid gain in height ... quite frightening ... a cold sweat on my forehead – WHY? Looking through my window I saw a wartime runway receding below me that was criss-crossed with metal sheep hurdles and hundreds of the white woolly animals. A miscalculation by our King's Flight navigator nearly caused an accident, with incalculable consequences, by directing the pilot to a disused airfield restored to farmland. We landed safely at Yeovilton, billeted according to rank and woke refreshed on the Saturday morning. The chat and banter at breakfast was abuzz with our experience of the flight on the King and Queen's posh aeroplane.

From that sublime luxury to everyday discomfort as our rattling old Bedford coach bumped and squeezed through narrow country lanes to a Somerset village (I wish I could remember where), festooned with bunting celebrating a traditional festival. We were to play cricket on a picturesque village green resplendent with be-flagged marquees that dispensed a choice of refreshments – tea and sandwiches, cream teas or local cider according to tradition and taste.

In the 'now' of writing I find that I am 'seeing' some of the wonderfully contrasting scenes, people and colours I experienced during those two days in July 1948. First: from the photograph of twenty-two cricketers at Jesmond, among the white flannels, colourful club blazers and smiling faces is the dour image of a cricket captain whose selfish caution ruined a game of cricket that had, until then, been enjoyed by players amateur and professional from North and South.

Second: "no pilots ... what do you mean NO PILOTS!!" The pale, taught, moustached face of our angry Air Commodore which changed into a ruddy-complexion, framed in azure blue uniform splashed with gold, as he emerged triumphant from his confrontation with the incompetent flight schedulers ... followed by their Majesty's silver aeroplane enhanced by an interior of rich creams and royal blues which flew our cricket team over the amazing panorama of hills, fields and rivers that make our *green and pleasant land* so special. Then top lit by a blazing sun the colourful scene on the Somerset green; men in white chasing a hard red ball to the applause of country folk attired in floral skirts and breeches brown, while high between the trees the multi-coloured bunting danced in the cooling breeze. Ah!! Country Life in Somerset – I loved it!

My affection for London was waning, especially when in early August rain caused the Lord's match against the Army to be abandoned and, in September, demobilisation was postponed until further notice. When posted from Stanmore to the Operations Room at Uxbridge on September 15th I had already served two months more than the standard two years of conscripted service. One week later the Operation Room's personnel, not used to parades, were inspected by the Commanding Officer before he announced that due to the Russian blockade of Berlin all demobilisation was cancelled for three months. It was 'demob day' for one of our colleagues: he had already returned his bedding and other equipment to the quartermaster's stores – now he had to book it all out again, return to his Nissen hut and make his bed.

The political and military row between the Allies and Stalin's Soviet hierarchy over the partition of Germany had escalated to dangerous levels with potentially disastrous consequences. On 24th June the Russians had closed off all road and rail access to Berlin through their occupation zone. Berlin was located some 200 kilometres from the British and American boundaries to the west. At the post-war Potsdam Conference it had also been agreed that Berlin be divided into British, French American and Russian administrative sectors. The complex disagreements that followed were based on strongly held but diametrically opposed plans: the Americans sought to rebuild Germany as the economic centre of a stable Europe whereas the Soviets, fearful that a rebuilt and rehabilitated Germany could create another war, sought to reunify the demilitarised State under Russian economic and military control.

The President of the United Sates, Harry Truman, initiated a massive airlift of supplies to the beleaguered military and civilian personnel in Berlin, ultimately amounting to 277,804 flights carrying 2,325,809 tonnes of food and supplies until the Russians lifted the blockade on May 11th 1949. But in spite of the escalating disputes between the Allies and Russia over the future of German territory, the flow of my life at that time focused on cricket, planning our marriage, dance teacher's exams and being demobbed as soon as possible.

However, when on duty as a plotter at Uxbridge that autumn, the critical nature of the Berlin situation was evident due to the exponential increase in mock defensive exercises. We had entered the age of jet-propelled aircraft, more advanced radar technologies, developments on V2 type rockets and the atom bomb – although Russia did not test their first A-bomb until September 1949.

I remember sitting in the canteen at Uxbridge one evening after duty, having a quiet think and concluding that we, the human species, were self-deluding, self-destructive and self-propelled towards extinction. After two world wars in thirty years that resulted in millions of lives lost and more maimed in body, mind or spirit ... even after all that collective human agony we were still intent on killing each other on an even bigger scale. "Nuts – we're all bloody nuts," I kept saying to myself.

In comparison cricket was sane; not mortal combat but a serious-friendly-competitive battle on a green-brown pitch where the greatest danger was a minor injury to body or a dent in one's pride. After the battle, players of both teams shared a beer, a chat and fond tales of deeds past, lengthened by the shadows of time as the dusk of another convivial day faded into the darkening night. My daily life heaped contrast upon contrast: on the one hand family, friends and cricket exemplified Life and Happiness – whilst on the other – Fighter Command's Operations Room typified Danger and Death.

Having celebrated the end of the European and Pacific world wars only three years earlier so that, thankfully, and in reality, the slaughtering and maiming of millions of dads, brothers, mothers, sisters *by other* dads, brothers, mothers, sisters had ceased – *why* are we intelligent humans still behaving so self-destructively??

WHY? WHY? WHY?

"Nuts – we're all bloody nuts!!"

~~~~~~~~~~

Wyn and Betty
at Dudley Road, Finchley, 1947

The family home
27 Dudley Road, Finchley, 1947

The new generation at Elmer Farm, 1947
Alan in RAF uniform, Betty, Derek and Michael Bolger
with the farmers Kezie and Doris

CHAPTER 30

TWO CONTRACTS

Our dreams unfurl into the reality of a future as yet unknown.

Thankfully, in contrast to my philosophising about 'Nuts', daily life in the family home and Arden Field was sane, happy and hopeful. However, one day in August 1948 destiny disturbed our pond of normality with a splash that created ripples of change into my near and distant future – and that of my fiancé.

I recall the moment when I saw the bulky form of the Chairman of Hampshire County Cricket Club enter the East End Road gate of Arden Field, walk impolitely in front of the Member's Enclosure during play, then ascend the pavilion steps to meet Finchley's top brass, Tom Birkin, Josh Levy and Cyril Harvey.

Desmond Eagar, the captain and secretary of the Hampshire club, had written to Cyril Harvey, secretary of Finchley Cricket Club, to request a meeting between his chairman, Mr WK Pearce, and senior members of the Finchley's committee. My parents had also received a letter requesting an informal meeting with Mr Pearce, presumably to assess my background and character before deciding whether or not to offer me a professional contract. I was not consulted because legally, at the age of twenty, I was still a 'minor'.

I was quite cross about this antiquated and undemocratic process. I knew next to nothing about the Hampshire club and had many questions I wished to ask. Although I had played twice against their second eleven and found the Hampshire players to be friendly, I had no knowledge of the club's policy regarding young professionals or my prospects of being selected for the first team in the next two or three seasons. I received no detailed feed-back of the meetings, but burned into my emotional memory is the condescending manner in which the Hampshire chairman addressed a few guarded words to me before he left Arden Field.

Cyril Harvey, a respected friend and mentor, was a civil servant of liberal mind and cheerful manner who lived opposite our house in Dudley Road. The next time we met I questioned him eagerly about the meeting with Mr Pearce: he emphasised that the discussion went well and there was a strong possibility I would be offered a two-year professional contract with the county club. Then Cyril surprised me with a remark that drilled itself into my memory: "Alan, some of us are worried about your future, because if you do sign as a professional you will then become working-class."

Despite antiquated protocol and questionable manners the outcome of that visit to Finchley by the Hampshire chairman radically changed the direction of my life, that of my future wife Betty and – later – the social environment that influenced the upbringing of our children.

I was somewhat confused by Hampshire's unexpected interest and needed to seek out Frank Lee for some advice. But Mr Lee was umpiring at Taunton. "What to do? ... oh, I'll take a chance and go to Hove today to see if I can find Mr Patsy Hendren for a chat." It was then about 8.30am on Monday 30th August; I was not on duty at Stanmore that day and I told Mother I was going to Hove to watch Sussex play Yorkshire. She responded with her usual kindness and made me some sandwiches. A fast train from Waterloo and a taxi from Brighton station enabled me to enter the County Ground well before lunch and seek out the Sussex coach.

Although Mr Hendren was surprised to see me, the cricketing legend with kind heart and bubbly humour ushered me to a quiet spot in the pavilion and listened attentively to my story. He answered my questions about Hampshire cricket and named a number of pre-war players who would soon retire. He also pointed out that Desmond Eagar was keen on building a young team of talented players, all of whom would have to be excellent fielders. I then asked a rather cheeky but serious question: "Do you think there is any possibility of joining the Sussex staff, Mr Hendren?" He laughed and said that, although several Sussex professionals were near retirement, the county already had a crop of very good young players waiting their opportunity to play in the first team. Although he gave me no definitive advice, our discussion had cleared my head and I decided that, if offered a contract, I would sign for Hampshire.

By coincidence the letter from Hampshire CCC confirming the offer of a contract arrived the same week in September that demobilisation was cancelled. Betty and I, forward-looking and now even more highly motivated, made plans. First we would put up the banns at St Mary's Parish Church to announce our wedding in five weeks' time – on Saturday the 23rd of October. Second, I would accept the terms of the contract offered by Hampshire CCC, providing the Committee agreed to the following:

1. To provide acceptable accommodation at a reasonable rent.
2. To arrange winter employment through interviews with prospective commercial employers.

Mr Eagar replied to my letter saying the Committee agreed to those requests and that the two-year contract from March 30th 1949 carried a year-round wage of five pounds per week, less a deduction of four shillings and eleven pence for the National Insurance stamp. Small bonuses of win and talent money applied to first-class matches only. All travel and hotel expenses were paid by the county when playing for official Hampshire teams. I wrote again to Mr Eagar, enclosing a letter of consent from my father, accepting the terms of the contract and stating I would be available to sign the documents in Southampton during the week beginning October 25th while on honeymoon in Bournemouth.

Betty and I rarely went to church but attended mattins at St Mary's on the first Sunday that our banns were being read. After the long service we made an appointment with the rector to discuss the marriage service. We then returned to Dudley Road and announced the date of our wedding to Sam, Wyn and Tricie. Father's immediate reaction: "You can't get married, my boy, you're too young!"

"Well, Father," I replied, "the banns were read this morning and we are looking for accommodation in Finchley until March because, as you know, Betty and I have decided to accept the terms offered by Hampshire."

"Well, I suppose that means you'll have to go back to Lever Brothers when you are demobbed ... but will you earn enough money playing cricket to provide a home, my boy?"

The ice broken, Wyn and Tricie congratulated both of us with polite hugs while Derek, now eleven and at the County School, was more interested in the news about Hampshire cricket than the wedding. Once over the shock, Father relaxed and poured sherries all round to propose a toast:

"To Alan and Betty — may they be happy and successful in all the years ahead ... cheers!"

During the next four weeks Betty and I had so much to think about and prepare, not only for the church ceremony, the reception and honeymoon but also to find a home of our own that we could afford. We followed up an advertisement in the *Finchley Press* and rented, for three pounds a week, two furnished rooms with kitchen and shared bathroom at No.7 Hamilton Way, West Finchley. From a hotel guide and a map of Bournemouth we booked a week at the Cumberland Court Hotel on the west cliff near the sea. Betty borrowed a wedding dress from a friend, I booked the photographer and two cars, Wyn and Tricie offered to organise the reception, and cousin Doris Bolger the food for forty guests at our family home in Dudley Road.

The great day arrived: the important aspects forever memorable, yet much of the detail wiped from my memory – Betty's, too. To respect the tradition that the groom should not see his bride until the church ceremony I breakfasted with the parents of John Gardner, a friend and neighbour in Dudley Road. I remember dressing soon after dawn – bursting with happiness – my mind busy with the list of things to do, yet reflecting for a moment that I was leaving my parents' home and starting a new phase of life with new responsibilities in a new place. It was as though we were disembarking from an ocean-going family yacht into an eight-foot sailing dinghy intent on reaching an island faint on the horizon in uncertain weather conditions.

Thankfully the weather was sunny and warm on Saturday October 23rd 1948. In mid-morning John and I walked down The Avenue past the park to St Mary's church to check arrangements with the verger and my old choirmaster Ivor Richards. All was well. After a light lunch with the Gardners I changed into my new dark-grey suit, a white shirt with separate stiff collar and silk tie. The Padgate drill sergeant would have approved of my gleaming black shoes. At one-fifteen a capacious Austin sixteen, dressed with wedding ribbons, conveyed me, my best man and four groomsmen to the church where I chatted to guests and members of the choir as they arrived. At five minutes to two Ian Bedford and I took our places in the front right hand pew at the head of the nave – the buzz of excited conversation in the congregation did not abate until seven minutes past the hour. Betty had arrived at the west door.

All heads turned towards the bride: Ivor Richards began to play the first sixteen bars of Wagner's *Bridal Chorus* pianissimo – then crescendoed to mezzo forte as Joan Elizabeth Griffin joined me at the chancel steps. My sweetheart bride was radiantly beautiful!

The wedding dress and other fashion details were aptly described in the *Finchley Press*:

> The bride, who was given away by Mr Harold Hoffman (friend of the family), wore a dress of white brocade with train and long embroidered veil. She had a head-dress of white carnations and carried a bouquet of pink carnations. Miss Jillian Addison was bridesmaid. She wore a pink lace dress and carried a posy of deep red carnations.
>
> Best man was Aircraftman Ian Bedford (friend), the Middlesex cricketer. Groomsmen were Mr Peter Sutherland, Mr David Limbert, Mr John Gardner and Sub-Lieut Edward Fox. The reception was held at 27, Dudley Road, and was attended by 35 guests. The honeymoon destination was Bournemouth. Among the presents was a chiming clock from the Transport Division of Lever Bros & Unilever Ltd and a table lamp from No.11 Group Filter Room, Fighter Command.

A full complement of our relatives, friends and cricketing team-mates were present in the church. Harold Hoffman, who gave Betty away, was a director of the Transport Division of Lever Brothers at Unilever House where Betty and her friend Jill Addison were employed as clerks. The rector, Michael Ridley, conducted the service in a warm and engaging manner; the choir sang enthusiastically; the bride's elegance enhanced by her dancer's poise; the bridegroom remained calm and aware of the serious significance of the occasion. I had, after all, witnessed scores of marriage ceremonies from the choir-stalls.

Alan and Betty,
Bride and Groom,
St Mary's Church,
Finchley,
23 October 1948

The Wedding Group at St Mary's, Finchley: Wyn Rayment; Sam Rayment;
Jill Addison; Alan & Betty; Ian Bedford; Tricie Griffin; Harold Hoffman

Three distinct moments are filed in my memory: one spiritual, one a practical accident and one romantic. At the end of the ceremony, as Betty and I knelt at the altar for prayers and the Blessing, I felt a gentle loving 'presence' hovering above my right shoulder – an invisible personal benevolent energy that remained in place through the prayers to the end of the Benediction.

The second moment was 'down to earth' in several aspects: confetti thrown high and floated down on a patch of grass in the churchyard where we had assembled for the photographs. The official photographer waved his arms to position people in groups – then disappeared under his black hood to expose the plates. Disaster: many of his photographic plated spilled from his unfastened leather satchel and were ruined as they crashed to the ground. Fortunately a few guests, and brother Derek with a Kodak Brownie, took both posed and casual photographs at the reception, thereby redeeming the disaster of the 'blown' plates. Three short speeches temporarily halted the buzz of happy chatter swirling among young friends and older relatives until it was time for Betty to retire and change, for me to check our luggage and thank everyone for their good wishes and presents – especially Wyn, Tricie and Doris and their helpers for creating such a wonderful buffet in times of rationing and austerity.

The romantic moment: there were ooo's and ah's when the bride rejoined the guests in an unforgettable 'going away' outfit. In 2010 Betty recalled: "My outfit was really special ... a red worsted ballerina skirt with matching peplum jacket topped by a black pill-box hat." Very New Look – therefore *comme il faut* that a grey Daimler, ordered by Mr Hoffman, arrived for the fashionable bride and her blond groom to 'go away' through familiar streets of North London to Waterloo Station. More confetti and fond farewells – the hubbub of everyone talking at once – then a moment of silence as the Daimler eased quietly past Arden Field and the Manor Cottage pub – then release as Betty and I hugged and joked about being *husband and wife*.

It was Betty who remembered 'The Waterloo Story'. Alighting from the Daimler I caught the eye of a friendly-looking porter who placed our suitcases on his two-wheeled sack truck and led us through the concourse to the platform of the Bournemouth train. Having chatted with the ticket collector who inspected our pre-booked tickets, the porter led us along the platform – then stopped to have a word with a uniformed steward who picked up our suitcases and told us to follow him. I tipped the porter – we followed the steward through three carriages until he indicated that we enter a first-class compartment. "But we have third class tickets," I exclaimed. "That's all right sir ... compliments of British Rail. Enjoy your honeymoon, sir ... madam."

At the Cumberland Court Hotel I proudly signed the register: *23rd October 1948 – Mr and Mrs Alan Rayment – 7, Hamilton Way, Finchley N3.* The hall porter carried our suitcases to *Room 23* ... my sign-ificant number ... and returned with a light meal and a pot of tea on a large tray. With no experience and little information love-making was a passionate learning curve from virgin naivety to athletic success. Hand in hand, we explored Bournemouth's beautifully landscaped central gardens, the pier, the beach and the western promenade leading to Alum Chine. We discovered Fisherman's Walk in Boscombe where I carved a heart with arrow and initials 'A-B' on a tree; took a smoky steam train to Swanage where spray from rough seas made us dive into a greasy-spoon cafe; danced on the perfect sprung floor at the Pavilion and cuddled up in the back row of the Odeon cinema to watch Moira Shearer and Robert Helpmann dance in the film *Red Shoes*.

From romance and dancing in Bournemouth Betty and I turned our attention to the business of cricket in Southampton. On Wednesday 27th of October we were met at Southampton's Central station by Arthur Holt, a former professional footballer with Southampton FC and capped Hampshire cricketer who was now the county's coach. Following his warm and jovial greeting we were pleasantly surprised that Arthur proceeded to take us on a sight-seeing tour of the county borough he so loved. The new car smell in his Morris Minor Traveller epitomised our experience in the here and now of this special week in our lives.

Starting at the impressive modern Civic Centre, Guildhall and Clock Tower, Arthur explained that the final wing of the building was completed in 1939 – a grand symbol of the community's pre-war confidence only a year before the Luftwaffe flattened vast areas of the nearby docks and lower town. He then drove through the shopping area of Above Bar where many properties had been rebuilt since the Luftwaffe raids, round the 12th Century Bargate – part of the Old Port's historic walls – and on through bomb-devastated areas towards the docks. Arthur presented a pass to the guards at one of the dock gates and we entered another world; a world of ships, cargoes and cranes, of little steam engines shunting railway stock, big lorries being loaded and unloaded – and hundreds of busy dock workers animating the mechanical cacophony. To walk the length of the RMS Queen Mary in dry dock was an unforgettable experience.

Arthur Holt, acknowledged by all who met him as an all-round generous and wonderful man, certainly charmed Betty and me long before we entered the gates of the Hampshire County Cricket Club's headquarters in Northlands Road. My first impression was the nakedness of the playing area – grass with few clothes. There were only two small but attractive red-tiled, white-painted, double-tiered stands for members and a dilapidated wooden structure that was part offices and part groundsman's mower shed. Around the remainder of the moderate-sized playing area were four tiers of scaffold and plank seating to accommodate the paying public. My first thoughts were: "This is a pleasant county cricket ground … needs dressing up with spectators … maybe it's on a par with the Sussex ground at Hove but not as attractive as Worcester-by-the-Severn."

Arthur Holt
Hampshire CCC coach,
1949-1965

Desmond Eagar
Hampshire CCC captain and secretary,
1946-1957

The County Ground, Northlands Road, Southampton
as it was on Alan's Hampshire debut in 1949

Arthur the Coach ushered the newly weds into a small outer office where two men dressed in well-cut dark-grey suits and county club ties greeted us with friendly handshakes. The chairman I had met: the other I recognised from team photographs in *Wisden* as the thirty-year-old captain and secretary of the Hampshire club, Mr EDR Eagar. When courteously invited into his office I was impressed by the framed photographs lining the walls depicting Hampshire teams from the 19th century to the present day. A junior female clerk brought in tea and biscuits and during the 'getting to know you' preliminaries I noted that Betty, though excited, felt at ease and joined in the light-hearted social conversation. Desmond Eagar exuded a powerful positive passion for the game in general and a vision of Hampshire's future: "We're building a new team – a mix of experienced and young players with potential – everyone must be a good fielder – Hampshire are going to be the best fielding side in the Championship." His enthusiasm and dynamic energies reminded me of my RAF skipper, Alan Shirreff: I knew they had played against each other in the Varsity match of 1939 – also that Alan had played a few games for Hampshire under Desmond Eagar's captaincy. I politely mentioned the fact that I had enjoyed playing for RAF teams captained by the Squadron Leader.

The only other topic of conversation that I remember was my concern about the cost of accommodation in Southampton and employment during the off-season. The Hampshire captain and chairman assured me, and Betty, that they would recommend suitable accommodation early in the New Year and ask members of the committee to suggest potential opportunities for employment during the close season of 1949-50. Thus reassured, I signed both copies of the two-year contract and thanked the three men of Hampshire for the opportunity to develop my abilities and, hopefully, to achieve my ambition to become a county cricketer. The affable Arthur Holt drove us to the railway station, wished us well and waved as our 'Battle of Britain' class 4-6-2 engine pulled away, emitting clouds of steam as though celebrating the signing of two contracts in one week: 'Marriage and Hampshire CCC'. The new Mr and Mrs celebrated with a jig in the empty carriage then cuddled up in the corner to enjoy the autumnal New Forest landscape unfolding through the screen of the window frame, symbolising the unfolding of our dreams towards the reality of fulfilment.

Three days later the reality of Waterloo station, noisy, drab and crowded, ended our quiet romantic interlude in the beautiful Hampshire countryside by the sea – though not the daily romantic adventure of our young lives. The freshness of domestic life together, of new routines and responsibilities, of creating our first home in West Finchley whilst planning the move to Southampton next March was exciting. The adventure of studying and training together for our ballroom dancing teacher's examinations, the novelty of inviting family and friends to visit our home – and being acknowledged and respected in our community and places of work as a married couple helped our adjustment to new roles and tasks.

On the other hand we returned to established routines: Betty travelled by the Tube to her desk and friends at Unilever House; I cycled to RAF Uxbridge for my duties in the Operations Room – except in foul weather when I travelled by bus and the Metropolitan Line.

Betty and I continued to receive both dancing and ballroom theory lessons from the Andrew brothers at Helen Wills' studio in Golders Green and faced the Imperial Society's examiner Josephine Bradley in December ... Betty passed, I failed. However, I passed the NATD Associate Teachers examination before we moved to Southampton, being able to devote more training hours when back in civvy street.

Demobbed – at last! On December 31st 1948, at a demob centre somewhere in South London, I hung around for ages with hundreds of other blokes waiting to be processed, signed some official papers and collected a double-breasted, brown tweed suit, two white cotton shirts, a brown tie and shoes and, oh my – I've remembered *the piece de resistance* – a cheeky pork-pie hat with a feather. I retained my RAF uniform because the majority of conscripts were still officially listed as 'reserves'.

Free – free at last! I was so exhilarated when I left the demob centre that I hopped and skipped through the Tube station's corridors and wanted to hug people on the train – but didn't, of course. Arriving at West Finchley station about 9.00pm I ran to Hamilton Way, changed out of uniform into my best suit and ran round to Gordon Hall to join Betty and friends for the New Year's Eve dance. The joy of being together and being free to choose our way forward in 1949 was blissful: boy-o-boy, did we enjoy dancing that evening! The next morning I said to Betty: " *'Out with the old and in with the new'* signals the end of end my RAF career and the beginning of our married life – and a new career as a professional sportsman. Yippee! This is a really Happy New Year!"

In the year now past the people of our nation had continued to experience food and fuel rationing. A prolonged strike by dock workers increased prevailing austerity and reduced the meat ration to six pence (fresh) and six pence (tinned) per person per week. In June, motorists were rationed to 90 miles per month and serious housing shortages necessitated the introduction of prefabricated dwellings. The Attlee government nationalised the railways, the steel and electricity industries and the National Health Service became a reality. Regional Health Boards now controlled 2,751 hospitals. Employers and employees contributed a weekly sum to the National Insurance Scheme, introduced by the government to cover health costs and state pensions. The Ministry of National Insurance opened 992 offices in Britain. The Olympic Games were held in London and the first post-war Motor Show at Earls Court was a great success. Betty and I attended the *Daily Mail*'s 25th Ideal Home Exhibition at Olympia – the family still have Waverley's eight-volume set of *The Book of Knowledge* and a facsimile of the 1455 AD Gutenberg Bible we purchased that day.

In the United States democrat Harry S Truman began his second term as President; pilot Colonel Chuck Yeager broke the sound barrier in a Bell XS1 jet-rocket airplane; 'transistors', invented at the Bell Laboratories, began to revolutionise the electronics industry and replace thermionic valves. Up to 900 aircraft per day continued to fly supplies to Allied forces and civilians in Berlin as the dispute with Soviet Russia entered its fourth month. Communists gained power in Czechoslovakia and Yugoslavia; the rebel communist forces of MaoTse-Tung continued to defeat Nationalist forces in China; Mahatma Gandhi was assassinated in India; the Israelis under Ben Gurion proclaimed a 'New State of Israel' in Palestine on the last day of the British Mandate to protect the territory. World War II had ended three years earlier but 'peace on earth and goodwill to all men' was seemingly unattainable.

In the first months of 1949 Betty and I enjoyed the exuberance of our new life together but felt we were treading water, waiting for moving day. Metaphorically we were at the foot of a bridge called *'Between'*. ... *between that which is no longer and that which is not yet*. We were longing to cross the bridge to begin our adventure in Hampshire but had to commute by Tube to central London every working day and grind away the hours in boring jobs. No doubt I was more bored than Betty who, thankfully, continued her clerical work among friendly colleagues and her mentor boss, Mr Hoffman, who had walked her down the aisle on our wedding day. However, early in February Betty resigned and found an uninspiring clerical job with a leather goods wholesaler in Barnet – two stops from home on the Northern Line. The journey to Blackfriars had become uncomfortable because she was pregnant ... gee-whizz ... we were going to be parents ... sometime in October ... a baby ... gee-whizz ... would the baby be a boy or a girl? The other advantage of the short commute for Betty was that, at the beginning of the January term, she began teaching ballroom dancing two evenings a week at Barnet's Adult Education classes.

On reflection, I commend myself for grinding out the hours of tedious boredom as a sales clerk for Lever Brothers in an office near Finsbury Square. Ten working weeks ... ten! I detested the job ... and assure you, dear reader, that I rarely use that word. Seventy men, many old ... well, over 40 ... sitting at desks in a high-ceiling room, each recording 'sales projected and sales achieved' for two or more on-the-road salesmen. Stifling central heating – no windows open for ventilation. On most days I fell asleep after lunching on a couple of sandwiches and a cup of tea. In my third week I approached the sales manager, Mr Plunket, in his corner office, reported that the big room lacked ventilation and asked permission to open three top vents of the tall windows. Permission granted, I grasped the long pole topped with brass boating hook and advanced through rows of desks in the style of a standard bearer at the Trooping of the Colour. Work stopped, silence fell, heads turned to witness the enactment of this folly by the young blond newcomer. Kerdonk – kerdonk – kerdonk ... three top vents open. Fresh air – well, as fresh as it gets in central London – filtered slowly into the room as the stale warm air crept out. As I returned the pole to its home in the corner the silence was replaced by a wave of mutterings broken by a single exclamation, "You can't do that," followed by louder murmurings between the older men now on their feet addressing each other across the aisles. I sat down, opened another box of index cards and tried to focus on the job in hand.

Not to be! To the accompaniment of grumpy harrumphs a Colonel Blimp look-alike emerged from the little group of discontents, picked up the pole and worked his way unsteadily through the aisles towards the window vents. Klunk – klunk – klunk ... vents shut. Murmurs of "well done" ... "I should think so" ... "young upstart, who does he think he is?" *He* felt challenged, amused and mildly angry ... in modern parlance, 'pissed off'! *He* waited for the murmurings to fade into work focused silence, then rose from his desk, quickstepped to 'pole corner' and waltzed to the windows ... kerdonk – kerdonk – kerdonk ... vents open!

A few stifled 'hurrahs' indicated that I had supporters who, standing by their desks, became engaged in increasingly noisy finger wagging arguments with the Colonel's home guard as he, with his aide-de-camp, headed for Mr Plunket's office. The vents were shut again. My turn to knock on the manager's door and, not caring whether or not I got the sack, boldly presented my view that the lack of ventilation in the big room was not only unhealthy in a general sense but, at times, also induced a drowsiness that affected my concentration. Mr Plunket listened attentively and offered a diplomatic compromise: he would allow me to go outside and walk round Finsbury Square when I felt sleepy ... but not to take advantage of this privilege, of course. I thanked him, proceeded to the front door (I wondered what Blimp's troops were thinking) and walked briskly down Finsbury Pavement, left into South Place and back up Wilson Street to the Square – fifteen minutes of damp smutty air to clear my head – and exercise to revive my energies. During my few remaining weeks as a bored sales clerk I took time out from the office many times and discovered three fascinating second-hand bookshops where, pleasurably, I idled away the minutes on rainy days.

Away from the work scene Betty and I were neither bored nor idle. In preparation for our home in Southampton we stripped an old leather three-piece suite and recovered it with a green-and-white herring-bone pattern fabric that Sam obtained from remnant stock at Martin & Savage. From an old table, a beautiful piece of Brazilian mahogany, I made a four-socket chandelier and an oval coffee table – the latter still in use in my flat. Every week we paid a few shillings into a Post Office savings account from our joint income of seven pounds, plus a huge fifteen pounds from Betty's Adult Education dancing classes that term. At one of the regular Sunday lunches with our parents and Derek at Dudley Road, Sam even commented favourably about our diligence – maybe because he was surprised.

The lack of diligence by the Hampshire cricket committee certainly surprised Betty and me because, by the last week in February, they had failed in their promise to recommend suitable accommodation in Southampton. Desmond Eagar, embarrassed and apologetic, agreed to arrange for copies of Southampton's *Daily Echo* to be mailed to our address. Betty and I responded to several advertisements by telephone and made an appointment for a viewing at 22, Burgess Road the next Sunday, March 6th. On that cool bright morning we were in high spirits when we alighted from the steam train at Southampton, excited by the prospect of inspecting a potential home near the County Ground and a bus ride to the sea. Having purchased a local street map we decided that it would be pleasant to walk up The Avenue beside The Common to Burgess Road – pleasant yes but three miles was further than estimated. Passing the Cowherds Inn we joked about being Fred and Judy ... Astaire and Garland... who performed a famous musical number in the recent film, *Easter Parade* ...

> *We are a couple of swells, we stop at the best hotels,*
> *But we prefer the country far away from the city smells ...*
> *... the Vanderbilts have asked us up for tea*
> *We don't know how to get there, no siree ...*
> *No siree ...*
> *We would drive up The Avenue but we haven't got the price ...*
> *We would ride on a bicycle but we haven't got a bike ...*
> *... So we'll walk up The Avenue, yes we'll walk up The Avenue*
> *And to walk up The Avenue's what we like ...*

... and for a few minutes we skipped along hand in hand singing, "so we'll walk up The Avenue 'til we're there."

Number 22 was a small detached house squeezed between the road and the northern boundary of The Common. The owners, Mr and Mrs Dear, were a pleasant and polite couple in their late forties who, having welcomed us warmly became reluctant to accept us as tenants when we shared the news of a baby due in October. I proposed a compromise, saying that because I had to report to the county club in three weeks' time, would they agree to letting us the two rooms until we had settled in our new environment: we would then seek other accommodation in June or July. Thankfully they agreed: we agreed to pay two pounds ten shillings per week for the two furnished rooms with shared use of the kitchen and bathroom.

Betty and I gave due notice to employers and landlady: the news that I had resigned from Lever Brothers to join the staff of Hampshire County Cricket Club caused a buzz among my fellow sales clerks – even Colonel Blimp offered congratulations and shook my hand. Our parents, never openly emotional, wished us 'all the luck in the world': my brother Derek, now twelve and playing football at the County School, gave me a hug and said he looked forward to seeing me play at Lord's. Bob Holmes, a new friend who was a pupil at Betty's dance classes, had offered to drive us to Southampton (his father owned a Vauxhall main dealership in Southgate). So on Saturday 26th of March we squashed our essential possessions in Bob's Austin Ten, weaved our way past familiar North London landmarks – Golders Green, Swiss Cottage, Lord's and Hyde Park, across the Thames – then the unfamiliar South London conurbation to Guilford, over The Hog's Back, round Winchester's pre-war by-pass to arrive in Burgess Road three and a half hours later. Bob helped us unpack, celebrated the occasion with a cup of tea and swiss roll before waving goodbye, promising to visit us when he had saved sufficient petrol coupons.

Eager to find the nearest beach on Sunday we enjoyed the short train ride to Netley on the eastern shore of Southampton Water, but although the sea air was bracing and the big ships exciting the actual beach was disappointing. On Monday we explored the main shopping area: Betty favoured Mayes' large clothing store adjacent to The Bargate and Tyrell & Green in Above Bar – and she remembers being surprised that there were trams in High Street travelling to Woolston Floating Bridge and Millbrook. We were both attracted by the design of the imposing modern Civic Centre and walked boldly up the steps into the Guildhall for a peek at the huge dance floor.

On Wednesday morning at 9.30 I said farewell to Betty and caught a bus down Hill Lane, walked through the footpath into Northlands Road, entered the County Ground gates by the groundsman's cottage and reported to the Assistant Secretary, Dick Court. My confident self gave way to my shy side, and I felt somewhat embarrassed when introduced to capped players who had played under Lord Tennyson's leadership in the 1930s. The coach, Arthur Holt, emerged from the group and said he would take me to the room for uncapped players at the east end of the Ladies Stand. We entered a scruffy small dark room – known as The Black Hole – in which a group of young players were chatting, smoking and laughing. Arthur introduced me to Jimmy Gray who, when he could get a word in over the volume of raucous banter, named names – some of whom shook hands with me. All were outwardly friendly but those who spoke in broad provincial accents seemed wary of my relatively posh London tones and traditional manners. Another newcomer, six-feet-five at the age of fifteen, Malcolm Heath from Walton-on-Thames, also sounded a bit 'plummy'. In contrast the other newcomer with a distinct regional accent was Cliff Walker, a twenty-nine-year-old Yorkshireman from Huddersfield. Cliff had played a few first-class games with Yorkshire but, not gaining a regular place, signed professional forms with Hampshire, even though he was a director of a chain of family cinemas and could afford to drive a new Jaguar.

Half an hour later Arthur Holt popped his head inside the door of The Black Hole, yelled "QUIET!" He announced that all twelve of us were to join the capped veterans in their dressing room. The Hutch, a small room perched above the mower shed beside the Member's Stand, was now overcrowded with a vociferous bunch of professional cricketers. Desmond Eagar delayed his pre-season talk because there was one absentee. When Jim Bailey and Lofty Herman called out, "He's coming Skipper," all eyes turned to the window overlooking the playing area to watch a small man with light wavy hair, splayed feet and a rolling gait, stroll across the square towards the stairs of The Hutch. Johnny Arnold, Hampshire's leading batsman, double international and senior professional, was greeted with a burst of high-spirited banter – "obviously a popular character," I thought to myself. The Skipper began to speak enthusiastically about his expectations for the coming season. With tact and diplomacy he referred to the fact that some of the younger players had a great opportunity to establish the places in the team because several of the veterans would soon be retiring. He also emphasised that one of his priorities was to build the best fielding team in the Championship.

Arthur Holt then presented the schedule of activities during April before the first Championship match on May 7th -10th, to be played against Glamorgan at Cardiff.

> From tomorrow: 10.00am to 12.00 batting and bowling in the nets; 2.00pm to 4.00pm physical training, six-a-side soccer and fielding practise – all dependent on weather conditions. The Easter Coaching Classes for schoolboys at Northlands Road, Dean Park, Bournemouth and Portsmouth Grammar School will take place from Monday 11th through the following Easter weekend (except Easter Sunday) to Saturday 23rd. Four two-day practice matches have been arranged: Sussex at Hove, The Royal Navy at Portsmouth, an Over 30s versus Under 30s match at Northlands Road among the staff plus available amateurs followed by a Minor Counties game against Gloucestershire at Southampton."

I revelled in every aspect of the pre-season programme, discovered holes in my defence when batting in the nets against Derek Shackleton and Charlie Knott, that my seam bowling was played with nonchalant ease by Johnny Arnold and Neville Rogers but that I was quicker and more accurate than anyone in ground fielding and throwing skills – except wicket-keeper Leo Harrison who was also a superb outfielder. The soccer was fun and competitive – the PE minimal and almost laughable. I was already fit and became marginally fitter. In general I felt accepted by the uncapped pros and realised I had had the experience of adjusting to so many individual and team personalities in the previous four seasons – though mostly in an amateur setting. Now there was a hint of professional competitiveness and the likelihood that some of us would not progress to a regular place in the championship team. I was thankful for my two-year contract.

After the schedule for the Easter Coaching Classes was announced, I was taken aside by Desmond Eagar and formally introduced to Neil McCorkell with whom I was paired to travel to Portsmouth Grammar School's playing fields at Hilsea. Neil, who made his debut in 1932, was in the top echelon of wicketkeeper-batsmen throughout his career. I am forever grateful for that propitious opportunity to spend travelling time with Neil, a quiet, thoughtful family man soaked in cricket experience and worldly wisdom. He became my first mentor in my new world of Hampshire cricket. I thoroughly enjoyed coaching the boys aged between eleven and sixteen; my enthusiasm and burgeoning teaching skills, enhanced through dance teacher training, not only improved their batting and bowling and fielding techniques but, I hope, encouraged their love for the enigmatic game of cricket. I had the privilege of watching Michael Barnard, a fifteen-year-old boy being coached by Neil in the adjacent net. Michael was an outstanding batsman and amazing fielder for his age. I learned that he also excelled at rugby and soccer.

"What did you do during our first months in Southampton?" I asked Betty during Christmas lunch in 2011.

"I remember so little of that time," she replied. "I suppose I walked across The Common quite often to the County Ground – wouldn't risk that today ... made friends with Marion Walker and Dick Court's wife, cleaned our rooms and shopped for food across the road ... and later in April began to search for alternative accommodation. I don't know why I didn't look for a job, even part-time, because our money was very tight."

"Ah yes," I replied, "I have told this story so many many times, Betty ... that after the war in the '40s and '50s, if a young man had some talent and a powerful inner drive to play first-class cricket as a professional, and indeed, if a young man or woman had a similar passion to be an actor or actress, a ballet or stage dancer, or classical musician ... then he or she had to *do it for love – not money.*' You will remember, Betty, that from April 1949 my weekly wage was five pounds and that we had forty pounds in a Post Office Savings account. Our weekly rent was two pounds ten shillings (£2.50), the National Insurance stamp four shillings and eleven pence (25p), which left us with two pounds five shillings (£2.25p) per week for food and domestic items, bus fares, clothes and cricket equipment (no sponsors for any tools of trade). It is important to remember that I had to dress smartly all the time. I could choose between a dark grey suit with waistcoat, a lighter grey two-piece suit, a dark navy-blue blazer with light grey flannels – also a fine dogtooth-pattern Daks sports jacket I had bought at a sale. And always a semi-stiff or soft collar with a modest tie – usually a club tie. I possessed two decent pairs of shoes – one black, one brown – and another pair of scruffy brown walking shoes ... oh yes, and a pair of white plimsolls. You were able to maintain a stylish low-cost wardrobe, Betty, because you were a very good dressmaker and got cracking when Bob Holmes delivered your Singer treadle sewing machine during that first Easter weekend in our new home. So yes, we were poor: we had to budget for every penny but we were happy, positive in attitude and bounding with youthful energies."

Net practice intensified during the last week in April, followed by the Under versus Over 30s game – a seriously competitive affair for the twelve uncapped professionals: John Taylor; Jim Gray; Ralph Prouton; Reg Dare; Leo Harrison; Derek Shackleton; Harold Dawson; Tom Dean; Dick Carty; Malcolm Heath; Cliff Walker and myself. Four uncapped amateurs were available: David Blake; Revd John Bridger; Vic Ransom and David Guard.

Who among the Black Hole inmates might show good enough form to be selected for the first few championship matches – even to replace one of the ten capped players, who if fit would almost certainly play the first ten matches? The capped professionals were: Johnny Arnold; Jim Bailey; Neil McCorkell; Gerry Hill; Ossie Herman; George Heath; Neville Rogers and Gilbert Dawson – the amateurs Desmond Eagar and Charlie Knott.

I was enjoying every moment on and off the field – bursting with energy and confidence. The banter between all the players was friendly – similar to that experienced in club and RAF dressing rooms. Friendships were developing with Jimmy Gray and Ralph Prouton, both of whom were local ex-grammar school boys and soccer professionals. Jimmy surprised me one day with an unanswerable question: "Alan, where do you get your confidence from?"

Walking home I asked myself: "Do I have a 'high and mighty' attitude ... am I cocky or talk too much? I don't think so, in fact I am quite shy in some respects ... though I like people and get on well with most types. I do exude a confident energy because I am fit and happy, married and playing cricket, enjoying this way of life – especially when comparing today against working in the gloomy sales office at Finsbury Square. Why should happiness and confidence be a problem to any of my colleagues?"

I did not expect to be selected for the senior practice game against Sussex at Hove nor the match against the Royal Navy at Portsmouth. But I played for the Under 30s, batted and fielded well (there are no records of this match but scored 50-plus in one innings), and in the Minor Counties game against Gloucestershire at Northlands Road on May 4th and 5th. Batting at number five in the first innings I scored 45 in a century partnership with centurion Cliff Walker. Arthur Holt and Gerry Hill complimented me on that innings – and my fielding – but in the second innings, and with only twelve runs to win the match, I was deceived by Arthur Milton's slower ball on 16 and walked off the field and up the stairs into The Hutch, smiling and chatting cheerfully with team-mates. But my happy demeanour was not pleasing to some of the onlookers.

As soon as the game was over Arthur Holt told me I had to report to Desmond Eagar in his office. The Skipper's beaming smile signalled that he was in a good mood, but I did not expect the very firm handshake accompanied by the words, "Congratulations Alan, you have been selected for the first six championship matches. You will report here tomorrow at 10am to board the coach for Cardiff. It is a long journey so, although lunch is arranged, I suggest you pack some sandwiches. I am delighted that the selectors are giving you this early opportunity to gain experience as a batsman ... actually your brilliant fielding and enthusiasm tipped the scales. However, I have to reprimand you about a matter brought to my attention by the senior professionals: they cannot understand why you still smile all the way back to the pavilion when you get out for a low score. Remember Alan, you are no longer an amateur club cricketer – or playing for the RAF with Alan Shirreff's chaps and their 'jolly good show' attitudes. Of course I want you to enjoy your cricket with Hampshire, but cricket is now your job and, as a professional, has to be taken more seriously."

My mind was buzzing with questions as I cycled home up Hill Lane having 'a mobile think': "How come I've been selected to play at Cardiff, the Oval and Taunton – and at Northlands Road against Notts? I didn't expect to play in the first team until I had made two or three hundreds in the second eleven but, as the Skipper said, 'this is an opportunity to gain experience.' Gee, what an opportunity – I'm thrilled and determined to do my utmost best for the team – and myself. But why do those friendly old pros think I'm not serious when playing cricket? Of course I'm serious when doing any job ... Father's saying about always doing a job properly is part of who I am, as intrinsic as saying 'please and thank you'. Was I not serious when I made that billiard table – or sang in the choir – or studied for the dance teacher's exams – or asked Betty to marry me? And am I not seriously happy that Betty is pregnant? But when I think about it there is serious and *serious*. That our country might have been invaded by the Nazis was *serious* – as was the Blitz and the horrendous loss of life in the war. Those wartime events were *seriously unhappy* – the consequences, too. Oh my! – life gets complicated sometimes."

I jumped off my bike and ran indoors to give Betty a swinging hug – round and round with her feet off the floor while babbling away with my news: "I'm off to Cardiff tomorrow ... in the first team for six matches ... playing first-class cricket ... against so many famous players ... it's really happening for me, for us, Betty my love."

We were seriously happy!

Following the usual noisy chat and banter during that long coach ride to Cardiff there were quieter moments when I ruminated about my childhood dreams of playing county cricket when I grew up. My happy thoughts drifted into memories of Arden Field and Lord's before the war; of Patsy and Denis and Learie, chuckles when I thought about Frank Lee and the 'big wigs' – then became silently thankful for my years with the Finchley Club and Colts. Oh, and so thankful to those wonderful veteran club players and mentors who had encouraged and supported me and who, in an organically natural way, had provided an environment in which I had imbibed so much about the skills and values of this beautiful, competitive and fair-minded game. Would my love of life and cricket now slip downhill because, as a professional, I was supposed to put on an act of being anxiously serious? Instinctively, and as yet without knowledge of the behavioural sciences, I doubted that playing cricket every summer's day would cause me to be less happy – more likely inspire my youthful energies to overflow with cheerfulness.

And Punchy? Well, first I have my parents to thank for the secure and happy background that established my well-mannered cheerfulness which, combined with displays of athletic fielding, won over the senior pros who initiated the nickname 'Punchy' during my fourth county game at Taunton – a sub-title that identified me in the cricketing world through ten seasons with Hampshire and continues to be used today among family and friends.

Back in the 1950s 'Punchy' meant either 'punch-drunk' or a person characterised by zestful energy and drive – 'lively spirited and vigorous', according to one of the dictionaries. And maybe I was something of a puzzle, an enigma, to those friendly old Hampshire pros. First I was lively spirited but not boisterous, well-mannered but not a prude, had the voice and confidence of an educated Londoner – and three initials – but was neither posh nor an amateur. "He plays football, he's married, his wife's having a baby, but he's a bleedin' dance teacher – I thought dance teachers were poofters ... and he's brilliantly 'nuts' at cover point with a hell-of-a-throw to the keeper. He's bloody Punchy!"

Thank you Jim Bailey, Johnny Arnold, Lofty Herman, Neil McCorkell and Gerry Hill for the nickname that stuck – a moniker that fits well with my Geminian personality.

"Father, what did you do in the First Great War?" was the first line on the first page of this book.

"What did you do from the age of twenty, Grand-dad?" may well be the question posed by some of our grandchildren in the second decade of the twenty-first century.

I have to laugh to myself, dear family and friends, because Punchy's stories about life from the 1950s onwards will fill two more books. I will start, and

finish if I am destined to live a few more years and and am blessed with staff –
joking – but perhaps a cheerful and patient friend to assist with the research and
the shopping. But for now I will close this really enjoyable writing marathon by
answering my daughter Valerie's question:

"Dad, why on earth did you have to stick 'Punchy' between your first and
last names as author of this book?"

Well! By 2005 I had written the first drafts of five chapters and began to
think about self-publishing the final result … and wondered whether, in the
Hampshire Library Catalogue, there were other 'Rayments' listed as authors.
Curious, and in the hush of Lymington's spacious new library, I hit the keys
of the in-house computer and shattered the hallowed silence by exclaiming,
"OH SHIT!" when the name 'Alan Rayment' lit up on the monitor screen.
An autobiography!? Book title? … *It Happened To Me* … "gee, could be my
title … and … and there are three volumes … wow … what a coincidence! To
separate our identities I will have to add my nickname to the author's title
when, eventually, my book is printed."

I borrowed and read the first volume, contacted the author and visited him
at his home near Havant in East Hampshire. First impression: 'in build, facial
structure and general manner he is so like my Uncle Jack … Sam's brother …
definitely closely linked somewhere in our family tree.' Thirteen years older
than me the 'other' Alan Rayment had played a lot of club cricket and studied
psychology to understand and support a son with mental illness. By profession
he was a retired engineering consultant who had worked on secret developments
of equipment for the Royal Navy after serving in an anti-aircraft artillery unit
during WWII.

Now, in February 2013 I laugh again: "But Sam, my father, served in
the mobile Ack-Ack unit in WWI … what a coincidence … but I'm used to
serendipitous happenings and coincidences and feel as though I'm in the old
Bohemia cinema in Finchley at the end of the main film when the lights go up
and I turn to Betty and say –

"OK, love, this is where we came in – let's go home."

Our dreams unfurl into the reality of a future as yet unknown.

Alan, county cricketer in Hampshire CCC sweater, 1949

Index

Alan Rayment himself and his parents Sam and Wynn are not included.

A

Addison, Jill 360
Aird, Ronald 262
Aitken, Dr. George 177
Albert, Prince Consort 136
Alfonso V111, King 109
Ames, Les 214
Ames, Mr. 248
Anson, Geoffrey 336
Appleyard, Bob 204
Arlott, John 332
Arnold, Johnny 371,373,375
Asquith, Herbert 12
Astaire, Fred 369
Attlee, Clement 111,177,262

B

Babbington-Smith, Constance 228
Bach, Johann 178
Badoglio, Mshl Pietro 221
Bagrit, Shirley 225
Bailey, Jim 371,373,375
Bailey, Trevor 249
Baldwin, Harry 338-9
Baldwin, Stanley 107,110
Balfour, Arthur 12,15-17
Barling, Henry 114
Barnard, Michael 372
Barnes, Alison, née Rayment
41,43,44,47
Bartlett, John 328,330
Bastin, Cliff 236
Batchelor, Denzil 332
Beaverbrook, Lord William 195-6
Bedford, Ian 32,234,244,246,
270,273-4,276,328-9,335,368
Bedser, Alec 249,333,351
Bedser, Eric 245,246
Bernays, Revd.S 92,172
Beswick, Mrs 75,139
Beveridge, William 262

Bevin, Earnest 195-6,230
Birkin, Tom 265,357
Birrell, Jean 237
Bishop, Lionel 265
Blaithwaite, Mr. 203-4
Blake, David 373
Bleriot, Louis 11
Blunden, Mr 55
Bolger, Doris, née Rayment
139,359,362
Bolger, Larry 135,139
Bolger, Michael 139
Bowes, Bill 119
Bowyer, Basil 350
Bradley, Gen Omar 221
Bradley, Josephine 366
Bradman, Don 171,253,350-1
Braun, Eva 261
Bridger, Revd John 373
Brookes, Denis 27
Brown, Aline 248
Brown, Freddie 248
Brown, Sid 334,336
Brunskill, Kenny 112,129,140
Brunskill, Mr 122
Brunskill, Mrs 122

C

Cairns, David 245-6
Cardus, Neville 332
Carmody, Keith 248-9
Carnegie, Revd Herbert 178
Carter, Absolem 47
Carter, Charles 47
Carter, Emily 47
Carter, Emma 47
Carter, Hannah 47
Carter, Harriet 47
Carter, Sarah 47
Carter, William 47-8,69,82,112,132
Carty, Dick 370

Chalk, Harold 181,238
Chamberlain, Neville
110,147,151,152,171,174,196
Chaplin, Charlie 106
Chisholm, Jack 273
Churchill, Winston
12-13,103,106-7,111,177,183,
185-9,191-2,195-6,199,200,220,
228,230-1,236,241,261-2,332
Clarke, Dr CB 249
Clayton, Arthur 235,239,263
Cleghorn, Mr. 238
Collier, James 193
Colquhoun, Sqn Ldr. R 323-4
Comber, Miss 184
Compton, Denis
116,118,153,170,245-6,248-9,
267,297-9,332-7,339-40,375
Compton, Leslie 245-6,248-9,346
Constable, Bernie 310
Constantine, Learie 11-9,153,
170-1,249,267,278-282,373
Copson, Bill 119
Corns, Mr. 184,240
Court, Dick 370
Coutts, Ian 311
Cowan, Abel 208,263
Coward, Noel 342
Cowdrey, Colin 311,336
Craig, Ian 280
Cramphorn, Iris 287,290
Cristofani, Desmond 279-81
Cross, Brian 234,235
Cull, George 218,234

D

Dare, Reg 350
Dare, Reg 373
Davidson, Geoffrey 113
Davies, Jack 281,337,341
Davies, W/O 306-7,313-4
Davis, Bette 183
Davison, M 245
Dawkes, George 325,329

Dawson, Gilbert 373
Dawson, Harold 373
de Torre, Kenneth 189
de Zulueta, P 311
Dean, Tom 373
Dear, Mr & Mrs 369
Deighton, John 330
Dempster, Charles 248-9
Dewes, John 325,329
Dewhurst, Tommy 348,351-2
Dexter, Ted 336
Dickens, Charles 164
Dior, Christian 346
Disney, Walt 150
Dodsworth, Anne 39
Donat, Robert 183
Donitz, Adml Carl 261
Donnelly, Martin 278-80
Dowding, Air Mshl Sir Hugh 192-3
Drake, Ted 236
Duffield, John 296
Dumont, Santos 11
Dunham, Katherine 348
Dutton, Flt Lt 319-20

E

Eagar, Desmond 358,365,369,371-4
Edrich, Bill 116,267,279-80,308
Edridge, Mrs 59,135
Edward VIII, HM King 137
Edward, HRH Prince 137
Eisenhower, Gen Dwight 226,261
Elizabeth II, HM Queen 102,
Elizabeth, HM Queen 137,261
Elizabeth, HRH Princess
137,261,346
Enthoven, Henry 29
Evans, Victor 274

F

Fisher, Admiral Sir John 12
Fisher, Dr. G Bishop 93
Fishlock, Laurie
114,154,245-6,267,281

Foster, Mr. 142
Fowler, Archie 245-6,286
Fox, Edward 263
Franco, Gen Francisco 109,151
Freeman, family 47
Fry, Charles 288-9

G

Gandhi, Mahatma 367
Garbo, Greta 183
Gardner, John 359-60
Garland, Judy 153,183,369
George V, HM King 107,136
George VI, HM King 137,261
Gimblett, Harold 279
Goddard, Tom 332-3
Goering, FMshl Hermann
109-10,191,1193,196-8
Gover, Alfred 116,154,333
Graham, Denis 263
Granger, Stewart 174
Gray, Jimmy 350,370,373
Gray, Laurie 283-5,335
Greenaway, S 248
Griffin, Ben 291
Griffin, Tricie 291,345,359,362
Griffiths, Billy 281
Guard, David 373
Gurion, Ben 367

H

Halifax, Lord Edward 171,185-6,190
Hall, Miss (Boris) 255,271,293,296
Hammond, Herbert 296
Hammond, Walter
171,278-81, 295,329,336
Handel, George 178
Hanks, Betty 41
Hanks, Herbert 41
Hanley, Brian 283
Hanley, Jim 245-6
Hapgood, Eddie 236
Harding, Norman 336-8
Hardy, Cpl 315

Harrington, Bill 298-9,310,348,350
Harris Mr. 178
Harris, Air Mshl Sir Arthur 221
Harrison, Leo 371,373
Harvey, Cyril 357
Harvey, Neil 336
Hasset, Lindsey 278
Hawker, FC 299
Headley, George 118-9,153
Hearn, Peter 325,327
Heath, George 373
Heath, Malcolm 370,373
Heath, Ted 290
Hedges, Bernie 351-2
Helpmann, Robert 363
Hendren, Elias (Patsy) 113-6,118,
181,297-9,335,339,358,375
Herman, Ozzie 371,373
Hever, Norman 341
Hill, Gerry 373,375
Hitler, Adolf 106,109-10,147,150-1,
165,171,177,185-7,190,194-5,
197-9,200,221,224-5,261,342-3
Hobbs, Frank 113
Hobbs, Jack 67,247,288-9,309
Hoffman, Harold 360,362,367
Hollies, Eric 279
Hollies, Eric 281,299
Holmes, Bob 370
Holmes, Dr. 32-34,80-81,140-3,223
Holt, Arthur 350
Holt, Arthur 363,365,370-1,374
Hough & Richards 11
Howland, Mr. 182,223,239
Hughes, Howard 110
Hughes, Kathleen 224-5
Hulme, Joe 263,265,271,273
Humberstone, Derek 209
Husband, Brian 204
Hutton, Len 154,253,309,332,351

I

Ikin, Jack 335

J

Jakeman, Freddie — 351
James, Alex — 244
Jameson, Col M — 255,265,293,295
Jenkins, Peter — 277
Joffre, General Joseph — 16
Johnson Mr. — 213
Jones, Margaret, — 178,223
Jones, Mr. — 212-3,239,252

K

Kaizer, Wilhelm II — 12-13
Kaye, Danny — 348
Keitel, FMshl Wilhelm — 191
Kenyon, Don — 348
Kesselring, FMshl Albert — 198
Kilburn, Jim — 332
King, Charlie — 237,239
King, John — 83,164
Kingsley, David — 311
Kitchener, Lord Horatio — 13
Knott, Charles — 371,373

L

Lacey, Tom — 255-6,265,271,293,295
Lake, Norman — 247
Lambert, George — 245-6
Langridge, James — 279
Larwood, Harold — 272
Laurel & Hardy — 150
Lee, Frank — 267-8,270-3,282,285,358
Legeré, Mr. — 256-7,259
Leigh, Vivien, — 183
Lenglen , Suzanne — 291
Lenin, Vladimir — 106
Leopold III, King — 186
Levy, Josh — 225,357
Liddell, Alvar — 218
Limbert, David — 97,112,128,
140,202,210,247,336
Lloyd George, David — 107
Lock, Tony — 286
Loosemore, John — 99,140
Loss, Joe — 225,290

Lugg, Mr. — 167
Lumsden, Dr. Ian — 351
Lundendorff, FMshl von — 106
Lutyens, Sir Edwin — 103

M

MacDonald, A — 249
MacDonald, Ramsay — 107-8
Macey, Bill — 94,172-3
MacIntyre, Arthur — 341
MacKenzie, Alec — 270
MacKenzie, Tom — 209,225-6
Mann, Francis George — 337-8,340
Manners, John — 329,351
Mansfield, Lord — 22
Mao Tse-Tung — 367
Margaret, HRH Princess — 137,261
Marr, Mr — 263
Marshall, Peter — 246
Martin, Cmdr R — 351
Martin, Miss — 184,224,237-8
Marx, Karl — 106
Mary, HM Queen — 136
May, Peter — 328-30,336,351
McEvoy, Miss D — 248
McGlew, Derrick — 336
McIndue, H — 245
Melford, Michael — 332
Merryweather, George — 41
Michael, Grand Duke — 22
Miller, Keith
248,277-8,280,283,336
Mills, F/O Robert — 343
Mills, Sgt — 313-5
Montgomery, Gen Bernard — 221
Montgomery, James — 210
Morant, Miss — 258
Morrison, Herbert — 230
Mosely, Sir Oswald — 152
Mountbatten, Lord Louis — 346
Mountbatten, Prince Phillip — 346
Murphy, 'Potts' — 184-5
Murphy, Dr. Edward — 351
Murphy, Mrs — 34,36,95,184

Mussolini, Benito
106,109-10,186,190,221,226
Mustard, Miss 81

N

Nelson, Admiral Horatio 12
Nelson, Dick 99,100,118,
140,202,210,243,246,247
Newman, Arthur 44
Newman, Gwendoline 44
Newman, Joan 44
Noble, Denis 116
Northcliffe, Lord Alfred 11,14
Nye, Jack 296

O

Oldham, Miss 51
Olivier, Lawrence 281,316
Owens, Jessie 343

P

Palmer, Charles 286
Park, Air VMshl Keith 192-3
Parker, F/O Rowland 325,330,343
Parr, Frank 351-2
Payton, Revd Sqn Ldr Wilfred 351
Pearce, Tom 263
Pearce, WK 357
Pearson Sdn Ldr 306-7,314
Peebles, Ian 286
Peeling, Miss 184
Pepper, Ces 279-81
Perceval, Gen Arthur 220
Phillipson, William 281
Picasso, Pablo 110
Pilditch, Len 140,181,202,209
Place, Winston 335
Plunket, Mr. 368
Pollard, Dick 333
Pratt, Miss 49
Prescott, Mr. 44,217
Price, Frank 115,118
Prouton, Ralph 373
Pryer, F/O Barry 325,329

Q

Quilliam, Mr 184

R

Raeder, Admiral Erich 198
Rait-Kerr, Col Rowan 269
Rands, B 229
Ransom, Vic 373
Raper, James 351
Ratcliffe, Alan 276
Ratcliffe, Alan 276
Rawlinson, Cmdr. Alfred
9,14-18,22-26
Rayment, Alan 'The Other One' 376
Rayment, Albert, (b 1850) 39-43
Rayment, Albert, (Bert) (b 1886)
40-1,43-4,139,43,139
Rayment, Alice (Tilly)
43,78,83,135,164,210,319
Rayment, Alice nee Cropp 42
Rayment, Annie 39,42
Rayment, Bernard 43
Rayment, Betty, née Griffin
33,233,279,285,290-1,293,295,
304,308,311,317-20,330,345,348,
350,358-60,362-3,365-70,374,376
Rayment, Beryl 31,42,59,72,78,
82-3,133,135,139,152,164
Rayment, Charles 40,134,139,216-8
Rayment, Charlotte, née Mitchell 39
Rayment, Christiana 39,41
Rayment, Derek 29,31,35,41,
127, 142,154-6,158-9,164-5,
174-5,179,183,202,210,212,
214,218,245,345,359,362,369-70
Rayment, Doris (by Charles)
44,70,216-9
Rayment, Doris (by William)
31,42,59,72,78,135
Rayment, Eliza, née Everitt 42
Rayment, Emma, née Barnard 39
Rayment, Frank 40,43
Rayment, George (b 1824) 39
Rayment, George (b 1876) 39,42,44

Rayment, Harriet, née Harrington
39,40
Rayment, Henry (Harry)   39,41-2
Rayment, Isobella, née Johnson 39,41
Rayment, Joan, née de Torre
29-31,34,36
Rayment, John (Jack)
40,43,76,83,85,135,
159-60,162-6,319,376
Rayment, Kezie, née Chaplin
44,70,216
Rayment, Margaret (Maggie)   40,44
Rayment, Margaret, née Church   139
Rayment, Mercy   40,43
Rayment, Minnie nee Peachy   43
Rayment, Peter (b 1920)   43
Rayment, Samuel (Sam)   40
Rayment, William (b 1799)   39
Rayment, William (b 1879)
39,42,44,72
Reid, Cyril   293,295
Reid, John   336
Richards, family   210
Richards, Ivor   92-3,95,178,360
Ridley, Revd Michael   360
Riley, John   329
Rivera, General Primo de   109
Roberts, J   263
Roberts, David   285-6
Robertson, Jack   249,279,334,336
Robertson-Glasgow, Raymond   332
Robins, Mr.   139
Robins, Ray   139,263,273
Robins, Walter
249,269-70,277,282-5
Robinson, Peter   247
Roger, Roy   150
Rogers, Neville   371,373
Rommel, Gen Erwin   210,226
Roosevelt, Franklin   220
Roper, Arthur   249
Routledge, Reg   296-7,348,350
Russell, P   285

S
Salisbury, Lord Robert   12
Sandham, Andrew   294
Sandys, Duncan   228
Scott, Admiral Sir Percy   15-17
Scutt, Norman   263
Sealy, Jeffrey   118
Seymour, Dickie   234-5
Shackleton, Derek   371,373
Shaddick, Dr. Rowland   298-9
Sharp, Harry   296-7,310
Sharpe, Air Cmdr R   345, 352-3
Shipman, Martin   263,272
Shirer, W   184
Silvester, Victor   225,289-90
Simpson, Wallis   137
Sims, Jim   245-6,276,286,299
Sismey, Stanley   249
Smith, Geoffrey   285-6
Smith, Jim   114,118
Sondheim, Stephen   210
Sperrle, F.Mshl Hugo   198
Spofforth, Frederick   309
Stacey, John   276
Stacey, John   283,285,310-1
Stalin, Joseph   106,110,194
Stanley, Grant   128,225
Staples, Sam   350
Stewart, James   183
Stitch, Herbert   47
Stitch, Kate   47
Stitch, Walter   47
Stollemeyer, Jeffrey   118
Streisand, Barbra   131,210
Strudwick, Herbert   294
Sturdy, Mr.   184
Sueter, Cmdr. Murray   14,18
Sutherland, Peter   288-90,360
Swallow, Hannah   47
Sweet, Beryl   167-8
Swinburne, Algernon   164
Sylvester, Gwen   294
Symes, Mr.   54

T

Tarzan,   150
Tate, Maurice   271
Taylor, Alan JP   185,192
Taylor, Mr.   133,139
Taylor, Rose   36,133-4,202,204
Thompson, Alex   297
Thompson, Leslie   350
Thomson, Mr.   82,122
Tirpitz, Admiral von   12
Tobin, J   329
Tolton, Anne   41
Tolton, Mabel   41
Tolton, Thomas (son)   41
Tolton, Thomas   41
Tozer, J   311
Trott, Albert   280
Trueman, Fred   204
Truman, Harry   262,355
Two Stripes, Cpl   305,312-5

V

Valentine, Bryan   326
Vaughan, Jack   245
Vavasour, Commodore Geoffrey
                             325,330,351
Verity, Hedley   119
Victoria, HM Queen   12,44,48,136

W

Wakefield, Elizabeth   47
Wakefield, Emily   47
Wakefield, Emma   47
Wakefield, Hannah, née Swallow   47
Wakefield, Louisa   47
Wakefield, Robert (b 1810)   47
Wakefield, Rober   t 47
Wardle, Johnny   204

Warner, Sir Pelham   269,276
Warrener, Mr.   44
Washbrook, Cyril   332,335
Watson-Watt, Sir Robert   321
Watts, Edward   116
Weekes, Mr.   54
Weiss, Miss   100
Wellings, EM   332
Wheelan, Miss   248
Whitcombe, Phillip   329
White, Crawford   332
White, Hon Luke   329
Whitehead, Johnny   327
Whittle, Frank   321
Whitworth, Claude   286
Wignall, Bill   276
Williams, Glenys   115
Williams, J   43
Williams, Robert   279
Williams, Valerie, née Rayment   376
Willis, Henry   178
Wilson, Robert   263
Wood, George   245, 272
Wood, Sir Henry   144-6,279
Worth, Mr.   48
Wright, Alderman A   167-8
Wright, Douglas
        119,278-80,332,336-341,351

Y

York, HRH Duke   213,240
Young, David   40
Young, Jack   274,286

Z

Zeppelin, Count von   11
Zuchov, Gen. Georgy   261